Discourse and Identity

The relationship between languag⟨...⟩ ⟨...⟩ ⟨...⟩ ⟨...⟩ ⟨...⟩ ⟨...⟩ has always been a major area of sociolin⟨...⟩ ⟨...⟩ ⟨...⟩estigation. In recent times, the field has been revolutionized as previous models – which assumed our identities to be based on stable relationships between linguistic and social variables – have been challenged by pioneering new approaches to the topic.

This volume brings together a team of leading experts to explore discourse in a range of social contexts. By applying a variety of new analytical tools and concepts, the contributors show how we build images of ourselves through language, how society moulds us into different categories, and how we negotiate our membership of those categories. Drawing on numerous interactional settings (the workplace; medical interviews; education), in a variety of genres (narrative; conversation; interviews), and amongst different communities (immigrants; patients; adolescents; teachers), this revealing volume sheds new light on how our social practices can help to shape our identities.

ANNA DE FINA is Assistant Professor in the Department of Italian at Georgetown University. She has worked and published articles on political discourse, discourse markers, language contact, narrative, and identity. Her publications include *Identity in Narrative: An Analysis of Immigrant Discourse* (2003) and *Dislocations, Relocations, Narratives of Displacement* (edited with Mike Baynham, 2005).

DEBORAH SCHIFFRIN is Professor of Linguistics at Georgetown University. Her research interests include grammar, meaning, interaction, and Holocaust discourse. Among her published works are *Discourse Markers* (Cambridge University Press, 1987), *Handbook of Discourse Analysis* (2001), and *In Other Words: Variation in Reference and Narative* (Cambridge University Press, 2006).

MICHAEL BAMBERG is Professor of Psychology at Clark University. His research interests are in narrative and narrative methods; language and development; and discourse and the construction of identity among adolescents. His books include *Relating Events in Narrative* (edited with R. Berman and D. Slobin, 1994) and *Narrative Development* (1997).

Studies in Interactional Sociolinguistics

EDITORS
Paul Drew, Marjorie Harness Goodwin, John J. Gumperz, Deborah
Schiffrin

Discourse and Identity

Edited by

ANNA DE FINA
Georgetown University

DEBORAH SCHIFFRIN
Georgetown University

MICHAEL BAMBERG
Clark University

CAMBRIDGE UNIVERSITY PRESS
Cambridge, New York, Melbourne, Madrid, Cape Town, Singapore, São Paulo, Delhi

Cambridge University Press
The Edinburgh Building, Cambridge CB2 8RU, UK

Published in the United States of America by Cambridge University Press, New York

www.cambridge.org
Information on this title: www.cambridge.org/9780521541916

First published 2006
Reprinted 2007

Printed in the United Kingdom at the University Press, Cambridge

A catalogue record for this publication is available from the British Library

ISBN 978-0-521-83402-5 hardback
ISBN 978-0-521-54191-6 paperback

Contents

    Anna De Fina   351

14 Performing self, family and community
    in Moroccan narratives of migration and settlement
    Mike Baynham   376

15 Making it personal: shared meanings in the
    narratives of Holocaust survivors
    Brian Schiff and Chaim Noy   398

    References   426
    Index   452

Contributors

Michael Bamberg	Professor of Psychology, Clark University, Worcester, MA
Mike Baynham	Professor of TESOL, University of Leeds
Susan E. Bell	A. Myrick Freeman Professor of Social Sciences, Bowdoin College, Brunswick, ME
Liliana Cabral Bastos	Associate Professor, Letters Department, Catholic University, Rio de Janeiro
Anna De Fina	Assistant Professor, Department of Italian, Georgetown University, Washington, DC
Maria do Carmo Leite de Oliveira	Associate Professor, Letters Department, Catholic University, Rio de Janeiro (PUC-Rio)
Vivian Gadsden	Associate Professor, Director, National Center on Fathers and Families, Graduate School of Education, University of Pennsylvania
Alexandra Georgakopoulou	Reader in Modern Greek Language and Linguistics, King's College London
Janet Holmes	Professor of Linguistics, School of Linguistics and Applied Language Studies, Victoria University of Wellington
Greer Johnson	Associate Professor, Centre for Applied Language, Literacy, and Communication Studies, Griffith University, Brisbane.
Scott Kiesling	Assistant Professor, Department of Linguistics, University of Pittsburgh

Robin Lakoff	Professor of Linguistics, University of California at Berkeley
Elliot G. Mishler	Professor of Social Psychology, Department of Psychiatry, Harvard Medical School
Luiz Paulo Moita-Lopes	Associate Professor, Applied Linguistics Program, Federal University of Rio de Janeiro
Chaim Noy	Visiting Lecturer, Department of Communications, Hebrew University of Jerusalem
Branca Telles Ribeiro	Associate Professor, Intercultural Relations Program, Lesley University
Brian Schiff	Assistant Professor of Psychology, Saint Martin's College
Deborah Schiffrin	Professor of Linguistics, Georgetown University, Washington, DC
Stanton Wortham	Associate Dean for Academic Affairs, Graduate School of Education, University of Pennsylvania

Introduction

Background

Research on language and identity has experienced an unprecedented growth in the last ten years. The time when scholars in the field needed to advocate for the centrality of language in the study of identity (see for example, Benveniste 1971 in linguistics or Bruner 1990 in social psychology) seems far away indeed. Research in fields as diverse as anthropology, linguistics, psychology, sociology, history, literature, gender studies, and social theory, among others, has now firmly established the fundamental role of linguistic processes and strategies in the creation, negotiation and establishment of identities. It is impossible to give a comprehensive view of the theoretical work in all of these areas and of how it has shaped identity studies. Our aim with this introduction is more modest: we want to briefly discuss some of the approaches and concepts that have had the greatest impact on current visions of identity, beginning with background perspectives and then turning to central constructs underlying the chapters in the volume. We then present an overview of the volume and a conclusion recapitulating some of the common ground among the contributors.

Background perspectives

Here we describe several approaches to the study of discourse and identity that pervade the chapters in the volume. We begin with those that have become widely accepted in research on discourse and identity and conclude with some that produce potential divisions in the ways scholars examine discourse and identity.

Perhaps the most general perspective, one that provides a very basic way of thinking about identity, is *social constructionism* (e.g. Berger and Luckman 1967; Hall 1996; Kroskrity 2000): the assumption that identity is neither a given nor a product. Rather, identity is a process that (1) takes place in concrete and specific interactional occasions, (2) yields constellations of identities instead of individual, monolithic constructs, (3) does not simply emanate from the individual, but results from processes of negotiation, and entextualization (Bauman and Briggs 1990) that are eminently social, and (4) entails "discursive work" (Zimmerman and Wieder 1970).

Social constructionism has generated a great deal of research on the use of linguistic strategies in discursive work to convey and build identities, on the emergence in interaction of conflicting versions of the self, and therefore on the existence of "repertoires of identities" (Kroskrity 1993), and on the effects of interlocutors, audiences and other social actors on the unfolding of identities in concrete social occasions. In brief, social constructionism has contributed to dissipating transcendentalist conceptions of identity and to directing the attention of researchers to social action rather than to psychological constructs.

Recent scholarship has also emphasized that identity is a process that is always embedded in social practices (Foucault 1984) within which discourse practices (Fairclough 1989) have a central role. Both social and discourse practices frame, and in many ways define, the way individuals and groups present themselves to others, negotiate roles, and conceptualize themselves. Taking the concept of practice as central to processes of identity formation and expression entails looking more closely at ways in which definitions of identity change and evolve in time and space, ways in which membership is established and negotiated within new boundaries and social locations, and ways in which activity systems (Goodwin 1999) impact on processes of identity construction.

Another defining trend in recent research has been the analysis of processes of *categorization and membership definition*. Taking inspiration from early work by Sacks on category bound activities and processes (1972, 1995), scholars in the Membership Categorization Analysis movement (Antaki and Widdicombe 1998b) have drawn attention to the fact that identity construction is often related to the definition of categories for inclusion or exclusion of self and others, and to their identification with typical activities and routines. This, in turn, has prompted a reflection on the nature of identification categories and on the relationship between individual identity and group membership.

Recent approaches to categorization have highlighted the limitations of applying pre-established categorizations, emphasizing instead the locally occasioned, fluid and ever-changing nature of identity claims. Identity claims are seen as "acts" through which people create new definitions of who they are. Such a conception defies traditional sociolinguistic approaches that link already established social categories with language variables, regarding instead "the very fact of selecting from a variety of possibilities a particular variant (on a given occasion) as a way of actively symbolizing one's affiliations" (Auer 2002: 4). Thus identities are seen not as merely represented in discourse, but rather as performed, enacted and embodied through a variety of linguistic and non-linguistic means.

A third important trend in identity studies has been the development of an *anti-essentialist vision of the 'self.'* Work in gender studies and discursive psychology has been crucial in this respect. Gender studies have greatly contributed to our postmodern rejection of the self as something that people possess and that represents some kind of core essence of the person (Bucholtz *et al.* 1999). Gender scholars have shown that people can display "polyphonous" identities, i.e. simultaneously assume voices that are associated with different identity categories, and that they can "perform" identities, i.e. represent themselves as different from what their personal "visible" characteristics would suggest (Barrett 1999), therefore concluding that there is nothing given or "natural" about being part of a social category or group. The inadequacy of an essentialist notion of identity as being embodied in the 'self' has also been noted by discursive psychologists who move away from a "predefined model of the human actor" (Potter 2003) towards the investigation of how the psychological categories used to describe or define the 'self' are themselves configured according to specific social practices and relationships.

Work in these perspectives has also stressed the centrality of processes of *indexicality* in the creation, performance and attribution of identities. Indexicality is thus a fourth overarching concept subsuming many of the theoretical constructs used to study identities: it connects utterances to extra-linguistic reality via the ability of linguistic signs to point to aspects of the social context. The connection between indexicality and identity has been a focus of attention in linguistics and anthropology since early work on deixis, particularly on shifters (see Benveniste 1971; Silverstein 1976) pointed to the indissoluble nexus established by these linguistic elements between the speaker and the utterance act.

Both linguists and anthropologists recognize the importance of pronouns in anchoring language to specific speakers in specific contexts and in signaling the reciprocal changes in the roles of interactants through their performance of, and engagement in, communicative acts. For example, linguistic signs at this referential level (Silverstein 1976) identify speakers not only in terms of their conversational roles or gender identity, but also in terms of how they orient to elements of the speech situation such as time and place. By using locatives and time expressions – as well as personal pronouns – language users point to their roles not only as speakers or addressees, but also to their location in time and space and to their relationship to others (present or absent).

Incorporation of the context is in itself a dynamic process through which speakers build their positions within what Hanks (1992) has named "the indexical ground." By carrying out acts of reference, interactants continuously constitute and reconstitute their positions with respect to each other, to objects, places and times. Thus, indexing aspects of the context can never be reduced to a simple act of orientation in physical space or to the mere signaling of alternations in speech roles. Indexicality is a layered, creative, interactive process that lies at the heart of the symbolic workings of language. The idea that signs are indexical goes beyond simple referential anchoring to encompass the ability of linguistic expressions to evoke, and relate to, complex systems of meaning such as socially shared conceptualizations of space and place, ideologies, social representations about group membership, social roles and attributes, presuppositions about all aspects of social reality, individual and collective stances, practices and organization structures.

The approaches and concepts briefly outlined above rest on basic, and generally accepted, assumptions about the relationships between discourse, identity and social processes. However, scholars of identity are also deeply divided on several theoretical and methodological issues.

At opposite extremes are two approaches: the one sustained by scholars working within the frame of Conversation Analysis and the one advocated by scholars working within the frame of Critical Discourse Analysis. The division is not exclusive to the study of identity. Rather, it derives from different conceptions of the relationship between language and social life, of the role of the researcher, and of the methodology to be followed in data collection and analysis. Scholars in the field of Conversation Analysis advocate methodological restraint, according to which analysts need to "hold off from using all sorts of identities which one might want to use in, say, a political or cultural frame of analysis" (Antaki and Widdicombe 1998a: 5) and look exclusively for categories of identity membership that are made relevant in the local context by participants. In this view, identities are locally occasioned in talk-in-interaction, they are consequential for the interaction at hand, and therefore participants clearly "orient" to them. The researcher's task is then to reconstruct the processes of adscription and negotiation of identities as they are manifested within the activity in which participants are engaged. These arguments echo Schegloff's polemic stance against the imposition of ad hoc interpretive categories by "politically informed" analysts. Schegloff (1997: 168) argued that only after analyzing the interactional event "in its endogenous constitution, what it was for the parties involved in it, in its course, as embodied and displayed in the very details of its realization – can we even begin to explore what forms a critical approach to it might take, and what political issue, if any, it allows us to address." Accordingly, within this approach, the only relevant context to understand the emergence of identities in interaction is the local context.

At the other extreme of the spectrum are scholars who identify with Critical Discourse Analysis (Billig 1999). In their view, the contexts that are relevant to the expression, negotiation and perpetuation of identities are much wider, since identities are, in many ways, produced and often imposed upon individuals and groups through dominant discourse practices and ideologies. From their perspective, keeping the analysis at the level of the local interaction only means ignoring how power struggles and wider social circumstances constrain and frame the way identities are perceived and projected in specific interactions. The consequence of such a stance is that Critical Discourse Analysts tend to privilege the analysis of political and ideological contexts in the formation of identities and concentrate on the representation of identities much more than on their projection or negotiation in interaction.

Our aim in this volume is not to argue for one position against the other, or to promote a particular agenda, but to offer analyses and reflections that can be taken as a basis for discussion by scholars who endorse different perspectives. In this sense, the volume differs from other collections in its inclusion of a range of approaches and its coverage of a variety of identities and texts/contexts: rather than share a single theoretical orientation, contributors come from different traditions and fields and use varying methodological tools. As we describe in the next section, however, several constructs re-appear throughout the volume, thus providing some overarching theoretical and methodological frameworks for the volume as a whole.

Overarching themes, underlying constructs and persistent questions

Contributors to *Discourse and Identity* employ a variety of specific theoretical approaches and methodological orientations, including Narrative Analysis, Conversation Analysis, Interactional Sociolinguistics, and Critical Discourse Analysis. Yet all share an anti-essentialist orientation, a discourse and practice centered approach to identity, and a close focus on the interactional and local management of social categories and language along with consideration of the effects of global processes on the management of local identities. Before turning to an overview of the volume, then, we highlight some of the overarching themes and underlying constructs that find application in the volume and discuss their relevance to the linguistic analysis of identity. We present each construct as a general question that is answered through the concepts and methods (the tools, the "nuts and bolts") comprised through each construct.

Positioning: How do the relationships we "take up" through (a) linguistically realized action and (b) interactions with different facets of our social, cultural and ideological worlds contribute to "who we are"?

Analyses of positioning build on the insight that identity is socially constructed at several levels: through relationships between the speaker and what is being said (including both means of production and evaluative or epistemic stance); through relationships between self and other, or speaker and hearer, in face-to-face occasions of talk and interaction; through relationships represented in the propositional content of talk (what is one textual character doing to another textual character?); through relationships to the dominant ideologies, widespread social practices and underlying power structures drawn together as Discourse (Gee 1996). One of the goals of positioning theory is to more clearly identify the mechanisms through which linguistic and social processes become reified as observable products that may be glossed by others as "identities."

If the practices in which we routinely engage are viewed as central to processes of identity formation, what kind of personal agency is inscribed in these practices? While some researchers focus more strongly on social and institutional factors that constrain and delineate the radius of agency for individuals and groups of individuals, others credit groups and individuals with an agency that enables them to more than comply with such societal forces. This latter orientation is particularly interested in the agentive role of participants in interactions as being able to counter dominant practices, discourses and master narratives.

Scholars who have developed positioning theory (e.g. Bamberg 1997b, 2005; Davies and Harré 1990; Harré and van Langenhove 1999; Hollway 1984) investigate agency as bi-directional. On the one hand, historical, sociocultural forces in the form of dominant discourses or master narratives position speakers in their situated practices and construct who they are without their agentive involvement. On the other hand, speakers position themselves as constructive and interactive agents and choose the means by which they construct their identities vis-à-vis others as well as vis-à-vis dominant discourses and master narratives.

Positioning provides a central theoretical construct and valuable tool for analyzing identity in this volume. Authors investigate
the linguistic mechanisms and discourse strategies that allow individual speakers to place themselves in positions of acceptance or
rejection, for example, of ideologies of race, gender, or widely held
conceptions about family roles and relationships (Bell, Moita-Lopes,
Wortham and Gadsden). Linguistic strategies for projecting and
constructing particular personas include modalization, constructed
dialogue, meta-pragmatic descriptors and pronouns. Authors also
suggest that speakers build positions vis-à-vis their former selves
through the management of time categories in the reconstruction of
their life experiences, since they look back at what happened in the
past through the vantage point of their present experiences, therefore engaging in an ever evolving interpretation of their roles and
lives (Bell, Mishler).

Authors also address the theoretical ramifications of the concept
of positioning through discussion of the many facets of identity
that can be the object of discursive work. Interlocutors can assume stances not only towards ideologies, but also towards absent
others (e.g. characters and their actions in stories), and towards
each other. Thus, in different chapters, interviewers and interviewees are shown using strategies such as the application of labels,
the use of discourse responses or even silence after questions, to
position each other in particular ways (Baynham, Bell, Johnson).

Investigating levels of identity construction as a process of
positioning, and discovering the means adopted to enact various
positions, leads to reflecting on the many ways of doing identity,
ranging from the proclamation and open assignment of membership into social categories to the enactment of different kinds of
selves, to indirect conveying of alignments and disalignments, to
the implicit placement of social agents into pre-assigned roles.
Analyses of positioning can thus productively connect the local
focus of conversation analytic and the more global focus of critical
discourse analytic approaches. They can also help elucidate the
embrace of, or resistance to, imposed identities through narrative,
as well as through other discourse genres, discursive practices and
Discourse writ large. While positioning thus constitutes a sort of
umbrella for different ways of constructing identity in discourse,

other more specific constructs are also used by contributors in this volume to account for particular aspects of identity work.

Interaction order: "Who are we" when we are interacting with one another in face-to-face talk?

The investigation of the interaction order as a central site for the construction of identities provides a significant site of analysis, and area of reflection, in the chapters collected in this volume. Many authors illustrate how a multiplicity of identities are managed through social interactions by building upon Goffman's work as a fundamental point of departure because of his insights on the importance of reciprocity in communication and on the fundamental presence of the 'other' in the public management of the self. This relational view of communication has an immediate relevance for the analysis of identity work through the constructs of footing ("the alignment we take up to ourselves and the others present as expressed in the way we manage the production or reception of an utterance" (1981: 128)), and "face" (the positive social attributes that a person claims for him or herself in the course of social interaction (1967a)).

The management of this relational level underlies a great deal of identity work in private and public exchanges and conversations (Bastos and Oliveira, Holmes, Ribeiro). Authors illustrate how the presentation of a positive face to others underlies the choice of referring terms or the telling of stories or anecdotes and the provision of details within them: both can depict the self as a "figure" whose actions, interactions and relationships within specific story-worlds have potential relevance for the interaction. Also shown is how the identities presented by clients of public services, or by people in the work place, are shaped by the need to preserve an image of oneself which is consistent with the requirements and exigencies of the situation, the interaction, and the needs of the interlocutors. Problematizing and deconstructing face work, then, leads analysts to interpret the presentation and enactment of particular identities not so much as expressions of the 'self,' but rather as constructions that take into account both the objectives of interactional practices, and the constraints of institutional structures, that are "in play" when people communicate with each other.

Analysis of interactional processes is also based on a fundamental principle of intersubjectivity that allows identities to be
achieved and built through reciprocal moves between interactants
(Schiffrin). Partners in storytelling events may build dominant
positions within close knit groups by consistently taking up roles
as co-narrators or evaluators of the narratives told by others (Georgakopoulou). Interactants can project identifications or rejections
towards their partners through cooperative or uncooperative management of conversation (Johnson, Holmes). They can also confirm
and fine tune local identities that place them in relationships with
others (such as "expert" versus "novice") through the use of repair
in referring sequences (Schiffrin). Many chapters in this volume
show how the management of interactional resources, such as those
described above, can become central to people's intersubjective
construction of identities.

Footing, multivocality and intertextuality: "Who" is
speaking "whose" words and what role are they taking
in the "speech"?

The question of "who" is speaking "whose" words – and the incorporation of other voices and texts in the here and now – has been
examined from sociological, linguistic and literary perspectives,
many of which underlie the chapters in this volume.

One perspective drawn upon by contributors to the volume is
Goffman's work on participation frameworks and the deconstruction of the notion of "speaker" into more subtle distinctions.
Goffman (1981: 128) distinguishes between different aspects of
the self in discourse production: the author (the person who designs
the utterance), the animator (the person who speaks the words
that may have been designed by someone else), the principal (the
person who takes responsibility for the sentiments underlying
the words) and the figure (the character in a story or other text).
These aspects of self define how people engage in identity work
by taking up one or more relationships to an utterance. Speakers
may signal or convey, through a variety of linguistic means such as
reference, pronominal choice, or quotation, that they are assuming
"authority" with respect to interlocutors, for example by claiming
expertise in certain areas of knowledge or experience (Ribeiro,

Schiffrin). They can also signal their authority to represent others in a community, thus conveying that they are not just individuals animating their own stories, but also principals who are collectively committed to particular versions of the past (Baynham, De Fina, Schiff and Noy).

Goffman's differentiation among the speaker as the "author" of the present discourse, the "animator" as a participant in the inter-action at hand, and the speaker as "figure" or character in a past world evoked in the discourse, also appears in many chapters as a particularly productive resource for the analysis of speakers' *stances* with respect to ideologies and behaviors through narrative discourse. Contributors who examine narrative, De Fina, Kiesling, and Moita-Lopes, for example, show that because narrators can use their own characteristics or actions as protagonists in story-worlds as a point of reference to express evaluations of many facets of social experience, they are able to convey their position on a variety of social problems such as gender roles, race and ethnicity without openly asserting their views.

Other perspectives on "who" is speaking "whose" words and what role they are taking in the speech stems from the research of linguists Becker (1984) and Tannen (1989) whose work also harks back to Bakhtin (1986) on multivocality and Kristeva (1980) on intertextuality. As suggested by Tannen, all interactions are made up of prior texts that we draw upon in new ways: "both the mean-ings of individual words. . .and the combinations in which we put them are given to us by previous speakers, traces of whose voices and contexts cling inevitably to them" (1989: 100). This notion of intertextuality has a long and rich history in literary studies. Kristeva (1980), for example, pointed out that texts have not only a horizontal axis that connects author to recipient, but also a vertical axis that connects a text to other texts. As Fairclough (1992: 84) explains:

Intertextuality is basically the property texts have of being full of snatches of other texts, which may be explicitly demarcated or merged in, and which the text may assimilate, contradict, ironically echo, and so forth. In terms of production, an intertextual perspective stresses the historicity of texts: how they always constitute additions to existing "chains of speech com-munication" (Bakhtin 1986: 94) consisting of prior texts to which they respond.

Just as an utterance can draw upon previous utterances from distant prior texts, so too, can it provide material for future utterances (and/or texts) by a recipient at a later time or place. The interchange between different interlocutors (the horizontal axis) is thus crucial, as stated by Bakhtin (1986: 68):

when the listener perceives and understands the [language meaning] of speech, he simultaneously takes an active, responsive attitude toward it . . . Any understanding is imbued with response and necessarily elicits it in one form or another: the listener becomes the speaker.

Bakhtin's view recalls an earlier point about how information is managed through the alternation of participant roles, as well as the shared sense of meanings, actions and knowledge that are grounded in the sequential organization of talk-in-interaction. The difference, of course, is the deictic center of information and participation: the listeners and speakers who draw upon intertextual connections with remote prior texts – rather than the just-completed utterance from a prior turn-at-talk – need not be co-present. And this reduces the potential for evidence of shared meanings and shared recognition of multivocality. Regardless of this (in)ability to trace the source of prior voices and texts, however, a multiplicity of voices and words is interwoven into discourse. Thus even when one individual appears to be responsible for the production of utterances, prior voices and texts are fundamental to our understanding of identity as a process.

Various contributors to the volume work with more explicit means of exploiting multivocality as a resource for identity construction. One way is the quotation of the words of others to stress an idea, to evaluate behavior, to summarize an opinion. In connection with this question, Bakhtin's work on constructed dialogue and on dialogism in general, is a theoretical framework widely referred to by authors in the volume. Bakhtin introduced the very central concept that reporting speech is not a passive enterprise, but an active process of transformation. Any act of reporting is, in his view, at the same time an act of appropriation of somebody else's words, and a reformulation of the original act. Bakhtin (1981b) showed, for example, how reported speech in narrative can be presented on a scale of "objectivity," from a clear separation of the narrator's voice with respect to that of the speaking character, to a subtle mixing of different voices within the same text that may make it at times almost impossible to distinguish reporting from commentary. Thus, authors in the book apply Bakhtin's ideas about voice and dialogism to show that narrators can borrow the voices of others to construct their own identity in opposition to, or in agreement with, what figures of authority express in story-worlds (Baynham, Moita-Lopes, Ribeiro, Wortham and Gadsden) as well as to convey evaluations of their role and the roles of others within present and past experiences (Bell, De Fina).

Other contributors show dialogism, multivocality, participant framework and intertextuality working at a different level: as discourses or ideologies that confront interactants, as underlying voices surrounding their own identity construction and lending meaning to categories, metaphors or images that they use to describe themselves and others and to place themselves in the social world. Interactants evoke Discourses, and confront themselves with them, for example through recourse to shared cultural models (Holland and Skinner 1987) that allow the interpretation of experience, but also evoke the fixity of social roles and relationships.

Shared cultural models constitute preferred scenarios against which people interpret not only narratives and characters, but also the value and significance of terms and category-bound expressions. Thus identities are constructed in discourse through the subtle evoking of contexts that lend meaning to implicit gender and ethnic categorization of self and others (Kiesling, Moita-Lopes). Internalized, typical scenarios set expectations for the behavior and roles of individuals in both private and public spheres, determining certain interpretations about the identities of people occupying certain positions in domains of social interaction that range from restaurants (Lakoff) to schools (Johnson) to hospitals (Bell) and insurance companies (Bastos and Oliveira). And once public figures and processes begin to constitute the frame within which individual behaviors make sense (Schiff and Noy), they can become the basis for the interpretation and communication of highly personal experiences and identities. Processes of categorization also rest on the implicit construction of shared representations about self and others that are the basis for ideologies about race and ethnicity (De Fina). Thus contributors to the volume demonstrate that individual construction of identity is in constant interdependence with general social and ideological processes and their representation and reconstruction in public voices and discourses.

Indexing local and global identities: How do our interactions with others contribute to our reflection and construction of who we are? How is "who we are" in our face-to-face interactions related to broader membership categories and to social, cultural and ideological aspects of the world in general?

A central concern in many chapters in this volume is the investigation of relationships between locally expressed identities and more global, socially-shared identities. A social constructionist perspective underscores the processual nature of identity construction and its links to concrete communication events, but leaves open the question of how these relations emerge in discourse and what role different contexts play in their interpretation.

Contributors to the volume attempt to show that micro- and macro-identities constantly intersect in discourse. Such intersections are apparent when we look at how different levels of identity construction contribute to the interpretation of the roles that partners occupy in interaction. Borrowing Zimmerman's classification of different levels of identity (1998), we can distinguish "discourse identities" as those that are related to the moment-by-moment alternation of roles such as speaker–listener or questioner–answerer; "situated identities," as those that are instantiated in particular types of situations, such as interviewer–interviewee or client–healthcare provider representative; and "transportable identities" as those deriving from more general characteristics of the individual, such as gender or ethnicity. Different authors in the book show that these identities are not only constructed simultaneously in concrete occasions of interaction, but also that local ("discourse" and "situated") identities crucially contribute to the emergence of more global, transportable identities. Thus, people's moment-by-moment management of interaction, their assumption of local roles, has important consequences for the projection of their image at a more general level. Activity-based identities during an interview between two women on the importance of a local market contribute to the emergence of gender and class identities

(Schiffrin), just as managing local roles of story-teller, evaluator and co-teller demonstrates the incumbency of larger social identities of gender for teenagers in conversation (Georgakopoulou).

The concept of indexicality helps us understand how connections are established not only between language (as well as other modes of communications) and local identities, but also between language and global identities. Linguistic forms at all levels may be used to signal relationships of membership within, or dissociation from, particular groups via the association of those forms with ideologies, stances, attitudes, actions, and practices attributed to members of those groups. Any aspect of language can become indexical of social identities, from phonological variables to individual words, to complex discourse structures such as patterns of actions in narratives. Indexicality is thus a resource for the construction of discourse identities that link the micro and the macro level thanks to the shared nature of ideologies, cultural models, Discourses and social representations that assign roles, typical behavioral patterns, even physical or mental characteristics to social agents and that presuppose scenarios in which stereotypical social relationships are represented.

Like the other processes and constructs discussed above, indexing identity in everyday face-to-face interaction is both reflective and constructive of social reality. On the one hand, speakers use indexicality to project identities based on social norms and expectations about what it means to be a certain kind of person or to act in a certain kind of way; on the other hand, they can use the same tacit understandings to build new associations and therefore to construct new types of identities. Thus indexical relationships are never given, but are continuously negotiated and recreated by speakers because of the infinite possibilities inherent in the association of signs with meanings. As shown in many of the papers in this volume, processes of indexicality are deployed as resources to negotiate identities at different levels, from local relationships within the interaction to membership in social categories, domains and different communicative contexts, from spontaneous conversations to focus group interviews. Indexicality has thus pushed research in the direction of the analysis of the management of identity as a highly symbolic process subject to cultural and interactional constraints, but also in constant flow and change according to new perceptions, new norms and new allegiances.

Indexicality also reflectively points to the importance of the kinds of discourse practices in which people engage. Although a nexus between language and identities can be studied in many different types of discourses, narrative has had a prominent role in forging this intersection. Contributions to the volume reflect the widely accepted centrality of narrative as a privileged locus for the negotiation of identities. Authors explore the power of narratives as coping devices to create coherent identities (Bell), as institutional tools to regulate identities (Moita-Lopes), and as interactionally co-constructed texts to create community (Georgakopoulou). However, they also investigate the role of other types of discourse practices in framing identities, for example the telling of personal anecdotes to build a connection between personal and collective identities (Holmes), the writing of menus, recipes and cookbooks to configure ideal housewives or clients (Lakoff), or of institutional letters to define acceptable and unacceptable public faces (Bastos and Oliveira), and the management of interviews to negotiate authority and expertise (Bell, Johnson).

Summary

Discourse and Identity brings together a range of theoretical constructs and methodological approaches that collectively provide important insights about the nexus between what we say (at both micro- and macro-levels of discourse and Discourse) and who we are (including both transient and emergent presentations of self and our relatively stable identities). In addition to examining the interplay between local and global identities in different interactional contexts, social settings, and types of discourse, the volume provides opportunities for comparative analysis of particular cases across a wide range of possibilities. Authors analyze strategies of construction, co-construction, and negotiation of identities in different contexts (e.g. the work place, medical interviews, focus groups, educational settings, food-oriented texts), in different genres (e.g. narrative, interviews, conversations, accounts, menus) and among different communities (e.g. immigrants, patients, adolescents, fathers, Holocaust survivors). The volume thus builds upon the linguistic and ethnographic orientation of scholars such as Dell Hymes and Pete Becker – an orientation that seeks generalizations through the accumulation of "particularities," which are, in turn, discovered only through detailed microanalyses of individual cases.

Volume overview

Discourse and Identity uses a variety of constructs central to the construction and presentation of identity (e.g. reciprocity, intersubjectivity, the fluidity of time, indexicality, positioning) and methodologies (e.g. interactional sociolinguistics, conversation analysis, narrative analysis) to examine local and global identities as constructed by people under very different circumstances and from very different backgrounds. Several chapters deal with group identities: immigrants (Baynham, De Fina), adolescents (Georgakopoulou, Moita-Lopes), clients (Bastos and Oliveira, Lakoff), members of hegemonic (Kiesling) and non-hegemonic (Wortham and Gadsden) social classes, and Holocaust survivors (Schiff and Noy). They do so to illuminate both the processes through which people produce these identities and the ideological and social conditioning to which they respond. Other chapters investigate individuals as articulating plural, often conflicting, identities such as mother–patient–woman (Bell); professional–private person (Johnson, Holmes); and individual–client (Bastos and Oliveira).

The volume is divided into four parts: Part I deals with the discussion of theoretical and methodological issues that are central to current debates on identity. The other three parts are organized according to domains of identity formation and negotiation: the private–public interface (Part II), gender (Part III), and transitional identities (Part IV). Below we very briefly summarize the content of each part, which are then discussed in more depth in their introductions.

The chapters in Part I, *Overview: theory, method and analysis*, focus on theoretical and methodological issues such as the contexts pertinent to the analysis of identities in talk, the appropriateness of theoretical constructs for the study of aspects of identity, the relative focus on language and the role of linguistic forms in the negotiation of identities.

Mishler opens Part I by discussing the implications of different approaches to temporal ordering in narrative for theories about identity development. His analysis focuses on linear conceptions of time and on external-world event ordering as an organizational principle for narratives.

In the following chapter, Ribeiro discusses the implications of a number of theoretical and methodological tools for the study of identity. She examines different concepts that have been used in the literature to account for facets of identity, specifically the notions of positioning, voice and footing. These notions are illustrated and compared through the analysis of a telephone conversation on medical family matters between two brothers.

Like Mishler, Georgakopoulou takes narrative analysis as a starting point to discuss a theoretical question: the interconnections between the local managements of discursive roles and "pre-existent, socioculturally available, Capital D, Discourses." Analyzing storytelling practices among members of a group of adolescent girls, Georgakopoulou shows that the connections between local identities and larger social identities are recoverable through the analysis of participant roles.

Schiffrin's chapter starts with a problem of reference: how can a referring term index identities in the textual and social worlds? Her answer requires a perspective on 'self,' 'other' and interaction developed from a close reading of Erving Goffman's work, as well as some understanding of linguistic analyses of reference. To illustrate this interdisciplinary theoretical framework, Schiffrin analyzes how a single reference during an interchange in one interview is part of a complex array of identities at different levels, including animator/author (of a repair), situated role in activity-based sequences, and broad social categories (gender, social class and region).

The authors in Part II, *Private and public identities: constructing who we are*, focus on how discursive practices shape identities, on how personal and public identities interact in concrete social processes, on the degree to which public discourses constrain the definitions of personal identities and on the role of different participants in such social practices (both local interactants and removed addressees) on the way people define who they are. In the contexts analyzed, the process of identity building involves coping with the conflicting demands of professional and private images, with the different perceptions by interviewers and interviewees on the tellability and noteworthiness of aspects of one's identity, or with the need to create appropriate images for consumers.

Lakoff opens by looking at the interface between public discourse and personal identities that revolves around food and food consumption. She shows how discourse and practices focused on food reveal a collective shift in the identity of Americans from a people that conceives of food as simply a means of sustenance, to a people whose identity is much more defined by what they eat.

Holmes' chapter also focuses on the interface between public and personal identities, but takes as its research domain the workplace. In her analysis, Holmes looks at how anecdotes in talk at work are used to instantiate varied personal and collective identities. The analysis illustrates that identities are achieved through interactional work and also that the identity repertoire on which individuals draw is tightly related to the activity in which they engage.

The relationship between personal identities and the identities in which individuals are positioned in particular communicative contexts is taken up also by Bastos and Oliveira in their chapter, as they investigate the social conflict produced by differences in expectations about identity and social roles held by individual clients and by their Health Insurance Service Company in Brazil. The chapter invites a reflection on how institutional contexts determine entextualization rules that, in turn, shape acceptable and unacceptable identities and on how a critical reflection on such processes can greatly impact the way institutions relate to individuals in the real world.

Johnson shares Bastos and Oliveira's focus on the construction of public identities and on how institutional demands and expectations intertwine with individual negotiations about who we are. She illustrates the ascription of a "good-teacher identity" to a participant in a research interview and how such identity is elaborated through the collaboration of both interviewer and interviewee.

In her chapter, Bell reflects on another important aspect of the interface between private and public identities: the construction of individual identities against the backdrop of ideologies circulated in public discourse and in institutional practices. The author examines how a woman whose life has been profoundly altered by her mother's exposure to a highly dangerous estrogen (DES),

builds an image of herself as a parent and an individual that results from a complex interaction with dominant ideologies about
motherhood and health, the medical circumstances that have
dominated her life, and the dialogue that she establishes with the
interviewer.

The chapters in Part III, *The gendered self: becoming and being
a man*, share a focus on the construction of masculinity in different
circumstances and social worlds. In particular, authors analyze
how general cultural models underlie and provide the context for
the interpretation of locally displayed identities, how whiteness,
heterosexuality and masculinity are negotiated and enacted in collective narrative practices within institutional interactions, conversations between peers, and interviews, but also how identities are
shaped by these practices. Another common thread between the
chapters is a reflection on narrative resources as a primary tool for
building and negotiating gendered identities.

Like Bell, Kiesling is concerned with ways in which the construction and management of individual identities is affected by and
reflects social discourses. In this case, the discourses examined are
about race and gender. This author stresses the role of Cultural
Models in the negotiation of identities at an interactional level. The
discourse construction of hegemonic and subordinate categories of
gender and racial belonging is also the focus of the chapter by
Moita-Lopes. Focusing on interactional positioning, the author
looks at the construction of whiteness, masculinity and heterosexuality in the discourse of one adolescent boy in focus group discussions taking place in a Brazilian school. In his analysis, identities
are built under local and socio-historical constraints that make
different kinds of meanings available on the basis of how people
are positioned within relationships of power. Both Kiesling and
Moita-Lopes demonstrate, with different data, the centrality of
processes of opposition and differentiation in the construction of
hegemonic categories.

The interactional construction of gendered identity and the role
of narrative in this process are also a prominent theme in Wortham
and Gadsden's chapter. Like Moita-Lopes, these authors focus on
"interactional positioning" and propose a re-elaboration of the
concept in order to account for ways in which narrators project

and enact identities in discourse. They also reflect on how the discourse ascription of membership categories is based on culturally available positions represented by associations between domains and actions.

Part IV, *The in-between self: negotiating person and place*, is centered on situations where identity construction is related to processes of coping with changes, troubles, or life-time transitions. In particular, contributors deal with the discursive negotiation of identity by immigrants and Holocaust survivors. In these circumstances, discursive processes of identification also imply a search for new meanings and new representations of self and others. The three chapters also deal with the relationship between individual identities and socio-historical processes and ideologies.

The opening chapter by De Fina presents a reflection on the emergence of group identity in the narrative discourse of Mexican undocumented immigrants to the US. She studies self-representations that emerge through the establishment of connections between identities and actions in stories, but also advocates for a close textual analysis of performance devices as a means of uncovering narrators' stances about socially shared self-representations. A similar attempt to bring wider contexts into the analysis of identity without abandoning the focus on interaction is found in Baynham's chapter, the second in the section. Baynham uses narratives of migration told by Moroccan immigrants to Great Britain to illustrate the unsettling of received categories of identity, to stress processes of identity formation and the building of new selves through interactional work.

The relationship between individual identity construction and social processes is also a central topic in the last chapter of the section. Schiff and Noy investigate the relationship between narrative and individual/social identity through an analysis of the life story of a Jewish woman, Bella. The narrator reinterprets her past through the help of a metaphor of brutality and chaos offered by a character, Demjanjiuk, whose existence and deeds surfaced much after the time of her deportation. The authors show how narrative is socially constructed in the sense that people integrate shared meanings and metaphors within their individual accounts.

Conclusion and anticipation

The purpose of *Discourse and Identity* is to gather together scholarship that represents the variety and richness of current approaches to identity. Within this variety, however, we found several points shared by all the authors that may be taken as guidelines for future work on discourse and identity.

The first point stems from the shared view that the analysis of any aspect of language is inseparable from analysis of its use in contexts. This has a consequence for analyses of identity. Identity is not something that speakers "have," but something that emerges through interactional practices – including ways of using language – in contexts. Since identity is continuously and constantly produced and reproduced, sketched and designed, and often co-constructed by 'self' and 'other,' we should strive to demonstrate how identities are (re)produced through language (and other media) and how they come into existence through social interaction.

The importance of "practice" is a second point. Not only is it within social practice that identities are shaped, but also the construction and projection of identities are themselves interactional practices. The details of these interactions vary, as do approaches to their analyses. Yet practices as varied as narrative, life story, interviews, letter writing, and conversation all provide systematic (yet emergent) means of "doing" things through talk that simultaneously provide means of "being."

A final point brought forth through this volume is that processes of identities cannot be neatly bifurcated as individual or social: interconnections between individual and social levels pervade both processes and products of identity construction. The social theorist Anthony Giddens (1991) observes four general oppositions that are claimed to thwart our efforts to situate a 'self' in a meaningful way within our phenomenal worlds: unification vs. fragmentation, powerlessness vs. appropriation, authority vs. uncertainty, personalized vs. commodified experience. Giddens places some of the responsibility for these oppositions, and their resulting "tribulations of self," on the increasing availability of mediated information in modern society. Yet other features of modern urban societies (e.g. the increasing role of bureaucracies, the rise of consumerism, social and geographic mobility, alienation from traditional institutions) can also contribute to, and complicate, our definitions of who we are. What this volume demonstrates is how recent scholarship in linguistics, anthropology, sociology and psychology has shown that it is largely within discourse that we find particularized evidence of Giddens' oppositions, as well as efforts to reconcile (or change) them within the various social domains in which our claims to self-validity and social legitimacy are reinforced, challenged or altered.

Part I

Overview: theory, method and analysis

Editors' introduction

The chapters in Part I, *Overview: theory, method and analysis*, present broad (and sometimes challenging) perspectives on several issues pursued and relied upon in many analyses of discourse and identity, including those in the chapters in this volume. Mishler opens Part I by taking sharp and critical aim at the presumption – and privileging – of linear time in the structure of narrative and the formation of identity. Mishler points out that research on narrative and identity is dominated by a "clock/chronological" model of time that has consequences for identity theory. If we assume that a sequence of events provides a causal chain of "what happened," then the development of identity through narrative should mirror that process: early identities would provide the basic material out of which later identities develop. Mishler argues, however, that our stories do not represent temporal and causal chains leading toward the present. Rather, stories represent more recent (or possibly current) reflections that throw a different light on what happened. Events and plots have actually been selected from many possible configurations at each point in time. Thus the only way we know what events will serve as a beginning or middle of a story is by looking backwards from the end of the story. Likewise, our constructions of identity through narrative flow recurrently between the present and the past.

Whereas Mishler challenges the validity of depending upon chronological time as a scaffold for the construction of identity in narrative, Ribeiro (Chapter 2) examines the use of three central constructs through which people manage their identities not only in the "remembered time" (Mishler) of narratives, but also in the "real time" of face-to-face interactions. Ribeiro uses an analysis of a telephone conversation on medical family matters between two brothers to illustrate and compare these different means of mediating the self through language, 'other' and interaction. By viewing footing, positioning and voicing as contextualization processes in talk and interaction, Ribeiro argues that the three means of mediating self/other/language/interaction allow participants to convey different types of meta-messages. Rather than argue that any one of these processes is more central to analysis than others, Ribeiro points out that analysts may choose to examine participants' subtle shifts of alignment (footing), strategic interactional moves (positioning) or the salience of agency (voice) during an interaction.

Like Mishler and Ribeiro, Georgakopoulou begins with some well-used and familiar aspects of theory/methodology and then subjects them to careful scrutiny. By addressing the relationship between identity and narratives – especially the processes whereby ordinary stories that are co-constructed during talk in interaction help construct identities – Georgakopoulou tries to bridge the divide between two sets of sometimes polarized constructs: local and global identities; discourse and Discourse. Analysis of storytelling practices among members of a group of adolescent girls establishes that global (i.e. extra-situational, exogenous) identities can be traced in discourse through local details and sequential management of talk. Also crossed is the bridge between discourse (as language use about and beyond the sentence) and Discourse (as "socially accepted associations among ways of using language, of thinking, valuing, acting and interacting, in the 'right' places and at the 'right' times with the 'right' objects" (Gee 1999: 17)). Here Georgakopoulou uses narrative analysis as a point from which the local management of participant roles can be connected to pre-existent, socioculturally available Discourses.

By demonstrating that participants' exploitation of conversational (interactional) structures and mechanisms makes visible extra-situational resources, this chapter argues for a pairing of storytelling participation roles with larger social identities.

Although Schiffrin's starting point in Chapter 4 is language, her theoretical framework and analysis of a short segment of talk in interaction touches some of the same ground as Ribeiro and Georgakopoulou: the positioning and footing of a 'self' in relation to an 'other' during social interaction. Schiffrin's chapter starts with a problem of reference: how can a referring term index identities in the textual and social worlds? Her answer requires a perspective on 'self,' 'other' and interaction developed from a close reading of Erving Goffman's work, as well as some understanding of linguistic analyses of reference. Schiffrin illustrates this interdisciplinary theoretical framework by analyzing how a single reference during an interchange in one interview is part of a complex array of identities at different levels, including animator/author (of a repair), situated role in activity-based sequences, and broad social categories (gender, social class and region). Her analysis thus suggests that interactional practices (e.g. sequencing, turn-taking) and linguistic details of repair, grammar, lexis, and prosody can provide resources for negotiating multiple identities, ranging from microanalytic facets of footing to situated identities and to broad social categories that may transcend their specific instantiation in a localized interaction.

1

Narrative and identity: the double arrow of time

Elliot G. Mishler

1.1 Introduction

The metaphor of the 'double arrow of time' points to the problem I wish to explore in this paper, namely, the implications for research and theory about identity development of two contrasting approaches to the functions of temporal order in narratives: clock/chronological vs. narrative/experiential models of time. In discussing this problem, I will draw primarily on my studies of life history interviews with craftartists and sexual abuse survivors. I will argue that more is at stake for narrative theory and research in the choice made between these two models of time than the specification of narrative structure. And, as well, that the differences are consequential for theory and research on human development, raising questions, for example, about research strategies that rely on a clock-time view of causality and on prediction as a criterion of adequacy for such studies. Further, the alternative narrative-time model underlines the importance of context in the production of narratives by showing how temporal ordering is a function of both cultural preferences for well-formed stories and the situated nature of storytelling, for example, whether elicited in interviews or expressed in the course of naturally occurring conversations. Thus, addressing problems of time and temporal order leads us to general and complex issues about relationships between context, structure, and function in narrative studies of identity.

1.2 Narrative/experiential vs. clock/chronological models of time

The well-known heterogeneity of narrative studies is to some degree offset by general, though not universal, consensus among investigators that temporal order is the fundamental criterion that distinguishes narratives from other genres of discourse (Mishler 1995). If we probe more deeply, however, we find that this agreement fractures as it becomes clear that while this may be a necessary criterion it is not a sufficient one, particularly if we wish to make the further distinction between event sequences that are merely *lists* from those that are *stories*. That is, a narrative must be more than one thing following another. Some form of meaningful connectedness among episodes is necessary for hearers/readers and analysts to recognize a stretch of talk or text as a bounded whole or gestalt with a beginning, middle, and end, that taken together has a point. In specifying this distinction, different models of time and temporal order have been applied. I will focus on the implications for theory and research on personal narratives and identity development of using either a clock/chronological or experiential/narrative model of time.[1]

Two quotations, each from a prominent narrative theorist, clearly display the contrast between these perspectives. The first is from the seminal paper by William Labov and Joshua Waletzky (1967) on narratives of personal experience; the second from Paul Ricoeur's paper on narrative time (1980).

Narrative will be considered as one verbal technique for recapitulating experience, in particular, a technique for constructing narrative units which match the temporal sequence of that experience . . . a narrative . . . may carry out the referential function perfectly, and yet seem difficult to understand . . . it has no point . . . The *evaluation* of a narrative is defined by us as that part of the narrative which reveals the attitude of the narrator towards the narrative by emphasizing the relative importance of some narrative units as compared to others.   (Labov and Waletzky 1967: 13, 33, 37)

I take temporality to be that structure of existence that reaches language in narrativity and narrativity to be the language structure that has temporality as its ultimate referent . . . By plot I mean the intelligible whole that governs a succession of events in any story . . . A story is made out of events to the extent that plot makes events into a story.   (Ricoeur 1980: 169, 171)

[1] The implications of this contrast for studies of narrative have been explored by other investigators, for example, by Klaus Riegel in his critique of human development research (Riegel 1997) and Cheryl Mattingly in her study of therapeutic emplotment in the work of Occupational Therapists with paraplegic patients (Mattingly 1998).

Labov and Waletzky immediately follow their *reality–language temporal–matching* definition of narrative in the quotation with the qualification that a "narrative which serves this function alone is abnormal; it may be considered empty or pointless narrative." They then "distinguish two functions of narrative: (1) referential and (2) evaluative " (1967: 13). The latter, expressing a narrator's "attitude" by the relative emphasis given to different narrative units, is of equal importance. However, what is particularly significant about this qualification is that it does not in any way alter the chronological definition of temporal order, which remains the fundamental characteristic of a narrative in their approach. Their form of analysis relies on a clock-time model, where the sequence of episodes in the *real world* must be matched by the sequence of clauses as they actually appear in the narrative account that represents that world. Clauses that do not meet this requirement of correct sequential placement are defined as non-narrative clauses, which may either be redefined as evaluative or deleted from the analysis. The evaluative potential of a clause depends solely on whether and how it indicates the relative significance of the predefined temporally ordered set of events that constitutes the narrative.

Early on in his "Narrative time" paper, Ricoeur observes that approaches to narrative in history, literary criticism, and philosophy tend to rely on an "uncriticized temporal framework . . . that corresponds to the ordinary representation of time as a linear succession of instants" (1980: 170). Proposing an alternative perspective, that specifies different levels or types of time, he emphasizes the significance of a "plot," as governing how a sequence of events is made into a story. He too finds it necessary to go beyond sequence, but in a different direction than Labov and Waletzky's addition of an evaluative component to a still-privileged temporal order. Instead, Ricoeur asserts that: "every narrative combines two dimensions in various proportions, one chronological and the other nonchronological. The first may be called the episodic dimension, which characterizes the story as made out of events. The second is the configurational dimension, according to which the plot construes significant wholes out of scattered events" (178). Specifying how a plot functions, he states:

The plot's configuration also superimposes "the sense of an ending" . . . the recollection of the story governed as a whole by its way of ending constitutes an alternative to the representation of time as moving from the past into the future, according to the well-known metaphor of the arrow of time . . . invert[ing] the so-called natural order of time. By reading the end in the beginning and the beginning in the end, we learn also to read time backward, as the recapitulating of the initial conditions of a course of action in its terminal consequences.   (Ricoeur 1980: 179–180)

An important feature of Ricoeur's formulation is that it gives the ending of a story the primary function in how a story is plotted or constructed. To argue that a narrative is "governed as a whole by its way of ending," is significantly different than the function of evaluations of temporally ordered events in the Labov–Waletzky model. In offering this alternative to the "well-known metaphor of the arrow of time," Ricoeur asserts that "a plot establishes human action not only within time . . . but within memory" (180).

The basic assumption in contemporary theories and studies of narrative that "more than one thing following another" is necessary for a sequence to count as a story is itself a relatively modern notion (Kern 1983; Toulmin and Goodfield 1965). Early incomplete or pre-narrative historical accounts, such as annals and chronicles (White 1980), simply list events in their temporal order without an explicit plot or ending. And in classic epics and myths, the passage of time is not marked by the progression of discrete, uniform units and events may repeat or recycle (Bakhtin 1981b; 1986; Freeman 1998). With due recognition of its historical- and cultural-boundedness, it is nonetheless important to take the problem of temporal order seriously since it is a critical feature of current work (Mishler 1995, 1997). For example, the Labov–Waletzky model of narrative analysis has influenced many narrative researchers (Bamberg 1997a) whose studies constitute the recent surge of interest in sociolinguistics and the human science disciplines, sometimes referred to as the "narrative turn." Although Ricoeur's model has been equally influential among language philosophers, literary scholars, and historians, there is a noticeable absence of reference to his work among researchers who focus on the personal, social, and cultural contexts and functions of personal experience narratives. The contrast between the two models of time provides a point of departure for this inquiry into the problematic of temporal ordering in narrative studies.

1.3 The "sense of an ending"

Ricoeur took the phrase the "sense of an ending" from the title of a book by Frank Kermode, an eminent literary critic, and expanded on his argument that:

In 'making sense' of the world we still feel a need, harder than ever to satisfy because of an accumulated experience, to experience that concordance of beginning, middle, and end which is the essence of our explanatory fictions.   (Kermode 1967: 35–36)

Kermode, in turn, had drawn on psychological experiments about the responses of subjects listening to rhythmic "tick-tock" sounds, who could accurately distinguish the length of intervals between tick and tock but not between tock and tick. These findings, he argued, demonstrate that "we can perceive a duration only when it is organized," which leads him to the definition of a plot that Ricoeur elaborated:

The interval . . . between 'tick' and 'tock' is now charged with significant duration. The clock's 'tick–tock' I take to be a model of what we call a plot, an organization that humanizes time by giving it form; and the interval between 'tock' and 'tick' represents purely successive, disorganized time of the sort we need to humanize.   (Kermode 1967: 45)

And for a recent and succinct restatement of this view about the role of endings in the plots we construct about the relation between the past and present, that is, our need to "humanize time," we find the hero of E. L. Doctorow's (2000) novel, *The City of God*, observing:

If not in all stories, certainly in all mystery stories, the writer works backward. The ending is known and the story is designed to arrive at the ending. If you know the people of the world speak many languages, that is the ending: The story of the Tower of Babel gets you there . . . The ending of the story implies that there might have been a different ending . . . You allow as how since things worked out this way, they could have worked out another way. You create conflict and suspense where there wasn't any. You've turned the human condition into a sequential narrative of how it came to be.   (2000: 65)

Ricoeur's conception of narrative time, amplified and specified by a literary critic and novelist, cautions us against relying solely on chronology as an interpretive frame for making sense of a story. As Kermode and Doctorow point out, we must know how a "story" ends before we can understand how earlier events in the sequence function as beginnings and middles. Further, even prior to such an evaluation, we cannot determine which events "belong" in the sequence and which do not without having first defined its ending. From the standpoint of this more radical reconceptualization of the structure of narratives, it appears that the work of narrativization alters the standard, common-sense view of temporal ordering as representing a chronological sequence where events that precede others are independent, and potential causes or explanations of those that follow – the clock-time conception of how things happen in the "real" world.

The implications of this distinction between narrative/experiential and chronological/clock models of time go well beyond studies of narrative as a form of discourse, that is, as an object for linguistic analysis. The "uncriticized temporal framework" where time is represented as a "linear succession of instants" is omnipresent, usually as a tacit assumption, in psychology and the other human sciences where change or development are primary topics for theory and research – whether at the individual, cultural, or societal level. Thus, studies of learning, personality change, and identity development rely on the clock-time model to justify preferred research strategies and theoretical frameworks. Experimental pretest–posttest designs, prospective and retrospective prediction studies, cognitive-, linguistic-, and identity-development stage theories all ground their claims for adequacy on the taken-for-granted assumption that the earlier event – pretest or Stage 1 – is independent of and not influenced by later tests or stages.

This assumption seems self-evident, and questioning it risks being viewed as odd or perverse, or even more worrisome as a return to a long-rejected idea of teleology. Nonetheless, I think it is important to remember that the clock-time model is empirically justified through its application to the physical world, the event space of material objects that are not gifted and burdened with consciousness, reflectiveness, memory, and intentionality. Atoms do not consult each other so as to act collectively to display Brownian movements, nor do viruses plan their strategies of cell invasion. Thus, it does no violence to represent their trajectories through time as a "succession of instants." But it is a different matter when it comes to how conscious and reflective persons re-present and re-story their memories of events and experiences.

1.4 Life stories and the double arrow of time

With this contrast between the physical world and the world of human consciousness and experience, I wish to underscore the point of these introductory remarks, namely, that the use of a clock-time model in studying human subjects – and other living species with varying capacities for memory, consciousness, etc. – can only be warranted if we strip them, theoretically of course, of those capacities and treat them as material objects. But if we wish to understand how individuals learn, change, and develop then we must have an alternative to the linear temporal-order causal model, one that allows for their acting in the present toward a desirable or away from an undesirable future state of affairs. And it must also allow for their ways of reinterpreting the meaning of past events in terms of later consequences, through which they redefine who they are and revise the plots of their life stories.

It is not surprising that recognition of the problematic of temporal order should emerge from recent studies of personal narratives, accounts of past experiences elicited in clinical and research interviews, or sometimes written for other purposes. Constructed retrospectively, by looking backward from the present, their plots are "governed as a whole" by their ways of ending, that is, by the current situation in which tellers find themselves after what has happened to them in the past. They display and document the "double arrow of time" (Mishler 1992, 1999).

This is not a peculiar or rare process but a pervasive one. Indeed, it is an inherent and intractable feature of how we remember and continually restory our pasts, shifting the relative significance of different events for whom we have become, discovering connections we had previously been unaware of, repositioning ourselves and others in our networks of relationships. The past is not set in stone, but the meaning of events and experiences is constantly being reframed within the contexts of our current and ongoing lives – a view that not only reflects studies of narrative but has gained acceptance among neuroscientists and psychologists in the field of memory research (Schacter 1995; Schacter and Scarry 2000). The central tenet in studies of identity and human development that the past is the unchangeable bedrock for predicting the future is untenable.[2] A narrative/experiential model of time offers an alternative point of departure for narrative and human development research, one that raises new questions and requires new methods and concepts that may prove more appropriate for studying lives in context than those we have inherited from clock-time models and assumptions.

In such research, we need to be particularly attentive to the psychological, cultural, and social functions of how a story is told and of the particular contexts in which it is told. How a narrator selects and assembles experiences and events so they contribute collectively to the intended point of the story – the "why" it is being told, in just this way, in just this setting – is our central question, not a side issue.[3] The problem I want to address is how we might conduct such inquiries under the rubric of a narrative/experiential time model rather than a clock/chronological one.

---

[2] Although memory researchers agree on the malleability of memories and the effects of later experiences, the clock-time view of the past as fixed and independent of what follows is still strongly held in a variety of fields. For example, in his historical account of the concept of traumatic memory and the psychiatric diagnosis of Post-Traumatic Stress Disorder (PTSD), Allan Young (1995: 135) observes that "The description of PTSD in DSM-III-R presumes that time moves *from* the etiological event to the post-traumatic symptoms." Further, this view is retained even though "clinicians know that, in some cases, the relation of time to symptoms and events can be ambiguous" suggesting a "picture in which time flows in two directions: from a significant event out to its symptoms . . . and from a person's current psychological state back to the event, where it acquires a genealogy and a discrete set of meanings." He notes that this is actually an "old idea" going back to the nineteenth-century French psychiatrist Ribot and "his conception of the self as a made object that continues to remake itself by appropriating the past" (1995: 136).

[3] It is worth noting that Ricoeur's emphasis on temporality and narrative time was part of his critique of structuralist theories of narrative that treat the temporal ordering of events in a story as a "surface" structure, subordinate to and derivative of a "deep" structure, with variations in the former of less interest and significance. One commentator summarizes this perspective as follows: "Whereas the surface structure of the story is syntagmatic, i.e., governed by temporal and causal principles, the deep structure is paradigmatic, based on static logical relations among the

In brief, I will argue that the act of narrativizing reassigns meaning to events in terms of their consequences, that is, how the story develops and ends, rather than to their temporal place in the sequence of events. Another way to say this is that narrative time is central to how a story is structured and understood, and temporal ordering is simply one strategy for organizing the events into a plot.

1.5 Turning points

I want to illustrate the sorts of questions that emerge from a narrative/experiential approach by focusing on one recurrent feature of life history narratives that I and others refer to as "turning points." These incidents, often occurring suddenly and unexpectedly, may be reported in life history or clinical research interviews, as I found in my study of craftartists (Mishler 1999) and in collaborative work on sexual abuse survivors' accounts of trauma and recovery (Harvey et al. 2000).[4]

Here are two examples, the first (1.1) from an interview with an adult survivor of childhood sexual abuse and incest and the second (1.2) from a woman studio potter recalling her first experience in a pottery class:

---

elements" (Rimmon-Kenan 1983: 10). In contrast to this emphasis on an underlying structure, studies of how identity is represented in personal narratives take how a story is actually told as their point of departure.

[4] Similar turning points are reported by researchers studying the life impact of chronic illness, who refer to them as "biographical disruptions" (Bury 1982; Charmaz 1987; Charmaz 1991; Williams 1984). Parallels to these life events may also be found in other fields of historical study. For example, the geologist-paleontologist Stephen J. Gould rewrites the history of geological theories of the formation of the earth in terms of two competing models of time: a linear progression of small changes he calls "time's arrow," in contrast to a cyclical one, where the same processes are repeated over and over again (Gould 1987). He argues that an adequate theory requires both, but in addition must also allow for instances of "radical disruption," once characterized as catastrophes, such as a comet's impact leading to the extinction of dinosaurs.

Example 1.1

I was enraged over this business thing that happened. And I turned around–
hung up the phone and I turned around and said you=know 'How could he
do this to me?' And then it was like a light went off in my head that said
you=know 'What did he do to you before? What did you expect.'

Example 1.2

As soon as I put my hands on the clay, I knew 'This was it.'

Respondents report such events as changing their understandings of their past experiences. They open up directions of movement that were not anticipated by them and could not be predicted
by their previous views of their pasts, leading to a different sense of
themselves and to changes that were consequential for how they felt
and what they did. The potter found her future vocation by chance.
She was in graduate school studying to become a history teacher
when she took a two-week, between-semester, non-credit ceramics
course to take her mind off her distress at the break-up of a
relationship. She had no prior interest in art and her discovery that
"This was it" was the turning point in her life. She gave up her plan
to become a history teacher, became instead a studio potter, and has
continued to work at that craft for the past twenty years.
A metalsmith told me a similar story. He saw the work of an artist
potter and decided he "just wanted to make beautiful objects"
rather than accept a Fellowship he had just been offered to return
to graduate school. He too has continued to work as a craftsman
for the past twenty-plus years.

Sometimes, these turning points lead to a restorying of the past
and the adoption of a new identity that changes the meaning of
past relationships. For example, a fabric designer's early "love"
of art was pushed aside, first by her parents' anxieties about how
she would support herself as an adult woman, and later by her
responsibilities as a wife and mother. For twenty years she could
only pursue her love of art as a side-involvement. Her turning point
did not come until her mid-forties when she decided, after a particularly difficult move occasioned by her husband's change of jobs,
that she was "no longer going to compromise herself in a relationship." She changed her life, renegotiated the terms of her marriage,
and recentered her identity as a craftartist.

This shift in her identity also changed how she interpreted her early family life and her relationship with her parents. Earlier, she had thought of her mother during her childhood as the "perfect mother," but after her own change began to blame her for not being an appropriate role model since her artistically-inclined and talented mother did not pursue her art seriously, made her own mother–wife role central in her life, and told her daughter that taking care of the family should always come first. Still later, as she succeeds in her new career, she takes a more generous view, recognizing that her mother too may have felt disappointment and loss about not doing more with her art and feels angry at her father for the demands he made on her mother (Mishler 1999).

Among sexual abuse survivors, a turning point may be an incident that leads them to revise the story they had lived with to make sense of a father's persistent childhood sexual abuse and incest. I am not referring to so-called repressed memories that surface years after but to situations where women had not forgotten what happened but either had no name for it or gave it a meaning that was later undermined. An unexpected event may lead them to problematize and recontextualize their pasts, and they may then rewrite their stories in ways that reposition them vis-à-vis their parents, siblings, and other figures in their lives (Harvey *et al.* 2000). The abuse survivor I quoted earlier, who experienced a "light" going off in her head when her father reneged on a promise – more than twenty years after the abuse had ended – was able for the first time to name what happened as incest. Recognizing that she had been victimized by her father, she confronted him directly about the harm he had done to her. She now believes that her mother "knew" about what was going on and has also confronted her about her silence and nonintervention. Since identities are rooted within this matrix of relationships, such events set in motion the complex process for sexual abuse survivors of restorying their pasts, re-emploting their traumatic histories in the context of new "endings," and thereby also revising their identities.

This is particularly striking in the account of another incest survivor whose adoptive stepfather was the perpetrator. In her pre-turning point story of her experiences, she had cast herself in the role of a "sacrificial lamb," where she believed her compliance with and silence about her step-father's sexual molestation from early childhood through late adolescence would protect her younger sisters and preserve her parents' marriage. Some years later, after her parents divorced, she learned he had also tried to molest her sisters. Her original story no longer made sense, as she realized it "was all for nothing." Having lost that way of under-standing what happened, she could only refer to that significant aspect of her past history as a "bizarre event."

Later still, after the birth of her second child, her fury at her step-father resurfaced and she was propelled into action: she had her adoption annulled legally, removing her step-father's name from her adoption papers; confronted him directly about the harm he did; located her birth father and re-established a relationship with him before his death. In these ways, she restored the connection between her "beginning" and her present self. Through this process of restory-ing, she gave her past a new meaning and built a new identity for herself – one no longer centered on being an incest survivor.

Turning points are particularly striking examples of what goes on all the time, that is, the continuous process we engage in of reconstructing the meanings of past experiences and remaking our selves in both small and big ways. This ongoing, unending process of revising, and re-revising our life stories and our identities, as we come to understand what happened in terms of ever-widening contexts of what happened later, strongly suggests the need to rethink some key assumptions in life-span development theory and research, such as continuity in developmental trajectories and the related emphasis on prediction in both prospective and retrospective longitudinal studies (Mishler 1999).

The process of restorying that both marks and results from these striking turning-point incidents is a general feature of our multiple identities, each rooted in a different set of relationships that form the matrix of our lives. Each of our partial selves is a character in a different story, where we are positioned in different ways in our relationships with others who constitute our several social worlds. These several stories, with their different plots, intersect and may conflict with each other, creating tensions at various points in our lives. This relational conception, of a plurality of sub-identities, points to another problem with temporal-order models of progres-sive change: the tendency to treat identity development as a unitary process, as if each life could be defined by a single plot line. This view suppresses our multiple identities that reflect our positioning ourselves in different relational contexts and ignores overlapping sequences of events and their intersection with each other. Narrative analysts with a clock-time perspective tend to favor a master narrative that gives a unitary, coherent meaning to our lives, and some theorists even argue that such an achievement represents a higher level of personal integrity (MacIntyre 1984; Taylor 1991).

A more adequate understanding of how we change throughout our lives requires a relational conception of identity, one that locates the recurrent restorying of our lives within the flux of contradictions and tensions of the several social worlds in which we are simultaneously actors and respondents to others' actions. The life histories of the craftartists I interviewed display these tensions. Their work identities were forged and re-forged with reference to two primary axes of relationship: one is the larger cultural and socioeconomic context of craftwork within a mass-production, late-stage industrial society; the other, their more immediate family relationships. These are not independent of each other. Whether one is considered an artist or a craftperson is central in the present art–craft world and being labeled as one or the other has significant social and economic consequences. For example, artists show their work in galleries and can price their pieces higher than craftpersons who market their work in craft fairs and their own studios. The latter rarely earn enough from their work to support their families. The stories they told of their careers and of their current work as craftartists reflect the tensions between their family and work worlds and how they attempted to resolve them (Mishler 1999).

One artist furniture maker, nearing forty at the time of our interview, began his work motivated by the desire to make beautiful objects and be recognized for his creativity. Despite a successful career, he is now troubled by how little he has to show for it in the way of "financial rewards," feels he has worked hard and knows he can "get by" but now wants more than that. These feelings are stimulated not only by approaching mid-life but by the fact that his wife earns more than he does. In their household economy, they do not pool their incomes but each pays certain expenses and has the remainder for personal use. Because of the income differential, they cannot do things together that his wife can afford but he cannot, such as take expensive vacations. These problems led him to seriously consider changing his line of work to designing for mass-production, which would radically change his work identity as well as his marriage relationship. These tensions are not unique to him. Another furniture-maker spent a dozen years early in his career and marriage doing commercial woodworking so he could support his family. He had time only to make an occasional piece of his own for a show. Finally, depressed and drinking, he simply "walked away" from the woodworking business and stopped making furniture. It took him over twenty years to get back to what he sees as his own work and he observes he "almost waited too long." Such disruptions in career trajectories, like the turning points I referred to earlier, are not uncommon and suggest that both our models of identity development and our theories and methods for narrative research need to include these shifts off a progressive, linear path. Neither the trajectories of our lives nor the stories we construct to understand ourselves and others are smooth, continuous, and progressive. Each is marked by fits and starts, detours, and hiatuses.

1.6 No middles/no ends: contexts of storytelling

Turning points, and the ensuing re-emplotment of past experiences that changes their meaning and initiates shifts in personal identities, highlight the significance of endings both for tellers and listeners to stories. In calling on narrative researchers to pay attention to this, I am simply extending to our work what we all know from canonical examples in our everyday worlds, such as mystery stories, folk tales, and jokes. The solution to a mystery turns the sequence of prior events into the clues that lead to and justify the ending – and just that and no other ending. The ending, however, cannot be so over-determined that we are not surprised. To achieve this aim, the skillful writer misleads us with alternative possibilities that conceal the real clues, which must, however, be there to be found retro-spectively or we would feel she has not played fair with us – a process that depends on the storyteller knowing the end in advance. On the other hand, if our expectation of a fitting ending is not fulfilled – as when someone telling us a joke stops in mid-stream to say she has forgotten the punch line – we become annoyed by having been led on by an account of events that now makes no sense.

Nonetheless, these well-formed genres of stories – where the ends beget beginnings and there are coherent plots – do not exhaust the types of stories we encounter in our lives and in our studies. They display the orderliness of written narratives or repeatedly retold stories, bearing the imprint of an author's editing where successive revisions are directed to making it all hang together. In contrast, stories told in naturally occurring conversations where other speakers may interrupt with comments may not reach a recognizable ending and remain fragmentary or incomplete. Or, some life experiences may be so disruptive or traumatic that individuals are unable to or resist including them as part of a coherent life story.

For example, stories that depart from the well-formed, culturally normative structure are often found in the personal experience accounts of trauma survivors and individuals with chronic illness. Arthur Frank's studies of patients suffering from what he refers to as "deep illness," that is, a chronic condition that will not go away and is always there, led him to propose a three-fold typology of illness narratives that he refers to as: quest, restitution, and chaos narratives (Frank 1995). Stories of the first kind are organized thematically around an individual's sense of having achieved a new identity based on the illness experience, and a belief that what was learned might benefit others in similar situations. They are similar in form and intent to the post-turning point stories of sexual abuse survivors I described earlier. Tellers of restitution narratives view their illnesses as aberrations in their normal life course and project a future where they will return to being the same persons they were in the past. Through this mode of re-emplotment they erase this episode from their life stories, thus deleting the middle of the story. In chaos narratives, there is confusion and uncertainty. Anything might happen and there is a lack of predictability to the future course of events. Such stories lack a clear plot and resemble the pre-turning point accounts of sexual abuse survivors who report not being able to understand what happened, have no way to name it, and cannot integrate their experiences into a coherent life story.

Lawrence Langer's analysis of holocaust survivors' life history narratives, recounted to interviewers, documents their difficulties in including their death camp experiences in their life stories – this

profoundly painful middle part of their lives has no connection
with what came before or what came after. It is not forgotten, but
remains an undigested fragment of "frozen time" (Langer 1991).
Langer points to problems that interviewers – and others in survivors' lives – have with these fractured accounts, which do not have
the shape of our culturally expected and preferred stories. Interviewers express their discomfort by pressing respondents toward an
ending that will integrate this significant part of their lives into a
well-formed story, but holocaust survivors resist this pressure to
make what happened understandable. We found a similar pattern
in our studies of sexual abuse survivors of interviewer efforts to
elicit meaning-making endings and survivors' resistance to these
demands.

Clearly, these examples seem to run counter to the argument
I have been making about the functions of endings. A further
problem is explicitly raised by Elinor Ochs and her collaborators,
based on their studies of storytelling in natural conversations
(Ochs and Capps 2001; Ochs, Smith and Taylor 1989). Briefly,
their analyses of how stories are told in conversations among
participants in ordinary social situations – at the dinner table or
in the talk among friends – point to how they are produced and
shaped through the interactive process. The story turns into a joint
product, where the course of telling may be interrupted and the
account contested, temporal order may be violated by digressions
and flashbacks, and the ending may be uncertain and ambiguous.

Although I have not been telling a story, I would guess that
readers would be surprised – and perhaps feel misguided – if the
line of argument I have been pursuing was to end with the uncer-
tainties of these counter examples. As with a story, the conclusion
to an argument must fit with what has gone before. In this case, the
problems raised by narratives that are not well-formed and lack
middles or ends must be accounted for in ways that may complicate
but still preserve the central claim about the functions of endings
and plots.

Since this is the Coda to the paper I hope that these problems
will stimulate others to address the problematic of temporal order
in their theories and studies, I will be brief in stating the grounds for
believing that my argument remains cogent. First, in order to
extend the argument to cover these apparent discrepancies, we

must place endings and plots in a larger context that includes recognition of both the cultural frames we draw upon in our judgments of the adequacy of narrative accounts and their situated production. The preference of tellers for well-formed stories is evident in how they structure their accounts. But this is clearly a reflection of cultural and historically grounded norms about what makes a good story. The discomfort of interviewers, other listeners, and narrative analysts with accounts that depart from these ways of storying reflects these same norms.

Chronically ill patients whose narratives are marked by chaos and uncertainty are not immune to this cultural imperative and strive, though unsuccessfully at that point in their lives, to construct a better story that makes sense. The distress of sexual abuse survivors who have not been able to make sense of their experiences is partially reduced in their post-turning point narratives, through which they redo the meaning of what happened to them. Holocaust survivors recognize the desire, in themselves and their listeners, for a coherent story that will integrate their death camp experiences into the before and after of that time – but they are both unable and resistant to doing so since this would make the un-understandable understandable. And the primary storyteller at the dinner table has an end in view – otherwise why start the story – but has to negotiate her way through the questions and comments of other speakers that may lead to a respecification of her intended ending, which may indeed change the meaning of her story.

The range of variation in the structure of narratives – a function of history, culture, and the context of production – makes it clear that the concept of narrative is a "fuzzy category" with exemplars that include all the necessary criteria and other types that are defective in one or another respect but bear a "family resemblance" to the defining examples (Robins and Rutter 1990; Rosch 1978; Rosch and Mervis 1975). It seems to me that variants like those I began by calling counter examples further strengthen my argument that narrative theory and research requires a narrative/experiential model of time. It is very difficult to imagine how a clock-time model could make sense of them.

Finally, I wish to make explicit my perspective on the work of narrative analysis that I have alluded to at several points, namely, that there is a parallel between the telling of a story and its analysis.

Narrative researchers rely, in the same way and to the same extent as the narrators we study, on the ending of a story to make sense of it. We go back and forth, between our understandings of the whole and its parts, engaging in a repetitive recycling of interpretive moves towards a deeper and more comprehensive understanding of a story and how it is put together. In this process, as we learn more about how the plot is constructed and how it ends, we work toward an interpretation of how the sequence of events is connected together into a meaningful whole.

If we take seriously the close resemblance between the story-telling work of our research subjects and the work we do of making a coherent story of their stories, we may also be able to accept the inescapable limitations of our research findings and theories. They are not immutable, universal, and timeless but always tentative, continually revised by new discoveries that function like story endings that change our understanding of past knowledge and present new problems for study that had not been foreseen. From this perspective, the history and development of science cannot be adequately represented by a chronology of new findings, each simply added to earlier ones. Scientific practice is a form of life that is not exempt from the process of narrative time. In the spirit of that model of time, I hope that my observations on temporal order, endings, and turning points will serve as an invitation to join in the nonending process of retelling and rewriting our collective story of narrative studies.

Acknowledgments

For their helpful comments on earlier versions of this paper, I wish to thank Vicky Steinitz, my colleagues in the Cambridge Narrative Study Group and Cambridge Hospital Narrative Seminar/Workshop, and participants at symposia and conferences on narrative, identity, and human development at: the Radcliffe Murray Research Center of Harvard University; Clark University Department of Psychology; the Department of Communication Studies at Linkoping University, Sweden; and the Departments of Psychiatry and Linguistics at the Federal University of Rio de Janeiro and the Catholic University of Rio de Janeiro, Brazil.

2

Footing, positioning, voice. Are we talking about the same things?

Branca Telles Ribeiro

2.1 Introduction

In everyday conversation, participants continuously negotiate what is being said and done – how they are defining the situation and how they mean what they say. This social and conversational work conveys how participants frame interaction as they speak and are framed by others as well. This chapter discusses different framing processes in a telephone conversation between two brothers. It investigates the construction and performance of social and discursive identities in the delivery and reception of difficult news. While the brothers display alliance towards each other through their talk, tension is caused by the younger brother's responses. When the younger brother questions the validity of the older brother's report, a set of common premises needs to be established to avoid misunderstandings.

As a conceptual tool, frame analysis (Bateson 1972; Goffman 1974, 1981; Tannen 1986, 1993a) is particularly suited for understanding how people construct meaning from moment to moment. Interactants jointly signal their definition of a situation through framing. That is, as people speak and act, they signal to each other what they believe they are doing (e.g. what activity they are performing or what speech act they are producing) and in what way they want their words and gestures to be understood. The intricate ways in which framing is accomplished in verbal interaction is captured through Goffman's (1981) notion of footing, or the alignment that speakers and hearers take toward each other and toward the content of their talk. Interlocutors jointly construct frames by signaling their own ever-shifting footings while recognizing and ratifying those of coparticipants.

This chapter discusses contextualization processes in talk and interaction. It starts by discussing framing and footing. This discussion provides a background for analyzing the notions of positioning and voice. It points to ways in which these concepts are related. However, it argues for distinguishing footing, positioning and voice so as to grasp different types of metamessages which are at work in everyday talk. The layering of slightly different perspectives in an overlapping framework provides methodological tools that can refine our analysis.

2.2 Footing, positioning, voice

Perspective shapes analysis, Saussure (1994) alerts us. In discourse analysis, whether one focuses, for example, on the situated context of a telephone conversation, or on the institutional and professional macrostructures that configure the contexts of that call, is ultimately a choice in perspective determined by a research question. Whether one asks "what's going on here?" in an attempt to understand a specific speech event, or inquires "who owns meaning here?" to highlight agency and effective participation (or the absence of it) in an encounter, also reflects a choice. Different viewpoints are also at play when one chooses to investigate a participant's storyline and relate it to issues of power and interactional strategies, or to look at how participants' subtle shifts in alignment provide intricate contexts that shed light on coherence and the joint construction of meaning.

Concepts such as footing (Goffman 1981), positioning (Hollway 1984; Davies and Harré 1990; Harré and van Langenhove 1992, 1999), and voice (Bakhtin 1981b, 1986) have been used in sociology, psychology, and literary criticism to capture contextualization processes in everyday talk (or texts).[1] These concepts reveal the analyst's perspective on context: one may examine participants' subtle shifts of alignment (footings), or their strategic interactional

[1] Extensive research has been developed in the last 20 years using each of these frameworks (either footing, or positioning, or voice) to capture the social, interactional, and cognitive work that participants do in everyday talk. Also, researchers have appropriated these frameworks in different ways (varying in purpose and scope). Given the limits of this chapter, I present a few researchers that ground my analysis.

moves (positioning), or how they make their agency (voice) salient
in a conversation. Each one of these terms points to the dynamic
and reflexive nature of discourse. In many ways they work to fine
tune and reinterpret the sociological concept of role, or more precisely role performance (Hoyle and Ribeiro 1993; Harré and van
Langenhove 1999). While the notion of role seems to be attached to
our sociocultural expectations, closer to our knowledge schemata
(i.e. the role of the caretaker, the role of the lecturer, etc.), footing
and positioning are interactional concepts. They denote a framework that helps understand the ever-shifting moves of interlocutors
in the construction of self in interaction. Footing, positioning, and
voice provide ways of capturing what we mean by identity or
"doing identity work" in everyday conversation.

These concepts all derive from communicative models which
assume a dynamic, relational and interactional participant structure (Wertsch 1991; Schiffrin 1994). Such models capture the fleeting and emergent nature of context. Footing, positioning, and voice
take the view that context is not separate from interaction and is
not given *a priori*. Rather, interactants participate in creating the
very context in which they are acting. I will use footing, positioning, and voice to illustrate alternative perceptions of "what's going
on here" and "how I mean what I say." I will point that this
conversational and social work is related to doing identity work.
Ultimately what is at stake is the performance of our social and
discourse identities in interaction – what Erickson and Shultz
(1982: 17) have called our "performed social identities" – and the
need to understand meaning as situated.

In the following discussion, I use footing, positioning, and voice
to illustrate different types of assumptions present in the conversation. Footing captures subtle interactional work, elusive micro-shifts
in the older brother's reports and the younger brother's responses.
Positioning reveals the resource orientations of participants (closer
to knowledge structures or schemata), i.e. the brothers assume
differing places in the conversation due to differences in status
and expertise. Positioning orients talk in a given direction (where
meaning can be disputed, refuted, negotiated). Shifts in positioning
and strategy occur. Such shifts indicate major changes in participation structure (while footing indicates micro-elusive changes).
Finally, voice captures agency (or lack of it). It is both socially and

cognitively informed. Voice is particularly interesting to illustrate what happens in participants' expressive orientations (intentions and emotions). Specifically, we will see how the two brothers initially differ greatly in agency (the "I" in the matter) and progressively work toward a common voice (and an agreement). A voice perspective helps us understand the social work that underlies reflexivity.

2.3 The data

In this phone conversation, John reports to his younger brother Louis a diagnosis that a neurologist has just given their parents (mother Marie, 80; stepfather Edgar, 86) concerning the mother's progressively failing health and social skills. The telephone conversation continues for 5 minutes and 45 seconds. While John is talking to Louis, their parents are still in the process of ending the meeting with the doctor in his office. A conference call that had been planned between the neurologist, Louis, and John to explain the diagnosis and discuss the couple's future did not take place.[2]

Prior shared information between Louis and John includes concerns over their parents' failing health, the distance of the parents' home from hospitals and other medical care, and the sons' distance from the parents. For two years, Louis has increasingly assumed a role as the overseer of the parents' affairs. Recently, the mother had been diagnosed with "intermediary to severe brain atrophy."

The doctor received a memo noting the above information from John and Louis (and referred to in the conversation). Also, the mother had frequently asked to "go to California, where it's sunny and warm." Two months prior to this meeting, John had flown north to bring his parents to California, where he lives with his wife and children. However, even though the parents initially agreed to come to California to live, they soon changed their minds and have been talking about returning "home." A full transcript of the conversation is enclosed (Appendix 2.2), along with the transcription conventions (Appendix 2.1).

---

[2] The data was provided by a family member. All names have been changed; however, place and time references reflect actual information. My special thanks to both brothers. Louis taped this phone conversation because he had expected to record a conference call with the doctor.

2.4 A frame perspective

In this phone call the conversation and report frames are sometimes equally salient; at other times one predominates. The reporting frame is characterized by John occupying longer turns while Louis mostly presents minimum responses (often backchannels). The focus of John's report is the doctor's speech (what he said about the mother or her condition). John uses reporting verbs ("he said," "he believes") to preface his statements. Also, John's performed identity in recreating the doctor's utterances differs from his conversational footings. In the conversational frame, Louis takes longer turns and John is often the respondent (providing the second part of an adjacency pair). Also, turns tend to be more symmetrical. Here both brothers make personal statements.

In the report, John brings his brother new information about their mother's mental health: what her doctor has just told them (Marie, Edgar, and John). This report creates a paradoxical situation: on the one hand, Marie is deemed healthy, she only has a "mild cognitive disorder," that is she is basically fine. On the other hand, she is increasingly putting herself and Edgar at risk, "there is a social (problem)," with the consequent metamessage that she's not fine. The doctor's alignments to his patient, as reported by John, frame this paradox.

Not only does talk shift between a report and a conversation, but within John's report three other contexts surface as well: a medical frame, a social frame, and a legal frame. Each frame introduces different footings. Footing, in Goffman's words, is "the alignment we take up to ourselves and the others present as expressed in the way we manage the production or reception of an utterance" (1981: 128). It is the stance that speakers and hearers take toward each other and toward the content of their talk.[3]

---

[3] A frame is constructed through participants' signaling their footings and recognizing and ratifying another's footing – which often changes from moment to moment. Goffman uses quasi-synonyms for describing a change in footing: "participant's alignment, or set, or stance, or posture, or projected self" (1981: 128). Furthermore, Goffman suggests that interactants do not simply *change* footing, but rather *embed* one footing within another.

In the data, changes of footing are indicated by: 1) a change of pronoun for the addressee and addressor; 2) change of register (relatively formal legal and medical registers contrast with a relatively informal social register). Each frame elicits different types of response from Louis. Each helps capture "when is context" (Erickson and Shultz 1977) and "how we mean what we say" (Tannen 1986).

2.4.1 The medical frame: addressing a neurological concern

At the opening of the phone call, John reports the doctor's clinical evaluation of the mother:

Example 2.1

(a) JOHN he believes that by any number of neurologists' standards
                          [speaking very slowly]
(b)   that mom has mild ['hhh] cognitive decline ['hhh]
                          [acc]

(c)   ['hhh] *it's::: absolutely, positively not Alzheimer's.*
(d) LOUIS yeah.
(e) JOHN ['hhh] he said that-
                          [acc]
(f)   based on what he has seen, he had seen between him and
             Dr. Smith,
             [acc acc]
(g)   that there is likely to be improvement in her condition. (pause)

John takes a footing as animator of the doctor's beliefs. He paraphrases the doctor's words, using indirect speech. In partially animating the doctor's words, John presents the following supportive points for his account: 1) he provides clinical evidence "by any number of neurologists' standards," "based on what he has seen" 2) he brings in the opinion of a colleague and family doctor – strengthening Dr. Jones' evaluation as reflecting the opinion of two experts; 3) he rules out suspicion of a major neurological disorder; and 4) he concludes with a hopeful evaluation that "there is likely to be improvement in her condition."[4]

---

[4] Of course in this excerpt one can identify "frame leaks" (Tannen and Wallat 1993) in references such as "that mom has" and in the chain of

Such a report is expanded throughout the conversation:

Example 2.2

(a) JOHN ( ) he said that- ahm ahm that the ahm:
           [dec]

(b)   *the Zoloft* (pause) appears to have been causing a number of con ahm
           [dec]   [acc]

(c)   *problems.* (pause) one was it- one of which was raising her blood pressure.

(d) LOUIS mmm mmm.=
           [acc]

(e) JOHN =and since she's been off- since Smith has taken her off *all* her meds.
               [dec]   [acc]
     (pause) ahm: again, she's seen an *even* *increased* *improvement.*=

(f) LOUIS =mmm mmm.

New information about specific medication (Zoloft) is introduced. Again Dr. Jones' alignment with the family doctor is mentioned reinforcing the metamessage that both doctors work together as a successful team of experts.

John continues to animate the doctor's position as the expert:

Example 2.3

(a) JOHN okay. well. (pause) he ga- Louis, he gave her a battery of tests again today.

(b)   and then they talked about what's going on. and- what she remembers,
     . . . .

(c)   and he said it's only a mild cognitive disorder.
     [acc acc]

(d)   and he said- "it actually may improve now that you're off all these medications."
     . . . .

(e)   ah y'know based on all the things that *he sees.* (pause)
     [acc]

(f)   all the patients he sees,

adverbs disqualifying Alzheimer's ("absolutely, positively not"). Whether or not Marie has this major neurological disease, such a strong disclaimer is not expected in a medical register.

Several bits of reported information attest to the doctor's experience, competence and, most of all, expertise: "based on all the things he sees," "all the patients he sees." New examinations were done and new conversations took place. Again John restates the official diagnosis ("it's only a mild cognitive disorder") as well as a good prognosis ("it actually may improve now that you're off all these medications"). Here we see John fully animating the doctor's words, using direct quotation, involving a change in pronoun form (from "she" to "you").[5]

In this frame – as the animator of the expert's report – John uses a series of qualifiers to either emphasize or attenuate the doctor's stance in the medical frame. A series of adverbs –"absolutely," "positively," "not" – preface the noun "Alzheimer's." This is in sharp contrast with the phrase "only a mild cognitive disorder." The adjective "mild," modified by the adverb "only" as well as the indefinite article "a," create a relative and vague reference for a minor mental impairment. Implied meaning from this phrase is "it's not a big deal; it's fine."[6] Louis' responses are minimal. He uses a series of backchannels ("yeah," "mmm mmm"), mostly continuers, thus signaling his listenership.

2.4.2 The social frame: addressing a social concern

Let's look at the doctor's reported talk on a "social problem." Here is John's description:

Example 2.4

(a) JOHN   ahm- and ah- he said that there is- that there is not a medical
             problem here,
(b)   but a social one.
             [portable phone noise interference]
(c) LOUIS   what's the social one?
                        [acc]

---

[5] Tannen names this discourse strategy "constructed dialogue" indicating that "when speech uttered in one context is repeated in another, it is fundamentally changed even if reported accurately" (1989: 110).
[6] This reference sharply contradicts information given to the family two weeks before, where Marie was described as having "intermediate to severe brain atrophy."

(d) JOHN   ahm- the- what is- what is actually best for them.
              [acc acc]
(e)   he said- "y'know, you have to understand that you're o::ld and
              you're decl-
              [dec]   [dec dec]
(f)   going to decli:ne over ti:me. (pause) *you can expect that.*" he
              said but- ah:
                                      [acc]
(g)   but- and he said "you may not have the same quality of life
              between the two of you that you have had in the past. you may
              need some assistance."

This report raises a problem in the social world. It recreates the
doctor's words addressed to Marie and Edgar. There are subtle
shifts in the doctor's reported alignments to both of them, conveying either aggravation or mitigation of intentionality on the
doctor's part regarding a social concern. Prior to illustrating what
the "social problem" is, John prefaces with the discourse marker
"y'know," signaling attention and that more information will
follow (Schiffrin 1987); another attention claimer, "you have to
understand," mitigates the illocutionary force of what will follow.
This new footing is clearly indicated by the shift in pronoun
form to "you" addressed to Marie and Edgar, foregrounding
John's alignment as animator of the doctor's talk. Then a series
of evaluative statements are introduced "you're old," "you're
decl-" repaired as "going to decline over time," "you can expect
that." This certainty (as an overt face-threatening act described in
Brown and Levinson 1979) is counterbalanced by mitigated
phrases such as "you may not have the same quality of life,"
"you may need some assistance." The stigma attached to old age
and assistance is relativized by adverbs such as "(decline) over
time," the modifier "some," as well as the repeated modal "may"
(alluding to a possibility).

   Further information is presented some time later:

Example 2.5

(a) JOHN   and and he said, y'know,
              [acc acc]
(b)   he said to her *all kinds of things.* y'know,
(c)   he said "*your family is very much concerned.*" (pause)
(d)   ['hhh] and and he said, ah: (pause)

(e)		that ah that she should listen to us *very carefully* because- (pause)
(f)		we're much closer to the situation (pause) on a personal basis,
(g)		than *he is*, (pause) he's talking about *medical* (pause) [portable phone noise]
(h)	LOUIS	mmm mmm
(i)	JOHN	*issues,=*
(j)	LOUIS	mmm mmm.=
(k)	JOHN	=y'know.=
(l)	LOUIS	=yeah.=

John reports the doctor's social concerns about Marie and Edgar by using informal and vague references, as in "all kinds of things" and "medical issues," in contrast to terms typically used in a clinical frame ("neurologists' standards," "a battery of tests"). Also, a series of recommendations (indirect directives) unfold as to what action to take ("listen [to her sons]"), how to take this action ("very carefully"), and why (sons are "closer to the situation on a personal basis").

Regarding the topic "social problem," we see the doctor's reported difficulty in deciding between confronting the patient with a real problem – which the family has reported on extensively[7] – and letting the patient independently decide what is best for her and her husband. The social account also is particularly problematic as it becomes embedded within the medical clinical frame:

Example 2.6

(a)	JOHN	ahm- and ah- he said that there is- that there is not a medical problem here,
(b)		but a social one. [portable phone noise interference]
(c)	LOUIS	what's the social one? [acc]
(d)	JOHN	ahm- the- what is- what is actually best for them.

"What is actually best for them" *from their viewpoint* is not what this consultation was supposed to be about – at least not what the family expected to happen. A neurologist is not supposed to be

---

[7] Extensive conversations among Dr. Smith, John, and Louis about their parents living situation in Washington state were followed by a detailed memo from John and Louis to Dr. Jones explaining the difficulties ahead if their parents were to move back home.

concerned about the social world and social concerns. In this matter, Louis' responses to his brother's report are abrupt and confrontational. As the recipient of bad news, he provides minimal responses; he challenges his brother's assertions "what's the social [problem]?" and, implicitly, the doctor's assertions. Finally, Louis' disbelief in Dr. Jones' clinical expertise is blatant. In a crescendo, he deems the doctor unreasonable:

Example 2.7

(a) LOUIS   okay. (long pause) okay. (long pause)
             [acc]   [speaking quietly]
(b)   well I surely wouldn't like to be in a foxhole with him.
(c) JOHN   why is that now? (pause)
(d) LOUIS   *well*, HE'S A JERK. I guess- I mean- it's an ABSURD
             DIAGNOSIS.
                   [acc acc]
(e)   I don't believe a word of it. I think he's crazy. (pause)
(f) JOHN   JONES?=
(g) LOUIS   =*yes*.

Now, the question here seems to be: why does Louis align himself as the recipient of bad news, typically responding by a denial "I don't believe it" and by a challenge to the doctor's competence? Why a sequence of negative responses if, as John has extensively reported in the clinical frame, the mother's health evaluation is a favorable one?

2.4.3 The legal frame: addressing a potential judicial matter

A third frame must be discussed. It involves the doctor as a court expert:

Example 2.8

             [dec]
(a) JOHN   that ah that she would be rul- ruled as competent in *a court of
             law*::.
             [background noise interference] (pause)
                   [dec]   [acc]
(b) LOUIS   I don't believe that. okay=
                   [acc acc]
(c) JOHN   =yeah, well, that's what he's saying. he saying that
             b- y'know,

(d)   he's testified in these cases, that under any-
                 [dec]
(e)   that she would be- *ruled competent*. ['hhh] ahm:=
(f)   LOUIS   = then I'm a blue goose, but go ahead.

The reported alignment of Dr. Jones as a court expert may
have been triggered by prior information, presented to him in
John's memo. Briefly stated, after a year of concern over his parents' failing health and constant insecurity, Louis had started to get
information about conservatorship laws in California (regulations
for becoming his mother's guardian). Though this procedure is
briefly mentioned in the memo as something the family may do as
a "last resort," John's report of the doctor's talk indicates how
much the legal frame may have influenced the talk in the medical
and social encounters.

Here John reports the doctor's assertion that the court would
deem Marie competent. He indicates his own alignment with the
doctor's claim by repeating it and by providing further evidence to
support the doctor as an expert: "he's testified in these cases."

The claim of authority in John's alignment with the doctor as a
court expert sharply contrasts with Louis's responses. First Louis
states directly his disbelief. Then he requests more information
"okay," to signal "go on." He presents an irreverent and confrontational footing when John restates the doctor's belief ("then I'm
a blue goose"). This shift disqualifies John's report in three ways: 1)
Louis shifts to a colloquial register (thus not sustaining the formal
frame of the report); 2) he makes a nonsensical statement (implicitly indicating "to an absurd situation, one responds with absurd-
ities"); 3) he reasserts a direct authorship, the "I" in the matter,
thereby contrasting with John's indirect quotation.

This abrupt frame break is followed by a request for more information "but go ahead" – thus shifting back to the report situation.
However, it is no wonder that John can neither reframe talk
as court talk again, nor immediately re-establish what talk is
about:

Example 2.9

(a)   LOUIS   =then I'm a blue goose, but go ahead.
                 [acc]   [dec]

(b) JOHN ( ) he said that- ahm ahm that the ahm:
                [dec]
(c)   *the Zoloft* (pause) appears to have been causing a number of
             con- ahm
             [dec]   [acc]
(d)   *problems.* (pause) one was it- one of which was raising her
             blood pressure.
(e) LOUIS   mmm mmm.=

First John attempts to respond and "go ahead" with talk; however,
a sequence of hesitation markers indicates his difficulty. Finally
John shifts from providing detailed evidence animating the doctor
as a legal expert to reiterating and expanding information from the
clinical report. Adroitly he maintains Dr. Jones' claim of expertise,
shifting back to medical concerns.

2.4.4 Summarizing the three frames embedded in the report

Both medical and legal frames are constructed as reports of expertise. They present a lay interpretation of Dr. Jones' statements.
Sarangi and Clarke (2002) state that lay talk or lay perspectives,
though not specific, often capture a gamut of information available
to patients and their families (2002: 140). The registers used
(words, references, and levels of formality) convey Dr. Jones' institutional knowledge and professional experience. As discussed
above, these terms contrast with the social frame, which introduces
familiar, colloquial, and vague referential processes. Items from the
three registers include:

The lexicon in the medical register:
"he believes," "he sees"
"any number of neurologists' standards"
"a mild cognitive disorder"
"(the illness) is not Alzheimer's"
"your short term memory"
"(patient took) a battery of tests"
"(patient's future) cognitive decline"
(patient's) medication, the Zoloft
(patient's) blood pressure
"likely to be improvement in condition"

The lexicon in the legal register:
"(patient) would be ruled competent"
"a court of law"

"(doctor) has testified in these cases"
"between the two . . . for the near future they can function independently"

The lexicon in the social register:
"you have to understand"
"you're old"
"quality of life"
"some assistance"
"being off meds"
"your family is very much concerned"
"all kinds of things"
"listen very carefully to your family"
"families don't want to have anything to do (with this)"
"what is actually best for them"

John's major concern is to convey to his brother a report. He also wants to provide an explanation of why there will not be a conference call, since it had been planned carefully for two weeks. In this double orientation (reporting a talk/meeting and explaining a state of affairs), he proceeds to animate several of the doctor's different footings regarding the issues that were brought up in the meeting. John uses the reporting verb "he says," "he said," "he's saying," sometimes also transformed to "he believes," in each one of the three frames.

To summarize, the first part of this conversation (up to where we are now) is a report. John does not become fully an author or principal (Goffman 1981), stating his own beliefs about the doctor, his parents, the diagnosis, or its consequences. In every shift in frame, John animates (fully or partially) one or more alignments of the doctor toward his patient, or toward both Marie and Edgar, or toward the doctor's diagnosis and prognosis, as well as toward the family's role.

By the absence of explicit first-person mention and consistent reference to the doctor's stances, one infers that John is indirectly aligning himself with the doctor, as well as ratifying his expertise and competence in both the medical and legal frames.[8] Louis, however, responds by a reframing in the first-person active form. He speaks as principal and author. He expresses discredit and

[8] Prior information indicates that John's own doctor, Dr. Smith, had recommended Dr. Jones as a specialist. Thus, John would be expected to endorse both doctors as competent professionals.

disbelief, indirectly and overtly. Indirectly, he signals minimally his listenership and speaker's ratification by a series of "yeah," "mmm," "yes"; then he explicitly confronts the doctor's reported interpretation "I don't believe that," "then I'm a blue goose," "he's a jerk," "I think he's crazy."

2.5 Brothers' talk: negotiating differences in positionings

Why does Louis align himself as the recipient of bad news? Why a sequence of negative responses if the mother's health evaluation is a favorable one? These questions take us to the very opening of the phone call when John states "there's not going to be a conference call." This opening statement defines the social situation as: 1) decisions have been made among the consultation participants; 2) these decisions imply no conference call among Dr. Jones, Louis and John; 3) John will report the decisions to Louis. Louis receives the report as bad news as it contradicts prior expectations and he understands that he will not be involved in the decision-making process.

The concept of positioning captures the assigned and unfolding differences between Louis and John.[9] Harré and van Langenhove (1992, 1999) present positioning as a spatial metaphor. Participants' social acts (verbal and nonverbal) constitute a conversational grid which attributes "locations" to each member. Thus participants work with a set of expectations as to where to place the other in a given interaction. I use positioning to characterize John's and Louis' locations and most prominent footings (or projected selves) in interaction. John's and Louis' positionings

---

[9] Hollway (1984) introduces positioning as a psychological concept, stating that "discourses make available positions for subjects to take up. These positions are in relation to other people" (p. 236). Researchers have used the concept of positioning in different ways while preserving its relational and interactional properties. I use positioning to capture salient schemata (Rumelhart 1980; Tannen and Wallat 1993) and salient performed social identities in the conversation. Thus positioning orients major changes in participation structure. Given the limits of this chapter I do not attempt to further explore its interpretive possibilities (as, for example, Louis' and John's positionings as brothers, as sons, or as carers).

regarding the doctor's status and expertise reveal differences in orientations and schemata. We will see that repositionings (the brothers' shifts in orientation) indicate major changes in participation structure as the conversation develops.

The phone conversation, which opens by contradicting Louis' expectations, provides the larger frame for the medical, legal and social reports. It has the perlocutionary effect of removing Louis from participating in any decision-making process regarding his family. It positions the doctor as the expert, unavailable to discuss decisions and consequences with the family at large. It restricts the decision-making process to the doctor/patient relationship (or at best among the participants present to the consultation).

John represents Dr. Jones as the medical authority (declaring that Marie has a "mild cognitive disorder") and the legal authority (Marie would "be ruled competent in a court of law"). Louis (who is in fact a lawyer) first refutes Dr. Jones' competence as a legal authority:

Example 2.10

(a)	JOHN	that ah: that she would be rul- ruled as competent in *a court of law::*.
		[background noise interference] (pause)
		[dec] [acc]
(b)	LOUIS	I don't believe that. okay=
		[acc acc]
(c)	JOHN	=yeah, well, that's what he's saying. he saying that b- y'know,
(d)		he's testified in these cases, that under any-
		[dec]
(e)		that she would be- *ruled competent.* ['hhh] ahm:=
(f)	LOUIS =THEN	I'm a blue goose, but go ahead.

After listening to John's full report, Louis again discredits the doctor:

Example 2.11

		[speaking almost to himself]
(a)	LOUIS	okay. (long pause) okay. (long pause)
		[acc] [speaking quietly]
(b)		*well I surely wouldn't like to be in a foxhole with him!*

By wishing "not to be in a foxhole with" the doctor, Louis takes an ironic stance and asserts implicitly that the doctor is not reliable and cannot be trusted. He would not entrust his own life to him. Once more he disputes the doctor's authority and expertise.

2.5.1 Owning expertise and validating a report

The unfolding conversation reveals a difficult negotiation. On one hand, we have Louis with expertise as a lawyer and experience with his parents' failing health; on the other hand, we have John, who reports on the doctor's expertise. In addressing the question of who stands as the expert, positioning seems to be particularly helpful. Following the interaction analyzed above, John tries again to convey the good news brought by the clinical meeting:

Example 2.12

(a)   JOHN   okay. well. (pause) he ga- Louis, he gave her a battery of tests again today.

(b)   and then they talked about what's going on. and- what she remembers,
               [acc]

(c)   everything else. he said "your short term memory isn't (pause) very good."
               [dec]

(d)   he said. "but, y'know, between the two of you." (pause)
               [acc acc]

(e)   and he said it's only a mild cognitive disorder. and he said- "it actually may improve now that you're off all these medications."
                                                                                    [acc acc]

(f)   LOUIS   well: I I I *of course* I hope he's right. (pause)

John's response to Louis begins with three markers: "okay," "well" and a pause. Each indicates work John has to do to address his brother's sharp criticism and confrontation. The report – presented in a very fast pace – repeats previous information. Louis matches the fast pace and overlaps. He ratifies the report and his brother's realignment as author. Attending to John's previous statements, and displaying similar difficulties in articulating a response, Louis uses the marker "well" to signal a shift in positioning, making an emphatic and emotional assertion "of course I hope he's right." For the first time in this conversation, Louis shifts toward accepting the position of the recipient of good news. After a pause, however, he adds that this clinical encounter is not about "hope" (or wishful thinking), displaying again support for his previous confrontational positioning (and his expertise as observer in his parents' daily life):

Example 2.13

```
                                                              [acc]
(a)  LOUIS   but I don't think she can handle two pots on a on a kitchen
             stove,
             [acc acc]
(b)          not to mention er any other ['hhh] daily events.
```

Louis presents his mother's social incompetence as dangerous and severe. However, he goes on to specifically state where he stands in the conversation:

Example 2.14

```
(a)  LOUIS   but in any case, I mean,
(b)          we aren't we aren't arguing here. this is simply about what he
             said.
             [dec]          [dec dec]
(c)          and what he said is a fact. so, so be it.
(d)  JOHN    yeah.
```

In using first person plural pronoun and declaring "we aren't arguing" and "this is simply about what he said," he clarifies their relationship and his positioning in the conversation. Also, he declares that the doctor's report (whether trustworthy or not) is factual. It has an existence in the real world and will also have moral and social consequences. He concludes with resignation ("so," "so be it."). This formulaic expression captures Louis' state of acceptance and frustration.

The talk that follows has the same pattern as the segments discussed. John develops a series of supportive points to the doctor's arguments. Louis responds minimally ("mmm," "yeah"), then again restates his alignment with his brother and his own position as recipient of good news:

Example 2.15

(a) LOUIS well, I only I only hope that he is right his diagnosis is correct,
              that's all I can say. I mean,
(b) JOHN   I (. . .)
                                           [acc]
(c) LOUIS believe me, I'm not I'm not taking issue at all
(d)   *with you on in any way, shape or form.* (laughs)
(e)   I know you're reporting what he said.
                                           [dec]
(f)   and I know we both hope that she'll- that she will improve as
            he says.

A discourse marker "well" signals Louis repositioning to John and
John's report. Louis' response is very personal. In two utterances he
packages four references in the first person. He refers to his hopes
and their hopes as recipients of good news. Then Louis reasserts
where he stands. In the conversation frame, Louis explicitly ratifies
his brother's report and John's persona. Again he makes this very
personal (first person mention three times). His laughter is ironic,
intending to communicate "we may have a difference of opinion
concerning this doctor, but we certainly don't have a difference
between ourselves." He makes a statement of belief in John's effort
to convey a truthful report: "you're reporting what he said."

    However Louis' inner battle goes on:

Example 2.16

                    [dec]
(a) LOUIS and I know we both hope that she'll- that she will improve as
            he says.
                    [dec dec]
(b)   I I have grave doubts but I'm not a doctor, he is.

Louis' two last utterances capture this conflict. He expresses his
skepticism over the results reported; at the same time, he accepts
the doctor's authority in the diagnosis and prognosis.

    Positioning the doctor as expert is crucial in this conversation.
It brings the consultation to a close regarding future actions. It
also captures Louis' shifting moves, first as recipient of bad news
("I don't believe that." "I think he's crazy.") and then as recipient
of good news ("well, I I I *of course* I hope he's right").

2.5.2 Brothers' repositionings and reframings vis-à-vis the diagnosis

John also shifts positioning as talk gets more conversational and less about the report. He changes from presenting a report ("he said," "he believes") to evaluating the doctor ("he was well prepared") and then shifting to first person reference and evaluating his own conversational role ("I was sitting there thinking"). Toward closing, both John and Louis convey more involvement (Tannen 1989) and personal information:

Example 2.17

(a) JOHN   well, yeah, Louis, I::: she::::
(b)   I I was sitting there thinking how emotionally involved I am in all this because she is such a *pain* in the ass. (laughter)

Once more John addresses his brother by name, but now, for the first time, he expresses his personal involvement explicitly and places himself as author and principal. He also aligns himself with Louis by introducing a criticism of his mother. This personal reframing is well captured by the concept of positioning as again it indicates that a key change in participation structure has taken place. So when John starts to report again, it takes a different perspective: alerting the parents to listen to their sons.

Example 2.18

                [acc]
(a) JOHN   and he he said to her, by the way,
(b)   he said "you should listen very carefully to your family."
(c)   "the majority of families (pause) don't want to have anything to do"
                [acc]
(d) LOUIS   "don't have anything to do with this."
(e) JOHN   yeah yeah. and he said that's- y'know, something
                . . . .
                [dec]
(f) LOUIS   *so he was saying that we weren't-*
                [dec]
(g)   *that we were stepping into a slot that's uncomfortable for us,*
                [acc acc]

(h)   and that's what he was recognizing, I think, is that correct?
(i)   JOHN   yeah. no::: he was admonishing mom to to listen (pause)
(j)   to what we're saying.
                          [acc]
(k)   LOUIS   because we'd rather not say it if we did not have to.
(l)   JOHN   yeah. that's right.

Here Louis complements John's words. The two agree and they collaborate in animating the doctor's words. Their co-constructed report (as in a duet) includes acknowledgment from the doctor over the difficult role that the family has had to play.

Nevertheless Louis finds his brother's rendition of the doctor's advice to the mother laughably understated:

Example 2.19

                          [dec]
(a)   LOUIS   yes, I understand. okay, well. that was- that was accurate (loud
                 laughter).
(b)   that was certainly accurate. (laughter)
(c)   JOHN   oh yeah, right. (laugh)
(d)   LOUIS   we get a lot of pleasure out of this, thank you. (laughter)

Louis reiterates his understanding only to reframe it with irony (referring to the report) and complemented by loud laughter. He moves towards closing the conversation by asserting the concerns – and not the pleasures – that both brothers have in this mission.

As the conversation closes, Louis restates his double positioning (as recipient of good and bad news) vis-à-vis the report:

Example 2.20

(a)   LOUIS   well, okay: y'know, overall, it's it's certainly a good
                 report ah in terms of-
                          [acc acc]
(b)   well, we hope that's the way it is, and he's the expert. so
                 (pause) God bless.
(c)   so let's see:: (laughs).
(d)   it's a bad report in terms of wh- what it means they're going to
                 do. (pause)
                          [acc acc]
(e)   JOHN   I think so. yes. yeah. I really do.

John and Louis are then recipients of good and bad news. This is a salient location for both brothers as the phone call comes to a close.

The good news is the medical diagnosis and prognosis; the bad news is what will unfold if the couple decides to head back home. A series of considerations regarding their stepfather's decision unfold. Louis concludes by saying:

Example 2.21

(a) LOUIS   *we played our hand,* (pause) *brother.*
(b) JOHN   mmm mmm.

The above examples attest to a joint construction of talk. Both brothers have worked discursively to: 1) position the doctor as the expert in the matter (and accept its unfolding social consequences); 2) reposition themselves in concordance with each other; 3) evaluate the effects of the report on the family and the consequences for the safety and care of the parents. A shift to "us" and "we" marks the development of joint actions to pursue (or not pursue). Also, Louis alludes to common feelings ("there is nothing we can do," "there is no reason for us to be apoplectic"). To these points John agrees: "that's kind of where I am coming down right now." The two brothers conclude this final part of the conversation in consonance.

2.6 Voice: being an authority in the matter

Finally, let's turn briefly to voice. *Voice,* just like *frame,* captures implicit meaning, point of view, and intentionality, and presupposes prior knowledge. Both notions are defined as psychological (Bateson 1972; Bakhtin 1981b). Both capture the dynamic nature of communication. Also, both address reflexivity in language and context. While Bakhtin made the utterance a dialogic unit (containing the voices of both speaker and hearer), Bateson made framing a relational notion binding speaker/actor A and speaker/actor B. For both, understanding is dialogic in nature. Their models for communication imply that communicative processes are better represented by a dialogical model rather than in a transmission model (Wertsch 1991; Schiffrin 1994).

Assuming that these concepts account for communicative processes in similar ways, what does the concept of *voice* capture or highlight? One may say that Bakhtin asks, "Who owns meaning?" (Wertsch 1991) while Goffman (1974) would ask, "What's going on here now?" Turning to our phone conversation, the concept of voice gives prominence to what is omitted or to the participant who was excluded in the decision-making process. Voice, in addition, captures the two brothers' differences in expressive orientation (how the physical voice comes across), with one conveying emotionality and the other rationality.

2.6.1 Voicing emotion and reason: reflexivity at work

Louis' responses reveal at least two major problems, from his perspective, with John's phone call. First, it contradicted Louis' expectations regarding his mother's diagnosis (she went from having an "intermediary to severe brain atrophy" to having a "mild cognitive disorder."). Second, it contradicted Louis's expectations of a participatory role in the decision-making process. He would not have a voice in the matter, despite his role as main caretaker.

Viewed from this perspective, it becomes clear why Louis responds with strong claims and confrontations. He challenges the doctor's expertise as well as the decision-making process. The words are emphatic and so are his evaluative statements. Also, his tone of voice has contrastive qualities (italics in the transcript mean loudness; caps means extra loudness):

Example 2.22

(a)   LOUIS   okay. (long pause) okay. (long pause)[acc and speaking quietly]
(b)   well I surely wouldn't like to be in a foxhole with him.
(c)   JOHN   why is that now? (pause)
(d)   LOUIS   *well*, HE'S A JERK. I guess- I mean- it's an ABSURD
               DIAGNOSIS.
               [acc acc]
               I don't believe a word of it. I think he's crazy. (pause)

Contrastive pace (long pauses vs. accelerated pace) as well as contrastive emphasis and loudness provide intonational contours and paralinguistic cues that capture Louis' physical voice: what Linklater (1976: 1) called a "direct contact with emotional impulse."

Louis' responses not only voice an "I" in the matter (discussed previously in footings and positioning), but signal an emotional self, an intent to communicate urgency, concern, and ultimately pain. Louis' voice captures all features of spontaneity: "the natural voice is transparent, revealing, not describing, inner impulses of emotion and thought directly and spontaneously. The person is heard" (Linklater 1976: 2). This emotional and spontaneous voice that shifts from "HE'S A JERK. I guess- I mean- it's an ABSURD DIAGNOSIS" to half way in the conversation "well: I I I *of course* I hope he's right." signal how Louis processes the results of the diagnosis and its consequences.

It is interesting to contrast Louis' emotional statements to John's rational voice providing a detailed description, accentuating what in the report is relevant:

Example 2.23

(a) JOHN he believes that by any number of neurologists' standards
          [speaking very slowly]
(b)   that mom has mild ['hhh] cognitive decline ['hhh]
          . . . .
(c)   that ah: that she would be rul- ruled as competent in *a court of law::.*
          . . . .
          [dec]
(d)   *the Zoloft* (pause) appears to have been causing a number of con- ahm
          [dec]   [acc]
(e)   *problems.* (pause) one was it- one of which was raising her blood pressure.

The pace tends to be slow. Words are carefully selected and emphasis (vowel lengthening, stress) placed on key references ("ruled as competent in *a court of law*," "*the Zoloft*," "a number of *problems*"). These are also key references to the frames previously discussed. They are conveyed in a contrastive pace (slow to accelerated pace), with pauses in relevant places.

The large difference between Louis's physical voice (the emotional spontaneous voice) and John's (the rational reporting voice) is somewhat transformed in the course of the conversation. Toward the end we hear Louis coming to terms with facts as reported:

Example 2.24

(a) LOUIS   this is simply about what he said.
                [dec]   [dec dec]
(b)   and what he said is a *fact*.
               . . . .
(c)   I'm not a doctor, he is.

In an inverted image, we also hear John speaking of how emotionally involved he was:

Example 2.25

(a) JOHN   well, yeah, Louis, I::: she:::::
(b)   I I was sitting there thinking how emotionally involved I am in all this because she is such a *pain* in the ass. (laughter)

In parallel contrasting ways, both Louis and John shift voices as they make explicit statements that attest either to reason or to emotion. Louis voices reasoning ("I'm not the doctor, he is"). John voices emotional involvement (the first personal pronoun; addressing his brother by name; the lengthening of vowels). A voice perspective helps us understand reflexivity at work. Specifically here it captures their reflective expressive orientation: how Louis' emotional responses are also at work in his brother's understanding of the parent's situation, and how John's reasoned arguments also find echo within Louis' beliefs.

2.7 Conclusion

This chapter discussed the social and discursive construction of identity in a troublesome conversation between two brothers. It examined three frameworks (footing, positioning, voice) to investigate the implicit, dialogic, and multi-layered nature of communication. The analysis pointed to the central role of language in the construction and ratification of identities. Footing captured the brothers' alignment (stance, posture, projected shelf) to each other and to the content of their talk. Positioning conveyed the key set of expectations participants have on where to place the other in a given interaction. Voice indicated agency (or lack of it) and ways in which participants speak and are heard in talk and interaction.

What is gained in applying these concepts to a given conversation? I propose that we gain particular understandings when we look at the same data from slightly altered angles. Frame analysis points to the complexity of multi-layered discourses: how contexts may shift from moment to moment (between "this is a report" and "this is conversation") and how each reframing entails a different participation structure (in the report, John partially animates the doctor's words and Louis attends to this frame; a shift to a personal conversation alters John's and Louis' response to each other). To make matters more complicated, three contexts surface in John's report. Bits of a relatively formal legal register or medical register contrast with a relatively informal social register. Each one of these frames introduces different footings and addresses different topics. Each frame elicits different types of responses from Louis.

The unfolding conversation between the two brothers reveals a difficult negotiation. In addressing the question "Who stands as the expert here?" the concept of positioning seems to be particularly helpful. It requires participants to look at the schemas that are most salient for that interaction. On one hand, we have Louis, the younger brother, who holds expertise as a lawyer as well as information about and experience with his parents' failing health and social skills; on the other hand, we have John, who reports on the doctor's expertise. In the phone call, positioning the doctor as expert is crucial. It brings the consultation to a close regarding future actions. It also captures Louis' shifting moves, locating Louis first as recipient of bad news ("I don't believe that." "I think he's crazy.") and then as recipient of good news ("well, I I I *of course* I hope he's right"). At the end, after much interactional work, both John and Louis reposition themselves as recipients of both good and bad news (the good news is the medical diagnosis and prognosis; the bad news is what will unfold if the couple decides to head back home). This is a salient location for both brothers.

How do positioning and footing differ? In the data analyzed, positioning captures how each participant locates himself regarding what matters most in this phone call. Validating the doctor's decision is the most salient issue, followed by a reconciling of the differences of the participants. The two brothers position themselves and the other according to what is most salient in their schema for that conversation. These positionings then influence the types of footings that unfold. Thus, positioning characterizes speaker and hearer's most prominent stances (or projected selves) in interaction, the ones that participants would clearly be identified with or would use to identify the other. In this way, positioning would be less dynamic, less elusive than footing. Footings (the plural may be important) refer to the very micro interactional shifts, which would ultimately constitute positionings. Thus, a shift in pronoun use (from "he" to "I") and a shift in register (from a legal to a medical lexicon) would be a shift in footing but would not necessarily entail a repositioning. For example, in the report, John may partially animate the doctor's words as a clinician or as a court expert (implying a change in footing), but he is still positioned as reporting what was said ("I know you're reporting what he said"). Distinguishing footings from positioning may help us: 1) assign differing degrees of salience to inferential processes (i.e. thereby fine tune what we mean by contextualization processes); 2) probe further into the nature of inferences in conversation; 3) relate positioning to salient knowledge schemas (or storylines); 4) contrast the more elusive (slippery) shifts with strategic (intentional) ones.

Finally, we turn to voice. If one asks the Bakhtinian questions "who owns meaning?" or "who creates the text?" we see John, as the narrator, aligning himself with the doctor and reporting on the voice of medicine, the voice of the expert. The resulting analysis would be comparable to points brought up by positioning and footing. However, a voice perspective indicates that certain types of information and inferences previously kept in the background can be brought to the foreground. Two types of issues were briefly discussed: 1) how a key participant questions authority and expertise in the decision-making process; 2) what the discourse of emotionality and rationality looks like and how they are physically voiced (what are the linguistic and paralinguistic cues). A particularly interesting point is captured by looking at voice and emotionality. It points to reflexivity and its processual nature (i.e. marking progressive changes) as talk unfolds. Voice reveals an aspect of reflexive changes in tone in John's and Louis' argumentative discourse (Louis, who initially reacted emotionally, becomes more rational; John, in a counter movement, becomes slightly more spontaneous). A voice perspective seems to portray well such subtle but relevant changes.

Pulling apart these three conceptual frameworks provokes a rich methodological discussion. We see that these frameworks may work to complement one another and consolidate (and strengthen) the analysis. Several examples were presented in this chapter – mostly examining the relationship between positioning and footing. In looking at voice and positioning, often one can arrive at similar metamessages. In the data described in this chapter, I have shown that voice and positioning carry an implicit message about identity work – in this case, both function to convey a message of brotherhood that says "we can work together."

Appendix 2.1   Transcription conventions

.	sentence-final falling intonation
?	sentence-final rising and fall intonation (BP question pattern)
,	phrase-final intonation (indicating more talk to come)
-	glottal stop or abrupt cutting off of sound
(PAUSE)	noticeable break in rhythm with no speech; length of time was not assigned
[ACC]	spoken quickly
[DEC]	spoken slowly
['HHH]	audible inhalations
[HHH]	audible exhalations
ITALICS	emphatic stress
CAPS	very emphatic stress, loudness or shouting
/WORDS/	spoken softly
//WORDS//	spoken very softly
( )	transcription impossible
(WORDS)	uncertain transcription
=	two utterances linked by = indicate no break in flow of talk, latching;
——	overlapping speech: two people talking at the same time

Appendix 2.2   The phone conversation

      [off the mic – "there's not going to be a conference call"]
JOHN he believes that by any number of neurologists' standards
                   [speaking very slowly]

       that mom has mild ['hhh] cognitive decline ['hhh]
                    [acc]
       ['hhh] *it's::: absolutely positively not Alzheimer's.*
LOUIS yeah.
JOHN   ['hhh] he said that-
                    [acc]
       based on what he has seen he had seen between him and Dr.
       Jones,
       [acc acc]
       that there is likely to be improvement in her condition.
       (pause)
       [dec]
       that ah that she would be rul- ruled as competent in *a court
       of law::*.
       [background noise interference] (pause)
                    [dec]   [acc]
LOUIS I don't believe that. okay=
                    [acc acc]
JOHN   =yeah, well, that's what he's saying. he saying that b-
       y'know,
       he's testified in these cases, that under any-
                    [dec]
       that she would be- *ruled competent.* ['hhh] ahm:=
LOUIS =then I'm a blue goose, but go ahead.
              [acc]   [dec]
JOHN   ( ) he said that- ahm ahm that the ahm:
              [dec]
       the Zoloft (pause) appears to have been causing a number of
       con- ahm
       [dec]   [acc]
       problems. (pause) one was it- one of which was raising her
       blood pressure.
LOUIS mmm mmm.=
              [acc]
JOHN   =and since she's been off- since Smith has taken her off *all*
       her meds.
       [dec]   [acc]
       (pause) ahm: again, she's seen an *even increased
       improvement.*=

LOUIS =mmm mmm.
                     [dec]   [acc]
JOHN   ahm- and ah- he said that there is- that there is not a medical
            problem here,
            but a social one.
            [portable phone noise interference]
LOUIS what's the social one?
                                        [acc]
JOHN   ahm- the- what is- what is actually best for them.
            [acc acc]
            he said- "y'know you have to understand that you're o::ld
            and you're decl-
            [dec]   [dec dec]
            going to decli:ne over ti:me." (pause) *"you can expect that."*
            he said but-
                                [acc]
            ah: but- and he said "you may not have the same quality of
            life between the two of you that you have had in the past.
            you may need some assistance."
                              [dec]
            (pause) ['hhh] (pause) but- *but he said.* (pause) ahm.
            ah y'know based on all the things that *he sees.* (pause)
                              [acc]
            all the patients he sees, that ahm, between the two of them.
            (pause)
                                                                [dec]
            that at least for the *near* term future they can function
            independently.
            [strong phone noise interference in background]
LOUIS okay. (long pause) okay. (long pause)
            [acc and speaking sort of quietly]
            well I surely wouldn't like to be in a foxhole with him.
JOHN   why is that now? (pause)
LOUIS *well,* HE'S A JERK. I guess- I mean- it's an ABSURD DIAG-
            NOSIS.
                            [acc acc]
            I don't believe a word of it. I think he's crazy. (pause)
JOHN   JONES?=
LOUIS =*yes.*

[dec]

JOHN okay. well. (pause) he ga- Louis, he gave her a battery of tests again today.

and then they talked about what's going on. and- what she remembers,

[acc]

everything else. he said "your short term memory isn't (pause) very good."

[dec]

he said. "but, y'know, between the two of you." (pause)

[acc acc]

and he said it's only a mild cognitive disorder. and he said- "it actually may improve now that you're off all these medications."

                                            [acc acc]

LOUIS well: I I I *of course* I hope he's right. (pause)

                              [acc]

but I don't think she can handle two pots on a *on a kitchen stove*,

[acc acc]

not to mention er any other ['hhh] daily events. but in *any case*, I mean,

we aren't we aren't arguing here. this is simply about what he said.

            [dec]   [dec dec]

and what he said is a *fact*. so, so be it.

JOHN   yeah.   ['hhh] well, ah, *again*. now,

                            [acc]

now, we're going to see *Smith* after this.

[acc]   [dec]

now we're not going to see him *today*. (pause) but we're gonna- y'know,

[dec]   [acc]

he's he's- talked to- he got my letter. he read it.

                            [dec]

he had notes all over it. (pause) ah he talked to Smith (pause)

[dec dec]

er ah (pause) as well. (pause) about- prior to this meeting.

LOUIS   mmm mmm.   yeah.
      [acc]

JOHN   so I mean. he was- (pause) well prepared. (pause) ah::=

LOUIS =yeah.=
      [acc]

JOHN = ( ) ran her through the tests. and and he said, y'know,
         [acc acc]
he said to her *all kinds of things.* y'know,
he said "*your family is very much concerned.*" (pause)
['hhh] and and he said, ah: (pause)
that ah that she should listen to us *very carefully* because-
(pause)
we're much closer to the situation (pause) on a personal
basis,
than *he is,* (pause) he's talking about *medical*
(pause) [portable phone noise]

LOUIS   mmm mmm

JOHN   *issues,*=

LOUIS =mmm mmm.=

JOHN =y'know.=

LOUIS =yeah.=
                [acc]

JOHN =and and he said, y'know, he said but-
         [acc acc]
but er she has mild cognitive disorder. this is not Alzheimer's.
       [dec]   [acc acc]
it it it's- she's going to gradually *decline* but she has every
chance of stabilizing or even improving slightly now that she's
off these meds after a period of time.

LOUIS well, I only I only hope that he is right his diagnosis is
correct, that's all I can say. I mean,

JOHN   I (. . .)
                [acc]

LOUIS *believe me, I'm not I'm not taking issue at all with you on in*
any way, shape or form. (laughs)
I know you're reporting what he said.
                [dec]

and I know we both hope that she'll- that she will improve as
he says.
[dec dec]
I I have grave doubts but I'm not a doctor, he is.
(pause)

JOHN   well, yeah, Louis, I::: she:::::
I I was sitting there thinking how emotionally involved I am
in all this because she is such a *pain* in the ass. (pause)
[acc]
and he he said to her, by the way,
he said "you should listen very carefully to your family."
(phone noise interference)

LOUIS you faded there. I'm sorry.

JOHN   the majority of families (pause) don't want to have anything
to do
(   )
(phone noise interference)
[acc]

LOUIS don't have anything to do with this.

JOHN   yeah yeah. and he said that's- y'know, something
(they are coming out right now), yeah

LOUIS yeah.

JOHN   yeah.
                        [dec]

LOUIS *so he was saying that we weren't-*
                        [dec]
       that we were stepping into a slot that's uncomfortable for us,
                        [acc acc]
       and that's what he was recognizing, I think, is that correct?
       [background voices: John is talking to mother and Edgar, or
       listening to them ; the conversation goes on with mother and
       Edgar in background]

JOHN   yeah. no::: he was admonishing mom to to listen (pause) to
       what we're saying.
       [acc]

LOUIS *because we'd rather not say it if we did not have to.*

JOHN   yeah. that's right.
                        [dec]

LOUIS yes, I understand. okay, well. that was- that was accurate
       (loud laughter). that was certainly accurate. (laughter)
JOHN   oh yeah, right. (laugh)
LOUIS we get a lot of pleasure out of this, thank you. (laughter)
       well, okay:: y'know, overall, it's it's certainly a good report
       ah in terms of-
       [acc acc]
       well, we hope that's the way it is, and he's the expert. so
       (pause) God bless.
       so let's see:: (laughs).
       it's a bad report in terms of wh- what it means they're going
       to do. (pause)
       [acc acc]
JOHN   I think so. yes. yeah. I really do.
                              [acc]
LOUIS so::: I could assum- I I assume that Edgar is going to give
       notice and there's nothing that we can do about that (pause)
       and if Smith says something that eh is contrary then Edgar
       could revoke or retrack his notice and I think that's what
       we're going be left with.
JOHN   mmm.
       [dec]   [acc acc]
LOUIS I mean (pause) I'm thinking out loud now, but that that very
       well may be it and and there is no reason for us to be
       apoplectic if Edgar gives notice,
       there's nothing more we can do.
       (pause)
       [acc]
JOHN   er- er yeah:: well I want to talk some more about that.
                              [acc acc]
       but- that's kind of where I am coming down right now.=
LOUIS =yeah.
JOHN   that's ( ) ahm.
LOUIS yeah.
JOHN   mmm.
       [dec]
LOUIS *we played our hand,* (pause) *brother.*
JOHN   mmm mmm.
LOUIS may- maybe. [clearing throat]

JOHN   yeah. (so much for the other guy).

LOUIS   well, Smith, Smith is going to give a more reasoned approach
        than er than some guy who is in a neurological box.
                                        [acc]

JOHN   yeah, oh, yeah, er *exactly*. oh he said that as well.

LOUIS   mmm mmm.

JOHN   uhm er he he he said that as well. ( )
        he is in a box constrained by (pause) his specialty.

LOUIS   yeah. (long pause) yeah.
                        [acc]
        so:: (pause) I think that's actually gonna be much more
        interesting.
                            [acc acc]
        and I and I thought (pause) that that would probably be
        more interesting.
        I never met Jones. I don't know anything about him.
        but I have met Smith and I have a very high regard for his
        common sense as well as his medical wisdom.=

JOHN   =I I believe you'd feel the same way about this guy.

LOUIS   mmm mmm.

JOHN   uhm he was recommended by the first guy.

LOUIS   yeah.

JOHN   and ah: ah ah (y'know, and speaks extremely high of him),
        yeah.

LOUIS   yeah.

JOHN   and this is his area- of expertise.

LOUIS   yeah. (pause) well. so be it.

JOHN   yeah. okay. uhm. ( )

LOUIS   well, hey, I appreciated it. thanks very much.

JOHN   bye bye.

LOUIS   bye bye.

3

Small and large identities in narrative (inter)action

Alexandra Georgakopoulou

3.1 Introduction

Research on identities in narrative increasingly shares with the rest of discourse studies the view that identities are not given entities, static properties, or finished projects. Instead, they are practical accomplishments that are constructed – and even deconstructed – online in the "everyday flow of verbal interaction" (Widdicombe and Wooffitt 1995: 218). Emphasis on the emergence of identities in discourse, particularly in interactional sites, where they can present a multiplicity of meanings, brings together approaches to discourse as diverse as social constructionism and conversation analysis (Widdicombe and Antaki 1998: 201). Nonetheless, there is less convergence on how the discourse constructions of identities relate to factors that are external to a specific interactional situation (sic. *exogenous*). In studies of identity constructions through narrative, the dominant view seems to be that pre-existent, socioculturally available – capital D – discourses are drawn upon and employed by tellers in the course of narratives in order to construct, justify, and explicate a sense of 'self' and, when applicable, 'other' (e.g. see Kerby 1991). In this process, narrative is seen as a privileged mode for self-construction and a unique point of entry into trans-situational features of the self and identity as those emerge in a person's (ongoing) life story (for a discussion see Lucius-Hoene and Deppermann 2000: 201). In view of this exigency, the type of narrative that has monopolized identity analysis is that of autobiography. As a rule, (natural) autobiographical narratives or life stories occur in research interviews.

Studies of autobiographical narratives have been gradually moving away from representational accounts of the self (i.e. accounts of the type of person that a life story presents its teller to be) to the interactional and performative aspects of identity construction, that is, the ways in which narrators perform and locally occasion themselves through their stories (see Bamberg 1997b). Furthermore, the idea of the teller's and audience's co-drafting or co-authoring identities even in a largely "monologic" mode such as a research interview is gaining currency (e.g. see Mishler 1986). This is based on a view of narrative not as a self-contained and autonomous unit but as talk-in-interaction. This kind of direction of research has still a lot of avenues to explore. To begin, autobiographical stories are but one type of narrative activity that is itself associated with specific communicative features and tasks. As a rule, autobiographical stories are non-shared, personal-experience, past-event stories. In terms of participation roles, they seem to divide participants into a teller with strong floor-holding rights and an audience with primary and secondary recipients. Furthermore, they more often than not are (or expected to be) well-structured activities that develop in the fashion of a more or less classic narration, that is, move from the reported events and the complications within them to the high point, which they evaluate and resolve (cf. Labov 1972a). In stark contrast to that, stories in everyday talk present a fascinating complexity and multiplicity of tellings and conversational actions: they span the continuum from highly monologic to highly collaborative tellings; from past to future and hypothetical events; from long and performed to fragmented and elliptical tellings (Georgakopoulou 2003; Ochs and Capps 2001). It is fair to say that as analysts we know less about the right end of the above continua and more about the prototypical or "canonical" narration of past (non-shared) personal events. Thus, this study is intended as a step towards unraveling the complexities of identity work in narratives that do not fit the bill of such canonical narratives. Specifically, the data at hand comprise stories of future (projected) events and, embedded in them, more or less elliptically told stories of shared (known) events.

As suggested, the view of narrative that forms the starting point of this study is that of talk-in-interaction. This is closely linked with the idea that large (i.e. extra-situational, exogenous, "portable") identities can be best traced in discourse through an analytic emphasis on the "small," that is, the details and sequential management of talk (see Wooffitt and Clark 1998; Zimmerman 1998). In studies of narrative, details intrinsic or endogenous to the specific situation of a storytelling that have attracted attention mostly have to do with the teller's choices of code, register, and style (e.g. animating characters' voices, shifting tenses, switching codes) that render a telling more performed (e.g. Bauman 1986; Georgakopoulou 1998; Hill 1995a). Less attention has, however, been paid to the ways in which the participants' local interactional roles (i.e. the small, here-and-now identities) that have to do with the endpoints of a story (i.e. initiation, closing, follow-up, but see Jefferson 1978) and its internal components make available or provide a window to extra–situational resources (see Goodwin 1984 for a notable exception). This stands in contrast to the systematic exploration of the "loose coupling" (Goffman 1983, discussed and quoted in this context in Zimmerman 1998: 88) of local, micro-roles with larger roles and identities in various occasions of institutional talk (e.g. emergency calls, Zimmerman 1998; divorce mediation sessions, Greatbatch and Dingwall 1998). There, roles (sic. *discourse identities*) tied with the sequence of adjacency pairs such as questioner–answerer, speaker–recipient have been found to provide a platform for larger social identities (e.g. spouse, parent, layperson–expert, etc.).

Drawing on the idea that the participants' exploitation of conversational (interactional) structures and mechanisms makes visible extra-situational resources, this study will argue for and demonstrate a pairing of storytelling participation roles with larger social identities. It will be shown that the telling of the stories is jointly constructed by the participants but with differentiated actions and contributions from each of them. In other words, different participants contribute in varying degrees to different story components, particularly plotline and evaluation. Furthermore, the participants are differentiated in the degree in which their contributions are ratified and taken on board by others or, equally, challenged and delegitimated. It will be argued that these telling roles make visible and are based on the participants' larger social (particularly gender) identities; relative standing vis-à-vis one another; and relationships as close friends who share an interactional history. The study's findings are hoped to demonstrate the close link between identity construction in narrative and a) a story's sequential management;

b) shared interactional history (including shared stories); and
c) type of narrative activity engaged in.

3.2 Data

The data for this study come from the self–recorded conversations
of a group of three Greek women (a fourth female person joins in
occasionally but is not seen as a "core" member). The ethnographic
study of this group was conducted in the context of a larger study
of young people's peer groups in Greece. When the recordings
started (early 1998), the participants were 17 years old and living
in a small town (25,000 inhabitants) in Arcadia, South Greece.
At that point, they were re-sitting their University entrance exams
and, as such, were outside the school framework. Their daily
routine thus involved self-study in the mornings, private tuition in
the early afternoons, and socializing thereafter, that mostly took
the form of hanging out with one another and chatting at cafés.
This regular socializing over a long period of time (the participants
had known one another and, in their description, been "best
friends" for 10 years) had resulted in a dense interactional history,
rich in shared assumptions that were consistently and more or
less strategically drawn upon to suit various purposes in local
interactional contexts.

3.3 Projections: a case of dialogism and intertextuality

The most common type of narrative activity in the group (i.e. two
thirds of narratives) involves the joint planning of events to take
place in the (near) future. The taleworld of such projected events, in
the same vein as in stories of past events, is temporally ordered and
emplotted (i.e. with arising complications and reactions to them,
goal-based action, etc.). *Stories of projected events* or *projections*
present a lot of intertextual connections amongst them. To begin,
there is an obvious thematic preoccupation that runs through
most of them and that has to do with flirting, romance, and relationships with men. As such, projections are typically about planning a
meeting with and/or asking out the man that one of the participants

happens to be romantically interested in. This planning involves
a turn-by-turn co-authoring and negotiation of details in the taleworld, particularly of an orientation kind (e.g. time, place):

Example 3.1

(a)	T(ONIA)	Mori θa pezi i AEK ecino to vraδi, δe θa pis? INE AEK o Pavlos!
(a)	T	AEK ((basketball team)) are playing that evening, aren't you going to say anything? Pavlos SUPPORTS AEK!
(b)		ce ti θa leme mori peri ba:scetiku perieχomenu?
(b)		And what are we going to say man about ba:sketball?
(c)	F(OTINI)	I AEK pezi simera.
(c)	F	AEK are playing today.
(d)	T	Perimene (. . .) sto mikro teliko, – ton broimiteliko, ama kerδisi simera,
(d)	T	Wait a minute (. . .) in the semi final, – the quarter final, if they win today,
(e)	T	θa peksi c'avrio
(e)	T	they'll play tomorrow too
(f)	V(IVI)	Re to χune noris, δen do χune //arγa
(f)	V	The match is on early, not //late
(g)	T	Δe θimase pu iχane ton Olibiako edeka i ora?
(g)	T	Don't you remember, they had Olympiakos's match ((team)) at 11?
(h)	V	Gamo tin atiχia mas! Na to orγanosume j'ali mera, na ine iremos=
(h)	V	Bloody hell! Let's organize it for another day, when he'll be calm=
(i)	F	=Bori na mi θeli omos na to //parakolutθsi
(i)	F	But he may not want to //watch it
(j)	V	Apokli:ete!
(j)	V	No wa:y!
(k)	F	Bori na min ine fanatikos!
(k)	F	He may not be a big fan!
(l)	T	Re, ine ce se OMAΔA, kaθe Tetarti pezi
(l)	T	Man he's in a team himself, they play every Wednesday

As we see above, the participants are jointly constructing the
time and place of the projected meeting. Such negotiations tend
to not get resolved straight away as the contentious issues
are gradually shaped and revisited in the course of the storytelling
and as a function of other events in the taleworld under construction. In this case too, agreement is finally reached 80 lines later (see

2 below), once other details and events of the projection have been arranged:

Example 3.2

(a) v   *Re cita, na kanonisume me tom Pavlo, na pume kata tis δeka.*
(a) v   Look, we must arrange it with Pavlos, say for ten o'clock
(b) т   *Ce pame me ta koritsja meta?*
(b) т   And then go out with the other girls?
(c) v   *Ce prin, prin, jati me tom Bavlo na pume kata tis δeka.*
(c) v   No before, before, if we are meeting Pavlos at ten.

As will be shown below, however, this systematic co-authoring of events by active co-tellers does not mean that all participants participate in the same ways or effectiveness in the construction of the taleworld.

The plotline of projections consists of planned events and verbal interactions. The latter mostly involve interactions between one of the participants and the man she is planning to go out with. As such, they tend to take the form of "You will say – he will say" (Example 3.3 below), or, less frequently, "We will say – he will say" (Example 3.4 below) (to paraphrase Goodwin's (1990) famous format of "he-said–she-said"):

Example 3.3

(a) f   *Orea (..) vrisko eδo kapu to Maci (..) etsi?*
(a) f   Tell me now (..) we are talking serious. Okay (..) I bump into Makis right?
(b) f   *Milai o Pavlos me ti Vivi eci, c'o Macis ine eci, ce ti tu les, TI TU LES?*
(b) f   Pavlos is talking to Vivi, and Makis is there, and WHAT would you tell him, what?
(c) т   *Ta kalandra?=*
(c) т   The carols?= ((jokingly))
(d) v   *=Ta kalandra*
(d) v   The carols ((laughs))
(e) f   *Oçi ta kalandra re peδi mu, ama su tiçi prota ap'ola (..) daksi?*
(e) f   Not the carols man, assuming this is going to happen (..) right?
(f) v   *Θa tu milisis sti γlosa tu tu peδju, se pa:u*
(f) v   You'll speak to the guy in his language, I fancy you ((imitates the local accent))
(g) т   *U iδjus*
(g) т   It's me ((laughs, imitates the local accent))

Example 3.4

(a) F   >*oχi me to pu θa mas δi< θa pi: e koritsia ti kanete? Vjikate, irθate ja kafe?*

(a) F   >no the moment he sees us< he'll say: eh what's up girls? Come out for a coffee?

(b) F   *θa tu pume ne c'emis, ja kafe imaste, θa pi o Pavlos kaθiste parea θa pi*

(b) F   we'll tell him yes, come for a coffee, Pavlos will then say come sit with us

(c) F   *θa epimini o Pavlos, θa rotisi ksero γo, δe mas χalane tim barea re Maci?*

(c) F   Pavlos will insist, he'll ask, they are not imposing Makis, are they?

(d) F   *mas ti χalane? θa pume emis stin arχi, oχi re peδja ksero γo*

(d) F   To begin with, we'll say no guys

(e) F   *mi sas χalame tim barea ksero γo*

(e) F   we don't want to impose right?

(f) T   *θa pi o Pavlaras eci pera, koritsia KAΘISTE KAΘISTE*

(f) T   Then Pavlos will say, girls DO SIT DOWN SIT DOWN

The characters talked about in projections are invariably men, and fall into two categories: a) those that generate the "love interest" and b) the mediators, that is, men like Pavlos in Example 3.4 above, who are assigned a helper's role in the setting up of the meetings.

Another recurrent feature of the telling of stories of projected events involves their dialogical relationship with stories of shared (known) past events. More specifically, in the context of future narrative worlds, participants draw upon shared past narrative worlds, in order to support and legitimize their own projected version of events. As I have shown elsewhere (Georgakopoulou 2001), these are (re)told more or less elliptically. Sometimes, they are even referred or alluded to by means of a punchline, a characterization of a third party based on action in their taleworld, or a quoted set phrase that imitates or parodies a character's speech style. In this way, there is an embedding of storytelling activities going on: stories of projected events form the main narrative frame and stories of shared events the embedded frame, which is thematically relevant to the main narrative activity (for a discussion of embedded narratives, see Ochs and Capps 2001: 36–40). As Ochs and Capps put it, embedded narratives serve the illustration of a point, support an argument, make a comparison, elaborate, provide an example, etc. In other words, they act as argumentative devices. In Ochs and Capps' data, embeddedness of narratives refers to their integration into the topic of conversation. In the case of the data at hand, however, the embedding is of one narrative into another. That puts the two taleworlds in a dialogical relationship (Bakhtin 1981b): what happened in the past can inform or throw into sharper focus what may happen in the future. Consider the example below: the story of projected events in this case involves the planning and debating of a meeting between Tonia and the man she is romantically interested in. The views of Vivi and Tonia, with respect to this meeting, are clearly opposed: Vivi firmly believes that she should take the risk and ask the man in question out. Tonia on the other hand constantly draws on shared stories in order to support her view that she should not ask him out:

Example 3.5

(a) T *Na su po kati, irθane ta peδja, o Jorɣos c'o Kostas*
(a) T Shall I tell you something, when the guys came, George and Kostas
(b) V *Ne*
(b) V Yeah
(c) T *Pu irθane ce mas lene pame ja kafe*
(c) T when they came to us and said shall we go for a coffee?
(d) T *I anθropi stin arçi fenodusan oti δe mas vlepane filika re peδi mu, ala de borume na pume c'oti mas eroteftikan ce ceravnovola*
(d) T It was obvious that the guys were interested, but it wasn't love at first sight either
(e) V *E tus aresame*
(e) V they liked us
(f) T *Orea, lipon c'omos stin arçi filika θa vjename, c'emis ipame oçi tus aporipsame ce jelasame ce mazi tus*
(g) T Fine, and to begin with we'd go out as friends, nothing more, but we completely dismissed them and made fun of them
(h) V *Ne re Tonia, jati itane apo to puθena, irθane me tetjo malacizmeno tropo, akoma eδo isaste? C'itane ce karavlaçi edaksi? esi kamia sçesi*
(h) V Yes Tonia, cause they came out of the blue, and they had an attitude, the way they asked are you still here? And they were peasants right? No relation with your case

As can be seen in Example 3.5 above, stories of shared events are telegraphically referred to by way of mini-tellings: these comprise the story's narrative skeleton, that is, a quick reference or reminder to its main events (lines (a), (c), (d)–(e)) and their resolution (lines (g)–(h)).

In the light of the above, stories of projected events present numerous inter-connections in terms of theme, structure, characters talked about, goal of interaction, and, as will be shown below, ways of telling. In this sense, they emerge as a set of reproducible, mutually intelligible and recognisable activities that link characters, tale-worlds, and tellers across time and place. It could thus be argued that their connections link them into a coherent framework of meaning which, in Schiffrin's (2000) terms, can be characterized as an intertextual narrative: this is a non-contiguous story with a recurring theme (in our case relationships with men), featured across different narratives (in our case projections).

3.4 Telling identities

Storytelling in the group is by no means a monologic activity that grants floor-holding rights to a main teller. In fact, the distinction between a teller and an audience, so common in the analysis of (prototypical) everyday storytelling, is too restrictive for the co-construction that is going on in the participants' stories. This co-construction essentially runs through the internal components of a story, inasmuch as the participants assume *telling identities* or *participation roles* that have to do with a story's sequential management. At the same time, co-construction does not mean that the participants equally and in the same ways contribute to the activity under way. In fact, as will be shown below, they differ both in the degree of contribution to a specific story component and in their type of contribution.

As suggested above, projections form comparable narrative events which present numerous thematic and taleworld inter-connections. This comparability extends to their interactive organisation. In other words, the participants' agendas and types of contribution not only link stories across time and place but also position the participants themselves as "observably and subjectively coherent participants in jointly produced story lines" (Davies and Harré 1990: 48). More specifically, as the stories' qualitative analysis suggested, the stories' joint construction rests on

contributions to their *plotline* and *evaluation* (for a detailed analysis
of such contributions in the case-study of a tale of tomorrow, see
Georgakopoulou 2002). The plotline covers a story's projected
events, verbal interactions and, in contrast to Labov's (1972a) model
of narrative structure orientation (i.e. time, place). The latter, rather
than being backgrounded or embellishing material, constitutes
an integral part of the plot, on which the final arrangement
of events heavily depends. Furthermore, as shown above (see Examples 3.1 and 3.2), the process of positing orientation and that of
co-constructing the plot's events are interdependent.

Evaluation on the other hand lies in references to stories of
shared past events (i.e. embedded stories, as outlined above) and/
or assessments of characters talked about, particularly men. These
are positive or negative evaluations that are mostly based on personality traits that the participants are united in judging as good or
bad. For instance, a typical "bad" male attribute is that of being shy
(e.g. Makis in the story from which Example 3.3 above has been
extracted is frequently evaluated negatively by Vivi and Tonia as
being shy). On the other hand, being articulate and confident as a
man are highly valued and invoked as positive evaluations by the
participants.

With regard to the two categories of evaluation above (i.e.
embedded stories, character assessments), it is important to recognize that, in this case, evaluation mainly rests on assessing the
relevance of past events for the future taleworld as well as on
constructing a perspective on the events and characters discussed.
Therefore, devices that render the telling of a story dramatic and
enhance its tellability (i.e. internal evaluative devices in Labov's
(1972a) terms) do not form the most important component of
evaluation in the stories. In this respect, the stories seem to be "less
geared to narrative as performance and more to narrative as a
social forum for [. . .] piecing together an evaluative perspective
on an incident" (Ochs and Capps 2001: 36). Participants dwell on
a story's point almost as much as they do on its events. There is also
another important difference between the stories' evaluation
and narrative evaluation in the Labovian sense. In Labov's
(1972a) definition, evaluation encodes by more or less explicit
means the point of a storytelling. In numerous cases, this takes
the form of evaluating past events by reference to the possible,

i.e. to what could or might have happened. In the data, this is reversed: evaluation of the projected events and interactions between the characters (i.e. the possible) is normally conducted through references to past events (i.e. the actual). In other words, in this case, it is the past that is revisited (re-constructed and re-interpreted) in order to be locally mobilized as a "guide" for considering what may transpire.

To shed more light on the results of the stories' qualitative analysis, 50 narratives jointly told by the three participants (i.e. Fotini, Tonia, Vivi) were analysed quantitatively for the telling identities of each participant. On the basis of the qualitative analysis, three such identities had emerged as significant: a) initiation (of a projection); b) plot contribution; c) evaluation, which was subdivided into i) embedded stories (i.e. stories of past shared events, more or less elliptically referred to) and ii) (character) assessments.

Initiations typically consisted of an invitation for a co-construction, sometimes in the form of a question: e.g. F: *Guys (. . .) what are we going to do tomorrow?* This is in contrast to what has been suggested about stories of past non–shared events: these are typically initiated by a story preface in which an offer to tell a story is made followed by a request to hear the offered story (Sacks 1995). After a story's initiation, each participant's turn (regardless of its length) during a story's telling that contributed to its plotline or was evaluative counted as one contribution and was coded as b) or c) above. Since the story's telling was a co-authored enterprise, contributions to a story's internal components were negotiated and either delegitimated or ratified, sometimes over several turns. The outcome of every contribution was thus taken into account in the coding and the number of contributions ratified and/or challenged for each participant was counted. Contributions that were initially challenged but in the end agreed upon and ratified were coded as ratifications. If in the meantime the initial contribution had been revised in subsequent turns, to take into account challenges, only the final contribution – if ratified – was coded as such. For instance, in Example 3.6 below, Vivi's prior contribution to the time and place of the story's events (i.e. that Tonia should go and talk to the guy she is interested in at the bar where he works in the evening) is being challenged by Tonia (lines (a), (c)). As a result, Vivi revises her suggestion in two separate turns of plot contribution (line (b),

(d)1). After a new challenge (lines (e), (g)–(h)), she alters her suggestion for the third and final time (lines (i)–(j)). This contribution
is being explicitly ratified (line (l), *That's not a bad idea*).

Example 3.6

(a)	T	*opote δe boris na pas ce na tu milisis etsi (.) boris?*
(a)	T	so you ca:n't go and talk to him like that (.) can you?
(b)	V	*Mono otan δen eχi poli δulja (..) arγa to vraδi boris*
(b)	V	Only when he's not too busy (..) like late at night
(c)	T	*Bor::s?=*
(c)	T	But can you?=
(d)	V	*=Ore (.) δena mesimeri ekso*
(d)	V	Well (.) one afternoon when he's out
(e)	T	*Ton vle:po?*
(e)	T	Will I see him?
(f)	V	*ΔEN ton iδame ecino to mesimeri pu pijename stin Irini?*
(f)	V	DIDN'T we see him that afternoon on our way to Irene's
(g)	T	*Pote ton iδame RE (.) otan epeze tavli me to filo tu?*
(h)	T	*Ine δjaforetices i singiries*
(g)	T	When did we see him MAN (.) when he was playing backgam-mon with his friend?
(h)		It's different circumstances
(i)	V	*Ka:la: re TOnia orea (.) θ a pas ena proi stu Kanata*
(j)		*eci pu kaθete stim borta*
(k)		*θa ti stisis karauli sto Xondo*
(i)	V	That's okay TOnia (.) so you'll go one morning to Kanata's
(j)		when he stands at the door
(k)		you'll be waiting ((to catch him)) opposite at Hondo's
(l)	T	*Δen ine kako afto*
(l)	T	That's not a bad idea
(m)	V	*>Θa se δi θa ton δis< θa su pi po:s apo δo!*
(m)	V	He'll see you you'll see him he'll say what brings you here?
(n)	T	*Lipo:n θa tu po >pao na paro kati apo to Xondo<*
(o)		*θa pjasume tin guvenda γenikos*
(p)		*kala θa tu po (.) esi otan teljonis apo δo δe bas puθena?*
(q)		*((χa χa)) s' eχi fai to γalaktobureko=*
(n)	T	So:, I'll tell him I'm going to Hondos to get something
(o)		we'll strike up a conversation about this and that
(p)		then I'll say (.) you going somewhere when you finish here
(q)		heh huh or are you too preoccupied with the milk pies?=

On numerous occasions, ratification was implicit, as, for
instance, in cases of participants' collusion, where the next turn

Table 3.1. *Telling identities in projections*

Participants	Initiation (N=50)	Plot Contribution (N=1341)	Ratification	Evaluation (N=963)	Ratification
Fotini	15 (30%)	246 (16%)	61 (28%)	242 (21%) Embedded stories: 105 (43%) Assessments: 137 (57%)	70 (29%)
Tonia	9 (18%)	500 (33%)	172 (43%)	390 (40%) Embedded stories: 277 (71%) Assessments: 113 (29%)	180 (46%)
Vivi	26 (52%)	595 (41%)	458 (77%)	341 (39%) Embedded stories: 150 (44%) Assessments: 191 (56%)	276 (81%)

builds on and expands on the prior turn (e.g. see lines (n)–(q) in Example 3.6 above).

As we can see in Table 3.1 Vivi is the participant who initiates as well as contributes more to plots of stories (and on an equal basis with Tonia) to the evaluations of stories. More importantly, her contributions are ratified significantly more than those of the other participants. This is particularly evident in the case of evaluation: although, overall, Vivi and Tonia do not differ in terms of the number of their evaluative contributions, Vivi's telling role of an evaluator is ratified more. This means that Vivi is more instrumental in getting her evaluation agreed upon. In terms of types of evaluative contribution, Vivi and Tonia seem to be operating with different resources. As I have discussed in detail elsewhere (2003), Tonia mostly tells stories of past events to justify her own posited version and to delegitimize other people's versions (77% of her evaluative contributions). In this way, she throws the future plotline into relief by drawing on past storylines. In contrast, more than half of Vivi's (and Fotini's for that matter) contributions to evaluation are made up of character assessments. Tonia's references to shared stories are frequently delegitimized by Vivi, who offers a different interpretative or evaluative angle to them, thereby questioning their relevance for the future taleworld under construction (see lines 9–10, Example 3.5 above). Of the three participants, Fotini is the one with the least number and effectiveness of contributions to the stories' plots and evaluations. In terms of her own participation roles, she mostly initiates stories (30%, as can be seen above) and elicits rather than contributes to the plotline of a story (see discussion below). As will be shown below, the participants' telling identities in the course of their stories allow them to (re)construct, invoke, and sustain their social organization as best friends and members of a group with an internal hierarchy (Goodwin 1990: 110).

3.5 From small to larger identities

The starting point of this chapter was that local interactional roles and identities can provide a window to larger extra-situational resources, be they roles, relations, or identities. Those are frequently described as transportable (Zimmerman 1998: 90), as they are available to be carried across situations and speech events, and are potentially relevant in any spate of interaction. In turn, their relevance in a situation may be cued more or less explicitly and via the participants' locally assumed interactional roles. Such roles first bring into being and articulate with *situational identities*, linked to the topic at hand and the activity under way (Zimmerman 1998). In this case, both the topic of projected meetings with men and the participants' telling–specific identities bring into focus and make relevant situational identities that have to do with advice-seeking and -giving on one hand and expertise in men on the other hand. To put it differently, the interaction between the topic of projected stories and the participants' telling identities clearly positions them as advice-giver vs. advice-seeker and expert vs. novice. These arrangements are visible in the participants' turn design and choice as well as in their storytelling contributions. For instance, plot contributions are frequently elicited by Fotini in the form of questions that position her as an advice-seeker. For instance, in the story regarding the planned meeting with Makis (see Examples 3.2, 3.3

and 3.4 above), Fotini frequently poses questions regarding the form and content of her verbal interaction with Makis during the meeting: e.g. Pavlos is talking to Vivi, and Makis is there, "and what would you tell him though, WHAT?" (Example 3.3, (b)); "And what are we going to say man about ba:sketball?" (Example 3.1, (a)). In turn, Vivi invariably provides solutions and suggestions to such questions which, as already suggested, mostly – and in the end – have a positive uptake. In addition to the above interactional arrangements, participants display an orientation to the identity sets of advice-seeker vs. advice-giver and expert vs. novice by means of self- and other-identity ascriptions that they invoke in the course of their story-telling. For instance, in the same story Fotini refers to herself as a "proper" and "decent" girl twice, while there are jocular references to her virginity by Vivi and Tonia. Furthermore, Vivi's characterisation of Fotini as "clingy" (i.e. dependent, lacking in assertiveness) on Makis is echoed by Tonia and in the end accepted by Fotini too. On the other hand, Vivi triumphantly claims that she has got "a good man" and that "she can put men in their place."

This co-articulation of telling specific with situational identities, points to larger social identities that are consequential for the construction and interpretation of the stories. These have to do with the participants' group–internal roles, relations, and hierarchies on the one hand and their gender on the other. To take each separately, the participants' telling and situational identities are informed by, as well as make visible, a status–hierarchy within the group with Vivi occupying a leading position. As discussed, Vivi is the main adjudicator or assessor of the events and characters talked about, that is, the main teller of the evaluative component of a story. As such, her contributions are most instrumental in constructing the point of a storytelling: they gauge and assess the contingencies and consequences of past and future taleworlds. Making and being successful in evaluating in narrative events has been shown to be associated with positions of power (Ochs and Taylor 1992). In a similar vein, Vivi's contributions, be they to a story's plot or to its evaluation, are more likely to be ratified and taken on board in the process of co-constructing the taleworld.

This position of power is also evidenced in other discourse activities. Specifically, Vivi is the person who engages in language play and creative uses of language, which carry a lot of symbolic capital (Bourdieu 1977) in the group in question (cf. Bucholtz 1999a). She is also the record-keeper of the group: she keeps the Book of Minutes, the diary-like record of the group's exciting activities and moments, safe from prying eyes (i.e. of parents and guardians) and is responsible for updating it. When the group indulge in their favourite activity of registering their experiences in the format of poems (with rhyme), Vivi is the one who actually writes them down afterwards and perfects them. Vivi's leading position was also attested to during my interviews with the participants (as part of the group's ethnographic study). According to the participants, Vivi "knows best" when it comes to relationships with men as she is "street-wise, assertive," "makes the first move" and "has the upper hand when involved with somebody". On the basis of this, it is arguable that Vivi's position of an adjudicator, not only in the specific storytelling episodes but also in the triad, is intimately linked with her gendered attributes and roles that appear to have symbolic capital in this and other peer-groups at that age (cf. Eckert 2000; Thorne 1993). Specifically, Vivi enjoys popularity, particularly with men. At the same time, she positions herself and is positioned as an empowered woman, somebody who actively resists gender roles in the community that require women at that age to be chosen rather than choose, to be flirted with rather than flirt, to be asked out rather than ask out. Similarly, Vivi is the only one in the group who is vocally opposed to accepted gender ideologies according to which girls are not supposed to have sexual desires and engage in promiscuity (cf. Fine 1988). Dressing provocatively and dating older men are part and parcel of her personal rebellion.

On the other hand, Tonia works with a different model of relationships with men. She invariably opts out of flirting as she fears rejection. Although she openly aspires to Vivi's ideas about men and to her popularity – in fact, in numerous interactions, she echoes and seconds Vivi's positions (see Georgakopoulou 2002) – her accumulated disappointment in men, as inscribed in the narrative construction of her past, proves too much to ignore. This history seems to filter and play into Tonia's main telling identity, that is, her frequent appeals to shared stories from the participants' interactional history as models of future (inter)action and testimonies of her views. Finally, Fotini is positioned as the "proper" and "sexually inexperienced" girl. She tends to be respectful and thus not in direct conflict with her parents. A churchgoer (for which she is made fun of by Tonia and Vivi), she is less defiant than the other two and better academically. This profile links well with her telling identities through which she seeks the other participants', particularly Vivi's, views and suggestions and tries to learn from their experience. As shown above, she initiates projections more than actually contributing to their plot or evaluation.

In all cases, the participants' larger identities are not only indexed by their telling identities but they also inform and are brought to bear on them. In other words, shared assumptions about self – and other – attributes act as resources for legitimating and validating a future taleworld as well as the participants' contributions towards its construction. As can be attested to by the place of shared stories, shared resources are vital in the group and they mostly originate in interactional history. As such, they can be best described and understood as forming part of a community of practice (CoP, see Wenger 1998; also discussion in Eckert and McConnell-Ginet 1999). As a CoP, the participants over a period of regular contact and socialization have developed shared ways of doing things, ways of talking, beliefs and values. These are a repertoire of shared but negotiable resources that can be put to interactional use in order to constitute group membership, roles, and relations. It has been suggested that CoP can be productively linked with Bourdieu's (1977) concept of habitus (see discussion in Wilson 2001: 347). This embraces a set of dispositions and group norms that generate and regulate practices. Although systematically probing into the relations between a CoP and a habitus is beyond the scope of this study, it is notable that the participants' shared resources can certainly be seen as a habitus too, particularly at the level of recognizable and intelligible interpretations of experience and sets of belief that are to be found in their shared stories as well as in the "intertextual narrative" of their projections. In other words, stories afford an experiential logic (cf. discussion in Ochs and Capps 2001: 183ff) and as such they are an integral part of the individuals' and the group's identity construction. More specifically, as the above discussion has attempted to show, there is a three-way connection between stories, larger identities, and local storytelling roles. The latter two are mutually informed and operative for a story's construction. At the same time, larger identities have partly been constructed through lived and textualized narratives and have thus become part of the group's shared resources.

3.6 Conclusions

Currently, the cross-fertilization between narrative analysis and identity studies is largely informed by dynamic and locally contextualized views on both. With regard to identities, there is an increasing emphasis on how they come into being as local accomplishments in the course of telling stories. As far as narrative is concerned, the view that formed the starting point of this study is that of narrative as talk-in-interaction. In addition, the definition of narrative adopted here was sufficiently broad so as to cover cases of highly embedded, elliptical, and/or systematically co-authored stories. Analytically, the meeting point of narrative and identity was assumed to be found in the participants' storytelling roles. This was linked with the idea that extra-situational, "portable" identities can be best traced in discourse through a micro-analytic emphasis on the details and sequential management of talk.

The pairing of the small (micro-) with the large (macro-), i.e. of storytelling participation roles with social identities was argued for and demonstrated with respect to the conversational stories of three female best friends, aged 17. Their stories mainly comprised stories of future events (projections), which, as shown, presented numerous intertextual connections with regard to their theme, plot, characters talked about, and ways of telling. Two prominent features in their telling were their systematic co-construction by the participants and the embedding of stories of shared past events in them for argumentative and illustrative purposes. The qualitative analysis of the stories suggested that different participants contributed in varying degrees to different story components, particularly plotline and evaluation. Furthermore, the participants were differentiated in the degree in which their contributions were ratified and taken on board by others or, equally, challenged and delegitimated. These findings were further shed light on by the quantitative analysis of 50 projections with regard to the participants' telling roles of initiation, contribution to plotline, and evaluation. Here, evaluation was defined as the process of jointly piecing together a perspective on the events and characters talked about and it was found to mainly rely on embedded stories and character assessments. The analysis suggested that one participant (Vivi) not only contributed more to the telling of projections but, more significantly, had her contributions ratified more than the other two participants. The distinct telling roles for each participant brought into focus situational identities of advice-seeker vs. advice-giver and novice vs. expert (in the domain of relationships with men). In turn, the co-articulation of telling with situational identities made visible and were based on the participants' larger social identity of gender, relative standing vis-à-vis one another, with Vivi clearly having a leading position, and relationships as close friends. We argued that all those "portable" identities and the group's telling of narratives were interdependent, in the sense that the former both came into being through projections and formed an integral part of the participants' shared resources from their interactional history, including their narratives.

The implications of the above findings for identity analysis in narrative, first and foremost, are to be found in the close link between identity construction in narrative and a story's (emerging) structure, in this case, plot and evaluation. While such structural parts were initially postulated as analytical devices (e.g. as in Labov's 1972a model), subsequent studies have looked into them as participants' rather than analysts' resources: in this capacity, they have been shown to raise alternative tasks and types of action for different participants (see Goodwin 1984: 245). Further studies in this direction could shed light on how the relation between locally enacted participation roles and story parts bears on the tellers' identity construction.

The second important aspect in the relationship between narrative and identities that has transpired in this study has to do with the type of narrative activity the tellers are engaged in, which, in turn, can be safely assumed to be mediated and informed by social roles, practices, and relationships. In this case, local telling and situational roles were bound up with the activity of constructing future taleworlds as well as the theme of those tales (i.e. male–female relationships). It is arguable that, at a different level, the specific type of narrative activity is linked with the teller's age and age–related social activities, such as, in this case, exploring sexuality and relationships with men (cf. Heath 1986; Kyratzis 1999, for the importance of projections or event–casts for self–construction amongst school–age children and pre–schoolers, respectively. For a detailed discussion see Georgakopoulou 2003).

Finally, this study has shown the importance of the co-experienced (i.e. shared interactional history and assumptions, including shared narratives) for identity construction in current storytelling. In particular, the embedding of stories of past events in stories of future events provided evidence for the need to look into self-construction in narratives as part of a "long conversation" (Maybin 1996: 46), a trajectory of interactions, and a history of meaning-making, where previous stories can be used in a bricolage fashion in the telling of new stories. In addition, the shared-ness of experience and biographies that tends to accumulate in groups of intimates, as in the data at hand, calls for the opening up of the inquiry into self-construction in narrative to issues of collective memory and a relational narrativisation of the self.

Appendix 3.1   Transcription conventions

//	overlapping utterances
=	continuous utterances (latching)
:	extension or prolongation of a sound
::	longer extension
,	end of intonation unit, continuing intonation
.	stopping fall in intonation
?	rising intonation
!	animated tone
(..)	a pause greater than 0.5 of a second
(.)	a pause of less than 0.5 of a second
(( ))	editorial comments
< >	talk uttered more quickly than the surrounding utterance
CAPITALS	are used for louder speech
italics	Greek transcript

4

From linguistic reference to social reality

Deborah Schiffrin

4.1 Introduction

One of the fundamental tasks of talk is to refer to something in the world – a person, place, thing – in a way that will not only capture our own sense of what that something is, but will also allow our hearers to adequately recognize what we are talking about. So central is this task that Brown (1995: 62) assigns reference *priority* in understanding language: "the most crucial feature of each utterance, the feature which a listener must minimally grasp in order to begin to understand the utterance, is the expression used to identify what the speaker is talking about."

The linguistic form through which we convey what we are talking about is the noun phrase, either a full noun phrase (e.g. *the boy, a new family on the block, my high school friends, her house*) or a pronoun (e.g. *he, they, we, it*). Often what we are talking about are people, especially specific people with whom we have had some personal experience. When we do so, our nouns and pronouns do more than just refer to an entity that is "human" and "animate": they display characters who go on to reveal complex attributes, take specific actions, and form social relationships with other characters within a textual world that varies over time and across space. These very same characters, however, emerge within another site of social action and interaction: a concrete social world that forms its own microcosmic and fleeting world. And just like the textual world, the social world is also occupied by people ("you" and "I"), situated in a place ("here") and developing over time ("now").

This multiplicity – the embedding of people from the "real" world in both a world of representation and a world of social action – places reference at the crux of a set of problems underlying the study of discourse and identity. If reference plays a pivotal role in portraying the characters about whom a speaker is talking in a textual world, might it also have a role in constructing the "character" of the speaker him/herself in the interactional world? Clearly some references – the first and second personal pronouns, *I*, *you*, and *we* – do have such a role: at the very moment that they are embedding self and other within a textual world, they are also indexing the self and other of an interactional world. But this is a limited set of referring terms. What about full lexical nouns and third-person pronouns that index people other than speaker and hearer?

Since narratives (Baynham; Bell; De Fina, this volume; Schiffrin 1984, 1996) and life stories (Mishler; Schiff and Noy, this volume) are prime settings for identity construction, these are genres in which we would be most likely to expect third-person references to index speakers' identity. Indeed, prior research on one speaker's referring terms in a life story told during an oral history about the Holocaust (Schiffrin 2002) confirms this expectation: lexical choices, use of nouns and pronouns, and sequential patterns of third-person references revealed different facets of the speaker's identity that complemented other textual evidence of a distant relationship with her mother (cf. Schiffrin 2000) and a close and long-lasting relationship with her friends. The same research also argued that the speaker's relationships with these 'others' defined identities not only in her personal life-world relationships, but also in a broad matrix of historically emergent identities and cultural archetypes.

In this chapter, I discuss two theoretical frameworks that help us understand how referring terms project identity within the textual world of characters about whom we speak (including, but not limited to, narrative/life story genres) and within the social world of people with whom we interact. After reviewing a sociological approach to identity and linguistic approaches to reference (Section 4.2), I present a sample analysis showing how a single self-repair of a reference contributes to the construction of a complex array of identities during a sociolinguistic interview (Section 4.3). My conclusion reconstructs the analytical and theoretical paths between linguistic reference and social identity (Section 4.4).

4.2 Background perspectives

Two different areas of scholarship contribute to the perspective developed in this chapter: a social constructivist perspective on identity drawn largely from the work of Erving Goffman (Section 4.2.1); linguistic scholarship on reference that both separates, and unites, the language-to-world and language-in-text relationships (Section 4.2.2). I discuss each in turn, not only to develop a means of showing theoretical and analytical connections between social identity and linguistic reference, but also to provide a conceptual background for the analysis in Section 4.3.

4.2.1 The interactional basis of self and other

In this section, I describe a theoretical foundation, based largely on the work of the sociologist Erving Goffman, that will help us conceptualize "who we are" in the social world. When Goffman first began to publish his work, two views about the relationship between society and the individual prevailed among sociologists. One was that social structure and the individual were relatively independent: the former, the province of *sui generis* society; the latter, the province of each 'self.' The other view was more reductionist, basing the structures of society on psychological properties of individual agents. Neither perspective found it simple to explain the seemingly seamless continuity of social organizations despite recurrent changes in the occupants of their positions.

The alternative that Goffman proposed as a way to bring society and self into one conceptual framework was a sociogenic explanation of the self. By extending classic theories of Emile Durkheim (on social facts), Marcel Mauss (on reciprocity), Georg Simmel (on forms and meanings in social life), and George Herbert Mead (on human development), Goffman developed an account of the self as a social construction. This account helped bridge the theoretical and analytical divide between self and society by re-conceptualizing how 'other' and society are related to one another and how both are related to the 'self.' In brief, 'other' is a microcosmic representation of society; other/society and self are interdependent because the complementary needs of each are satisfied by the other.

A foundation for Goffman's view of the self/other/society relationship is Mead's social psychological theory of the development of 'self.' Critical to becoming a member of a community is the development of knowledge and behavior expected of one who occupies particular social positions in that community. This process is made possible by the symbolic resources provided through language and evidence of shared meanings as they become concretized, and acted upon, during communication. To simplify: we learn standards of acceptable behavior by observing how others respond to us, anticipating others' responses, developing responses that are designed *for* others, and integrating them into our own repertoire of actions and meanings. The recipient design of our responses is facilitated by our incorporation of a generalized other: "an organization of the attitudes of those involved in the same process . . . which gives to the individual his unity of self" (Mead 1934: 154). This incorporation of an abstract set of community standards and practices into the design requirements of what we do and say does not end once we are socialized: we continue to display awareness of a generalized other in the way we interact with others.

Before discussing how Goffman's work situates the self/other/ society relationship within social interaction, it is important to note that construing 'self' and 'other' as different entities creates some theoretical challenges. First, although I consider myself to be the "I," I am simultaneously the "you" to you. And since we recurrently trade participatory roles during interactions (i.e. we take turns speaking and acting), we each have a chance at being the "you" for whom communicative intentions and actions are designed and an "I" who is involved in the design process.

The simultaneity of the "I" and the "you," and the exchange of 'self' and 'other,' might be very difficult to combine were it not for two assumptions that pervade interaction: *intersubjectivity* and *reciprocity*. Intersubjectivity reflects Mead's (1934: 154) emphasis on being "involved in the same process": we assume shared knowledge and familiarity with information ("you and I share some common ground") and action ("I can understand what you have done"). Reciprocity, as developed from Mauss' (1967) account of the gift, assumes that not only does one's own action reflect and respond to another's prior action ("I will give you something in exchange for what you have given me"), but that it is also guided by a presumption of another's upcoming action ("I will give you something in exchange for what you will be giving me").

Although both intersubjectivity and reciprocity are foundational to social interaction, they are by no means static or taken-for-granted. Rather, they are continuously negotiated and co-constructed during ongoing social interactions that help provide participants with a continually evolving sense of "what we know" and "what is going on." We assume that we (both the "I" and the "you") can add to our base of common knowledge and that what we (again, both the "I" and the "you") do and say constructs sequences of mutual interdependency in which my actions are implicated by (and implicative for) your actions, and the role that I have just taken (e.g. as speaker) will next be one that I permit you to take.

Goffman's perspective combines Mead's view that society (i.e. generalized other) is internalized in the individual with Durkheim's (1966 [1895]) view of *sui generis* society, a unit greater than the sum of its parts. Like all social units, the unit on which Goffman focuses – social interaction – has properties that are not the sum of smaller units, i.e. not the cumulative properties of each person. In his classic work on the division of labor in society, Durkheim (1964 [1902]) argued that production tasks are distributed within a group based on either similarities (everyone can do the same work) or complementary differences (people can do different tasks that combine to produce a single product). The result of the latter arrangement (organic solidarity) is stronger and more dependable than the result (mechanical solidarity) of the former.

If we take seriously the idea that social units share fundamentally similar properties, then we can transpose these two types of solidarity onto social interaction. Intersubjectivity is a cognitive form of mechanical solidarity: it provides the stabilizing assumption that allows simultaneity ("I" am the "you" to another "you" are the "I" to yourself). Reciprocity is an action-based form of organic solidarity that facilitates the trade-off of 'self' and 'other' in social interaction (your action did/will complement mine). Thus the basic assumptions underlying 'self' and 'other' rest upon, and continuously reinstate, the two forms of solidarity that are critical to society in general: not only does intersubjectivity and reciprocity bring 'I' and 'you' together as internalizations of society, but they also contribute to the stability of interaction.

Goffman himself does not present this argument: he does not discuss intersubjectivity or reciprocity, mention mechnical and organic solidarity, or relate Mead to Durkheim. However, what Goffman does do is locate the structural basis of interaction in an interdependence between self and other that builds upon both self/ other similarities (mechanical solidarity) and their differences (organic solidarity).

Consider, first, how an utterance contributes to an interaction: whereas some information is given intentionally (i.e. communicated by the speaker), other information is given off (i.e. expressed) *un*-intentionally (Goffman 1959, 1963: 13–16). Since "most concrete messages combine linguistic and expressive components" (Goffman 1963: 16), utterances are built upon a fundamental division of informational labor with "the proportion of each differing widely from message to message." The varying distribution of information within and across messages has a consequence for recipients and for the outcome of interaction. Recipients of messages are faced with a set of strikingly different choices depending upon which aspect of information they focus upon to construct a response: they can draw upon either (or both) as the basis from which to infer meaning and design their own utterances. By assigning the 'other' a role in directing the course of an interaction as potentially potent as that of the 'self,' what happens in interaction can thus be the result of a fundamental differentiation of participant stances toward information: what I intend on a linguistic level may not be the message you infer on an expressive level. This differentiation of responsibility can be reallocated again and again: once I reply to you, I have the same opportunity to manage the direction of interaction by selecting what facet of your utterance will be the basis of my response.

Also allowing the other a pivotal role in communication is Goffman's view of face and ritual. Face, the positive social value a person claims for him/herself, is "diffusely located in the flow of events in the encounter and becomes manifest only when these events are read and interpreted for the appraisals expressed in them" (Goffman 1967a: 5). Just as face depends crucially upon interactions with the 'other,' so too does self/other interaction itself depend upon face: "the maintenance of face is a condition of interaction, not its objective" (12). Interpersonal ritual also links self and other together. Here the connection is due not to the face needs of a 'self,' but to a reciprocity between 'self' and 'other' linked in "a chain of ceremony, each giving deferentially with proper demeanor to the one on the right, what will be received deferentially from the one on the left" (Goffman 1967a: 85). What we take to be our unique being of 'self' is "thoroughly a product of joint ceremonial labor" (Goffman 1967a: 85).

Discussion thus far has been relatively abstract. We can become more concrete by observing how Goffman (following Simmel's (1950) focus on micro-level forms and meanings in social life) reveals how material and symbolic resources within the minute details of everyday life support "who we are." Material resources are found in the layouts of social establishments (e.g. homes, offices, stores, restaurants) and the objects housed within them. Our division of self into a public character and a private performer (Goffman 1959, Chapter 3) depends upon material resources that are built into establishments (e.g. service elevators, back doors) as well as those that are portable (e.g. mirrors placed in the front halls of our homes; cabinets whose doors can close upon a television, refrigerator, or piles of old newspapers). Our ability to embrace (or retreat) from a situated role (Goffman 1963) can depend on how we position and comport ourselves in relation to such resources, e.g. what seat we choose in a classroom, on a carousel, in a church and how we position ourselves once we are seated.

Also important are the symbolic resources provided through language and other communicative modalities. In addition to providing continuous evidence that we share a symbolic system, language also gives/gives off information that mediates between self and other to help alter the course of an interaction. The various ways in which we express and adorn ourselves, speak, act, and move, and place ourselves and our belongings (including not only physical objects, but also information itself (Goffman, 1971)), work together to enact the recurrent rituals through which we construct socially viable selves (Goffman 1967b). Likewise, our routinized exchanges – in which we greet or take leave of others, make requests or offers, issue warnings or apologies – all have ritual value through which we support positive valuations, or remedy negative valuations, of self and other (Goffman 1971).

Goffman's later work on the self (1981) turned attention from analyses of self/other to deconstruction of 'self.' And rather than focus on material and symbolic resources as the basis for divisions of self, Goffman focused solely on how we divide the labor underlying the production of an utterance. Goffman proposed that we author (design what is said), animate (present what another will hear), act as principal (commit to the meanings of what is said) and become a figure (a character in a textual world). Basing divisions of self on the productive labor of an utterance provides a link with sociolinguistic analyses of contextualization cues (Goffman 1981: 126–127), presages work on positioning theory (see Ribeiro, this volume) and informs linguistic studies of evidentiality (Schiffrin 2006). It also returns us to the textual world. Central to the textual world are not only the author who constructs that world, the animator who voices it, and the principal who commits to its information, but also the figure, the self-referential character in that world. What thus reframes, re-keys and laminates that textual world at both sentence and textual levels (Goffman 1974, Chapter 13) is the author's verbal production, the animator's presentation, the principal's propietary rights to information and its implications, and the figure's attributes, actions and relationships.

We began this section by asking how to conceptualize "who we are" in the social world. Goffman's scholarship has provided some answers. By immersing 'self' within multiple levels of social organization, and deconstructing traditional notions of 'self,' Goffman's work has established that "who we are" is not just a product of stable social structural organization. Identity is a fragile construction of different facets of 'self' and 'other' within social units such as interactions, encounters and situations during which we draw from numerous material and symbolic resources, including but not limited to language, for continuous substantive and ritual support. The forms and meanings accrued through the processes and products of ordinary social interaction, including its recurrent attestations to intersubjectivity and reciprocity, work together to construct a 'self' and the various identities that modify that self and display facets of it to others in various situations and through complex textual worlds. In the next section we turn from Goffman's perspective on the social world, and its brief attention to the first-person "figure" in the textual world, to perspectives on how linguistic reference establishes connections with a pre-existing world of persons, places and things, as well as connections between words within the textual world.

4.2.2 Word to world and word to text

Given the centrality of reference to language and communication (noted at the outset of this chapter), it should not be surprising that its study has been pertinent not only to linguists, but also to philosophers and psychologists. Even within Linguistics itself, reference is a topic of study in various subfields: semantics, pragmatics, variation analysis, computational linguistics and discourse analysis (including in the latter, those interested in grammar and interaction, discourse processes, text structure and narrative). And in keeping with its inter- and intra-disciplinary breadth, methodologies for studying reference within Linguistics include philosophical introspection and argumentation, the development and testing of formal models and algorithms, corpus analysis, conversation analysis, and numerous approaches within both discourse analysis and pragmatics.

An important distinction in the linguistic study of reference is between *external* and *internal* perspectives: the former examines the "relation between symbols and the objects they represent;" the latter, the "relation of coreference between symbols" (Kronfeld 1990: 3). Although these perspectives are often separated in both theory and analysis, they also intersect with one another. Before discussing the intersection, let us learn a bit more about each one independently.

The term "reference" itself invokes the *external* perspective: a relation between language and something in the world. Hence, in keeping with the view of semantics as the study of how signs are related to the objects to which they are applicable (Morris 1938), the study of reference often falls to the linguistic subfield of semantics. Yet who is it that relates signs to objects and realizes their applicability? If we view the speaker – and not the linguistic signs themselves – as the critical conduit through which signs are related to objects, then the study of reference might belong more properly to pragmatics, defined in Morris' (1938) terms as the study of how interpreters engage in the "taking-account-of" designata (the construction of interpretants) of sign-vehicles.

Locating the analysis of reference in one linguistic subfield, however, assumes that those subfields are discretely bound areas of inquiry. Yet the boundaries between semantics and pragmatics are notoriously amorphous, depending to a large extent on what theory/model is adapted in each: formal truth-conditional vs. cognitive semantics; the largely Anglo-American view of pragmatics as based on Grice's maxims or the more continental view of pragmatics as language use. Various aspects of meaning and use get caught up and differently allocated to each subfield (e.g. semantic vs. pragmatic presupposition); different relationships between the two are proposed, challenged and defended.

Reference is one aspect of meaning that has been entangled in the semantics/pragmatics quagmire. In his two-volume text on semantics, for example, Lyons (1977: 184) states that "the fundamental problem for the linguist, as far as reference is concerned, is to elucidate and to describe the way in which we use language to draw attention to what we are talking about." Privileging the speaker within semantics is based on the belief that "it is the speaker who refers (by using some appropriate expression): he invests the expression with reference by the act of referring" (Lyons 1977: 177). A strikingly similar perspective is offered by Givón, but as part of pragmatics, rather than semantics:

Reference in a Universe of Discourse is already a *crypto pragmatic* affair. This is because every universe of discourse is *opened* ('established') – for whatever purpose – by a *speaker*. And that speaker then *intends* entities in that universe of discourse to either refer or not refer. And it seems that in human language it is that *referential intent* of the speaker that controls the grammar of reference. (emphasis in original)   (Givón 1989: 175)

Although the semantic and pragmatic perspectives noted above both emphasize the role of the speaker, other areas of research that also assign speaker actions and intentions a necessary role in reference are quick to point out that it is the *hearer* who adds a sufficient condition for reference. The psycholinguists Clark and Wilkes-Gibbs (1986), for example, speak of referring as a collaborative process: whereas a speaker can propose a referent, the identification of the referent is an outcome of mutual knowledge that may need to be achieved through speaker–hearer interaction (see also Brown 1995; Sacks and Schegloff 1979). Thus, the external process by which expressions refer to an entity "involves the cooperative exploitation of supposed mutual knowledge" (Green 1989: 47) that may emerge in concrete sequences of speaker–hearer interaction.

In contrast to the word-to-world relationships addressed by the external perspective, what is added by *internal* analyses of reference are language-in-text relationships: how does a current referring expression evoke the same referent already evoked by a prior referring expression? If there are multiple prior referring expressions, hence multiple entities already in the textual world, how does a hearer know which is the right antecedent? With this shift in focus comes a shift in analytical perspective: whereas external analyses often draw from semantics and pragmatics, internal analyses often draw from discourse analysis. The reason for this discursive turn is simple. The link between an initial referring term and the 'real world' has already been established in a prior text. Hence possible links between a subsequent referring term and the initial referring term are delimited by the characters, activities and scenes already evoked in the textual world.

The examples below (altered from Brown 1995: 12) illustrate how discourse plays a role in resolving the internal problem of locating the textual antecedent, and thus the referent, of the pronoun "*they*," first seen in Example 4.1, line (b):

Example 4.1

(a) As Mom and Dad drove up to the house, the boys had just started their cowboy game.
(b) Instead *they* ran out back to the car.

In line (a), *Mom and Dad* are driving up to a house, inferable as their home, while *the boys* are engaged in *their cowboy game*. Within this textual world, we build upon our knowledge of how kin terms lead to upcoming relational inferences (cf. Sacks 1972 on membership categorization devices) to infer a domestic familial scene in which *the boys* are "children of the parents." This inferred relational connection allows other inferences: whoever is evoked by *they* is running towards *Mom and Dad* because they are eager to greet them; since children are eager to see their parents, *they* in Example 4.2, line (b) is co-referential with *the boys*.

In Example 4.2, line (a), differences in referent and activity reconstruct the textual world in which an antecedent for *they* (in line (b)) is sought:

Example 4.2

    (a) As the police drove up to the house, the boys had just started their robbery attempt.
    (b) Instead *they* ran out back to the car.

In line (a), the referent (*the police*) and boys' activity (*robbery attempt*) re-construct the textual world as one in which *the boys* would not be running towards those driving *up to the house*. Thus the antecedent of *they* is less clear: we can imagine that it is either the police running towards (i.e. chasing) the boys, or the boys running away from (trying to escape) the police. Hence either *the police* or *the boys* can be running *out back to the car*. Thus *they* in Example 4.1, line (b) and Example 4.2, line (b) has different possible interpretations because of the different characters, activities and scenes in the textual worlds already established in the discourse.

To summarize: the external perspective on reference focuses on the link between a word and the "real" world that is typically made in the first mention of a referent in a text; the internal perspective focuses on a "next" link between a word and a referent, crucially, a link mediated through a prior word and its "first" link to the "real" world, as well as the position occupied by that referent in the textual world. Notice that putting the external/internal difference in terms of order of mention in a text recasts them as different phases of one communicative goal: interlocutors seek to achieve general agreement about what referent is being evoked by a referring term. And the way this goal is accomplished requires a multi-faceted process in which a speaker uses a referring term that is intended to be interpreted by another person within an emergent textual world constructed during an ongoing interaction with that other person.

4.2.3 *Summary*

In this section, we have reviewed two different areas of inquiry as a prelude to our analysis of identity and reference. Some preliminary connections should already be apparent. For example, just as we observed that language is an important symbolic resource through which we construct "who we are" with others during social interactions, so too, we invoked social interactional identities (such as speaker, hearer, interlocutors) when discussing how we create references. Recall, also, Goffman's suggestion that messages differ widely in their proportion of linguistic (intentionally given) and expressive (unintentionally given) components. Like other aspects of messages and the language used to convey them, then, it is reasonable to assume that the nouns and pronouns that evoke the figures – "who we are talking about" in a textual world – can also take their place within the collection of semiotic resources that provide expressive information about "who we are" when we are talking to one another within the social world.

4.3 Reference and identity in a sociolinguistic interview

In this section, our discussion of reference and identity comes together in an analysis of a problematic referral that contributes to the construction of identities within a sociolinguistic interview. Since the analysis encompasses various facets of the discourse (the linguistic form/meaning of the referral, the repair process, the sequencing of turns and moves) it may help to anticipate its main findings: a single reference helps to construct identities through a repair that is part of a brief story, that joins a second-story, to support an assessment about a local market.

Also helpful is a brief description of the context of the segment – a sociolinguistic interview. Although all interviews share a common core (i.e. gathering information through questions (Schiffrin 1994, Chapter 4)), there are also differences among them and the identities that both motivate and emerge within them. Sociolinguistic interviews are a type of research interview: their long-term goal is to seek information that will advance a body of knowledge already reified as an academic discipline. Sociolinguistic theory and methodology developed together during the 1970s as William Labov and his associates searched for empirical methods to study the underlying structures of vernacular speech (the language variety first acquired and then used in daily life). The sociolinguistic interview provided a means through which to attain large corpora of spoken language in which informants from a particular community speak in a variety of styles. Included is a "casual" style that resembles how people speak when they are not monitoring (and possibly modifying and correcting) the way they talk. When efforts to elicit a wide range of styles are successful, sociolinguistic interviews gain a "blended" or mixed quality, reflecting the goals, practices, form and content not only of research interviews, but also of conversations.

Although transient and subtle shifts between interview-like and conversation-like situations are clearly recognized as having academic value for the overall research goals of sociolinguists studying community-wide language patterns, their value for studying discourse and identity has not always been recognized within the research paradigm driving sociolinguistic analyses of speech communities. What is prescribed instead is a relatively narrow and fixed view of "who we are," in which identity is typically viewed as relatively static and categorical. Two types of identities are usually relevant to sociolinguistic interviews. One is situational: *a linguist* (a scholar with an interest in language) talks with *an informant*. The other differentiates informants in terms of broad social categories (e.g. class, gender, age, ethnicity, neighborhood) and language background and views them as exemplars of subtypes of those categories.

In addition to being static and categorical, sociolinguistically ascribed identities have typically played only a "boundary" role in research design and practice, appearing only at the inception and conclusion of a research project. As a project begins, people are chosen for interviews on the basis of their social class, age, gender, race, ethnicity, neighborhood, and language background. As a project ends – once the data has been collected, analyzed, and aggregated – linguistic patterns are explained on the basis of aggregated identities (e.g. working class vs. middle class, men vs. women). As we see below, however, a range of temporary and locally situated identities intersect with the more stable social categories of identity to pervade a single interchange from a sociolinguistic interview.

In the interchange to be analyzed, Anne and Ceil are driving around Philadelphia. Anne is a middle-class graduate student studying Linguistics; she is from California and in her early twenties. Ceil is a working-class woman from Philadelphia in her forties. Although Ceil and Anne have spent many hours talking in Ceil's house, here Anne is driving Ceil around the city so that Ceil can act as an informal "tour guide" and provide an "insider's" perspective on different areas in the city. The constantly changing setting defines the means by which Anne gathers information from Ceil. Rather than use questions to prompt and elicit information from Ceil, what provides the impetus for information-gathering is the changing milieu of the city: Anne drives Ceil to an area about which Ceil either comments on her own or is invited by Anne (through an observation or a question) to provide a comment. The information-seeking function of Anne's sociolinguistic interview with Ceil is thus mediated by the changing scenes and visual material that appear as Anne and Ceil move through the city in Anne's car.

In Example 4.3 below, Anne and Ceil are approaching a neighborhood known as South Philadelphia, home to many working-class Italians whose houses Ceil has admired. The main analytical focus in the segment will be Ceil's self-initiated and self-completed repair of a referring term, beginning with *the-* (line (s)) and ending with *them two* (line (bb)).

Example 4.3

(a)	CEIL	This is Washington Avenue.
(b)		Now here's a great section.
(c)		Over at Ninth Street.
(d)	ANNE	Right.
(e)		That's- that's the Ita[lian market, huh?
(f)	CEIL	[Yeh, Italian market.
(g)		And I wish we had one up, where [we lived at.
(h)	ANNE	[Yeh.
(i)		Oh, I do, [too.
(j)	CEIL	[Oh:, I'd love to have one up there because-
(k)		oh, I enjoy its-
(l)		I love to come down there.
(m)	ANNE	Yeh.
(n)		It's fun. It's fun. No kidding.
(o)	CEIL	It really is.
(p)		I mean, like uh-
(q)		We used to come down on the trolley cars.=
(r)	ANNE	Yeh.
(s)	CEIL	=And bring *the*-
(t)		like we only had-
(u)		like Ann and I, we-
(v)		my cousin, Ann?=

(w)	ANNE	Mmhmm.
(x)	CEIL	=We-
(y)		like she had Jesse
(z)		and I had my Kenny.=
(aa)	ANNE	Mmhmm
(bb)	CEIL	=And we used to bring *them two* down on the trolley car.
(cc)		And bags of uh, [groceries.=
(dd)	ANNE	Is that [so?
(ee)	CEIL	=Carry all the bags, right?

The segment opens as Anne and Ceil are entering an area of several city blocks on which vendors sell produce in an open air sidewalk market. Ceil's identification of the area begins at one street (*This is Washington Avenue* (line (a))) that is evaluated (*Now here's a great section* (line (b))) as they are approaching its intersection *Over at Ninth Street* (line (c)). Since this identification fills the official purpose of the situation – describing sections of Philadelphia to Anne – here Ceil is enacting her official position within this sociolinguistic interview as tour guide and expert. Anne reciprocates by staying within her visitor/novice position: she conveys some familiarity with the market through *Right* (line (d)) and then requests verification of its identity *That's- that's the Italian market, huh?* (line (e)) that Ceil confirms (*Yeh, Italian market* (line (f))) midway through Anne's turn.

The segment continues with Ceil and Anne praising the market in assessment sequences in which overlapping turns (lines (g)–(o)) display their involvement with the topic and highlight their agreement on the market's virtues. At first it is Ceil who takes the lead in praising the market and Anne who follows pace. Ceil wishes for a similar market in her neighborhood (*And I wish we had one up, where we lived at* (line (g)), *Oh:, I'd love to have one up there* (line (j))) and then conveys desire (*I'd love to come down there* (line (l))) to shop at the market. After each of Ceil's endorsements, Anne adds agreement tokens: *Yeh* (line (h)), *Oh, I do, too.* (line (i)), *Yeh* (line (m)). When Ceil does not continue to praise the market after Anne's second *Yeh* (line (m)), however, it is Anne who opens another round of assessments by praising the market (*It's fun. It's fun. No kidding.* (line (n))) and it is Ceil who then endorses the assessment (*It really is* (line (o))).

Although both Ceil and Anne have initiated rounds of praise for the market, Anne's *It's fun* (line (n)) has a dual reading: it can also serve as an explanation for the positive assessments of the market (e.g. one reason we enjoy something is because it is fun). When *It's fun* has its explanatory reading, it fills a vacated slot from prior talk. Ceil had earlier begun to explain her desire to have such a market in her neighborhood (*I'd love to have one up there because-* (line (j))), but she had abandoned that reason, first, for *oh, I enjoy its-* (line (k)), and next, for a wish to visit the market (*I'd love to come down here* (line (l))). Ceil does eventually explain why she likes the market (*Because you can do better down there* Example 4.4 line (rr)), but only after telling two anecdotes that establish an experiential basis for her claim.

It is in Ceil's first anecdote that we find the problematic referral. After endorsing Anne's *It's fun* (line (n)) with *It really is* (line (o)), Ceil uses two discourse markers that preview the functions of an upcoming anecdote about trips to the market: *I mean* previews an elaboration (Schiffrin 1987, Chapter 9) and *like* previews an exemplification of a more general point (Schiffrin 1982: 270–286). Ceil then introduces a past activity (*We used to come down on the trolley cars* (line (q))) and begins to add detail to her anecdote with (*And bring the-* (line (s)). But she then interrupts the object noun phrase initiated by *the-*.

Ceil's sequence of repairs, beginning with *the-* (line (s)) and ending with *them two* (line (bb)) is sequentially ordered to allow a cumulative set of referents to accrue. The definite article *the* typically indicates speaker's assumptions that a hearer can identify and recognize the entity that the speaker has in mind. But instead of following *the-* (line (s)) with a lexical noun that will be similarly recognizable, Ceil interrupts her own *the-* and switches to *we only had-* (line (t)), a clause type often used to introduce a new referent (Schiffrin 2006). Yet rather than complete the clause with a noun, Ceil interrupts *had-* (line (t)) and begins to specify *we*. Ceil then self-interrupts *we* (lines (u) and (x)) twice to deconstruct the plural referent. She describes one member of *we* as *Ann my cousin* (line (v)); she dissects two members of *we* (through repetition of the earlier cut-off "X had" clause structure) when she separates *we only had-* (line (t)) into *she had Jesse* (line (y)) and *I had my Kenny* (line (z)). It is the two boys, Jesse and Kenny, who are represented by *them two* of the repair-completion (line (bb)).

Ceil's repair illustrates the external/internal links, and the collaborative nature, of reference discussed in Section 4.2.2. Repairable is a definite noun phrase: it began at *the*, an article that prefaces a referral to a specific entity assumed to be recognizable to the hearer. What Ceil's repair provided is the background information needed to make that referent recognizable, i.e. "who" is being evoked. Because she could not assume that Anne would recognize the referent until she knew who "we" are ('Ann and I'), who "Ann" is ("her cousin"), who Ann "had," and who she "had," she built up internal links within the text: she introduced *my cousin Ann*, Ann's son *Jesse*, and her own son *Kenny*. Ceil's dependence upon an external link is revealed by her use of familiarity anchors (Schiffrin 2006) to link referents to herself: Ann is presented as *my cousin*, and one of the boys is *my Kenny* who *I had*. Ceil thus created a backdrop of familiar information that would allow Anne to draw the correct inferential link between *them two* and its textual antecedent, the most recent plural nouns, *Jesse* and *my Kenny*.

Ceil's repair cooperatively exploited shared and familiar information in still another way. She used repetition to embed the completed referral within a textual world parallel to the one interrupted in the repair initiation:

REPAIR INITIATION	line (q)	we used to come down on the trolley cars
	line (s)	And bring *the-*
REPAIR COMPLETION	line (bb)	we used to bring *them two* down on the trolley car

In the repair completion, line (bb), Ceil repeats an agent (*we*), a habitual (*used to*) action, directionality (*down*), and the instrument of locomotion (*on the trolley car(s)*). She also maintains the proximal deictic verb (shifting from *come* to *bring*) to establish her physical closeness to the market. Thus the referent initiated by cut-off *the* in (line (s)) – the entities who Ceil and Ann *used to* (lines (a) and (l)), *bring* (lines (c) and (l)) *down on the trolley car(s)* (lines (a) and (l)) – is provided as *them two* (line (bb)) only after sequentially implicative and cumulative self-completions of several other referrals are introduced and explained, and after the details of the very same textual world are re-established.

Once Ceil has completed her repair, she continues her anecdote by adding that it was not only the boys who were part of the trip, but *bags of uh, groceries* (line (cc)), *all the bags* (line (ee)) that the two women used to *carry* (line (ee)) on public transportation (*the trolley car* (line (bb))). These details portray Ceil in a domestic realm: she is a member of an extended family (a mother with a cousin) who is providing food for her family. But they do not portray the shopping experience as positive. This is puzzling since the story had been prefaced as support for positive assessments of the market, including the evaluation of the market as "fun." As we see below, Ceil's brief anecdote about the struggles of the past works in tandem with a next story: it provides an evaluative preface for a second story about a more recent past in which the possibility of going to the market went unrealized.

Ceil begins a second anecdote (in Example 4.4, line (gg)) right after Anne mentions that women from *Port Richmond still um, go down that way* (line (ff)) to shop:

Example 4.4

(bb)	CEIL	And we used to bring them two down on the trolley car.
(cc)		And bags of uh, [groceries.=
(dd)	ANNE	Is that [so?
(ee)	CEIL	=Carry all the bags, right?
(ff)	ANNE	A lot of women from Port Richmond still um, go down that way.
(gg)	CEIL	That's like Tom said to me a few weeks ago.
(hh)		He said, "I was gonna take you down Ninth Street,"
(ii)		he said, "but I didn't think you'd want to go."
(jj)		I said, "Oo:=
(kk)	ANNE	Oo.
(ll)	CEIL	Oo: y'know like-
(mm)	ANNE	"Dummy.
		Of *course* I wanted [to go.=
(nn)	CEIL	[Dummy.
(oo)	ANNE	=Let's just go down here."
(pp)	CEIL	I said, "I wish you had've told me,"
(qq)		I said, "I would've went down."
(rr)		Because you can do better down there.

As shown by the direct quotes, expressive vocalization, dramatization and overlapping turns, the second anecdote shifts the mode of interaction between Ceil and Anne from its interview and "guided tour" frames to a "teasing" frame in which both participants inter-weave their contributions within a shared floor. Although Anne had supported Ceil's assessment earlier in their interaction, here she co-constructs enthusiasm for the market by co-authoring and co-animating Ceil as a figure in a past interaction between Ceil and her husband Tom.

In the performance, Tom *said* that his intention to take Ceil *down Ninth Street* (line (hh)) (a local way of referring to the Italian market) was thwarted by his thought that Ceil wouldn't *want to go* (line (ii)). Ceil and Anne join together in voicing Ceil's response to Tom. Their co-animated and co-authored performance of Ceil as a figure in the textual world uses Tom's unstated offer as a vehicle through which to present Ceil's enthusiasm for the market, thus authenticating the positive assessment of the Italian market from earlier talk. The form and substance of their performance moves Ceil and Anne from their situation-based identities as expert (Ceil) and novice (Anne), and activity-based identities as co-assessors of the market, to identities that are not only locally emergent, but also globally categorized: Ceil and Anne engender their identities because they are jointly satirizing cross-gender communication.

Anne and Ceil enact a dialectic between silence and speech that typifies a cultural stereotype about the differences between men and women. Tom is silent and his actions are shrouded by what he does not say: he presents a counterfactual offer (*I was gonna take you down Ninth Street* (line (hh))) that was not actualized because he presumed that Ceil would turn it down (*I didn't think that you'd want to go* (line (ii))). Anne and Ceil perform Ceil's response to Tom, first with Ceil's *I said "Oo:* (line (jj)), that is echoed by Anne's *Oo* (line (kk)), and re-echoed by Ceil's *Oo:* (line (ll)). Anne and Ceil then characterize Tom through the pejorative term *Dummy* (lines (mm) and (nn)) that also suggests a lack of ability to speak: some-one who can neither hear nor speak is "deaf and dumb"; marion-ettes whose voices are ventriloquized are known as "dummies." Each has parroted the other: whereas Ceil first says *Oo:* (line (jj)), it is Anne who first says *Dummy* (line (mm)). Ceil then voices her hope for more open expression of Tom's intentions (*I wish you had've told me* (line (pp))) that would have allowed her to accept his offer (*I would've went down* (line (qq))).

The narrative about Tom functions in relation to Ceil's first story and to her joint assessments with Anne about the market. Whereas the first anecdote narrated Ceil's struggle to get to the market, the second anecdote narrated Ceil's response to someone thinking that she would *not* want to go. The two story-worlds thus establish an ironic contrast between Ceil's own willingness to struggle to get what she wants and the fact that an easy opportunity to get those same "goods" was unrecognized by someone close to Ceil. In addition to providing evidence for Ceil's devotion to the market, the two stories also provide an economic incentive (*you can do better down there* (line (rr))) for liking the market that differs from Anne's reason for liking the market (*it's fun* (line (n))). Thus Ceil is not only an expert: she is an expert whose everyday domestic circumstances give her good reason to be so.

In sum, we have examined a reference that had no direct "external" link with speaker or hearer, but nevertheless had multiple roles in their social interaction. The reference was the object of complex self-initiated and self-completed repair. The repair began at *the-*, an article that typically conveys a speaker's assumption that a recipient would be able to identify the specific entity about to be mentioned. Rather than test this assumption (by saying, for example, *the boys*) Ceil used a cumulative sequence of nouns to create a higher likelihood of recognizability for Anne. Although the immediate textual antecedent of *them two* was *Jesse* and *my Kenny*, these two referents had already gained entry to the textual world by being anchored to Ceil through *we, my* in *my cousin Ann* and *my Kenny*, and *I had*. Also facilitating the eventual replacement of *the-* by *them two* was Ceil's repetition from earlier text of crucial semantic information: who (agent) did what (action), how (instrument) and where (location). Thus, Ceil's repair of her reference depended on the semantics and pragmatics of text/context pairings within (and across) the sequence of utterances throughout the interchange.

Once Ceil's referent was available to Anne, it was able to gain roles in the larger textual and social worlds emerging during Ceil and Anne's interaction. The referent became part of a first-anecdote providing support for an assessment already shared between Ceil and Anne. The first-anecdote became part of a discursive construction of irony through a next-anecdote that joined Ceil and Anne in a gendered evaluation of a husband's diminished means of voicing an offer to his wife and established Ceil as an expert on the values of the market. Thus joining the reference in the construction of identity were turn-by-turn sequential contingencies and performance styles, both of which created local activity-based identities and indexed broad social identities. A single reference that gave information about an entity in a textual world thus contributed to a complex of discursive acts that gave off information about "who" in the social world was speaking to "whom."

4.4 Reference and identity in discourse

In this section, I reconstruct the analytical and theoretical paths between linguistic reference and social identity. Although the identities that emerged during the interchange between Ceil and Anne were not separable in practice, it is helpful to summarize them based on facets of text/context and aspects of identity: *author, animator, principal* based on utterance production; *expert* based on situated activities; *working-class woman from Philadelphia* based on language structure and use. A final discussion of reference, identity and discourse then suggests how referring terms provide bridges to the multiple social worlds in which identity is constructed.

Ceil's repair revealed a differentiation of self based on the varying tasks underlying the production format of a reference. Ceil composed (as author) and voiced (as animator) information supporting her commitment (as principal) to information that would meet the interpretive needs of her hearer. The trajectory of her repair adhered to Levinson's (2000) principle of "say less, mean more": speakers reduce the amount of information in a referring term if they can assume that information from text and context is inferentially available (through communicative maxims of quantity or relevance (Schiffrin 1994, Chapter 5)) to supplement what is "said" through the referring term itself. Thus Ceil was able to use the relatively uninformative pronominal *them two* only after cooperatively providing, and then exploiting, a cumulative sequence of self-completed repairs of referrals and re-establishing the reference in an identical textual world. Since Anne participated by using *Mmhmm* to ratify Ceil's identification of two key parts of her referral – who *we* were, who we *had* – both speaker and hearer built upon an emergent base of shared knowledge in which "meaning more" by "saying less" had been interactionally warranted.

Completion of the repair, and use of *"them two"* as a character in the textual world of "going to the market," was relevant to Ceil's emergence as a local expert in her interchange with Anne. The potential for Ceil to speak to Anne with a voice of authority had already been created by the institutional frame of the sociolinguistic interview, in which a researcher typically seeks information from a member of a local community. Driving around the city enhanced that potential simply because of the physical availability of the material about which Ceil was more knowledgeable than Anne. Despite this situational potential, Ceil's voice became authoritative only through the locally emergent activities of assessing, supporting an assessment, and telling stories. It was in Ceil's story about herself and her cousin on public transportation, carrying bags, that *them two* appeared, adding to what was already a cumbersome trip. Ceil's story about the difficulty of past trips to the market, together with her next-story about her husband's presumption that she would not now want to go to the market despite the ease of getting there, provided the experiential base for her authoritative voice.

Ceil's expertise about the market also depended upon a finely tuned differentiation of self partially grounded in group identities buried within her references. We can view the "I" of Ceil's assessment (*I wish we had one up, where we live at* (line (g)), *I'd love to have one up there* (line (j))) as a singular principal committed to a sentiment. But what attested to this assessment was the immersion of Ceil as a figure in a textual world of collective domesticity: the figure *I* appeared taking action with a cousin, nephew, and son and interacting with a husband. And it was only after constructed dialogue (e.g. *Of course I wanted to go* (line (mm))) allowed the figure to animate commitment that the principal's position could be justified. And rather than do so for reasons of "fun" (cf. Anne's *It's fun* (line (n))), a characterization that would view food shopping within a domain of "leisure," Ceil justified her commitment to the market by again immersing herself in a collective (note the use of indefinite *you*) whose reasons for shopping at the market (*you can do better down there* (line (rr))) are based on rational economic preference.

If we view experts as people who can provide valuable information to someone who has no access to that information, then another potential for expertise inheres in the research goals of the sociolinguistic interview itself. Sociolinguists choose people to interview based on the belief that their social characteristics (e.g. region, social class, gender) are correlated with ways of speaking about which they would not otherwise know. Put another way, the linguistic information that sociolinguists seek can be provided only by samples of speech from informants typifying specific social categories. Since sociolinguists know how to identify one's region and gender, and measure one's social class, there is often an assumption that these identities – once assigned to people – remain stable throughout an interview. In the segment from the interview between Anne and Ceil, however, each of these categories became more salient through different means of expression, such that some parts of what Ceil said were more indicative of her membership within these broad categories of social identity than others.

Ceil's regional identity as a Philadelphian appears through lexis and syntax. Consider, for example, the term she used for the market. Although Ceil had initially verified Anne's identification (*Yeh, Italian market* (line (f)) of the market, *Italian market* is not an insiders' term for the market: Philadelphians usually label shopping areas by street name, not by neighborhood or salespersons' ethnicity. Ceil herself used the more local term for the market when quoting her husband Tom during their reported interaction: *He said, "I was gonna take you down Ninth Street"* (line (hh)). Notice, also, that Philadelphians often use motion verbs plus the spatial preposition *down*, but without the *to* preceding the destination (as in *come/go down* [to a location]). Although Ceil and Anne both used *go down* with spatial pronouns (*come/go down here/there* (lines (l) and (oo))), it was only Ceil who said (when animating her husband Tom): *I was gonna take you down Ninth Street.*

Also emergent during Ceil and Anne's interchange was social class. Ceil used nonstandard grammatical forms associated with socio-economic status and education (two indicators of social class). A common feature of working-class speech, for example, is the grammatical case of *them two*, Ceil's self-completed repair of *the-*. Since the standard form would have been either the objective *them* ("bring them") or the nominative *those two* ("bring those two"), Ceil's *them two* is a non-standard form suggestive of working-class status. Ceil's use of other nonstandard features of English include *had* instead of modal *would* (*you had've told me* (line (pp))), past tense of *go* ("went") rather than past participle ("gone") in *would've went down* (line (qq)), and the postposed preposition in the "where" clause (*where we lived at* (line (g))).

Whereas region and class appeared through grammar and lexicon, gender appeared through topic and means of performance. In Ceil's first anecdote, the description of the shopping trip, including reference to *them two* (Ceil's son and cousin), situated her in a domestic realm of motherhood, child care and provision of family needs. Gender emerged more dramatically in the second anecdote through the reported interaction with Tom and its means of performance with Anne: Ceil and Anne co-animated a narrative about Tom's communicative style and performed a gendered dialectic between speech and silence. Because Anne could jointly author and animate Ceil in a staged teasing about Ceil's husband (an act typical of people in a close relationship), their co-performance also conveyed solidarity based on a gendered alignment quite different than either their static identity as "women" or their interviewer/ interviewee relationship.

In sum, facets of Ceil's identity emerged through various linguistic forms that were situated in specific sites of social activity and interaction. A differentiation of self based on production format, and coordination with recipient responses, emerged through the sequential production of a baseline of intersubjectivity vis-à-vis a reference. The reference itself fits into interactionally situated activities of shared assessments and storytelling. The form and content of the two brief stories not only provided experiential bases that provided authoritative warrants for the assessment, but also provided a gendered critique of communicative style and displays of characters grounded in both domestic and economic worlds in which the need to provide for a family can be further hampered by the need to conserve financial resources. Use of specific syntactic forms and lexical items reflected Ceil's membership in broadly based social groups arising from her upbringing and socialization in a regionally based, and socially stratified, community in which such forms were conventional parts of the grammar that she acquired.

What are we to make of these various aspects of identity, their various linguistic manifestations and bases, and their appearance in different aspects of social worlds? And how can we account for the role of linguistic reference in the construction of social identities? In earlier work on discourse markers (Schiffrin 1987), I proposed a model of discourse in which different domains, as well as relations among them, provided a system within which markers function. This model may help us here.

In the model, an *ideational structure* concerned propositions; an *information state* concerned the organization and management of speaker/hearer knowledge and meta-knowledge. A *participation framework* focused on the more social sides of speaker and hearer: their alignments, relationships to each other and to what they are saying. An *action structure* incorporated structured knowledge about what "counts as" particular actions, as well as their constrained sequential contingencies. Finally, *an exchange structure* concerned the organization of turns at talk and the distribution of speaking/hearing rights. My design of the model reflected my interest in discourse markers and their multi-functionality, i.e. markers can display relationships between units in more than one domain at a time. This multi-functionality stems partially from the linguistic properties (semantic, lexical, deictic, grammatical) of markers and partially from the units that they bracket.

We can use this model to help account for the relationship between referring terms and social identities in two ways. First, we can reconfigure what we have been calling the textual and social worlds as discourse domains. Although the textual world corresponds to the ideational structure, the social world is a vast over-simplification: it includes worlds as potentially different as those in which we perform actions, exchange turns and moves, organize information, and orient ourselves to one another and to our utterances. Second, the model can recast the questions underlying this chapter. If reference plays a pivotal role in an ideational domain (and its evolving information state), might it also have a role in constructing identity in the action structure, exchange structure and participation framework? And if so, how?

The new set of questions can be answered by drawing upon the sociological and linguistic perspectives reviewed in Section 4.2. These perspectives suggest two reasons for the multi-functionality of referring terms in discourse domains: the processes underlying different discourse domains resemble each other; the communicative properties of referring terms allow references to be salient in more than one domain at once.

Discourse domains share crucial properties and undergo similar processes. Of course the people who we talk about, and who we talk to, are not always one and the same: unless we are directing actions (e.g. warnings, requests) toward an 'other,' we usually talk about people other than those with whom we are interacting at the moment. But each world creates a set of characters – linked by intersubjectivity and reciprocity, simultaneity and exchange – that provides an 'other' in relation to whom we define a 'self.' In each world, the 'other', as generalized other, serves as a microcosmic representation of societal structures that are larger, more complex, and more abstract than the interaction in which 'other' appears as a hearer. Both macro-level and micro-level social phenomena – again, in each world – reflect social organizational and structural processes that guide self/other in what is said and done. Likewise, the identities that become salient in both worlds include those that stem from macro-level societal processes of structural differentiation (e.g. gender, social class) as well as those more locally constrained by institutional and/or sequential contingencies of ongoing talk in interaction. Put another way, what happens in the textual world is not all that different from what happens in the social worlds of action, exchange and participation framework.

Although communication is a multi-modal process, drawing from a rich array of material and symbolic resources, it is only language that allows us to simultaneously construct a text, move fluidly among different types and levels of contexts, and make use of a text in more than one context at the same time. What language thus allows us to do is represent what I and 'others' have already said and done (or will say and do) in a textual world that can be reflected or acted upon, denied or supported, desired or dreaded, in the social worlds in which we are currently speaking and doing. "Who" we are is constructed not only by what I and 'others' say and do in the world of social interaction, then, but also by how

I represent (as author and animator) and commit to (as principal) what I (as figure) and different 'others' say and do in the textual world. Thus, the language of our textual world allows us to see each other in our social worlds in relation to many other categories of 'others.'

Referring terms initiate the process whereby we see others in different domains. They do so because of their communicative properties: they connect language to an external world of people, places and things that is typically assumed to exist independently of each particular mention in language. The linguistic job of a referring term is thus to set up a word-to-world connection: a referring term evokes an entity from the world, an external link to a part of the world that it denotes. Once a word-to-world connection is established by speaker for hearer, and an entity has been evoked through language, it is an object of attention. But we do not stop there: we expect something *to be said about* the entity to which we are attending.

Given all the different domains in which what we say has an impact, and is interpreted by 'other' as a basis for a next contribution, it is hardly surprising that a referent can have more than one thing *said about it* at a time: it can evoke a character that takes action, has attributes, and interacts with other characters; it can become part of co-constructed sequences, actions, turns; it can contribute to adjustments of speaker/hearer relationships. Like a discourse marker, then, a referring term connects to more than one domain of discourse: the textual world of the entity being represented and configured based on the current state of information between participants; the social worlds of actions, turns, and relationships in which the reference is produced and interpreted.

In sum, we give off information about who we are in the "here" and "now" of the multiple contexts that are co-constituted by what we say and do. One way of doing this is to give and give off information about 'self' and 'others' in the "there" and "then" of the textual world. Thus who I am "here" and "now" is not only a result of interaction with a co-present 'other.' It is also a result of interactions among displaced 'others', all evoked by reference, from the "then" of different times and the "there" of different places. The role of reference in understanding language, then, is even more important than stated by Brown (1995) in my initial quote. Reference is indeed a crucial feature of an utterance as part of a text: a reference introduces and continues to display identities of those in a textual world. But who we talk about, and what we say about them, also becomes part of our social worlds. Thus a reference must be grasped to begin to understand not only the meaning of an utterance in text, but also how the contextual meanings of utterances contribute to the social worlds in which we construct our identities.

Appendix 4.1 Transcription conventions (adapted from Schiffrin 1987; Tannen 1989)

.	indicates sentence-final falling intonation
,	indicates clause-final intonation ("more to come")
!	indicates exclamatory intonation
?	indicates final rise, as in a yes-no question
...	three dots in transcripts indicate pause of 0.5 second or more
´	accent indicates primary stress
italics	indicate stress
í	accent on words already in *italics* shows emphatic stress
[	brackets show overlapping speech
]	reversed brackets show no perceptible inter-turn pause
:	colon following vowel indicates elongated vowel sound
::	extra colon indicates longer elongation
-	hyphen indicates glottal stop: sound abruptly cut off
" "	quotation marks highlight dialogue
( )	parentheses indicate "parenthetical" intonation: lower amplitude and pitch plus flattened intonation contour
hhh	indicates laughter (number of hs indicates duration by second)
=	equal sign at right of line indicates segment to be continued after another's turn; equal sign at left of line indicates continuation of prior segment after another's turn
/?/	indicates inaudible utterance
→	highlights key phenomenon

Part II

Private and public identities: constructing who we are

Editors' introduction

In the general introduction we talked about the interconnectedness of individual and social processes in the formation and presentation of identities. The chapters in Part II look closely at ways in which social processes, ideologies and institutions interact with individual histories, behaviors and needs in the discourse construction of identity in different contexts. The discursive configuration of the self can take shape at many levels and in many ways. It may result, for example, from direct use of categorization devices through which people assign themselves and others to different social groups or sets of social networks. However, often identity claims are made indirectly, for example through the careful insertion and management of stories or through recourse to shared assumptions and social knowledge about the meaning of words used to describe self or others. Also, importantly, identities projected and constructed in interactional situations are the result of reciprocal positionings by the interlocutors and of their negotiations over the pertinence of roles, actions, attitudes and behaviors in certain social situations. Finally, identities interact with ideological prescriptions about roles and relationships in specific domains of social action that assign preferred properties, needs and desires to individuals.

The pressure of ideologies and social conventions on identity production is at the center of Robin Lakoff's contribution (Chapter 5). Lakoff investigates the social domain of food preparation and consumption, as a defining aspect of people's *minor identities,* i.e. identities that do not involve central aspects of their social definition such as race or gender affiliation, but rather more peripheral characteristics such as dress code or musical preferences. Lakoff uses the example of food to show how identities are socially framed through complex interactions between material conditions, social practices and ideologies. Thus, in this case, evolutions in the material conditions of the middle classes such as its relative social wealth, and therefore its access to different kinds of foods, its reliance (or lack of it) on domestic service and the position of women in its social networks determine ideological representations about what a good wife is supposed to know and to do with respect to food. These changes also affect the shape of menus and cookbooks, the attitude towards eating and the kind of preparation and presentation techniques that are seen as acceptable at different points in time. These attitudes and practices are, in turn, taken as points of reference for the definition of certain aspects of people's identity. Lakoff explains, for example, how globalization and the increase in import and export possibilities has produced a major shift in American customs with respect to food consumption that has directly affected the configuration of socially accepted food-related identities, determining a change not only in cookbooks and menus, but also in the way waiters and patrons present each other and interact in restaurants. Thus menus and cookbooks are shown to encode expectations about the characteristics of their users, while users are pushed to adapt to social expectations about what kinds of people they should be when it comes to food consumption and appreciation. In that sense, one of the most important points in Lakoff's chapter is the illustration of how individual attitudes and displays of "food identity" always establish a dialogue with existing ideologies and power relationships.

Interactions between individual identity presentation and social pressures and expectations are also at the center of Janet Holmes' contribution (Chapter 6). Holmes analyzes a particular arena for the construction of identity: the work place, an especially interesting social setting for identity negotiation since it poses the need for a delicate balance between personal and social roles, individual and collective images. In response to these institutional requirements, individuals work at the projection of different identities that may be consistent with their jobs and responsibilities as workers and as members of a community of practice. The theoretical tradition in which Holmes places her investigation is Social Identity Theory (Giles and Coupland 1991; Hogg and Abrams 1988; Meyerhoff and Niedzielski 1994) that views individual identities as resulting from the interaction of different group and personal inventories variedly called upon and dynamically activated according to social contexts and the characteristics of specific interactions. This model coincides with other interactionist perspectives represented in this book in recognizing the shaping force of contexts on the deployment of identities and in denying any stable relationship between the persona and the characteristics and qualities that are presented as constitutive of it in specific circumstances. Thus, individuals are seen as actively engaged in the work of producing identities that fit into the frames provided by shifting contexts.

Holmes analyzes the display of personal and group social identities through talk and work in a variety of New Zealand workplaces. The genre studied are personal anecdotes, narratives that are used in the workplace both to construct and instantiate a variety of personal and professional identities, and to strengthen a collective sense of self through "relational practice" (Fletcher 1999), i.e. interactional work aimed at constructing and fostering rapport among individuals who belong to the same community. As shown in the chapter, narrators deploy a variety of discursive strategies that allow them to present identities pertaining to different spheres of action: from the domains of professional performance to those pertaining to personal experience. The author demonstrates how both interactional storytelling strategies (such as monologic or cooperative modes, audience participation and involvement) and strategies of self-presentation in the story-world (such as the use of pragmatic markers, intonation contours, plot organization, evaluation and elaboration of events) concur in the dynamic enactment of types of identities. But one of the most important contributions of the chapter is the exemplification of the interaction between individual and group identities in relational practice. Anecdotes tell stories about how individuals want to be seen by their colleagues, create occasions for social sanction or negotiation of these representations, but also provide an arena for the creation of solidarity and therefore for the shaping of collective images about the team as a whole. Thus collective and individual identities continuously emerge in interaction, not as isolated constructs but in constant interdependence.

Bastos and Oliveira (Chapter 7) focus, again, on the presentation of social identities within institutional contexts. However, here the

authors look at a written genre: letters sent to an insurance provider
by customers, and the responses issued by the company. In this kind
of context, the processes by which the participants construct their
identity become crucial to mutual understanding and to the validation of the service provided. Goffman's (1967a) notion of face as an
image of the self that individuals continuously manage in interaction is particularly relevant here since individuals use impression
management to achieve their personal goals in their interaction
with the institution. The strategies employed for the construction
and communication of certain kinds of personae are related in the
letters written by the costumers to their ideologies about health and
fair treatment. The authors closely analyze how clients strategically
build narratives about their encounters and experiences with health
services that emphasize what kind of people they are and what
kinds of antagonists they encounter. Like in Holmes' chapter, the
analysis looks at event organization, the descriptions used to characterize protagonists and antagonists, the presence and type of
story evaluation, the use of emotional language.

The identities that emerge in the letters reflect a vision of fair
treatment as involving, for example, consideration of the writers'
social situation, such as their role as parents, or as patients. As
Bastos and Oliveira show, the letters issued by the clerks in the
health provider company reject the pertinence of personal and
social identities for the evaluation of service. They reflect a vision
of health relationships as guided by contracts and laws, and therefore a definition of fair treatment as action in accordance to
established norms. In the responses by the health provider, writers
do not project any specific identity, but rather present themselves as
principals (Goffman 1981) on behalf of the company. Bastos and
Oliveira demonstrate not only the close ties that bind identity
construction to the goals and objectives of specific interactions
and contexts, but also how mismatches in identity perception
and construction between individuals and institutions reveal alle-
giance to totally different ideologies about duties and rights that
lead not only to communication failures but also, ultimately, to
social injustice.

Johnson (Chapter 8) also deals with institutional identities, those
taken up by teachers, but focuses on how these are constructed
moment by moment in interactional exchanges. The data analyzed

refer to a research interview conducted with a teacher who is asked to reflect upon and explain her pedagogical practices. The theoretical coordinates taken as a point of reference in the chapter are Ethnomethodology and Conversation Analysis. In accordance with these perspectives, interactional contexts are seen as arenas for people's ongoing display and negotiation of multiple identities and the researcher's task is to explicate those displays rather than impose pre-given categories on the data in a "top-down" fashion (Miller 1997: 258) that presupposes that identity is a fixed entity waiting to be uncovered.

Thus, Johnson points to the emergence in interaction of different teacher identities that develop in accordance with the negotiations that the interviewer and the interviewee engage in. The role of the interviewer is important in setting certain parameters for the discursive development of the teacher's identity and the teacher is seen reacting to the interviewer "positioning" of her and gradually developing a more autonomous voice and a more "agentive" self. The analysis of how identities are projected and managed is based on a turn by turn examination of how use of conversational resources at a micro level such as reformulations, the issuing of agreement tokens, discourse markers, and silence allow speakers to set, orient to, or challenge definitions of teacher practices and identities. Identities are therefore shown as emerging as a result of collaborative talk. However, Johnson, like the other authors in this section, also points to the presence and manifestation of social and institutional constraints both at the level of the inventories of identities available to the teacher and the interviewer, and at the level of the existence of shared understandings about what belonging to these social categories means. Particularly interesting in this respect is the use of culturally loaded metaphors to describe activities or procedures. Thus although subjectivity develops within talk-in-interaction, it is, as the author stresses, inserted into the wider ideological frames within which individuals work.

The complex relationship between identities and ideologies is also discussed, from a different perspective, in Susan Bell's contribution (Chapter 9). The author studies the narrative discourse about mothering of a "DES" (diethylstilbestrol) daughter, Hannah Fisher, who had been exposed pre-natally to this synthetic estrogen later banned because of its destructive effects on pregnancies. Bell revisits an interview that she did with Hannah in the early eighties as part of a study of the social and emotional consequences of living with the negative effects of exposure to DES. The theoretical perspective on identity within which Bell inscribes her work is that of Narrative Psychology (see Bruner 2001; Gergen and Gergen 1997; Mishler 1999). The proponents of this approach, who generally focus on autobiographical discourse, see narrative as central to the expression of identity, since they conceive of the self as a discursive construction in continuous evolution not only within specific interactional encounters, but also across time, given that individuals review and reconstruct their selves looking back from the perspective of the present (see Mishler, this volume). Narrative psychologists have also emphasized the constitutive role of the discursive exchange between participants within the interview in the construction of specific identities (see Mishler 1986) and this is an important issue in Bell's chapter as well. In fact, the author looks in parallel form at the identities built and deployed in discourse by Hannah Fisher, at her role as interviewer in the co-construction and interpretation of those identities at the time of the interview, and at her reading of the interactional event twenty years later. Thus she is able to point to the complex interactions between Hannah Fisher's positioning on her experiences as mother in the interview and the systems of ideas about motherhood dominating the eighties: on the one hand the ideology of "intensive mothering" as the only fulfilling role for women, and on the other hand the rejection of traditional feminine roles. Through analysis, for example, of the metaphors and terms used by Hannah to describe her body, Bell shows how this woman draws on the scientific and ideological discourses about women and mothering prevalent at the time to present herself both as a victim of devastating experiences with the medical world, and as a survivor, someone who is capable of facing any difficulty in order to be a good mother.

An interesting aspect of Bell's chapter is the incorporation of her own positioning as an interviewer and as a woman into the analysis. The author demonstrates how her own perspective on motherhood guided her questions and reactions to what Hannah Fisher was telling her and how, because of her own ideological stance at the time of the interview, she ignored or did not pursue certain clues that her interviewee was giving her about the centrality of motherhood in her inventory of identities. At the end of the chapter Bell advocates for an approach to identity that both "seeks to recognize the multiplicity of social experiences and perspectives [and] tries to make statements about regularities in the social world." Interestingly, this conclusion seems to provide a general description of the main analytical focus adopted in the five chapters presented in Part II.

Identity à la carte: you are what you eat

Robin Tolmach Lakoff

5.1 Food in history and culture

Once upon a time, not all that long ago, human identity was generally viewed rather simply. It was assumed that identity achieved its final form in the course of childhood and adolescence, culminating in the famous Eriksonian "identity crisis," the successful resolution of which ushered in a competent adulthood.[1] While experts disputed just when and how the larger aspects of individual identity congealed – gender identity for instance – and argued as well about the relationship between individual and group identity, identity was not seen as something adults actively worked on or typically experienced conflict over.

In recent years, prodded by feminist and queer theorists,[2] students of identity have radically changed their views. Increasingly they see human identity as a continual work in progress, constructed and altered by the totality of life experience. While much of the work in support of this belief concentrates on the larger aspects of identity – especially gender, ethnicity, and sexual preference – in fact human identity involves many other categories. Identity is constructed in complex ways, more or less consciously and overtly. Some aspects of identity, in particular those listed above, are applicable both to individual identity and a person's identification as a member of a cohesive and coherent group.

---

[1] As discussed in Erikson (1950), especially chapter six.
[2] Cf. for instance Bucholtz, Liang, and Sutton (1999); Butler (1990); Anzaldúa (1987); and Barrett (1999).

Other aspects of individual identity are more subtle, perhaps less prone to being problematized, and not linked to group membership in any obvious way. While these have been given less attention than the others – perhaps with reason, since they are less apt to create either pride or distress – nonetheless they form a significant part of who we are and how we think of ourselves, and our selves. We might think of the first, more obvious, aspects of identity formation – e.g. race, gender, and sexual preference – as composing a person's *major identity*, and these latter as aspects of a *minor identity*. Examples of such cases might be musical preferences, style of dress, and – the area I will discuss here – taste in the consumption and preparation of food.

The psychoanalysts, who were the first social scientists to consider identity closely, famously declared that sexuality was the most significant aspect of human identity and human intrapsychic and interpersonal behaviors. But here, too, a century after Freud's original statements, we are learning that human beings are not as reductive as early theorists had claimed. We have other salient needs that are only sometimes capable of direct and uncomplicated expression, and which, like sexuality, must sometimes be sublimated or otherwise distorted if we wish to conform to group norms. One such category is that of food and how we feel about it. What we can and cannot eat, what kinds of edibles carry prestige, how much we are expected to know about what we eat – all of these are aspects of individual and group identity that may remain stable in a society for long periods of time, or may go through abrupt shifts. In this arena, as in others, socially competent individuals learn to bring their self-presentation into conformity with the ethos of the group in which they live. Those who wish to maintain their standing as competent persons learn to change their behavior with the times, in eating as in sexual or conversational style. Thus the attitudes and behaviors of individuals both mirror those of the larger society, and create them in microcosm.

The ways in which identity is formed have also lent themselves to more sophisticated analytic practice in recent years. Within the last quarter century or so, the roles that language plays in human interaction and individual self-awareness have become more apparent to social scientists, and have become more amenable to scholarly scrutiny as techniques for studying abstract linguistic behavior have been developed – methods as diverse as discourse and conversation analysis, speech act theory and conversational logic. Earlier studies of identity tended to focus on the evidence available from psychopathology or analytic case histories. But increasingly research focuses on the forms of linguistic expression, oral and literate, formal and informal, spontaneous and planned, as evidence of the capacity shared by human beings for differentiating themselves from others and connecting themselves with others – the businesses of making, recognizing, and maintaining identity. Discourse of all types is a potent creator and enforcer of identity, and it is the sum of our daily linguistic interactions that, to a very large degree, creates us and recreates us continually.

My focus here is on the formation of individual identity: how each of us decides who he or she is, what her or his values and preferences are, on the basis of interactions with one another. But even when we concentrate on our individual selves, we are, knowingly or not, working toward the creation and re-creation of our group ethos. And the values, attitudes, and behaviors identified by the groups in which we acknowledge or desire membership will in turn influence our individual choices and our evaluations of those choices. Thus, in the areas I am discussing, as in others, the constructions of individual and group identities are closely linked and bidirectional.

This paper examines some of the ways in which individuals in one American subculture (at least some of the white, middle-class residents of Berkeley, California) form their food-related identity, and how food attitudes are part of the creation of a sense of social cohesion within that subculture. I will use mostly written documents: restaurant menus, cookbook recipes, newspapers and magazine commentary.

5.2 Changes in gastrolinguistics

America once was a country in which, it could reasonably be said, food was not a significant locus of personal (or group) identity. As late as the 1960s, undue concern with food, discrimination in one's eating habits, and interest in its preparation were apt to mark an American, and especially an American male, as either un-masculine or un-American, probably both. While women's magazines contained recipes, and cookbooks were big sellers, both tended toward preparations that were fast, simple, and gastronomically unadventurous. Ingredients were simple, and the corner grocery or the neighborhood supermarket was unlikely to offer exotic products or boutique vegetables. Restaurants tended to provide the same kinds of foods we were accustomed to eating at home, except for ethnic restaurants where one could get chop suey, spaghetti and meatballs, and not too much more.

But by the early 1960s things were already beginning to change. Craig Claiborne's *New York Times Cookbook*, containing a wide variety of challenging and adventurous recipes, was first published in 1961. The nascent Public Broadcasting System's Boston affiliate, WGBH, started to air Julia Child as *The French Chef* a few years later; in 1966, with her collaborators Simone Beck and Louise Bertholle, Child published the first volume of *Mastering the Art of French Cooking*. By the mid 1960s, it was possible to find dim sum and Szechuan restaurants in the Boston area; by the early 1970s one could count ten varieties of lettuce in at least one supermarket in Berkeley, California. These communities were atypical, of course, but could be seen as bellwethers of an American culinary reidentification. By the early 1980s, nouvelle cuisine was more or less available even as far from the bellwethers as Bloomington, Indiana.

In 1971 Alice Waters opened a small Provençal restaurant, Chez Panisse, on an otherwise unremarkable stretch of Shattuck Avenue in Berkeley. The rest, as they say, is history. By the early 1990s, the unmarked American attitude to food had undergone what is currently called a sea change (or a quantum leap). At my Berkeley supermarket this week I could get:

> white truffles
> poussins
> ostrich
> white asparagus
> broccoli rabe
> fresh tarragon
> soy milk
> Spanish cheeses
> French lemonade

super-premium dulce de leche ice cream
Valrhona bittersweet chocolate
pad-Thai mix
pappadums
Australian wines
at least ten different kinds of artisanal baguette
at least six kinds of balsamic vinegar

a list off the top of my head, not at all exhaustive; but none would have been available in the supermarket whose place the current one took, as late as the mid-1970s. So it is reasonable to conclude that something significant in the culture's regard for food has shifted.

To the degree that academic recognition of a field confers official status on it as *interesting*, the recent publication of several scholarly collections on food and its place in Western culture signifies this shift (Beardsworth and Keil 1997; Griffiths and Wallace 1998; Inness 2001), as does the creation of a new journal, *Gastronomica*, published by the University of California Press. At a more popular level, one can point to the creation of the Food Channel on cable television, as well as the near-saturation of cooking shows on Saturdays on PBS.

Nor would it be the first occasion of such a shift. Just as language change is a mark of cultural flux, so is gastronomic change. Tobias (1998) documents the role of cookbooks in colonial America. He notes that between the end of the colonial period and the mid-nineteenth century, the role of food and cooking underwent a marked shift, from something to which very little attention was paid (as measured by the sparsity of cookbooks during the period), to a matter of significance as manifested by the publication of many cookbooks and the development of detailed recipes and, by the end of the nineteenth century, precise measurements, oven temperatures, and cooking times. This shift not only signaled a change in the role of food in the culture, but also marked an increase in the prestige of private life relative to public, with hearth and home (and with them, mealtime) playing an increasingly important role in both men's and women's lives; and in the job of the middle-class woman, who increasingly was having to depend on fewer servants, but acquiring modern conveniences that removed some of the drudgery from kitchen tasks, allowing aesthetic considerations to play more of a role in the cooking process. Being a "good cook," possessing arcane knowledge (secret recipes, special techniques), began to be a mark of the superior housekeeper and a point of pride – an important aspect of a woman's identity.

Restaurants, too, have undergone successive metamorphoses. Hardly extant in America at all until the mid-nineteenth century, they have reperceived their roles more than once in the intervening century and a half. What constitutes an appropriate and appealing "menu" and how the waiter and the customer should interact – crucial aspects of the dining experience – have changed greatly more than once over this time. A series of articles appearing in the *New York Times* in 1998 and 1999 (Grimes 1998, 1999; Hesser 1998) discusses some of these trends; the very fact that the paper of record has seen fit to devote very long articles (two of the three, with related articles and sidebars, occupy two pages each in the "Living Arts" section and the last is almost a page in length) itself signifies the importance of food as a cultural artifact at the dawn of the third millennium. Grimes (1998) discusses changes in menu style and content, as well as in the way in which a reader (or patron) is supposed to respond to the menu under inspection.

Ordering from a menu used to be routine. No more. It is becoming a journey into the unknown, a junior division of the adventure-travel industry, as chefs working with new cuisines and new ideas reconfigure their menus, creating new categories, offering new combinations of dishes and befuddling the unwary.

Originally (the article reproduces a menu from one of New York's first restaurants, Delmonico's, from 1834, to prove its point) menus were spare: offerings were familiar; the reader did not need to know more than simply what was available and how much it cost:

Cup tea or coffee	1	(cent)
Soup	2	
Beef Steak	4	

on up to

Roast Chicken, at an imperial 10 cents.

It is true that some of the things assumed to be too familiar to require commentary in 1834 seem distinctly strange to us today, and are unlikely to appear in any form on even the toniest or most venturesome modern menu: Fried or Stewed Heart (3 cents) and Pigs Head (4 cents); but most of what appears are old standbys.

By 1887 Delmonico's menus had been upgraded and Frenchified, as illustrated in the same article. Foods are now assigned to designated courses: Potages, Hors d'oeuvre, Poisson, Relevé, Entrée, Rôti, Froid, and Entremets Sucrés.[3] There is, nonetheless, only one choice in most categories. Prices are not indicated. But while the level of consumer has apparently risen greatly (you are expected to know some French, and the appropriate order of a meal), not much needs to be said about the items on the list: they are familiar to the new type of patron (or at least, he or she had better pretend to familiarity): Palmettes à la varsovienne; filet de boeuf à la Bernardi; Bécasses au Cresson. Neither the 1834 nor the 1887 versions looks very familiar to us, however. While the idea of the "restaurant" and the "menu" has, in some sense, remained constant over two centuries, our roles in and expectations of both are clearly very different from those of our ancestors.

Amanda Hesser's article, appearing the week after Grimes', offers further commentary on the new art of the menu. It concentrates less on its formal structure and more on style. The article comments specifically on the decline of the simple "salad" in restaurants, replaced by "witty new renditions," salads "made with humor and irony." So the food itself, or at least its verbal representation on the menu, has become a literary form. It has certainly not been commonplace to be able to think of food – salads, perhaps, least of all – as demonstrating wit, humor, or irony. But if we accept this idea, then the food itself becomes discourse. How can a salad be "witty" or "ironic," you ask? Well, what if it consists of a chunk of iceberg lettuce – but instead of the thousand island dressing of yore, it is lapped in "buttermilk-blue cheese dressing" and accompanied by "bacon and scallions." It's not quite retro, but a commentary on retro. You have to be gastronomically sophisticated, aware of the last fifty years of the American salad, to get the

---

[3] While a century ago (and probably until the 1960s) French was the only foreign language an American restaurantgoer needed to display sophistication, today's foodie requires a knowledge of the kitchen vocabularies of at least five or six languages: French, Italian, Spanish, Chinese, Japanese, and perhaps Hindi or Thai.

joke. So we no longer go to restaurants just to eat – we go to *interact* with, to engage in *discourse* with, our food. We are expected to play with our food, or at least respond to it playfully.

Grimes' second article, appearing almost exactly a year after the first, takes on another aspect of the restaurant experience. Even in the highest temples of gastronomy, the formality and hushed reverence expected of old has largely given way to informality. A frequent diner at such establishments ventures, "In the past, you felt that dining in a top restaurant was a rare privilege, and you'd better behave. Now, there's a warmth and an interaction that wasn't there before." Grimes continues, "In a city where intimidation is nine points of the law and one-upmanship is the coin of the realm, pleasing the customer counts as a revolutionary idea." The balance of power, in other words, has shifted from the establishment (personified by the waiters) to the patron: the former must accommodate the latter, not the other way around.

One index of the importance of an artifact in any culture is the proliferation of new words around it. That has certainly been the case with food in America over the last quarter century. There are, as suggested in the list given above, innumerable new words for new foods, or new forms or appreciations of old ones, words that were certainly not in the common American English vocabulary at the start of this period, but which are now in general use among everyone with pretensions to gastronomic culture:

> pain de mie
> Muscovy duck
> chanterelle
> heirloom tomato
> cold-press extra virgin olive oil
> mesclun

There are words for methods of getting, keeping, or making food:

> forager
> Wolf range
> Sub-zero refrigerator
> sweating (e.g. onions)
> mounting (or monter) [a sauce]
> garde-manger

>   fond
>   caramelization

Most of these terms existed previously in the vocabularies of professional food workers, but it is only recently that they have made their way into the active vocabularies of consumers (as demonstrated, for instance, by their use without definitions on television cooking shows).

And words have been developed for those who produce or consume the final product:

>   foodie
>   Chez Panisse Mafia
>   food Nazi
>   Gourmet Gulch (or Ghetto)

So all the signs suggest that food occupies a pivotal spot in the consciousness of Americans; and that being willing and able to talk at length and correctly about it, as well as knowing how to order, eat, and often cook it, are both relatively new modes of personal interaction and shibboleths of group membership in that culture.

As with other forms of discourse and more generally social interaction, forms of behavior are normally ambiguous: they can, in different contexts, signify any of several different things. So knowledge of a type of food, or a technique, can mark not only ethnic or professional identity, but increasingly, also be used as a marker of education and sophistication, or as a means of creating secret-handshake identification with an interlocutor (like slang or professional code). In a more and more overarching way, we are what we eat – our identity is predicated on what we know about food. A menu can be merely a list of what is available at a given establishment, or can be the opening gambit in a game between restaurateur and patron: who are you, here's who I am, here's what I want from you, here's how we'll behave toward each other.

5.3 Reading the menu

A restaurant menu communicates a number of things to its reader. Some of these are present or inferable on all menus; the presence of others depends on the nature of the menu and the restaurant.

It is always necessary to indicate that what is being perused *is* in fact a restaurant menu: food is available for a set, non-negotiable price. While the creators of the menu, the restaurateurs, can safely assume that the nature of the establishment is obvious to visitors, and that what one goes to a restaurant for and how one behaves there is likewise presupposed, nonetheless a piece of paper entitled "menu" or something similar makes the point inescapable. Further, the handing-over of the menu to the patron is one of the most significant explicit steps in the restaurant game, along with: making a reservation; greeting by the maitre d'; ordering; eating; paying. But since the first two of these are not part of every restaurant experience, and are in a sense preparatory to the chef d'oeuvre, the true business at hand, it is the handing-over of the menu that truly initiates the experience of "eating out at a restaurant." It is, moreover, the first clear opportunity for the restaurant to identify itself to the patron and give an indication about what kind of establishment it is, and, therefore, what kind of patrons they anticipate serving, in terms of their prior knowledge and interactive behavior. In accepting the menu, the patron implicitly agrees to the terms of the restaurant, and is assumed to know what is expected and be willing to comply.

The menus I have collected range between two poles. On one side there are relatively few choices, but much information is given about those choices. On the other there can be many choices, but much less information. Consider as Exhibit A a menu from Chez Panisse in Berkeley, California. Chez Panisse is a kind of temple of gastronomy: it is a shrine to which pilgrims come to worship – pilgrims who are both affluent (the prix fixe weekend menu is $75.00, plus wine, tax, and 18% service charge) and knowledgeable.

Example 5.1

> FRIDAY, APRIL 13 [2001] $75
> An aperitif
> Asparagus with scrambled eggs and *migas*
> Spicy Catalan fish soup
> Grilled Paine Farm squab with green olives, leeks, and wild mushrooms
> Blood orange–walnut crêpes à la Panisse

If you don't understand the CP mystique, the above menu is both curiously vague and oddly specific. A CP menu offers no choice:

you eat what is put in front of you, and your acceptance of the menu signifies your acceptance of those terms. But how can the prospective patron give informed consent to the first item, listed as it is only as "an aperitif"? One must be in awe of the environs and therefore fully trusting, and openminded (and open-palated) enough to accept whatever turns up.

The next item seems straightforward enough except for the "*migas.*" My Spanish dictionary (and presumably the patron is expected to know (a) Spanish and (b) that the word is Spanish, when (c) Spanish is not one of the languages ordinarily expected of the gourmet)[4] defines *miga* as "crumb." Then why not simply call a crumb a crumb? Perhaps *miga* provides a segue into the next item. Or maybe a "*miga*" isn't *exactly* a crumb, or exclusively one. So a menu entry that at first glance seems to be reasonably informative on second glance is revealed to be almost as mysterious as the first.

The next course is pretty straightforward (except that it doesn't mention which spices, or what fishes, compose the "spicy Catalan fish soup").

The fourth item is pure Chez Panisse. The meat is exotic, "special" in a way that nothing preceding has been: squab, not mere chicken. (Indeed, except for the wild mushrooms and the blood oranges in the dessert, this is the only unusual or exotic item on the menu.) But more, it is "Paine Farm squab." The Chez Panisse downstairs restaurant weekly menu (from which the example above is excerpted) contains a legend in italics at the bottom: "*Most of our produce and meat comes from local farms and ranches that practice ecologically sound agriculture.*" So whatever it tastes like, eating the squab is an act of civic virtue; the patron, in accepting the menu, shows him- or herself to be not only a person of taste and refinement, but of consummate ecological sensitivity. "Paine Farm" further signifies that the meat we will be eating is not mere generic squab, but rather squab specially raised to be particularly toothsome. (We don't know just how, but it must be so: by the rules of Conversational Logic (Grice 1975), the menu wouldn't

---

[4] While the last footnote suggested that a sophisticated restaurant patron should know some Spanish, that knowledge is typically confined to a few terms, e.g. *tacos, mole poblano, refritos* – the language of Mexican or Latin American restaurants. *Migas* would not normally be recognized.

be this explicit unless the explicitness foreshadowed the gustatory experience.) The reader is assumed to be aware of that specialness as a true appreciator.

Indeed, almost all of the menus listed on the sheet from which this example is taken offer similar specificity at least once. Monday, April 9: *Larsen Ranch* pork shoulder; Tuesday, April 10: Spit-roasted *Dal Porto Ranch* leg of lamb; Wednesday, April 11: *Liberty Ranch* duck. On Thursday, the convention takes a break, but on Saturday, April 14, we find a double dose: Grilled *Dal Porto Ranch* spring lamb with *Chino Ranch* fava beans, artichokes and peas.

The menu is highly specific in other ways as well. It tends to mention all the identifiable ingredients found in a dish: "with bacon, braised endives, green lentils, and turnips." Another kind of menu might merely refer to "mixed vegetables." Moreover, the specificity is often meaningful only to the *cognoscenti*, as in "green lentils" – vs. the normal browns.

The menu presumes a worldliness on its readers' part: there is much use of foreign languages, and not only words from common cuisinary languages or terms of cuisine. Monday is Italianate, with *Torta Pasqualina; Costoletta di maiale alla toscana;* and Meyer lemon *pasticcini* for dessert. Tuesday's dessert is French: *noyau* and amarena cherry souffle; Thursday's is an apple and hazelnut *tourte*; on Friday there are the *migas;* and Saturday's dessert is a cardamom *baba au rhum.* So the patron must be linguistically sophisticated and titillated rather than put off by opaque terminology.

Now consider a menu from a restaurant across the street from Chez Panisse, but a universe away: a humble Chinese takeout. At Chez Panisse, you have one choice and only one per evening. At the Oriental Restaurant, there are ninety-seven numbered dishes from which to make your selection: you may choose as many as you wish. At CP, if you don't know what aioli or tangelo is, unless you are very courageous, you'll just have to be surprised. But the Oriental Restaurant states its philosophy on its cover: "There are pictures displayed in our store to make your selection easier." They are in full color and detailed. A very different relationship is being created between restaurateur and customer, and a very different sort of customer (or, perhaps the same customer but in a different frame of mind) is presupposed. For one thing, customers are not assumed to be trusting: they need to know exactly what they will be getting.

They are more in control: they make the choices, from a very broad range. There are broad categories: Appetizers, Soups, Noodle Plates, Fried Rice Plates, Claypot, Main Entrees (subdivided into Vegtarian [sic] Plates and Traditional Plates), and Oriental Plates. Within each category are at least five or six choices, in one case over thirty. Among the many Traditional Plates we can find:

Example 5.2

1. Vegetable w/ shrimps, chicken, beef, pork *or* squids
2. Celery and pineapple w/ shrimps, chicken, beef, pork, *or* squids
3. Mushrooms w/ shrimps, chicken, beef, pork, *or* squids

and similarly for tofu, bell peppers, snow peas and black mushrooms, green peas and black mushrooms, green peas and tofu, tofu and black mushrooms . . . well, you get the idea. (All of these are $9.96 regular, $16.20 special.) So doing the math, each of 26 of the "traditional plates" should be multiplied by five, resulting in a truly gargantuan range of options.

Although customers are given *carte blanche* as far as choice is concerned, in other ways they are treated less munificently. The vegetables and meats are simply generic, with no *appellation* provided. No method of cooking is specified. So there is no indication that the patron is one to whom deference or respect is due: no presumptive arcane knowledge, no developed appreciation.

Indeed, the very design of the menus signifies the difference in role. The CP menu is elegantly calligraphed with striking print and lots of luxurious white space around it. The Oriental Restaurant menu is much more compact: smaller and darker type, packed close together. (The typo "Vegtarian" itself signifies diminished expectations, for the restaurateur himself and for his patrons: "Who cares?") But that's what you can expect for $9.96, as opposed to $75.00.

So the menu interaction creates a relationship between patron and restaurateur. Each comes to the table (as it were) with pre-existing expectations of character, interaction, and role to be played; the menu merely validates and underscores those assumptions and sets the stage for the main act, the food and the eating of it, again according to personal expectations. The Chez Panisse and Oriental Restaurant menus are no more interchangable than the restaurants they represent. It is probable that, if one were presented with a Chez Panisse-type menu at the Oriental Restaurant, it would be almost as disconcerting as the reverse would be. Both would create identity confusion.

Many of us, of course, patronize both kinds of places, and many in between. In that sense our gastronomic identities remain plastic and malleable. But that does not mean that we are comfortable with whatever transpires at a restaurant. If the menu we are handed doesn't meet our prior expectations, the entire meal may suffer: we have not been treated as the people we believe we are.

In intermediate cases, a patron must be flexible, indeed, to be several kinds of people at once. There exist cluttered menus with exotic names and more or less elaborate descriptions. There are Asian restaurants that have adapted to the terrain and provide elaborate and descriptive menus, using some of the same kinds of ingredients one might expect to find at Chez Panisse (but with the many choices characteristic of the Chinese menu). Thus with Kirin, an upscale Chinese restaurant in Berkeley. As with the Oriental Restaurant, offerings on the menu are organized into categories: Appetizers, Cold Appetizers, Soup; Mu Shu, Beef and Lamb, Pork; Vegetables and Tofu, Fowl; Seafood; Rice, Chow Mein and Chow Fun. But for the items in these categories, rather than presenting a stark description according to main contents, Kirin's menu offers descriptions that include a summary of ingredients, methods, and flavors. Interestingly, unlike the simpler place (which is likely to cater to many Chinese students), Kirin's menu gives Chinese characters alongside the English names of the dishes.

Example 5.3

Hot and Sour Soup [characters]
A Northern Chinese mixture of shredded chicken, shrimp, tofu, peas, willow tree fungus in a peppery and tangy chicken broth finished with whipped eggs.

Unlike Chez Panisse, and like the Oriental Restaurant, Kirin offers many choices (so, e.g., soups can be ordered in three sizes). Courses are à la carte. But the menu's descriptions are reminiscent of those of gourmet western-cuisine restaurants. One way to read such a menu is to see it as intended for a bilingual and bicultural consumer – one conversant in the communicative presuppositions of both ordinary Asian restaurants and Chez Panisse. Kirin's price range, too, is intermediate. While the Oriental Restaurant's prices are very low (small hot and sour soup is $2.30, large $3.60), Kirin's are higher (but nowhere near the celestial cost of Chez Panisse: the small hot and sour soup is $5.95, medium $7.25, and large $12.00). Berkeley restaurant patrons can assume several different identities, depending on what they want to eat and how they want to eat it.

But relationships and expectations shift like fashions in dress. In another recent article on mediated restaurant–patron relationships William Grimes (2002) writes about a shift taking place at some upscale New York restaurants: instead of loading the menu with informative content, the latter has been assigned to the mouth of the waiter.

This sort of encounter [over-informativeness on the part of a waiter] is becoming more common, and I should have seen it coming. A few years ago, restaurant menus reached the limit in text-heaviness. Every dish was explicated and annotated, with commentary sometimes running to a full paragraph. Gradually, the pendulum swung the other way, and chefs began identifying their wares by a simple word or two. In extreme cases, the menu might simply name the principal ingredient and the cooking method. Further details would be offered tersely, in very small type underneath. "Roast cod" on a menu of this sort carried the implied message, "Need we say more?"

While this shift has not yet reached Berkeley, one can understand it. Extreme informativeness on a menu was originally devised to convey a message that may be glossed:

We know that you are a connoisseur and a person who knows his/her way around a kitchen. You therefore need to know precisely what is involved in the production of a dish, even as a literary critic needs to know the sources and references in a poem. Both activities are a kind of scholarly enterprise. By our specificity, we recognize you as a scholar of cuisine, one who cares as much as we do, knows as much as we do – viz. *one of us.*

The message was intended as one of inclusion, a kind of inclusive *we.*

But this sort of explicit inclusiveness is problematic in the negotiation of relationships. As Grice (1975) has noted, if you choose to make a statement, your hearer necessarily assumes that there was a *need* to make it – things could be otherwise. And by saying, in effect, "You and I – we're the same," the restaurant's menu might be read (by the insecure gastronome) as more deeply implicating, "Maybe so, but it's not all that obvious. We have to spell it all out for you, as we would not for ourselves." So the pendulum swings to facilitate the patron's sense of belonging: by saying as little as possible, the restaurant conveys intimacy. Respect is never having to say, "Niman-Schell Ranch." At the same time, though, the restaurant needs to have a means of slipping the full information to the patron, a task that has now been entrusted to the waiter.

5.4 The recipe for happiness

The reciprocal of the menu, in a sense, is the recipe. The reader becomes the means of production rather than consumption, but the end product is similar. As with menu construction, recipe-writing is an art-form that has changed over time, and as with menus, the changes are related to the writer's assumptions about the relationship shared with the reader.

Before the beginning of the twentieth century recipes tended to be enigmatic, at least by modern standards. Quantities, times, and methodological details were normally lacking, wholly or in part. Fisher (1968:16) quotes in full a seventeenth-century recipe for Herring Pye:

Put great store of sliced onions, with Currants and Raisins of the sun both above and under the Herrings, and store of butter, and so bake.

To us this seems incomprehensible, instructions that leave us hardly better off than before we read them. But old cookbook writers could afford to be enigmatic; or rather, for their presumptive audiences, they were not enigmatic, but adhering perfectly to the Gricean Maxims as demanded of instructional texts. Their intended readers were professional cooks, who had been taught to cook as children by their mothers, and who needed only the most general guidance, since they did their cooking intuitively.

By the mid-nineteenth century, however, servants were disappearing from the middle-class American household. Those servants who remained tended to be young immigrant women, who, even if they had been taught to cook by their mothers, certainly could not provide the kind of food demanded by American families of that era. Young wives were not generally educated as specialized cooks, and the kitchen was a place of mystery to them. In order to be able to cook, they had to be told precisely how to produce even the most familiar dishes. They required specifications of ingredients, times, and methods. The first cookbook to do this in a modern way is generally considered to be Fannie Merritt Farmer's (1896) *Boston Cooking-School Cook Book*. Farmer standardized traditional terms like "cup" and "teaspoon," and offered detailed recipes not unlike those familiar to cooks of a century later. We can understand the revolution, for such it was, as a response by writers of cookbooks to a changing readership: people whose primary identity was not as professional "cooks" and who therefore could not be presumed to be coming into the kitchen with a lot of prior knowledge. Rather than a partnership of peers sharing a profession and the arcane knowledge that is a part of it – writer and reader of the twentieth-century cookbook had a nonegalitarian and nonintimate relationship. The writer typically was a professional; the reader, an amateur. For the writer, cooking was life; for the reader, it was either one of many useful skills, or an adjunct to her otherwise busy life. (And the reader, though not the writer, was normally assumed to be female: the home kitchen until very recently was a woman's preserve.) Quite often, cooking was seen as something the busy housewife had to do, without much desire or pleasure, as efficiently and swiftly as possible (Hence the popularity of Peg Bracken's early 1960s *I Hate to Cook Book*). Recipes tended to be cobbled together of precooked canned or frozen ingredients: canned tuna and Campbell's Cream of Mushroom Soup topped with crumbled potato chips; thawed frozen green beans with canned French-fried onions; the ubiquitous green Jell-O mold with canned fruit salad.

Beginning in the 1960s, the relationship between cookbooks and cooks, and cooks and their kitchens, underwent a dramatic change. Although, as I noted above, Julia Child is often credited with the birth of American gastronomy, others made significant contributions. Craig Claiborne's *New York Times Cookbook* was published in 1961. But the publication date is a bit deceptive, as the book represents a compilation of many years of recipes published in the newspaper, so the renaissance (or rather, naissance) really started in the 1950s – the era immortalized by Betty Friedan in *The Feminine Mystique*, in which college-educated women had to find ways to deal with confinement to the home, without going crazy. One way was to apply the perseverance, intelligence, and analytic skills developed through higher education to the role of homemaker – a word that had just come into vogue. And the most attractive aspect of homemaking from that perspective was cooking, which has attributes of both art and science. Food preparation, which a half century ago had changed from professional to amateur status, was now shifting to pro-am. Betty Fussell's *My Kitchen Wars* (1999) eloquently and hilariously documents the competition among academic wives at Princeton in those times to cook the hardest, most exotic, most expensive dishes. But contestants in these games needed exact directions and specifications – especially since, often, they had never actually seen the dishes they were executing prepared, or even tasted them.

Even for those who were not playing Fussell's game, interest in food and its preparation grew exponentially during the 1960s and succeeding decades. People were beginning to travel, and even live, in foreign countries and became familiar with their cuisines and wished to reproduce them; foreign restaurants sprang up in many cities, and those who frequented them became curious about how the food was made, even venturing to attempt it themselves; they began to wander into Chinatown and other exotic parts of town, examining wood ears and tiger lily buds, la yu and hoisin sauce.

So the American relationship to food and its preparation had shifted greatly since the 1950s. We began to look to cookbooks not only to enable us to create new kinds of foods, but also to ratify the new, post-1960s *us*. "You are what you eat" was a popular, if confusing, slogan of the counterculture. Some of us took it literally.

The best recipe for someone wanting to use cuisine as the springboard to a classier identity was the diametric opposite of one aimed at a professional cook who wanted to produce only familiar dishes others like her had been cooking for centuries – the assumption behind the seventeenth-century cookbook. Now the reader was an amateur for whom cooking was a hobby, but a deadly serious one. It had become important to produce – for family or friends – food of "restaurant quality," using unusual ingredients and complex techniques; but the cook had to be led carefully through the process, often starting from the composition of the shopping list. The author was skating on thin, and ambiguous, ice: the reader had to be addressed as a sophisticated novice. Cutting corners, as recommended in American cookbooks of the 1950s, was passé.

Substitution of common American products for exotic ones – say, canned beef gravy for demiglace – was unthinkable. Yet the reader's time and patience were limited, and experience frequently minimal. Cookbooks of the 1960s through the 1980s found various ways to make the necessary adjustments.

To get an idea of the range of options, let us examine similar recipes from three cookbooks of very different persuasions. The differences will suggest the ways in which each writer constructs her reader, and the triangular relationship (reader, food, writer) that the latter is creating through the form of the recipe she chooses. I will look at the following three cookbooks, each representative of a type:

> Irma S. Rombauer and Marion Rombauer Becker (1964) *The Joy of Cooking.*
> Simone Beck, Louisette Bertholle, and Julia Child (1966) *Mastering the Art of French Cooking*, volume 1.
> Alice Waters (1996) *Chez Panisse Vegetables.*

The recipe under comparison is one for potato gratin: sliced potatoes, baked with a liquid and often onions, cheese, and/or butter (and other optional ingredients).

Example 5.4

Joy of Cooking 1964: 291–292.

SCALLOPED POTATOES
4 Servings
Preheat oven to 350°.
Grease a 10-inch baking dish. Place in it, in 3 layers:

> 3 cups pared, very thinly sliced potatoes

Dredge the layers with flour and dot them with butter. Use in all:

> 2 tablespoons flour
> 3 to 6 tablespoons butter

There are many tidbits you can put between the layers. Try:

> (1/4 cup finely chopped chives or onions)
> (12 anchovies or crisp bacon – but then reduce the salt in the recipe)
> (1/4 cup finely sliced sweet peppers)

Heat:

> 1 1/4 cups milk or cream

Season with:

> 1/4 teaspoon salt
> 1/4 teaspoon paprika
> (1/4 teaspoon mustard)

Pour the milk over the potatoes. Bake them for about 1 1/2 hours. They may be covered for the first 1/2 hour.

Example 5.5
Mastering the Art of French Cooking 1966: 523–524.

GRATIN DAUPHINOIS
[Scalloped Potatoes with Milk, Cheese, and a Pinch of Garlic]
There are as many "authentic" versions of *gratin dauphinois* as there are of *bouillabaisse*. Of them all, we prefer this one because it is fast, simple, and savory. It goes with roast or broiled chicken, turkey, and veal. With roast beef, pork, lamb, steaks, and chops you may prefer the *gratin savoyard* which follows, since it is cooked with stock rather than milk. Although some authorities on *le vrai gratin dauphinois* would violently disagree, you may omit the cheese. If you do so, add 2 more tablespoons of butter.

For 6 people

Preheat oven to 425 degrees.

> 2 lbs. "boiling" potatoes (6 to 7 cups when sliced)
> A fireproof baking-serving dish about 10 inches in diameter and 2 inches deep (if recipe is increased, dish must be wider but no deeper) 1/2 clove peeled garlic
> 4 Tb. butter/1 tsp. salt/1/8 tsp. pepper/1 cup (4 ounces) grated Swiss cheese/1 cup boiling milk
> Peel the potatoes and slice them 1/8 inch thick. Place in a basin of cold water. Drain when ready to use. _____ _____ _____ _____
> Rub the baking dish with the cut garlic. Smear the inside of the dish with 1 tablespoon of the butter. Drain the potatoes and dry them in a towel. Spread half of them in the bottom of the dish. Divide over them half the salt, pepper, cheese, and butter. Arrange the remaining potatoes over the first layer, and season them. Spread on the rest of the cheese and divide the butter over it. Pour on the boiling milk. Set baking dish over heat and when simmering, set in upper third of preheated oven. Bake for 20 to 30 minutes or until potatoes are tender, milk has been absorbed, and the top is nicely

browned. (As the oven is hot, and the dish shallow, the potatoes cook quickly.)

May wait for half an hour, loosely covered, over simmering water. For a longer wait, stop initial cooking just before all milk has evaporated. Set aside uncovered. Shortly before serving, dot with 2 Tb butter, reheat on top of stove, and set in a 425-degree oven for 5 to 10 minutes to finish cooking.

Example 5.6

Chez Panisse Vegetables (1966: 248).

POTATO GRATIN

Rub an earthenware gratin dish with smashed peeled garlic and butter. Layer overlapping slices of potato cut 1/8 inch thick. Season with salt, pepper, and thyme leaves. Make another layer of potato slices, and season again. Moisten with cream, cream and chicken stock, or milk to the top level of potatoes. According to taste, sprinkle the top with grated Parmesan or Gruyère cheese, and distribute thin shavings of butter on top. Bake 45 minutes to 1 hour in a preheated oven at 375°F., until nicely browned.

Many variations are possible: potato and turnip (page 302), potato and celery root (page 89), potato and winter squash (page 276), potato and leek, potato and black truffle, or potato and sweet potato. Try adding a layer of some other delicious thing between the potato layers: sorrel, green garlic or roasted garlic, grilled chicory. sautéed wild mushrooms, caramelized onion, kale or chard, black olives, artichoke hearts.

On the surface these recipes seem similar, and indeed their finished products are likely to be very similar to one another. But the ways in which the authors approach the subject of potato gratin are quite distinct, largely because the imagined reader and user of each recipe is seen as a different kind of person.

The Child recipe is the most complex of the set, although by the standards of the cookbook as a whole, it is unusually short. (The recipe for Cassoulet is, famously, about six times as long, counting introductory matter.) Still, it is more than twice as long as either of the others (373 words to *Joy*'s 122 and *Panisse*'s 152). It is very detailed and precise in terms of what to do, when to do it, and how much of it to do it with, or to. While *Joy* is content to allude to "3 layers," *Mastering* describes the structuring of the gratin layer by layer. It is also the only one of the recipes to concern itself with the pre-preparation of the potatoes. While *Joy* offers the reader options for "tidbits" to place between the layers, *Mastering* is more rigid, and only very tentatively in the introduction offers the risky option (don't offend a French "authority"!) of omitting the cheese. Child and her collaborators would seem to be writing for someone without much kitchen experience (the most specialized term in the recipe, "simmer," is defined at the beginning of the book), but with the patience and obedience to follow detailed and precise instructions to the letter. Recall that the two books were published nearly contemporaneously, and reflect on their titles: The *Joy* of cooking: it's not as bad as it's made out to be – in fact, it might be that most American of virtues, "fun"; vs. *Mastering the Art* of French cooking: it is a daunting task, but possible; and what is learned is an "art," not a mere skill or daily drudgery. Both books, though, comment in their titles about the kind of activity their readers are going to be engaged in when they use them; the third, *Chez Panisse Vegetables*, has as its title a simple description of its contents, without any promises made to the reader about what (s)he is about to embark upon or how it will feel to do it.

All three recipes involve about the same amount of work and the same amount of difficulty. But the explicitness of *Mastering*, while on the one hand demystifying the process and leaving nothing to chance, at the same time makes the process more daunting, especially to the neophyte. For instance, while *Joy* trusts the reader to know how thin "very thinly sliced" potatoes are, *Mastering* defines them as exactly 1/8" thick. The style of *Joy* is rather brusque and straightforward by comparison: ingredients are incorporated syntactically into the instructions, where in *Mastering* the reader needs to flip from left to right, creating the impression of extra steps. The fact that both *Joy* and *Panisse* encourage the reader to make free choices among optional ingredients suggests that both of these have more trust in the reader's judgment and competence than does *Mastering*; and that, therefore, the former two consider the reader more of an equal and a colleague than does the third.

Chez Panisse Vegetables was published forty years after the other two, and reflects the changes in our relationship to the kitchen that the others, and similar works, brought into being. It is quite short, and much less concerned with clarity of exposition or demystification of ingredients or technique. As with the CP menus, less is more – more collegial, that is. Waters can assume that the user of her recipes is conversant with complex cooking techniques and ingredients – ingredients that Rombauer and Becker would never have considered at all, and Child and her collaborators would have dismissed as either inaccessible to, or too weird for, the American kitchen: you can read the entirety of the other books without running into a single reference to black truffles, green garlic, or grilled chicory, but *Panisse* treats all of them, and more, as completely unremarkable and familiar – not requiring explanations or excuses. If *Mastering* were to call for any of the above, it would describe them in detail, either in the body of the recipe itself or, more likely, in an introductory paragraph (or several). *Panisse* assumes that all of these exotica are as familiar to the cook as to Waters herself. While both *Joy* and *Mastering* are specific about ingredients and methods, *Panisse* is considerably vaguer – leaving many decisions, in postmodern fashion, up to the reader.

As often in *Panisse*, quantities are not given, and technical description is allusive rather than detailed. On the other hand, the equipment is specified in somewhat more detail (no mere "baking dish," but an "earthenware gratin" dish). Both identically specify the desired appearance of the final product, "nicely browned," as *Joy* does not.

The aim of *Joy*, I think, is to convince the reader that there is no mystique – just do it; of *Mastering*, that there is plenty of mystique, but the reader can overcome it with the writers' help; and of *Panisse*, that professionals like *us* are aware of the mystique, but we're beyond being bothered by it. The three very different recipes for a very similar product reflect very different kinds of communication, based in turn on different assumptions made by each author (or set of authors) about who the reader is, what the writer's relationship with the reader and the reader's relationship with the kitchen is, and what the reader therefore wants and needs. And the reader in turn constructs his/her identity as a "cook" on the basis of that conversation: I am someone who needs precise guidance in the kitchen in order to get the job done (*Joy*); someone who looks for exacting detail in order to achieve *Mastery;* someone who is already professional in all but literal truth, who simply needs a little advice from a professional colleague (*Panisse*).

By comparison with the 1960s models, the *fin-de-siècle Panisse* may seem a striking novelty. But we have seen that those books were following the model provided by Fannie Farmer, who represented a striking change from the prevailing style of her times. That vague and imprecise style of menu writing was, as we have seen, intended for a reader who herself was a professional in the kitchen and therefore needed no more than general hints about ingredients and procedures. From this long-term vantage point, we can perhaps understand the ways of *Panisse* as the opening wedge of a post-millennial future, one in which home cooks have been, in a sense, re-professionalized (as their ability to recognize and use arcane terminology demonstrates). The cook has returned to a role and status in many (though by no means all) ways more similar to that of the professional for whom pre-Fannie Farmer cookbooks were written than to the cooks for whom *Joy* and *Mastering* were written.

5.5 Summary and conclusion

In this paper, I have discussed activities through participation in which we daily engage in the making and changing of our sense of who we are – our identities. While the construction of major aspects of human identity – sexuality, race, ethnicity, gender – may have more striking consequences, "minor identities" like culinary preferences and sophistication contribute significantly to our sense of ourselves: who we are, how competent we are, who our friends are or should be, whom we admire or disdain. Cuisine has in many ways affected our language, both our vocabularies and the way we construct discourse around food, its procurement, and its preparation. Some of us are more avid "foodies" than others; but even those who are proud to proclaim their disinterest in such things are aware that – in many circles, at any rate – theirs is a minority attitude, one that marks its possessor as a bit of an oaf. It has not always been the case in America that an appreciation of *haute cuisine* was a marker of intellectual and aesthetic achievement, but that is the case in many social milieux today; and consequently, being able to participate knowledgeably and volubly in the discourse of food, and knowing how to make sense of the menus and recipes one encounters, marks one as a serious person in the early twenty-first century.

6

Workplace narratives, professional identity and relational practice

Janet Holmes

6.1 Introduction

Narrative creeps into the most unexpected interstices of social interaction. Consider, for instance, the request in example 6.1[1] from Sandy (JS) to Neville (NS) to tell "a tale of his weekend".

Example 6.1

Neville's weekend

Context: Meeting of regular project team in a commercial organization.

(a) JS   but we should I guess start in the traditional manner
(b)   and have Neville give us a tale of his weekend
(c) NS   oh there's no tales to tell# mind you last night
(d) ALL   [laugh]

One might deduce from this invitation that the two men are involved in a social event, but this is far from the case. This exchange takes place at the beginning of a weekly project meeting in a commercial organization, and Sandy is the chair of the meeting.

Workplace talk serves many functions. In their everyday interactions, individuals at work are engaged in the complex business of developing and maintaining professional and social relationships with co-workers, while also attending to the serious and overtly ratified purpose of workplace activity, the organization's explicit objectives. In addition to these social and transactional functions,

---

[1] Transcription conventions are supplied in Appendix 6.1. All names are pseudonyms. Some minor editing of examples has been undertaken to eliminate irrelevant detail and improve readability.

workplace talk also provides an essential means of constructing and negotiating diverse social identities in the workplace. This chapter describes some of the ways in which people use stories, or "workplace anecdotes", as effective vehicles for reconciling the varied and sometimes competing demands of their professional roles at work.

Researchers working within the framework of social identity theory have been engaged over the last ten years or so in exploring the relationship between an individual's personal identities and their group identities (e.g., Giles and Coupland 1991; Hogg and Abrams 1988; Meyerhoff and Niedzielski 1994), and especially the ways in which this relationship is evident in everyday talk. As Meyerhoff (1996) says,

Social identity theory treats an individual's various group identifications as central to a development of self and as the basis for many kinds of behaviour, not the least of which is linguistic behaviour. (1996: 204)

Using this approach, individuals are regarded as having a range of social identities which link them to social groups, and a number of personal identities which are based on more one-to-one relationships with others. Individual identity is thus conceived as a unique complex of interacting aspects of different group and personal identities (Meyerhoff and Niedzielski 1994). In any interaction, while all facets of an individual's social identity are potentially relevant resources, individuals tend to present or focus on particular aspects of their social identity, sometimes emphasizing gender (e.g. Meyerhoff 1996), sometimes ethnicity (Gallois and Callan 1981), sometimes power, authority or professional status (e.g. Holmes, Stubbe and Vine 1999), and sometimes organizational or institutional identity (e.g. Gioia and Thomas 1996). The approach is a dynamic one, allowing for constant flux and interplay between different aspects of an individual's diverse social and personal identities in response to contextual influences.

The personal and group identities which make up an individual's persona are not static, but rather can be activated or called on to different degrees depending on the situation. (Meyerhoff and Niedzielski 1994: 319)[2]

---

[2] The model was initially developed to account for factors contributing to the creolization of pidgins.

Thus, individuals draw on different aspects of their social and personal identities in different interactions; different ingroups and outgroups may be brought into focus in different contexts, or even at different points in the same interaction. Individuals can be regarded as constantly engaged in the process of constructing aspects of interpersonal and inter-group identity. The analysis in this chapter makes use of the framework to explore the complexity of the identities people construct in the workplace, focusing in particular on the ways in which workplace anecdotes contribute to this process.

I first briefly describe our data set and methodology, and then explain how "workplace anecdotes" were identified. I then illustrate the ways in which such anecdotes function to construct the individual's professional identity at work, and their social functions in workplace relationships, including their function in managing potential conflicts between different aspects of an individual's complex identity. Finally I demonstrate the function of workplace anecdotes as an effective means of mediating the public–private interface in an organization, and the ways in which they achieve this.

6.2 The dataset

The data used as the basis for the analysis in this chapter is taken from the large database of workplace interactions which comprise the Wellington Language in the Workplace Project Corpus. The project aims to analyze features of interpersonal communication in a wide variety of New Zealand workplaces (Holmes 1998, 2000a), and to this end the methodology has been designed to record workplace interaction as unobtrusively as possible (Stubbe 1998). Typically, with the explicit knowledge and agreement of all involved, volunteers tape-record a range of their everyday work interactions over a period of time. In addition, wherever possible, workplace meetings are video-recorded.

At the time of writing, the dataset comprises 2500 workplace interactions, involving more than 500 participants recorded in a number of government departments and commercial white-collar organizations, as well as in small businesses, and in blue-collar factory environments. It includes social talk as well as business or task-oriented talk, and the length of recorded interactions ranges from short telephone calls of less than a minute, to long meetings which last more than four hours. The data analyzed in this chapter is taken from normal everyday business talk in six different workplaces: two government departments, two private-sector corporations, one semi-public organization and one factory.

6.3 Identifying workplace anecdotes

Narratives have been defined as stories concerned with "spontaneous personal experience" (Coates 1996; Johnstone 1993). But, in terms of purely structural criteria, such as those proposed by Labov (1972b), which have been widely adopted in narrative research, workplace anecdotes are often difficult to distinguish from business reports (e.g. Bamberg 1997a; Edwards 1997; Goodwin 1990; Herman 2001; Marra and Holmes 2004; Linde 1993). Both typically involve the core components of a complicating action and an implicit or explicit evaluation, for instance (Marra and Holmes 2004; Labov 1972b). Nevertheless, anecdotes do have features which can be used to distinguish them from reports. Adopting the model proposed in Holmes (2000b: 37) for distinguishing business talk from phatic communion and social talk, workplace anecdotes can be classified as strictly-speaking "dispensable" in the context of transactional workplace talk such as meetings. They cannot be regarded as an intrinsic component of the business at hand; they are not *required* accountings (cf. Heath 1986; Polanyi 1985: 20). In other words, workplace anecdotes are essentially digressions from the business talk which constitutes the core of workplace interaction.

At least some of the functions of workplace anecdotes can also generally be distinguished from those of business reports. While they serve many functions, as will be illustrated below, the function most relevant for distinguishing workplace anecdotes from oral reports is probably their function as entertainment. Workplace anecdotes are generally told to provide at least interest, and often amusement, for colleagues. Like humor and small talk (with which they frequently overlap), they provide relief from the core business of the workplace (see Holmes 2000b; Marra and Holmes 2004, 2005). To justify telling a narrative, there has to be something holding the listener's attention (Labov and Fanshel 1977: 105); or, as Polanyi (1985: 20) points out, a story, as opposed to a report, must have *impact*.

In discussing criteria for identifying workplace anecdotes, then, we conclude that in terms of Labov's structural criteria, a workplace anecdote minimally includes "complicating action" and an (implicit or explicit) evaluation; it is not institutionally ratified "on-task" core business talk; it is strictly speaking dispensable (i.e. not a required accounting); and it functions to interest or entertain co-workers (Marra and Holmes 2004). Typically, the workplace anecdotes identified in our sample were produced as entertaining or interesting, if typically brief, digressions from core business talk. Often, they could also be characterized as marginal or peripheral talk in terms of their positioning and status in relation to transactional or core business talk, a point discussed further below.

6.3.1 Constructing social identity at work

Most talk is multi-functional, and workplace anecdotes are no exception. This section explores the ways in which anecdotes may contribute to the construction of the professional identity of people at work, while recognising that they may simultaneously serve other functions as well. As the research in this volume attests, narratives are widely recognised as one important resource in identity construction. Moreover, as CA researchers have pointed out:

the fine-grained analysis of speaker turns and utterances [can] shed light on such general notions as institutional identity and the ways in which participants orientate to institutional settings. So doctors, for example, take on their doctoring identity as they present themselves as questioners of patients. Or the prosecutor designs her turns in such a way to implicate the defendant or witness. The social facts of workplace life such as decisions, institutional roles, standards or what counts as 'success' are not givens or simply the product of external variables but are interactionally accomplished.   (Sarangi and Roberts 1999: 7)

This is equally true of the professional identities that individuals construct in their everyday interactions in business meetings and organizational contexts (cf. Dyer and Keller-Cohen 2000; Holmes and Marra 2005). Workplace anecdotes contribute to the construction of "the professional self" (Dyer and Keller-Cohen 2000), though the precise way this is achieved tends to differ in different workplace cultures or communities of practice (Holmes and Marra 2002; Wenger 1998). The difference in emphasis in the anecdotes reflects the different interactional practices in which they are embedded, and from which they emerge (Holmes and Marra 2005). Just three examples must serve to illustrate this point.

6.3.2 Constructing professional identity

I begin with a workplace anecdote recounted by a manager in a New Zealand factory, pseudonymed Tallows. Tallows is very hier-archically organized with clearly demarcated professional roles for staff at different levels. The interactions we examined in this work-place focused on a particular production team, pseudonymed the Power Rangers. The team manager, Ginette, was universally recog-nized within the factory as outstandingly good at her job (see Stubbe 2000), a recognition well supported by our detailed ethno-graphic observations, as well as promotions during the time we collected the data analyzed in this chapter. Ginette's authority as team leader was unquestioningly accepted by her team. While she provided abundant positive and encouraging feedback, especially to individuals, when the team performed well, she was a straight-talking and authoritative manager who dished out direct and ungarnished criticism when the team failed to meet its targets or made errors. She did not suffer fools gladly, nor tolerate lateness, slack work, or stupidity, as the following workplace anecdote illustrates. In this excerpt Ginette presents one important facet of her professional identity as a team manager.

Example 6.2

Sam and the hopper

Context: Ginette (GT), the team manager, is working in the scales area of the packing line and talking to other members of the team.

(a) GT   and it wa- I think it was yesterday or the day before +
(b)   he had Sam up there
(c)   there must have been a blockage in the hopper
(d)   and Lesia and I were standing
(e)   (and Sam) was banging away +
(f)   I said to Lesia why the fuck is he banging the dust extraction pipe
(g)   know that big thick pipe

(h)   HW   yeah
(i)   GT   instead of banging the hopper
(j)   HW   /[laughs]\
(k)   GT   /he was banging the pipe /[laughs]\
(l)   HW   /[laughs]\
(m)   GT   [laughs]: and I said to him: what's the matter Sam
(n)   [mimics Sam]: oh hopper's blocked
(o)   powder's not coming through to the head:
(p)   so why are you banging the dust extraction pipe
(q)   [mimics Sam]: oh:
(r)   HW   [laughs]

Ginette here entertains team members, and particularly Helen
(HW) who is her immediate neighbour on the packing line, with
a story which exposes a third (absent) team member Sam to
ridicule for stupid behavior. The story is a simple one, told in a
way that holds Helen's attention, and it clearly succeeds in providing amusement, as the laughter throughout indicates. An
examination of just *how* the tale is told, however, indicates that
it is doing more than serving as entertainment. In particular, the
strategies used to elaborate and evaluate the events provide interesting insight into the kind of professional identity Ginette is
constructing through her narrative.

Ginette first provides the physical context and relevant background information (the orientation), explaining how she and
another team member Lesia observed Sam banging on a pipe (lines
(a)–(e)), and her inference (line (c)) *there must have been a blockage
in the hopper*. She then uses an expletive to signal her astonish-
ment at Sam's stupid behavior to Lesia *why the fuck is he banging
the dust extraction pipe* (line (f)). The next few lines ((f)–(k)) are
oriented to Ginette's audience to check that Helen can follow her
story, that she knows what is being referred to, and hence can
understand why Ginette considered Sam's behavior to be so
stupid. All this is achieved very concisely, with minimal elaboration: *instead of banging the hopper, he was banging the pipe*
(lines (f) and (k)). However, Ginette then proceeds to mercilessly
expose Sam to ridicule by reproducing the exchange she conducted
with him in a way that clearly demonstrates his lack of common
sense.

Ginette constructs her own complicated role very skillfully. At
one level, she represents herself as asking an apparently innocent,

interested question: *what's the matter Sam* (line (m)). Sam's response *hopper's blocked powder's not coming through to the head* (lines (n)–(o)) is then directly juxtaposed to her devastatingly direct challenge exposing his illogical behavior *so why are you banging the dust extraction pipe* (line (p)). Sam self-evidently betrays himself and his stupidity without any help from Ginette. But, because she has already indicated (in line (f)) her reaction to what he is doing, it is clear that she is not in fact guileless – she has set Sam a trap. The story is capped off with Ginette's wicked mimicking of Sam's dim-witted response as he finally gets the message *oh* (line (q)). Ginette thus plays a dual role: she presents herself to Sam as an innocent observer who gives him the opportunity to explain himself, but Helen and Lesia (and we) know that she has already worked out what Sam is doing and why, and judged it as very silly behavior.

Sam is thus presented in the final exchange as a bit of an idiot who cannot see the stupidity of his behavior until Ginette spells out for him quite explicitly that his actions are not well directed to solving the problem.

So Ginette presents herself as a tough manager. Her story focuses on a weak team member and exposes his stupid behavior for others' entertainment. In team meetings, too, Ginette provides acerbic evaluations of unintelligent behavior, and indicates that she will not tolerate mistakes, especially those which could damage the team's record or adversely affect their productivity. She constructs her professional identity as a hard taskmistress with very high standards, "a bit of a tartar" who is intolerant of errors and expects perfection from team members. Her direct, focused, unelaborated style is well illustrated in this narrative, which is told with remarkable economy. There is only one phrase, namely the intensificatory *the fuck* in line (f), which is not crucial to the addressee's basic understanding of events (though even that is important in comprehending the point of the story). There is not a single attenuating hedge, no mitigating devices, and no spare descriptive adjectives. Even the reported speech is presented with the minimum of speech attributions, i.e. using one phrase: *I said to him* (line (m)). The remaining dialogue attributions are achieved through Ginette's mimicking of Sam's speech, a device which simultaneously allows her to convey her evaluation of Sam's (lack of) intelligence. This is discoursal instantiation of Ginette's direct, no-fuss, authoritative managerial style. In this anecdote, she conveys her stance as a tough professional with little tolerance for incompetence or stupidity.

This story thus provides insight into one facet of Ginette's identity at work – her professional identity as a team manager. It also, of course, simultaneously negotiates other aspects of her identity, such as her gender identity, and her membership of a factory team or community of practice (Holmes and Meyerhoff 1999; Wenger 1998). It is clear that Ginette presents herself as anything but stereotypically "feminine". Indeed, her gender identity, as reflected in this anecdote, is consistent with the tough, "masculine" style which she frequently adopts in the indubitably "masculine" community of practice in which she operates (see Holmes and Stubbe 2003). The workplace culture of the factory reflects its goals, and the means by which they are achieved – namely material outputs (material products) and heavy machinery. From a management perspective, talk is a secondary activity, only justified to the extent that it facilitates productivity. Ginette's direct, concise and highly focused style – even in her workplace anecdotes – is an interesting verbal instantiation of this orientation. Moreover, factory team members are highly interdependent in their work. One person's task typically provides the input for the next person's. Hence Sam's stupid behavior threatens the team's productivity. Ginette's focus on a team member's less than intelligent way of approaching a task thus has an important underlying message, one which is consistent with her overt message and her self-presentation as a demanding tough team manager in other contexts.

Example 6.3, which is analyzed more briefly, illustrates the complex identities which individuals construct at work in a very different community of practice, namely a white-collar, commercial organization.

Example 6.3

Marlene, Renee and the phone call

Context: Weekly team meeting in a large commercial organization.

(a)   MA   I got a phone call from someone
(b)   who thought that I was Renee

(c) cz [drawls]: oh:
(d) ma and at first I didn't realize
(e)   cos they just sort of asked kind of general questions
(f)   and then by the time I realized
(g)   sort of as I was just about to get off the phone
(h)   that they thought I was Renee
(i)   I thought this is going to be too embarrassing
(j)   for this person now
(k) cz [drawls]: oh yes yes:
(l) ma I quickly rushed off and told [laughs]: Renee:. . .

In this workplace anecdote, which, interestingly, is directly concerned with issues of professional identity, Marlene (MA) recounts an embarrassing experience in which her identity was mistakenly construed by a caller as that of her colleague Renee.

The story is encapsulated in the first two lines (the "abstract" in Labov's terms); the remaining ten lines provide an elaboration of the narrative, indicating Marlene's attitude to the event described, and some insights into her management of her workplace identity. Three points are worth noting, all of which suggest that Marlene presents a very sensitive, caring, but self-aware workplace identity. Firstly, the content of Marlene's story provides evidence of this. (One cannot imagine Ginette responding to a caller in this way, for instance.) Rather than asserting her identity, Marlene allows the caller to continue to assume she is Renee, even after the mistake has become evident to Marlene. Secondly, in this short anecdote there are a number of pragmatic signals of embarrassment and discomfort, indicating that Marlene is self-aware and conscious of threats to her own face needs. In addition to the overt disclaimer *and at first I didn't realize* (line (d)), there is also a distinctive prosody in the form of high rising intonation contours, and a number of attenuating hedges and mitigators, *sort of, kind of, just* (lines (e) and (g)), which all indicate that Marlene is less than comfortable with the situation. Thirdly, Marlene presents herself in a number of ways as a person who is sensitive and responsive to the opinions and feelings of others. She indicates, for example, that she does not wish to embarrass the caller *I thought this is going to be too embarrassing for this person now* (lines (i)–(j)), and she is similarly concerned to inform Renee at once of what has happened *I quickly rushed off and told Renee* (line (l)), suggesting she does not want to be badly thought of, or to be misjudged as having impersonated

Renee. Moreover, her disclaimer (line (d)) also signals concern that her addressee should be aware that she did not deliberately mislead the caller. In this brief anecdote, then, Marlene enlists a range of strategies which indicate her sensitivity to people's face needs, including her own, and in the process she contributes to the construction of a professional identity which is consciously polite, caring, and responsive to the needs and feelings of others. It is hardly necessary to point out that such an identity is much closer to "feminine" than "masculine" gender stereotypes, and the contrast, with Ginette's anecdote is very clear on this dimension as on others.

Finally, it is worth noting that in a community of practice where talk is central to the accomplishment of workplace objectives, Marlene's anecdote is directly concerned with talk and identity. Her anecdote provides an interesting example of the way in which workplace talk can simultaneously contribute to the achievement of transactional goals or workplace objectives and more personal goals such as identity construction.

The next section focuses on yet another aspect of workplace talk, the social or interpersonal dimension. Here too workplace anecdotes make an interesting contribution. Whereas in this section the stories were told by individuals about past events (in the storyworld), and served to contribute to the construction of the individual's professional identity at work, in the next section the stories are, at least partially, joint constructions (embedded within the storytelling world), and appropriately illustrate the important social functions of narratives in managing workplace relationships.[3]

6.3.3 Constructing social relationships

In addition to serving as a strategy for constructing the complex professional identities of individuals at work, workplace anecdotes also serve the important function of developing and maintaining workplace relationships. The opening Example 6.1 illustrates nicely that rituals which embrace off-task talk, including anecdotes, may be integrated into the ongoing process of constructing

---

[3] I owe this point to an insightful comment from Deborah Schiffrin.

good relationships between team members in an organization. Sandy opens the meeting by inviting Neville to contribute "a tale of his weekend." By his use of the phrase *in the traditional manner* (line (a)), Sandy signals that this is part of a regular routine for this team, or community of practice, one way in which they have established their distinctiveness and "belongingness" as a group. Sandy's invitation clearly expresses approval of Neville's contribution to the team's spirit and rapport, and Neville himself sustains the good-humoured key by first declaring he has no tale to tell (line (c)), but then, without taking breath, immediately signaling with the discourse marker *mind you* that he does in fact have a contribution to make. In her book *Disappearing Acts*, Joyce Fletcher (1999) draws on relational theory (Gilligan 1982; Miller 1986; Miller and Stiver 1997) to develop the notion of "relational practice." Relational practice (RP) refers to the many overlooked and unnoticed strategies used to foster and strengthen interpersonal relationships at work, in ways that also facilitate the achievement of workplace objectives (see Holmes and Marra 2004). Among the various kinds of RP she identifies, the type of most relevance to this analysis is RP directed to *creating team* (Fletcher 1999: 48) or "creating the background conditions in which group life [can] flourish" (74). This includes all the typically unobserved behind-the-scenes behaviors which foster team spirit and the development of a group's esprit de corps – activities such as taking the time to listen and respond empathically to non-work-related information, creating opportunities for collaboration and cooperation, interfacing or facilitating productive interaction, and defusing potentially confrontational situations. Workplace anecdotes have an obvious place in such a list, since they provide ways of building and strengthening team spirit, and constructing strong workplace relationships.

Two contrasting examples will serve to illustrate the contribution of workplace anecdotes to "creating team". The first example is taken from the interactions of a high performing and highly qualified computer development project team in a white-collar, commercial organization. The team members are discussing plans to have dinner together at a restaurant, a social event arranged by their organization. In order to understand this exchange, the reader needs to know that Eric has a reputation for invading the restaurant kitchen and "helping" the chef on these occasions.

Example 6.4

Visiting the restaurant kitchen

Context: Regular weekly meeting of a project team in a white collar commercial organization. The example is preceded by a discussion of the seating plan for a company dinner to be held in the near future.

Pre-amble

(a)	JA	I wanted to get er maybe your opinion
(b)		we can do open seating or we can do assigned as far as dinner
(c)		do we want to do er assigned or do we want to do open
(d)	ER	how are you going to assign it. . . . . . .
(e)	BA	we'll just make it open won't /we\
(f)	ER	/yeah\
(g)	JA	(great) /that's easier\
(h)	CA	/(you'll but)\

Anecdote

(i)	CA	you'll be off to the kitchen pretty quickly though /won't you\
(j)	ER	/yeah\ I know yeah
(k)	BA	cooking
(l)	ER	after that third bottle of wine I'll be in there /( )
(m)	BA	/[laughs]\ [laughs]: making dinner: [laughs]=
(n)	ER	/I haven't I haven't done that kitchen so /that'll\ be one=
(o)	CA	/yeah\
(p)	ER	=for the collection
(q)	BA	[laughs] /[laughs] you /can't you can't\ remember it:
(r)	ER	/( ) [laughs]
(s)	MC	there's a lot of kitchens he doesn't remember

This anecdote illustrates a number of points. Firstly, it is concisely accomplished; its content can be summarised very briefly: i.e. when Eric reaches a certain state of intoxication, he regularly invades the kitchen in restaurants where the team is having a social meal in order to "assist" with the cooking. Callum introduces it with a reference to Eric's established practice of visiting the kitchen in restaurants where the team eat dinner *you'll be off to the kitchen pretty quickly though won't you* (line (i)). Eric and Barry respond in ways that indicate they understand exactly what Callum's inexplicit utterance refers to (lines (j) and (k)). Eric contributes the information that he hasn't yet "done that kitchen" and hence he can add it to his "collection". The excerpt is closed by humorous gibes from

Barry (line (q)) and Marco (line (s)), both of which elaborate the context in which Eric makes his contribution to restaurant cooking. So while it is brief and very enigmatic to an outsider, the anecdote presents no problems of interpretation to these team members who know each other well, and, like any well-integrated community of practice, have a good deal of shared history (Wenger 1998). The anecdote is a re-run story serving the function of reinforcing and maintaining collegial relations between team members. This is evident not only from the fact that its content is clearly already known, but also from the way the anecdote is constructed and conveyed. It also simultaneously, of course, contributes to the construction and maintenance of Eric's persona in the team as a maverick "performer" who, on social occasions, enacts a routine familiar to his team mates or co-participants (Goffman 1959: 16), a role Eric clearly relishes.

The anecdote is jointly constructed; it is Eric's story but it is introduced by Callum (line (i)), and elaborated both by Barry (lines (k), (m), (q)) and Eric (lines (l), (n), (p)), with a final contribution from Marco (line (s)). The joint construction underlines the fact that, while its focus is Eric, this is part of the team's shared experience. This aspect of the delivery is further sustained through the use of inclusive and cooperative pragmatic devices: e.g. Barry's use of a "facilitative tag question" (Holmes 1995) *won't you* (line (i)); and his completion of Eric's clause *I'll be in there* with the phrase *making dinner* (line (m)). The clearly humorous key (Kotthoff 2000) which is developed by all four contributers provides additional evidence of the collegial nature of the construction. Indeed the gibes at Eric first keyed by Callum's introductory comment *you'll be off to the kitchen pretty quickly though* (line (i)), are sustained by Barry *you can't remember it* (line (q)) and Marco *there's a lot of kitchens he doesn't remember* (line (s)). These strategies are consistent with the argument (outlined in Holmes and Marra 2004a) that the way members of this particular community of practice do relational practice is through contestive and competitive humorous repartee.

Hence this brief excerpt simultaneously constructs Eric's identity as a source of entertainment on the team's social outings, and reinforces the team's esprit de corps, or in Fletcher's terms "creates team," both through its content and its manner of construction.

The organization within which this project team operates has a reputation for being very competitive, and the workplace culture is widely characterized as distinctly "masculine". This team instantiates this masculine culture in a variety of ways, as this workplace anecdote indicates. The contestive humour involved in its delivery is very masculine in style (see also Holmes and Marra 2005). The anecdote has Eric as its focus, but unlike social identities constructed in more "feminine" workplaces, the facet of Eric's identity constructed both by himself and his team mates in this excerpt is a very masculine identity, and it is not an overtly complimentary one. The characterization of Eric's drunken assaults on restaurant kitchens is at best ambivalent, and it is certainly very distinct from his professional identity (which is that of team expert on particular aspects of the company's computing programs).

This anecdote thus serves a range of complex functions. By focusing on a facet of Eric's behaviour which contrasts markedly with his work performance, the anecdote complexifies and elaborates Eric's role as an individual within the team. As a jointly constructed, familiar, and much-told tale, it also serves the function of creating team or strengthening team solidarity. This workplace anecdote thus contributes in a variety of ways to the construction and maintenance of the distinctive socio-cultural relationships and identities of the members of this particular community of practice within the larger commercial organization.

A second example is taken from a different private commercial company. Example 6.5 occurred at the beginning of a regular weekly meeting of a highly rated project team.

Example 6.5

Golden Globe awards

Context: *Weekly team meeting in a large commercial organization.*

(a) NS   actually did you see that um that actress from um [tut] Chicago
(b)   Hope was in the toilet when she /got her award=
(c) MA   /mm\
(d) NS   =shit that was funny see that?
(e) JS   no
(f) MA   she missed it so /Robin Williams got up for her
(g) XM   /(*says something indicating amazement*)\
(h) MA   /yes he did\

(i)   NS   /the whole crowd\ was going /where is she\
(j)   MA   /yeah her husband\ went up
(k)   and then Robin Williams /went up and pretended to
           be\=
(l)   NS   /(and then Robin Williams got up)\
(m)   MA   = like this Spanish waiter going [*in Spanish*]: eh eh (blah)
           Signorita Leate [*Spanish accent*]: your (award) is waiting:
           [laughs]:
(n)   like this into the podium he was being really funny:
(o)   NS   shit that was a laugh ( ) //( )\
(p)   JS   /did they\ did they have the camera in the toilet
(q)   just to catch her /the facial expression\
(r)   PG   yes they /did\
(s)   SH   ironic
(t)   ALL [laugh and talk at once]

This is a relatively self-contained section from a long humorous interchange around the topic of the Golden Globe awards. The excerpt illustrates how such anecdotes contribute to the construction and development of social relationships at work. Firstly, it is worth noting that the anecdote introduces a topic which is not even peripherally work-related – it is pure social talk. Nor does its content involve any of the participants; it is rather gossip about well-known public figures, in this case movie stars. The talk is nevertheless licensed by the meeting chair, Sandy (see, for instance lines (p) and (q)), and contributed to by almost all those present. This is typical of the social talk which takes place regularly at the opening of meetings in this team; such anecdotes are regarded as perfectly acceptable in this community of practice, and they clearly serve to warm people up at the beginning of meetings, and to (re-) establish good rapport between team members.

Secondly, it is worth noting how this example too is a jointly constructed anecdote. Although the anecdote is set up by Neville (lines (a)–(b)) Marlene picks it up and completes the Labovian "abstract" at line (f) *she missed it so Robin Williams got up for her*. The two then contribute alternately through lines (i)–(p), at which point Sandy asks a humorous question, to which Peg and Seth respond. The contributions of Marlene and Neville nicely complement each other at some points and overlap at others: for example, they both produce almost exactly the same words *and then Robin Williams went up*, at almost exactly the same time in lines (k)–(l). It is always clear, however, that they are "in tune" with each other and working together to present the story in an amusing way. This is underlined by Neville's appreciative comment *shit that was a laugh* (line (p)) following Marlene's skilful imitation of Robin William's rendition of a Spaniard (lines (m)–(n)).

This anecdote is pure entertainment; it serves to strengthen the social ties between members of this cohesive project team. No team member is the butt of the humour and the participants provide good evidence in their various contributions that they are all on the same wavelength. And again, this anecdote is a good reflection of the positive and dynamic workplace culture which characterizes this community of practice. This is a high-energy team and a mutually supportive one. Anecdotes – typically humorous – are one important means by which the team constructs and maintains the positive social relationships which ensure they work together effectively.

At the same time, this anecdote contributes to the social identities which individuals have developed within this community of practice. For example, by not ruling this discussion irrelevant and insisting on proceeding with the agenda, Sandy, the meeting chair, covertly plays his usual role in this team as facilitator of strictly off-topic, amusing stories, a pattern seen above in Example 6.1. Similarly, Neville is fully involved (with Marlene) in the recounting of the anecdote, using his skill to make the story amusing. Again this is consistent with his identity as team story-teller which was also evident in Example 6.1. In other words, while this jointly constructed anecdote most obviously serves a social function of strengthening team solidarity, it simultaneously contributes to the construction and maintenance of different facets of the individual's interpersonal and professional identities (cf. Goffman 1959).

We have identified a number of examples of such non-work-related anecdotes serving primarily social purposes but also contributing to the construction of the individual's identity. One particularly telling example involved the story of an April Fools' Day trick which Ginette, the manager discussed above, successfully perpetrated on a number of her team members. She persuaded them to phone the number of the local zoo (without their realizing where they were ringing) and ask for Mr. Lion. The story was told and re-told with great glee for several days afterwards and clearly served to strengthen team solidarity, while also indicating and reinforcing Ginette's status as a core member of the team, one of the "jokers," an important and highly-regarded status within this team. Anecdotes thus serve a range of (usually simultaneous) functions in the workplace, from the construction of personal, professional and social identities, to the establishment, maintenance and strengthening of interpersonal, social relationships between those who work together. In the next section, I consider the distribution of workplace anecdotes in the recorded data, and the significance of the distributional patterns in relation to the function of workplace anecdotes.

6.3.4 Workplace anecdotes as off-record work

Workplace anecdotes can be considered marginal in several senses in workplace interaction. Firstly, their content may bear no overt connection with workplace business, as clearly illustrated by the examples in the previous section. Secondly, their position within workplace talk is frequently at the margins of "official business" or serious transactional talk at work. And, thirdly, they can often be characterized as functioning at the organization's public–private interface, acting as the conduit between people's private lives and their professional identities. I deal with each of these points in turn.

The content of workplace anecdote in our data is very variable. Some anecdotes deal with material which has little or no relation to workplace business, as illustrated by Examples 6.4 and 6.5. Others recount experiences at work which qualify as interesting or amusing, as illustrated in Examples 6.2 and 6.3. Despite the fact that these instances are concerned with work-related issues, it is clear that they are nonetheless topically marginal to the ongoing business of the organization. They may be used to illustrate a point, or to illustrate qualities of the character of a team member (as in Example 6.2), but these anecdotes are not part of the team's core business. They are strictly speaking dispensable or "de trôp." One anecdote from a non-government organization, for instance, involved two team members describing how they were badly treated by members of an external organization who invited them to a meeting which turned out to be a confrontational set-up. While this example comes close to engaging with the team's serious core business, even in this instance the anecdote can be characterized as dispensable. The point that was being made – that the external organization was not to be trusted – could have been made without the anecdote.

Anecdotes qualify, then, as canonical examples of relational practice in Fletcher's terms. They are generally regarded as dispensable, irrelevant, or peripheral, and in some cases even distracting, in the workplace context (see Holmes and Marra 2005). Their marginal and off-record status is sometimes even signaled explicitly by the use of discourse markers such as *to get back to the point, to get back on track, enough digressing, enough (of that)*, or, less overtly, by markers associated with digressions, such as *so, anyway, right, well, now*, and so on. In one workplace the phrase *moving right along* had clearly developed as a routine marker of the end of a digression. When such discourse markers accompany workplace anecdotes, they provide clear evidence that the anecdotes are perceived as off-topic digressions. Further evidence is provided by the fact that workplace anecdotes are never recorded as part of the official record of the meetings in which they occur. Even when used to illustrate an important point or to make a valuable contribution to people's understanding, they are typically not regarded as components of core business. Like relational practice more generally, workplace anecdotes tend to be treated as peripheral in workplace interaction.

In terms of when and where they occur, workplace anecdotes are often literally positioned at the peripheries of core workplace business. They typically occur at the interstices of official or serious business talk at the boundaries of meetings, in passing in the corridor, and so on. Example 6.5, for instance, occurred at the beginning of a meeting, while Example 6.4 comes from the end of a meeting. Even when they occur within meetings, workplace anecdotes, like small talk and humor, tend to mark transition points (see Holmes 2000a; Marra 2003). They are marginal in this literal sense, therefore, as well as in their assessed contribution to the transactional goals of the workplace.

As with other instances of relational practice, the important interpersonal and social work that anecdotes perform within organizations generally goes unrecognized. I have indicated in the two previous sections how workplace anecdotes firstly provide a means of constructing and instantiating the personal and professional identities of workplace participants, and, secondly, contribute to the construction and maintenance of workplace social relationships by "creating team" and strengthening solidarity within work groups. By serving these different functions, workplace anecdotes provide a conduit between an individual's personal identity and their public or professional identity as a member of a community of practice in the workplace. Moreover, as Goffman (1959) noted, these two functions are inter-connected; the characterization of Eric in Example 6.4, for instance, as a drunken joker who misbehaves in restaurants on semi-formal social occasions organized by the company, is interestingly positioned at the end of a meeting in which he has overtly demonstrated his expertise, and where his outstanding performance has been explicitly referred to. One colleague recounts, for instance, how Eric had received "a standing ovation" for a recent presentation he had undertaken, and another comments "and now he's developed a whole project around it . . . talk about empire building." The restaurant anecdote could thus be regarded as counteracting a professional identity which threatens the team's cohesion, serving as way of reconciling an overly successful professional performance and Eric's identity as a well-integrated team member. Similarly, in a very different organization, a section manager recounts a self-deprecating anecdote at the end of a meeting where she has explicitly exercised her managerial authority in a community of practice with a very overtly articulated, democratic and egalitarian culture (see Holmes 2000c; Holmes and Stubbe 2003). Anecdotes can thus provide an interface between different worlds, sometimes reconciling conflicting aspects of a person's professional and social identity, sometimes allowing people to smuggle the expression of personal concerns into a public context, and sometimes legitimating the discussion of private issues or off-work topics by providing an acceptable (even if marginal) position for them within transactional work space.

6.4 Conclusion

Though often relatively brief, and typically perceived as peripheral to ratified workplace business, workplace anecdotes serve complex functions. In Meyerhoff's terms, they provide strategies for constructing and instantiating the varied personal and social identities evident in ongoing interpersonal and intergroup interaction (Meyerhoff 1996). Workplace anecdotes provide a means of doing one's professional identity, while simultaneously doing gender, workplace culture, and personal identity. They provide a means of constructing the professional identities of others as good or poor, competent or incompetent team members. They provide a legitimate and acceptable, but unofficial and off-record, outlet for dissatisfaction, jealousy, or irritation in the workplace. And they allow team members to construct team cohesion by building strong interpersonal bonds at work.

From a different perspective, the concept of "relational practice" (Fletcher 1999) indicates how workplace anecdotes function as instances of relational work, often at the boundaries or the interstices of workplace transactional business. Though typically overlooked, marginalized and erased from the official record, workplace anecdotes may make an important contribution to constructing workplace solidarity, or "creating team" in Fletcher's terms. They may also contribute to the better understanding of ratified workplace objectives, though this contribution is rarely recognized.

In sum, I have suggested that workplace anecdotes may contribute to the construction of complex personal, professional and social identities for workplace participants, allowing them to emphasize particular facets of their social identities and different dimensions of social meaning – professional status, team solidarity, authority responsibilities, gender category, group affiliations, distinctive workplace culture, and so on. Although workplace anecdotes are strictly marginal aspects of workplace interaction, the analysis has demonstrated that they comprise a valuable resource for (re)producing or enacting the various facets of an individual's personal, professional and social identity, that they may serve as effective and socially acceptable discursive strategies for reconciling conflicting aspects of identity, and that they often provide an important interface between the personal and public dimensions of an individual's socio-cultural identity.

Appendix 6.1. Transcription conventions

YES	Capitals indicate emphatic stress
[LAUGHS] : :	Paralinguistic features in square brackets, colons indicate start/finish
+	Pause of up to one second
. . . / . . . .\ . . .	Simultaneous speech
. . . / . . . .\ . . .	
(HELLO)	Transcriber's best guess at an unclear utterance
?	Rising or question intonation
-	Incomplete or cut-off utterance
. . . . . .	Section of transcript omitted
#	signals clause completion but no pause
XM/XF	Unidentified Male/Female

All names used in examples are pseudonyms.

Acknowledgements

This paper has benefited greatly from comments by colleagues, especially Meredith Marra, Anna De Fina and Deborah Schiffrin. I also express appreciation to other members of the Language in the Workplace team who have been involved with the project development, data collection, processing and transcription, including Maria Stubbe (Research Fellow), Dr. Bernadette Vine (Corpus Manager), and a number of research assistants. I also thank those who allowed their workplace interactions to be recorded. This research is supported by a grant from the New Zealand Foundation for Research Science and Technology. More information about the project can be viewed on our website *www.vuw.ac.nz/lals/lwp/*.

Identity and personal/institutional relations: people and tragedy in a health insurance customer service

Liliana Cabral Bastos and Maria do Carmo Leite de Oliveira

7.1 Introduction

There is much more to late modernity than the comfort it has brought to our daily lives: this age of rapid and sometimes radical change in which we live has also rendered more complex the interactions between human beings. One example of this complexity is the bureaucratization of interpersonal relations, brought about by the expanding commercialization of services. Modern society all too often trivializes the contact between service providers and clients, and this has resulted in efforts to make direct contact between individuals and organizations more frequent. In past decades, high-quality relationships with customers were considered a key element of success in bureaucratic organizations (Dubar 2000: 113). Yet the focus on the customer has further problematized the question of communication in individual–organization interactions. The client's evaluation of the service is directly related to his/her expectations, which are invested with subjectivity. The success of the company's engagement in providing a service that will satisfy the client depends, therefore, on communication that favors a better reciprocal understanding and a shared sense of the actions of the participants (Zarifian 2001).

The focus of this chapter is on communication in a health insurance service. One relevant aspect of this communication is the negotiation of the sense of health and the contractual conditions that regulate the client/company relationship. In this context, the processes by which the participants construct their identity become crucial to mutual understanding and to the consequent validation of the service provided. We examine how participants construct identity through their communicative behavior in two exchanges: two letters written by customers describing tragic events in which they thematize health problems, and the letter of response they elicit from the company. We examine how codes of reference are negotiated, specifically those that affect understanding of what is a fair treatment (cf. Schneider and Bowen 1999).

7.2 Identity and narrative

7.2.1 Identity

In current reflections on identity the term has been used to refer to different realities and phenomena such as social class affiliation, interactional roles or psychological orientation. In the present chapter, in accordance with most recent research in sociolinguistics, social psychology and cultural studies and indeed with the position taken by other authors in this volume, we define identity as as a performative act, realized when people expose who they are at each moment in specific social interactions (Erickson 1966; Schiffrin 1993, 1996). We also see it as a negotiated process of exposure and interpretation of social positions, affiliations, roles, status, and other social categories (Ochs 1992, 1993).

Traditional views of identity conceive of it as fixed and continuous, something that belongs to the individual (Mishler 1999: 111). However, individuals position themselves differently at different moments and places, in accordance with interlocutors, topics, situations and the variety of roles that they may be playing (Woodward 2000). Giddens (1991) remarks that *self-identity* is neither a distinctive trait nor a set of traits, but rather a person's understanding of his/her biography, thus the stability of the *self* is given by a sense of autobiographic continuity which the individual communicates to others. The identity of a person is therefore linked to his/her ability to keep a given life story going (see Mishler, this volume). According to Giddens, this sense is at the same time strong and fragile: even if it can be maintained through moments of tension and transition, it is only one possibility among many others.

But identity also results from the cooperative and dynamic social presentation of individuals in interaction, as Goffman clearly saw. His notion of "face": the positive social attributes that a person claims for him or herself in the course of social interaction is particularly useful to understand identity work in institutional settings. Face is preserved through strategies used by participants to construct and maintain a favorable image of themselves and provide support to (or question) the identities projected by other participants as the interaction develops (Goffman 1959, 1967a). In institutional contexts such as the one under analysis here, the work of claiming and maintaining positive self-images is very important since individuals use impression management (Goffman 1959) to achieve their personal goals in their interaction with others.

7.2.2 Narrative and identity

By telling stories, we convey to others a sense of who we are, of our beliefs and values. Narratives of personal experience have been related to many forms of social identification such as cultural belonging and gender affiliation (Tannen 1980,1989; Johnstone 1993, 1996, but also see Kiesling, De Fina, Holmes in this volume) and more in general, have been shown to provide a central "resource for the display of self and identity" (Schiffrin 1996: 168).

Work in social psychology developed within a constructionist approach to identity has shown that narrative not only organizes experience (Bruner 1990: 35), but also allows individuals to actively shape the configuration of their self-conception, to construct themselves as specific persons in everyday interactions (Bamberg 1999) and to stress their agentivity in dealing with social coercive structures (Davies and Harré 1990: 52).

In healthcare contexts, investigation has concentrated mainly on narratives told in medical and research interviews (Capps and Ochs 1995; Mishler 1986; 1999; Ribeiro 2001; Young 1999). Whether in clinical, psychological or psychiatric contexts, this strand of research has shown how narratives work to build both who patients are and how their conditions are classified and perceived. In our analysis, we deal with a different health-related context and data: written letters exchanged in the bureaucracy of a health insurance company. Despite these differences, narratives in this context also play an important role in the construction of patients' identities and in the configuration of company/customer relations. When telling stories, the narrator is at the same time the agent who makes and transforms the world, and the individual who responds reflexively to conditions in it (Mishler 1999: 17–20). This duality reflects the fact that narratives are socially-situated actions but also occasions for individual identity displays that relate to very personal conditions and needs. As we will see in the analysis presented below, customers, although acting in accordance with general social-cultural values and beliefs, are also engaged in very local and personal issues. The particular dimensions of their identities which are foregrounded in each of the narratives are closely related to the problems they want to solve.

7.3 Customer satisfaction and face needs

Like other service providers, health insurance providers are concerned with attracting and keeping customers through the delivery of quality services which ensure their satisfaction. The literature on services marketing offers numerous models of customer satisfaction, and customer communication has been recognized as a useful dimension in evaluating that satisfaction (Grönroos 1995; Lee and Ulgado 1997; Zeithaml and Bitner 1996). The Internet has also introduced new paradigms for customer services and consequently new criteria to measure satisfaction. Of special interest to the present work is the Customer Needs Model, developed by Schneider and Bowen (1999). This model is based on two principles:

(i)   Customers are people before they are clients;
(ii) People consider their basic needs more fundamental than their specific expectations as consumers.

Not only does this model have the merit of recognizing the existence of several identity dimensions: it also de-emphasizes a social identity based exclusively on the role of "customer." As the authors state, service providing has to juggle three basic needs: security (feeling of protection against physical or economic damage), justice (need to be treated correctly), and self-esteem (desire to maintain and improve self-image). The needs for justice and self-esteem greatly impact interaction. The need for justice encompasses:

a) Distributive justice: the evaluation of outcomes by the customer. Evaluation of distributive justice may involve the combination of three internally inconsistent rules: equity (the right to receive the same treatment as some customers); equality (the right to receive the same treatment as all other customers); and need (the right to be treated differently from all other customers).

b) Procedural justice: the employment of equity of rules and procedures that determine fair outcomes.

c) Interactional justice: the compliance with rules of fair interaction between employees in any given company and customers on a personal level.

The evaluation of procedures and interaction encompasses obligations such as keeping promises and commitments, being flexible when dealing with extraordinary requests, helping when required, establishing bonds of friendship, acting with honesty, and being polite and respectful. The need for self-esteem includes the several forms by which a company can reinforce the personal value of the customer, making individuals feel intelligent, competent, important, comfortable and free to make choices.

Schneider and Bowen's conception of the need for justice and self-esteem is remniscent of the notion of face (Goffman 1967a), specifically as developed in the work of Brown and Levinson (1987). According to these authors, a model person is a fluent speaker who has rationality and face. The model person must be able to distinguish between the goals and the means to reach the goals. In addition, this model person has two face-related wants: the want to have a positive self-image and the want to be unimpeded.

Brown and Levinson, like Schneider and Bowen, work with pre-established and fixed categories to explain in an abstract and non-situated manner the nature of face work. Although we believe that the need for a "positive self-image" underlies how customers want, or do not want, to be regarded/treated in their interactions with a company, we also believe that this need may be carried out in different ways. For example, to claim recognition of the value he/she believes to have, the customer may show himself/herself as abandoned. The evaluation of what counts as fair treatment is, therefore, directly related to the communicative strategies that support, reinforce or threaten situated identities.

7.4 Fair treatment and health

Societies whose focus is profit and market success are characterized by a continual search for business opportunities. Within this context, health has become an attractive niche: there is a guarantee of payment for service provided irrespective of whether or not the human and material resources offered are actually accessed. In countries such as Brazil, in which health has not been a priority for governments, and where the cost of medical treatment is outside the purchase power of the majority of the population, health insurance services have proved to be great business.

The data analyzed here were collected from the customer service office of a health insurance company. This health insurance provider is associated with a pension fund in a large public foundation. It provides health insurance to about 300,000 civil servants and their legal dependents throughout the country. Most are low-income individuals with little schooling. The customer support service, which was being implemented during data collection, employed six female operators who, in addition to answering phone calls, handled the correspondence directed to the health plan.

Although health insurance providers try to maintain an image of medicine as not being associated with an economic activity (advertising is very illustrative of this position), health is indeed their business. The representation of health as a commercial activity has an impact on the way the service provider presents itself to users and on the relationship it establishes with them. From the company's perspective, the relationship is guided by a formal contract, signed by both parties, which defines their rights and duties. The contract establishes what the company offers, such as medical appointments, accredited outpatient clinics and hospitals, and coverage of a limited number of tests, procedures and treatments. The contract also defines the conditions for the delivery of these services. Therefore, fair treatment can be interpreted in relation to the provisions outlined in the contract.

The commercial nature of such service is also anchored in a bureaucratic plan that (among several negative aspects) mediates the interaction between the customer and the company. Very often, the people making decisions or dealing with the customer's anxieties have little or no medical knowledge, making the exchange even more difficult (Cicourel 1999).

However, in a broad sense, the main factor hindering communication between a health service provider and its users may be the conflicting representations of health. For the customer, health is not a utility (equivalent to telephone, gas, or electricity, for example). Health is not an unessential luxury: it is a basic need of all human beings and as such a right of all citizens. Differently from other consumer goods/services, health should not be used as a mechanism contributing towards social inequality, excluding those who cannot pay and contributing to increased distance between those who depend on public services and those who can pay for private services. Provision of service should not be constrained by any type of restriction: access to different types of procedures or number of tests should not be denied due to exaggerated installments that are not compatible with the customer's financial status. In addition, the provision of medical consultations should not follow the logic of the market, which pushes for fast visits to compensate for the low rate paid to health professionals by the health insurance provider. The customer's logic, according to which health is a right, demands that healthcare be guided by neither the clock nor the economy, but rather by the personal needs of the customer. The individual who pays for health insurance wants the best treatment – that which ensures prevention, and, whenever possible, cure from disease.

These conflicting representations of health suggest that, from the viewpoint of the customer, the rules that operate in the evaluation of fair treatment are:

(i)   The customer considers it fair to be treated as some customers – those who can pay privately for the services provided.

(ii) The customer considers it fair to be treated differently from all other customers – his needs may justify the bending of contractual rules.

The combination of these two rules will impact the evaluation of what is fair treatment in procedures and interaction. Along this line, customers will judge treatment as unfair when:

(i) Bureaucratic procedures delay, prevent, or hinder the provision of, or come in the way of service, making the customer feel impotent, that is, not in control of the situation

(ii) The service provider or its representatives are inflexible when responding to requests for exceptions to rules stated in the contract

(iii) Operators, physicians, nurses and other health professionals act in a negligent, indifferent, and even inhumane manner, at least from a perspective according to which all customers are important and deserve all the attention and care they need.

It is based on this perspective of fair treatment that customers choose the identities through which they will expose themselves and define the manner in which these identities will emerge in interaction.

7.5 Customer narratives

According to Goffman (1974:503), "what the individual spends most of his spoken moments doing is providing evidence for the fairness or unfairness of his current situation," presenting to listeners a version of what they have experienced. Goffman calls these versions "replayings," since they are not mere reports of past events, but rather "films" of personal experiences made from a personal point of view. Customer letters often contain reports of past events, or replayings, in Goffman's terms. These letters have many of the elements traditionally attributed to narratives, such as the introduction of characters and settings, character actions, and temporally ordered specific events (cf. Labov 1972c; Mishler 1986). Just like in face-to-face service encounters (Bastos 1997), such narratives have strategic applications (Cook-Gumperz and Gumperz 1997) since the report of unfair experiences functions as an argument to support claims and/or complaints from customers.

Here we focus on two specific narratives that appear in written letters to the insurance company. One formulates a request that presupposes the possibility of fair treatment. The second is a letter of complaint expressing exasperation in the presence of unfair treatment. Both narrators positively project themselves as responsible and sensitive individuals, simultaneously revealing their hypotheses and expectations about what is acceptable in each specific context. Both narratives also strategically unveil the emergence of tragic events, by relying on strong feelings of emotions/affection, and introducing evidence supporting the credibility of the reported facts. As we will see, not only do the two letters present narratives, but they present the typical structure as described by Labov. In each letter, two short initial paragraphs function as "abstracts" of what is to be described; the next paragraphs present "complicating actions," since they contain references to a temporal sequence of events. Also present are "orientation" (the introduction of characters and settings) and "evaluation," statements concerning the emotional atmosphere, which suggest the reason for the narrative. Closings in the two letters function as "codas," marking a departure from the narrative world. The codas are followed by moral considerations and (re)statement of requests or complaints. Finally, both narratives recount "reportable" events: they refer to dramatic (not ordinary) events; their point is to show the tragic unfairness of the situations described. The events and their point justify the complaints and requests conveyed through the letters.

Like most of the customers of our specific health insurance provider, the narrators/signees belong to the lower middle class and have little schooling, which is reflected in their poor mastery of written language and in the reference to financial problems. They also have little familiarity with the genre "letter directed to an organization." Both texts are thus hybrid, in the sense that they mix formal aspects of written language and informal markers of oral narrative.

7.5.1 Supplication

In the first letter to be analyzed, the signee/narrator, whom we will call João Reis,[1] not only requests, but begs that his debts be

---

[1] The names of all people, institutions, and locations involved have been omitted or changed.

pardoned, justifying his supplication with a tragic report of his son's path from hospital to hospital following a car accident and of the consequences of these events for the family. The original Portuguese version of the letter is transcribed at the end of the chapter.

Example 7.1

Bom Jardim, February 10, 1998.
To the President, X Health
  I am writing this letter to inform you of my conditions whereby it will be difficult to pay off the debt which I am being charged by X Health.
  Since the accident when my son stayed 18 days in a deep coma at the Neurology hospital with no sign of life except through the machines, where they generated many expenses for which I had to spend what I didn't have, X Health could not cover all tests, and this made it even more difficult for my financial condition to pay for the tests they made on him. I do not have belongings that I can sell to settle my debt, because all I had I sold to pay for the tests when I was asked, I live in the interior, spent money on transportation, sometimes slept at the hospital's reception area, because I had no money to pay for the ticket to go to the home of my relatives which is far, the little money I had was for food for me and my wife.
  Then he was transferred to another hospital from the same group, still in the ICU, but did not react, did not speak after he came out of the coma, still does not walk today that is three years on the 2nd of February of 1997, and I will have expenses, in the beginning he did not recognize anybody it was when I became really desperate because he was in one of the best hospitals and, I paid for the health insurance and the doctors didn't do anything and even his foot was broken in the accident and the doctors didn't see it purely because of carelessness.
  Now he is in a wheelchair and still without walking, he recovered speech a little, where we understand him a little. My debts are not all settled yet, because I wasn't able to I had to transfer to another state where he is doing physical therapy so that his nerves will not atrophy this was the diagnosis of many doctors from Fortaleza-CE. I cannot lift weight, because I am old, I have back problems, my wife after my son's accident was never healthy again because we cannot pay for a nurse to help us, we are in this situation where it becomes worse every day.
  The amount you are charging, I do not have and will never be able to pay, not even a rich person could pay.
  If possible read and analyze the situation, because I have not had peace since I received the letter from the health plan (X Health).
  My salary as a civil servant is not enough to pay the debt, because I haven't had a raise in three years and some months. If possible help me.
  With sincere thanks, Member: João Reis

João Reis's narrative is organized around the accident and treatment of his son, yet it is also a replaying of his personal experience as the father of a sick individual and member/payer of the health insurance plan. In addition to placing himself in the role of father of the individual who suffered an accident (*since the accident when my son stayed 18 days in a deep coma*), he describes himself as poor (*I had no money to pay for the ticket; I do not have belongings that I can sell*), old (*I am old*), physically hampered (*I have back problems*), and unable to stay close to his son (*I live in the interior*). Note that Mr. Reis plays the role of a traditional father, being the family member in charge of supporting the family. This role, as well as the affiliation to the social categories listed above, places him among the group of less privileged members of society, which influences the construction of his suffering. By making use of indirectness, however, Mr. Reis also introduces in his report attributes that are socially accepted as being positive (cf. Goffman 1967b). For example, he leads the reader to infer that he is a dedicated father (*I slept at the hospital's reception*), responsible, honorable (*I paid for the health insurance*), generous (*all I had I sold*), and humble (*if possible help me*). These roles, affiliations and attributes shape the identity of the narrator as somebody who deserves compassion, given both his social status and his moral integrity.

Mr. Reis, who projects himself as *poor but honorable*, is faced with a difficult, undeniably tragic, personal situation. From his perspective, in their fight for the recovery of their son, he and his family are facing opposition from both the health insurance provider, who takes away *his peace* with letters requesting payment, and from hospitals and physicians *who didn't do anything* and did not see his son's broken foot *purely because of carelessness*.

Identifying antagonists and opposers is one of the elements in the construction of identity in terms of broader social categories since by establishing binary categories, it provides an "us vs. them" relationship with other social groups. That which is described as different, "the other," is excluded, depreciated, equated with negativeness. In the discourse of racism and discrimination, for example, the other is the black individual vis-à-vis the white individual, or women vis-à-vis men (Hall 1996: 109–111). Similarly, presentations of self and constructions of a positive image are frequently carried out parallel to negative presentations of the other (Sarangi and Roberts 1999: 69; Bastos 2002; and Moita-Lopes, this volume). However, it is important to observe that this resource is not over-used by the narrator: there are only the two mentions cited above. Although this narrator explicitly aligns himself with his family and occupation, he does not emphasize the exclusion and decrying of others.

The text's emotional load is constructed, above all, through the telling of the situation being described: the accident which left Mr. Reis' son bound to a wheelchair, speaking with difficulty after three years of treatment at different hospitals in different towns. The sequencing/ordering of facts, which follows a crescendo of tragic elements, associating the son's treatment stages with the degradation of the family's finances, provides the dimension of suffering, "evaluating," in Labov's terms, the narrated events. Thus, the evaluation is carried out mostly indirectly, or, to use Labov's terminology, in an "embedded" manner: the narrator does not suspend the narrative flow to convey emotions, but from this very flow we are able to apprehend sensations such as sadness, concern with the son and wife, anxiety resulting from the increasing debt, and disappointment with hospitals and physicians.

In addition to the ordering of events, the contextualization of facts by the narrator – achieved by creating images or describing the scenario in which the events take place (cf. Tannen 1989) – also conveys embedded evaluation. These images are created through the introduction of details such as having slept at the *hospital's reception* since the relatives' home was too far; a back problem that prevents the narrator from carrying weight; the *wife who after the accident was never healthy again*. Thus the narrator conveys feelings of deprivation and discomfort that compose a scene of suffering.

There is only one direct reference to the emotion experienced, that is, there is only one moment of explicit evaluation. In the third paragraph, the narrator states that his son *did not recognize anyone* and that it was when he *became really desperate because he was in one of the best hospitals and* he *paid for the health insurance and the doctors didn't do anything*. This is the only direct reference to an emotion on the part of the narrator – despair – and it appears exactly at the point in which Mr. Reis associates the severity of his son's condition with the increasing expenses and the carelessness of physicians. The term *desperate* seems to encompass all the other negative emotions experienced by the narrator.

In parallel with the expression of his despair, Mr. Reis also provides the reader with evidence to support the credibility of the facts to which he is referring. Such evidence is represented by temporally ordered details included in the report, for example, by the citing of the names of hospitals and towns (*Neurology Hospital, ICU/ another hospital, Fortaleza*), the use of medical terms (*deep coma, nerve atrophy, physical therapy*) and reference to specific periods and dates (*18 days in a deep coma, three years on the 2nd of February 1997*). These resources are used towards the construction of the narrator's suffering, which includes physical (pain, discomfort, deprivation) and psychological sensations (despair). This suffering depicts the situation lived by Mr. Reis as unjust, since he presents himself as a dignified, responsible, sensitive man. The injustice of the situation authorizes Mr. Reis to beg for his debt to be pardoned, as a form of fair treatment by the company in view of his personal needs.

7.5.2 Resentment

In the second letter to be analyzed, the signee/narrator, whom we call Vera Silva, writes to X Health to complain about the medical care provided to her during a colonoscopy. Vera Silva's letter is also structured as a narrative.

Example 7.2

São Paulo Sept/7/98
  Dear Physician and Auditor
  I would like you to clarify what the *correct* procedure is for a colonoscopy.
  I have iron deficiency (xx), and my hematologist (Dr. X) asked me to see a proctologist. I was first examined by Dr. XY – Hospital X – Downtown. He asked me to have a colonoscopy and since I was there I scheduled it with the secretary. When I arrived at work, I called a different location and realized the procedure was different.
  Clinic Z only schedules appointments personally because of the necessary orientations, and the exam is done only under "GENERAL ANESTHESIA!!!".
  Since I didn't have a check to pay for the anesthesia, I looked for a different location that would not delay me that much. But before scheduling I called X Health and asked about the exam and the person

who answered my call told me that each place does something different, but that all use "almost" the whole procedure.

I decided to do it at Hospital X because they had openings on the day when I could get off early from work, or even miss work if that was necessary.

Clinic Z was out of the way because I work in Morumbi, and I wasn't able to go there just to schedule the appointment, and besides there was the check. I prepared myself during three days, I was started on the serum at 9:00, had to drink an awful liquid that looked like acid, but that was alright! After 2:30 pm I was taken to the examination room.

The nurse stuck a tube through my nose as if I was a "rag doll." She gave me a sedative but it had no effect. Dr. XZ did not wait until I fell asleep and did the exam anyway!

I asked her to wait for the effect of the sedative or to give me more, but *she didn't give me an answer!* At that moment, I wanted to die! I screamed, cried, begged for the love of God, but nothing helped.

The nurse held me so that I would not shake she saw my despair but didn't do anything either. When I got to the recovery area, another nurse asked why I was awake already! She thought it was strange but didn't do *anything*! I called the doctor and she told me that she had given me the necessary dose and that she couldn't have given me more.

I hated Dr. XZ's behavior and I would like X Health to act on that.

I called several places and all were appalled with the doctor's behavior. I know that the Regional Council of Medicine hides their professionals under their cover, but I will not be silent in the presence of such brutality! I am sure that not even an animal should be treated like that. Is she human? Of course not!!! Was her oath during graduation legal? Was it from the heart?

I thank X Health in advance, which has acted with correction and helped its members as best as it can.

Vera Silva

In contrast to Mr. Reis, Ms. Silva is herself the patient receiving care through the health insurance plan. She is the protagonist of the narrative of suffering, in the sense that she is at the same time the enrolled member and the individual being mistreated by the health-care team. She places herself in the role of customer. Note that Silva presents herself as a person who has an *iron deficiency* and who has a hematologist; however, she does not mention a "disease" or "health problems."

Also differently from Mr. Reis, Ms. Silva does not explicitly mention affiliations to social categories such as age group, socio-economic class, or family role. She does, however, refer to her work. She positions herself as a conscientious and responsible worker, choosing the day and location for the procedure according to her work schedule. These qualities help create a positive image, just like her ability to reason objectively, revealed at various moments in the report. She builds cause/effect relationships at several points in the text, comparing procedures and perceiving differences (*I called a different location and realized the procedure was different*), showing that her decisions are always based on concrete and objective reasons and motivations (*Since I didn't have a check. . . I looked for a different location*). In addition, by sending a complaint letter that exposes all her resentment and revolt at her unfair suffering, she presents herself as a courageous and determined person, who is capable of protesting, denouncing, and claiming rights. Thus, Ms. Silva constructs herself as a responsible professional who acts rationally.

In sharp contrast with Ms. Silva's objective and rational presentation of herself as a customer and a professional stands her emotional recount of the clinical exam she underwent. Considering emotion (or affect) as a social construct (Lutz and Abu-Lugod 1990) which refers, in general, to feelings, attitudes, and states of mind (Ochs 1989), we examine how it works in Ms. Silva's identity construction. Different discourse devices are used to index emotions, including evaluation (in the Labovian sense) of the reported events through images, reported speech, indirectiveness and irony.

Ms. Silva's despair during the exam procedure is expressed directly: *at that moment I wanted to die! I screamed, cried, begged for the love of God, but nothing helped.* The dimension of the nurse's inability is emphasized through an image (a strong image, despite being a cliché): *the nurse stuck a tube through my nose as if I was a "rag doll."* Her puzzlement concerning the different ways the colonoscopy was carried out is conveyed indirectly: *I realized the procedure was different. . . each place does something different, but all use "almost" the whole procedure.* There are several occurrences of reported (indirect) speech: *the other nurse asked me why I was awake already; I called several places and all were appalled with the doctor's behavior.* Not only do these utterances function to create a dramatic atmosphere, with scenes and speaking characters: they also function as evidence of the veracity and accuracy of the reported events.

The evaluative resources described above also function as strategies of involvement (Tannen 1989), creating emotional bonds between the participants of the communicative situation. By emotionally replaying her physical and psychological suffering, the narrator touches the reader, creating a favorable atmosphere for understanding and sympathizing with her indignant complaint.

The presence of emotions in discourse has also been analyzed as a marker of gender.[2] Although not explicitly affiliating herself to the social category "woman," the narrator performs her femininity by emphasizing affection, both when reporting her suffering and during the closing of her narrative, when she pronounces her moral judgment concerning the physician who performed the colonoscopy: *I am sure that not even an animal should be treated like that. Is she human? Of course not!!! Was her oath during graduation legal? Was it from her heart?* Whereas Mr. Reis makes only one direct reference to his despair, Ms. Silva's narrative is more explicitly emotional, thus revealing her different ways of acting out suffering.

Although we have focused thus far on the differences between Ms. Silva's and Mr. Reis's narratives and identity strategies, there are also similarities. Like Mr. Reis, Ms. Silva builds a positive image of herself, while at the same time discrediting the image of others, in this case the physician and nurses in charge of the procedure she underwent. The defamation of the other, however, is stronger in Ms. Silva's letter than in that written by Mr. Reis. Although there are differences regarding their affiliation to social groups, both narrators position themselves as workers. Such insertion, however, is carried out differently: Mr. Reis takes on the role of civil servant to justify his low salary, and Ms. Silva presents herself as a responsible professional. Finally, while Silva aligns herself with the company at the end of the letter by praising it (*I thank X Health in advance, which has acted with correction and helped its members as best as it can*), Reis does not seek such alignment: he only thanks and begs. More than the hospitals and physicians who provided care for his son, the opposing 'other' to him seems to be the company itself, which unfairly (to him) requests that he settle his debt.

---

[2] For discussion of the complex theme of the relationship between emotion and gender, see Lupton (1998).

In sum, the letters by João Reis and Vera Silva have been constructed by people whose personal dimensions and identities are
those made relevant through their narratives. Although each letter
was constructed by a different individual with his/her own personal
style, both of the narratives of suffering have the same objective:

(i)   To construct the customer as a person, for whom the main
      element of appeal is to another person, who is receiving the
      letter
(ii) To build an identity as a victim (but not a worthless person),
      based on experiences of physical or psychological suffering
(iii) To legitimate the needs of the customer as an argument for the
      fulfillment of a request or complaint
(iv) To elicit solidarity

The letters/narratives disclose human beings who are looking for
the solidarity of other human beings – based on the principle that
all have the right to overcome suffering and all have the right to
receive dignified care.

7.6 The responses elicited by the narratives

The letters written by João Reis and Vera Silva are directed to
persons, the "President of X Health" and "Physician and Auditor,"
respectively. Reis addresses the President (*I am writing to inform
you; if possible read and analyze the situation*), referring to
X Health as a separate entity (*X Health could not cover all exams;
I received a letter from the health plan*). Silva also opens her letter
by addressing a person – the physician and auditor (*I would like
you to clarify what the correct procedure is*) – but she closes by
addressing the organization (*I would like X Health to act on that;
I thank X Health, which has acted with correction and helped its
members*). By addressing specific people in their letters, Reis and
Silva assume that within an organization there will always be
people who can be sensitized to human suffering, especially when
that suffering is related to their right to receive dignified care.

The narratives in the letters, however, do not elicit the expected
response: the participant "organization" does not show itself as a
person; nor does it view Reis and Silva in their identity as persons.
Rather, the organization views them as customers. The company

ignores the personal accounts, the problems and feelings expressed in the narratives.

7.6.1 Response to the letter of supplication

Example 7.3

25 February 1998
Mr.
João Reis
Rua José Viana 317 – Santa Cruz
Bom Jardim - CE
Dear Mr. Reis,
We have received your letter dated February 10, 1998, reporting the problems you have been experiencing since your son's accident.
On this matter, we inform you that you are paying for a Health Loan.
Your dependent, XX, on suffering an accident on PE-96, was driving without a license, a fact confirmed by yourself on the declaration dated February 02, 1995, which you signed and sent to our Regional Office in Ceará.
To drive on a public road without a driver's license is an illicit act which is against the law.
As you know, item R in provision 25 of X Health's Rules and Regulations states that such situations are not covered by the plan. Therefore, X Health would not be obliged to cover the admission. However, since the patient's life was in danger, we chose to do that, provided you would reimburse to X Health the amount paid. You agreed to this and signed a "Term of Responsibility."
In our correspondence X-X-X/98, we inform you that the total expenses amount to R\$ 79,314.89 and that at this point you are only paying for part of your debt, equivalent to R\$ 2,800.00, and that in 50 installments. The installments were calculated taking into consideration your co-payment, so that the amount can be deducted from your paycheck.
Please contact our Customer Support Center at 0800-xx-xxxx – Toll Free if you require further information.
Sincerely,
Madalena Ferreira,
Supervisor, Customer Support Center

In the response to the letter of supplication, the customer's narrative is framed as a "problems report" *(your letter. . . reporting the problems you have been experiencing)*, without any reference to the impact of the suffering caused by these problems. There is no sign of solidarity with the pain experienced by the customer. The identity of the "organization" emerges in the objective manner of dealing with the problem. A review of all the facts serves to remind the customer of the responsibility he undertook and to uncover the illegitimacy of the request based on the contract's provisions. The representation of health as a business deal agreed upon by both parties therefore justifies the request for settlement of the debt as fair treatment. More than that, such a representation reinforces the evaluation of fairness by seemingly sharing with the customer the representation of health as a right: since *the patient's life was in danger*, the company *chose to cover the admission*. This "human face" put on by the company, however, does not hold, since a pre-condition had been established to warrant the exception: *provided you would reimburse to X Health the amount paid*. The slight bending of contract rules was possible only due to the guarantee provided by the customer's signature on the "Term of Responsibility," which ensured the viability of the deal. Thus, the customer's narrative does not fulfill its intent, because what governs the behavior of the company is the contract, with its clear rules, which are unchangeable and immune to emotion.

Let us turn now to the company's response to Vera Silva's letter.

7.6.2 Response to the letter of complaint

Example 7.4

22 September 1998
   Ms.
   Vera Silva
   Rua Tomás de Albuquerque 218/601 – Oliveiras
   São Paulo – SP
   Dear Ms. Silva,
   In response to your letter dated September 8, 1998, we regret the events that you experienced during your examination.
   We would like to inform you that the Digestive Endoscopy Unit at Hospital X in São Paulo will no longer be accredited by us starting on the 25th of September of 1998.
   Please contact our Customer Support Center at 0800-xx-xxxx – Toll Free if you require further information.
   Sincerely,
   Madalena Ferreira,
   Supervisor, Customer Support Center

In the response to the complaint letter, the report of suffering is renamed with the generic word "events" (*the events that you experienced during your examination*) and the "human face" of the company emerges in the formulaic "we regret."

It should be noted that, whereas the distant treatment given by the company to Reis is understandable, at least in commercial terms, in the case of Silva it is, also in commercial terms, inadequate. The poor care provided to her compromises the image both of the clinic and professionals she is denouncing, as well as of the health insurance provider who accredited them. The company's response, however, reveals that it takes no responsibility for the poor quality of the service provided. Silva's experience in the hospital damages the relationship between service provider and customer, but the company makes no effort to rebuild the social bonds by assuming its responsibility and apologizing for what occurred. The failure is framed as something trivial, and the company's regret is formal and distant. In addition, the company is not concerned with restoring the customer's dignity by associating the disaccreditation of the hospital with the complaint. The customer is merely informed of the fact,[3] without any connections being made between her suffering and the punishment imposed to the hospital.

In sum, we see that not all narratives elicit the compassion or compensation that the reports of suffering and the need for fair treatment justify. The response letters resemble a standard form that can be used to respond to any customer, under any situation. Except for the salutation, the letter can be used to address any person in the identity of customer. The closing is another evidence of this bureaucratic behavior. The information about the toll free number is embedded regardless of its relevance or coherence in the context of the situation. The availability of the company to interact with the customer is only technological and formal. Communicative strategies emphasizing clarity and distance have the following functions:

(i)   To build an impersonal identity for the company
(ii) To treat the user above all as a customer, not a person
(iii) To legitimize what the company understands as fair treatment provided to the customer

---

[3] We were told by company employees that the hospital lost its accreditation due to several other problems.

In the responses to the narratives, what prevails is the identity of a fictional participant – the organization – which is able to prevent people from mixing with business, or, as the saying goes, "friends are friends, business is business."

7.7 Final remarks

At the turn of the millennium, as we all talk about globalization and international identities, we may question the relevance of discussing handwritten letters describing personal tragedies and locally constructed identities. However, in late modernity, the access to technology is still a privilege of certain social strata, and handwritten text is a reality we have to address. Added to that is the fact that these texts are produced to fuel a certain type of interaction which is also specific to late modernity: the interaction between individual and organization. Not only does the issue of identity observed in concrete everyday interactions make evident the complexity of the relationship between communicative behavior and identity, it also highlights the problems and contradictions present in the management of these identities, especially in the type of interaction analyzed here.

One interesting question, for example, is the fact that participants' identities model interaction based on different ideologies about health. The narratives result from a model of person to person interaction (Reis–President; Silva–Physician and Auditor) in which health is treated as a right: all people have access to the resources that ensure the prevention/treatment of disease and to care that respects the dignity of human beings. The objective and formal responses of the company result from a model of non-person to non-person interaction (organization–customer) in which health is treated as business. It is from the identity of authority that the company speaks thus ignoring the needs and feelings of each customer. These models carry different beliefs and values about what is fair treatment, and as a consequence they affect what the participants do in the interaction.

Another interesting point is the way in which the human need for self-approval manifests itself in the context of the interactions analyzed. Our analysis reveals that although the customers try to present themselves as victims, they do not want to be seen as helpless, since they want their right to health and fair treatment to be respected. Yet the identity as "victims" justifies the claim to "fair treatment" – the relief from debt and the punishment of the guilty. The analyses also show that this "micro level unfairness" is associated with a greater unfairness: the providing of health services as a mechanism of social inequality that excludes those who cannot pay, and which does not always ensure dignified treatment to its members. By underscoring different aspects of the construction of identity in the interaction between customer and organization, we hope that our analysis has contributed to a theorization of discourse, narrative and identity that can lead towards a critical approach to interaction in similar settings.

Finally, dealing with real world issues requires that we address the impact that this kind of analysis may have on companies, workers and customers. We are aware of the complexity of the issues we are tackling, but we would like our understanding of what occurs in interactions within the context of organizations to contribute to the creation of more satisfactory working conditions, in which customers and employees can communicate with the least possible suffering. In problematizing the interaction between customer and organization we are proclaiming the need for critical reflection, which includes understanding how the less privileged members of our society present themselves and how the interaction between these individuals and business organizations occurs.

Appendix Letter 7.1

Bom Jardim, 10 de fevereiro de 1998.
    Ao Sr. Presidente XSaúde
    Venho através desta carta lhe colocar a par de todas as minhas condições onde ficará difícil de quitar esta dívida em que estou sendo cobrado da XSaúde.
    Desde o acidente o meu filho onde ele ficou 18 dias em coma profundo no hospital do Neuro sem dar nem um sinal de vida a não ser através dos aparelhos, onde acarretou muitas despesas em que tive que gastar o que não tinha, o plano XSaúde nem todos os exames podia cobrir, era quando dificultou ainda mais as minhas condições financeiras para pagar os exames em que lhe era submetido. Não tenho bens onde posso me desfazer para pagar a dívida, pois o que tinha me desfir de tudo para pagar os exames quando era pedido, moro no interior, gastava com transporte, as vezes, dormia na recepção do hospital, pois não tinha dinheiro para pagar

as passagens de ida e volta para casa dos meus parentes que era muito distante, o pouco dinheiro que tinha era para alimentação minha e de minha esposa.

Depois ele foi transferido para outro hospital onde era do mesmo grupo hospitalar, continuou na UTI, mas o mesmo não reagia, ficou sem falar depois, que saiu do coma, não anda até hoje completou-se três anos no dia 2 de fevereiro de 1998, onde continuo tendo despesas, no início não reconhecia ninguém foi quando meu desespero aumentou, porque estava num dos melhores hospitais e, eu pagava o plano e os médicos não fizeram nada, que até o seu pé foi quebrado no acidente e os médicos não viram por pura displiscência.

Hoje ele estar numa cadeira de roda continua sem andar, recuperou um pouco a fala, onde nós entendemos um pouco. As minhas dívidas não foram todas pagas ainda, porque fiquei sem condições tive que me transferir para outro estado, onde está fazendo a fisioterapia para que os seus nervos não venham a atrofia-rem assim foi o diagnóstico de vários médicos de Fortaleza-CE. Não tenho condições de pegar em peso, pois sou velho, tenho problemas de coluna, a minha esposa depois do acidente do meu filho nunca mais teve saúde, por não Ter condições de pagar uma enfermeira, para nos ajudar, estamos nesta situação em que se agrava a cada dia que passa.

O valor em estam me cobrando, não tenho e nunca terei condições de pagar, nem mesmo uma pessoa rica poderia pagar.

Se possível leia e faça uma analise da situação, pois não tenho tido paz desde que recebi a carta do Plano de Saúde (XSaúde).

O meu salário de funcionário público não dar para pagar a divida, pois não recebo aumento a três anos e alguns meses. Se possivel me ajude.

Agradece Atenciosamente,
O associado: João Reis

Appendix Letter 7.2

São Paulo 7/9/98
Sr. Doutor e Auditor

Gostaria que me esclarecesse o procedimento *correto* para se realizar uma colonescopia.

Tenho uma deficiência de ferro (xx), e meu hematologista (Dr.X) pediu que procurasse um proctologista. Fiz o exame inicial com Dr.XY – Hospital X – Centro. Pediu que eu fizesse a colonescopia, e aproveitando que estava lá marquei com a secretária. Chegando ao trabalho, telefonei para outro estabelecimento, percebi que era diferente o procedimento.

A Clínica Z só marcava pessoalmente devido as orientações necessárias, e o exame era feito somente com "ANESTESIA GERAL!!!".

Como eu não tinha cheque para pagar a anestesia procurei outro estabelecimento que não me atrasasse tanto. Mas antes de marcar liguei para a XSaúde e me informei quanto o exame e a pessoa que me atendeu disse que cada lugar trabalha de um jeito, mas todos usam "quase" todo procedimento.

Resolvi fazer no Hospital X porque tinha horário no dia em que eu podia sair mais cedo do trabalho, ou até mesmo faltar se fosse preciso.

A Clínica Z era contra-mão já que eu trabalho no Morumbi, e não tinha como ir até lá, só para marcar, além do cheque. Preparei-me durante três dias para a clínica fazer o exame, entrei no soro as 9:00, tive que tomar um líquido horrivel, que parecia ácido, mas até ai foi tudo bem! Depois das 14:30hs me levaram para a sala onde foi realizado o exame. A enfermeira enfiou um tubo no meu nariz como se eu fosse um "boneco de pano". Me deu um sedativo mas o mesmo não fez efeito. A Dra XZ não esperou que eu dormissi e mesmo assim fez o exame! Pedi a ela que esperasse o efeito ou que me desse mais sedativo mas ela *nada respondia*! Queria morrer naquela hora! Eu gritava, chorava pedia pelo amor de Deus, mas de nada adiantou.

A enfermeira me segurava pra eu não me sacudir viu meu desespero mas tambem nada fez. Quando eu cheguei na enfermaria, outra enfermeira perguntou-me porque eu já estava acordada! Estranhou mas *nada* fez! Chamei a Dra e ela disse que me deu a dose necessária e que não podia ter me dado mais.

Odiei a atitude da Dra. XZ e gostaria que a XSaúde tomasse as providências.

Liguei pra vários estabelecimentos e todos ficaram pasmos com a atitude da mesma. Sei que a CRM esconde seus profissionais embeixo dos panos, mas não me calarei diante de tal brutalidade! Tenho certeza que nem um animal deveria ser tratado assim. Será que ela é humana? Claro que não!!! Será que ela jurou na sua formatura de forma legal? De coração?

Desde já agradeço a XSaúde que tem sido tão correta e que ajuda seus associados da melhor maneira.

Vera Silva

Appendix Letter 7.3

Sr.
João Reis
Rua José Viana 317 – Santa Cruz
Bom Jardim – CE
Prezado Sr. João,
Recebemos sua correspondência datada de 10 de fevereiro de 1998, relatando os problemas que o senhor tem passado desde o acidente de seu filho.

Sobre o assunto, informamos que o senhor está pagando um Empréstimo Saúde.

Seu dependente, XX ao sofrer o acidente na PE-96, dirigia sem a Carteira de Habilitação, este fato inclusive foi confirmado pelo senhor, na declaração datada de 02/02/95 que assinou e enviou a Gerência Regional da X em Pernambuco.

Conduzir um veículo automotor por via pública, sem habilitação é considerado um ato ilícito e contrário à lei.

Como é de se conhecimento, o regulamento da X Saúde, artigo 25, item R, informa que esses procedimentos não são cobertos pelo convênio. Sendo assim, a X Saúde estaria desobrigada de oferecer cobertura para esta internação. Entretanto, tendo em vista que o paciente corria risco de vida, optamos por custear a internação, desde que posteriormente o senhor devolvesse à XSaúde o valor que pagamos. Essa proposta foi aceita pelo senhor com assinatura de um "Termo de Responsabilidade".

Em nossa correspondência X-X-X/98, informamos que o valor total das despesas chega a R$ 79.314.89 e que no momento o senhor só está pagando apenas parte do débito, no valor de R$ 2.800.00 e ainda assim em 50 prestações. O cálculo das prestações foi feito de forma a obedecer sua margem de consignação, permitindo assim o desconto no contracheque.

Colocamo-nos à disposição para maiores informações através do nosso Centro de Atendimento ao Cliente, telefone no. 0800-xx-xxxx – Discagem Direta Gratuita..

Cordialmente,

Madalena Ferreira,

Supervisora do Centro de Atendimento ao Cliente

Appendix Letter 7.4

22 de setembro de 1998

Sra.

Vera Silva

Rua Tomás de Albuquerque 218/601 – Oliveiras

São Paulo – SP

Prezada Sra. Vera,

Em atenção à sua carta datada de 7/09/98, lamentamos o fato ocorrido com a senhora durante a realização do exame.

Informamos que a Unidade de Endoscopia Digestiva do Hospital X de São Paulo está sendo retirada do nosso cadastro a partir de 25 de setembro de 1998.

Colocamo-nos à disposição para maiores informações através do nosso Centro de Atendimento ao Cliente, telefone 0800–xx-xxxx – Discagem Direta Gratuita.

Cordialmente,

Madalena Ferreira,

Supervisora do Cento de Atendimento ao Cliente

8

The discursive construction of teacher identities in a research interview

Greer C. Johnson

8.1 Introduction

Contemporary approaches view identity as a discursive construction that can be conceptualized further through a number of different data analysis frameworks. In relation to the understanding of teacher identities, the more familiar analytical approach has been generated from different versions of critical discourse analysis. Accordingly, the intention is to explore teacher talk as a space for the articulation and the repression of "voice" (Bloomfield 2000; Britzman 1992; Ellsworth 1989; McWilliam 1994). This can be considered as a "top-down" approach because the voices expressed and withheld – in interview talk, for example – are embedded in the wider ideologies and discourses of power that constitute educational and other cultural institutions. From this perspective identity is represented and shaped through the social and discursive practices that are available to individuals and groups at particular moments. Consequently, as members of particular discourses, individuals are positioned to speak, think and act in particular ways and are able to take up or refuse that positioning (Davies and Harré 1990; Gee 1996).

A much less familiar approach to teacher identity analysis is generated from ethnomethodology and conversation analysis (Baker 1983, 1984; Johnson 2002a, 2002b; Paoletti 2000, 2001, 2002). Using this "bottom-up" approach, researchers have become engaged in conceptualizing identity as "the set of verbal practices through which persons assemble and display who they are while in the presence of, and in interaction with, others" (Hadden and Lester 1978: 331). Widdicombe and Antaki (1998) ask "*whether, when,* and *how* identities are used" (195, emphasis in original) in particular settings, rather than, in the critical discourse analysis tradition, how discursive membership allows them to speak. This social interaction approach takes the local construction of talk between members in a particular social setting, such as the research interview, as the vehicle for the construction of a range of possible multiple identities. Therefore, members display their interpretation of identity discursively in "the *machinery*, the *rules*, the *structures* that produce and constitute that orderliness" (Psathas 1995: 2, emphasis in original), most often during naturally occurring talk and associated activities. The analyst's task is to explicate those displays rather than impose pre-given categories on the data in a "top-down" fashion (Miller 1997) that presupposes that identity is a fixed entity waiting to be uncovered.

This chapter demonstrates how identity is constituted through the language resources called upon by two participants, the interviewer/ researcher and the interviewee/teacher, in a research interview. Specifically, aspects of ethnomethodological and conversational analysis are used to examine a lengthy interview transcript and reveal that initially the identity work is done by the interviewer as she positions the teacher to take up the identities of critically reflective teacher and excellent research participant. "Positioning" is understood to be connected to the ethnomethodological enterprise in so far as speakers might take up agentive positions that in turn can be countered by other speakers.

Further analysis shows how the teacher accepts the interviewer's positioning and explicates it further through her explanation of dilemmas that concern how she and others at the school are affected by parental expectations for good student results when students are not academically able. As the interview proceeds the teacher's identity construction becomes increasingly agentive. She shifts from a dilemmatic discourse to a more positive construction of how her teaching practices help students to fulfill parental expectations, therefore positioning herself as a good practitioner.

8.2 Materials and methods

Each teacher in the study reported on here produced a self-authored and illustrated picture book, the topic of which was self-selected from any aspect of professional activity. Subsequently, the picture book was treated as an artifact to stimulate reflective discussion between the author/teacher and a researcher/interviewer (Johnson 2001, 2002b). The interviews were generated from the overarching research question, "Can a poststructural approach to critical reflection encourage teachers to become more critical?" (see Johnson 2001, 2002a; Smyth 1992). The research agenda, as shown in the interviewer's input in segment one, was to offer teachers an opportunity to engage in and to demonstrate a capacity for critical reflection. The intention was not to impose a question–answer sequence but rather to encourage a turn-by-turn interaction somewhat characteristic of everyday conversation. Essentially, the teachers were asked to describe what they meant by the different pages of their picture books. Later, they were encouraged to challenge their work-related assumptions about teaching and learning represented in the picture book. As interviewer/researcher I had made a decision, prior to beginning any of the interviews for the study, to intervene minimally and to act as a sympathetic and interested listener. However, no matter what the intention, interviews are understood as always co-constructed between the participants so that the reality produced is negotiable (Baker and Johnson 1998; Roulston 2000).

I have selected, from the corpus of 28 audiotaped interviews, four segments of the transcript that display how one teacher (whom I call Desley) and the interviewer work to co-construct good research participant and good teacher identities. The segments show Desley responding to the interviewer's invitation to talk about the aspects of her picture book that depict her teaching life. As she explains during the interview, her book was produced from photographs she took during a typical teaching day at her school. She selected appropriate images and added verbal text. During the interview we hear Desley refer to specific pages of her picture book in order to explain them further. The particular segments selected for detailed analytical treatment display the progressive construction of identity throughout the interview. The transcription of the segments relies largely on the notation symbols devised by Jefferson (1984), as often used by conversation analysts and ethnomethodologists (see Appendix 8.1).

8.3 Getting started: interviewer's formulation of a competent reflective practitioner identity

Desley begins the interview talk by asking the interviewer for guidance: she asks if she should skip over "anything that's not relevant" (line (a)).

Example 8.1

> I (Interviewer)
> D (Desley)
> Date: 26 April 2001

(a) D anything that's not relevant (0.8) about um
(b) I yep that's fine
(c) D when when I when I first got the (0.4) the question (0.4) or the you know the (0.2) the *ta:sk* I wasn't really sure (.) whether I wan whether *you* wanted me to actually look *critically* at my own teaching practice or whether there was something ((clears throat)) that I was missing [so
(d) I   [this is in
(e)   the picture book=
(f) D =this is [in the picture book=
(g) I   [when you did the picture book
(h) D yeah (.) so what I worked on was the assumption (.) *that* (0.6) I would look at (0.2) *my* teaching practices
(i) I yep
(j) D and *analyze them* (0.4) ah (0.2) through through the visuals um (0.4) a as the way I you know I saw things happening
(k) I yes
(l) D and that's that was where I went so it was *mainly* (0.2) the *purpose* of the of writing (0.2) ah doing the book the way I did was to look at my own teaching practice from a critical (0.2) point of view
(m) I yes um ((noise)) okay what some people did I'll just explain the *difference* (0.6) and this is where I say you're sort of (0.4) *different* from them .h they sort of *did* like um (0.2) um a non critical narrative of what happens say in their teaching *day* or so
(n) D mm
(o) I and then the interview was the kind of critique of it (.) whereas *you* have tended to critique already is that
(p) D mm
(q) I is that what you're saying
(r) D mm
(s) I in here
(t) D mm

(u) I   okay well do you want to just sort of (0.2) talk (0.6) about the sort
         of critical perspective that you um documented

(v) D   okay

(w) I   in the picture book and then perhaps go on to answer some of
         these more (.) um like you you picked out the contrasting dis(h)
         cour(h)[ses before

(x) D   [ha ha ha ha

(y) I   um you might like to talk about talk about that in particular

As a means of orienting herself to the research interview the
teacher (Desley) in line (c) presents her dilemma: she was not sure
of the parameters of the picture book task she was set and she is
not sure what the interviewer wants her to talk about now. In lines
(d)–(l) she takes more control of the talk by giving the interviewer
an account of her previous actions – that is, she describes the
critical perspective from which she produced her picture book.
She elaborates on what she understood she was doing as a participant in the author/interviewer's research project and justifies her
decision to look at her teaching through visual representation.
Overall, she portrays herself as doing reflective practice from a
"critical perspective." Opening with the discourse marker "yes um
((noise)) okay" in line (m), the interviewer accepts Desley's explanation (Beach 1993; Schiffrin 1987) and then proceeds to respond
to her dilemma by formulating an identity for Desley by importing
the category "competent critical reflective practitioner" that is
partly described in the teacher's talk about her previous actions.
This manoeuvre is managed through an explanation of difference
produced in the introduction of two contrasting categories. Desley
is explained as being "different from them" (the other teachers in
the study) who did a "non critical narrative (picture book)".

(m) I   yes um ((noise)) okay what some people did I'll just explain the
         difference (0.6) and this is where I say you're sort of (0.4) *different*
         from them .h they sort of *did* like um (0.2) um a non critical
         narrative of what happens say in their teaching *day* or so

The interviewer's use of pausing throughout line (m) helps to
separate the two different categories of teachers as reflective practi-
tioners. Those other teachers in the study who produced "a non
critical narrative [picture book]" are produced as *not* as critically
reflective as Desley, even though both categories are classifiable
within the same membership categorization device (Sacks 1995),

research participants. The continuation of the formulation work by
the interviewer, in lines (o), (q) and (s), then seeks the teacher's
acceptance of the contrasting categories. Desley then attempts to
reassure the interviewer, through back-channeling signals, articulated by repeating the agreement token "mm" in lines (n), (p), (r)
and (t), that her attempts to navigate the conversational topic are
going to be taken up subsequently.

(n)   D   mm
(o)   I   and then the interview was the kind of critique of it (.) whereas
          you have tended to critique already is that

(p)   D   mm
(q)   I   is that what you're saying
(r)   D   mm
(s)   I   in here
(t)   D   mm

    The interviewer's use of the term "contrasting dis(h)cour(h)ses" in
line (w) signals the possibility of more identity work and the specific
direction the talk might take. Overlapping laughter over the words
"contrasting dis(h)cour(h)ses" could mean that the interviewer and
Desley are orienting to a similar understanding of a critical reflection
identity, one that is derived from the poststructural nature of the
research question driving the study ("Can a poststructural approach
to critical reflection encourage teachers to become more critical?").
The interviewer returns to this positioning later in the interview.
    At the start of the interview Desley displays some confusion
about what it was she was asked to do in producing a picture book
and exactly what she is being asked to talk about in the interview.
In effect she asks for the interviewer's guidance about the nature
and direction of their ensuing conversation. The interviewer then
attempts some clarification by suggesting an identity for Desley (in
lines (m)–(w)) and tries to ensure that this is accepted so that the
purpose of the interview for research purposes might be achieved
(in line (y)). This section of the analysis has shown that the teacher
and the interviewer have treated the opening to a research interview
in a rather conventional manner. Given that Desley had engaged in
the production of her picture book alone prior to the interview
and that the talk in Example 8.1 is her first attempt to converse
about the artifact, it is predictable that she will use the opening
stages of the interview to orient to the genre. The local nature of the

talk shows that Desley is also orienting to the researcher's agenda, which is to facilitate and evaluate the construction of critically reflective teacher identities through the study. At this stage, however, although the scene is set for the uptake of a defined identity in the talk, the only observable identity work is being done by the interviewer, who produces specific descriptions of what can and cannot be named as a successful critical reflective practitioner identity.

8.4 The teacher's take-up of a critically reflective practitioner identity

There are a number of interactive options available to Desley at the juncture following Example 8.1. As she begins to reflect on the pages of her picture book once again Desley presents herself in another dilemma: that various external influences acted against her and others achieving ideal teaching goals. This time the dilemmatic discourse is related to her reflections on her teaching practice as opposed to the problem of how to act within the interview.

This dilemma is accounted for in what is apparently a complaining activity in Example 8.2. Here not only Desley but also all teachers at her school are institutionally entangled in practices that are less than ideal. While accounting for this institutional dilemma, Desley is able simultaneously to construct herself as critically reflective and as excellent interviewee in the terms laid out by the researcher/interviewer in Example 8.1.

Example 8.2 demonstrates the production of an account that premises the negative effects of external influences on the type of institutional identities un/available to teachers at Desley's school. However, since the macro talking frame is a research interview where the purpose is to account for and indeed evaluate the reflections represented in the teacher-generated picture book, it would be expected that the teacher's talk would be highly evaluative and possibly extend to complaints related to her institutional context. As Roulston (2000) has found, very few studies refer to the management of complaint stories in the research interview. However, the literature on the use of complaints in everyday naturally occurring talk is useful to my analysis (Drew 1998; Drew and Holt 1988).

Example 8.2

    I (Interviewer)
    D (Desley)
    Date: 26 April 2001

(a) D okay .hh well when I when I started to *do* this I I thought about the *school* (0.2) that I was in (0.2) and (.) *the* (.) um various external influences that were that were continually arising that caused (0.4) my teaching practice to be perhaps the way it is rather than perhaps (0.4) the ideal way

(b) I yes

(c) D um for *best* learning outcomes for students and so I I started off looking at at all of those things and I I thought about the *parents* because it is a *private* ((clears throat)) excuse me it's a private um (0.6) *sma::ll* (0.2) ah indep um ((church)) school in a *rural* (0.2) country area which means that the students that come to the school come from a a parent *family* group that perhaps (0.4) um have not had private education them*selve*s want private education and because they're paying money (0.4) *expect* um these brilliant results *because* they're paying money

(d) I yes

(e) D and that (0.4) has put pressures on on me and and staff at the school because we're being required to *achieve results* and kids are being channeled into perhaps *courses* that they don't really have the *ability*

(f) I oh yes

(g) D to do

(h) I mm

(i) D because of this parental expectation of excellence and I suppose it comes um as I've mentioned here basically from the materialistic world that we live in and if you don't have (0.4) or per*ceived* to have an um a university education or qualification you're NOT going to get a decent job so you're not going to have .h *money* and it's some of those things that *they* themselves haven't had

(j) I yes

(k) D so I suppose in a way it's it's it's the old American dream syndrome
(The interview continues without a break in example 8.3.)

In accounting for her dilemma Desley "complains" in the generic sense about the effects of external influences, even though in turn (a) she refers to "my teaching practice." The external influences are not pinned down. In a domino-effect description "the parents" (turn (c)) are introduced but not blamed for pressuring the teachers. In turn (i), Desley finishes the point she began in turn (e) about the pressures put on staff to have students perform successfully in courses for which they "don't really have the ability." She begins with the phrase "and I suppose" which serves to take away responsibility from the parents. Desley subsequently attributes responsibility for exerting pressure to the wider materialistic society in which "we live" (line (i)). With the use of the pronominal "we," she joins the parents as victims of a materialistic society that might cause them to put pressure on the teachers. In line (c), the parents' expectations are associated with "paying money" for a private education they had not had themselves, whereas in line (i) there is no mention of a parental value-for-money mentality. This perspective has been replaced with the more acceptable justification that the parents act this way so that their children will get a university education and an entrée into appropriate employment. The use of "I suppose" in line (i) could be heard somewhat in the same vein as Sacks (1995) attributes to the phrase "I guess": as an invitation to the listener to take up a position on this assessment. The interviewer's "yes" in the next line (j) displays a sympathetic hearing of the account of her dilemma. The process of justifying the dilemma is then summarised with the teacher's introduction of the figurative expression in line (k), "so I suppose in a way it's it's it's the old American dream syndrome." It has been found that idioms can enhance the legitimacy of the complaint (Drew and Holt 1998) and, in Desley's case, the idiom confirms her stance that it is no one's fault. Desley shows she understands where the parents are coming from even when she intimates that she might not agree with their motives. Rather, it is "parental expectations of excellence" generated from "the materialistic world that we live in" (Example 8.2, line (i)) that "causes pressures on us in the classroom" (Example 8.3, line (b)). In these segments, the dilemma in which Desley and her colleagues find themselves is accounted for as nobody's fault because no one is afforded any sense of agency.

Example 8.3

    I (Interviewer)
    D (Desley)
    Date: 26 April 2001

(a)   I   yes yes

(b)   D   and um so that's caused that causes us to (.) to look um or or causes pressures on us in the classroom the school is a new school so it's trying to *attract* people into the school and it doesn't really mind um who it *attracts*

(c)   I   yes

(d)   D   so therefore as long as they can *pay*

(e)   I   yes

(f)   D   um at this point in time they can come so they want us to have results also

(g)   I   yes

(h)   D   in order to um (0.6) to *promote* the school

(i)   I   yes

(j)   D   so those two (0.6) ah very much impinge on what happens in the in the classroom

(k)   I   yes

(l)   D   and you and that's perhaps not a good thing

(m)   I   mm hm

(n)   D   um

(o)   I   so that's something that you wanted to reflect on

(p)   D   mm

(q)   I   in this

(r)   D   mm

(s)   I   journal (0.3) diary

(t)   D   well it is

(u)   I   whatever you want to [call it

(v)   D   [yeah well it is with with particularly with some of the lower achievers

(w)   I   yes

(x)   D   okay (0.2) um and of course then teaching in the Senior School (0.8) I've also got the other external agency the Board of Secondary School Studies

(y)   I   mm hm mm that's fine

(z)   D   that's fine okay um which (1.0) obviously mandates that students have to have a set (1.0) (.hh) *outcome* and therefore all students have to have *the* (0.2) *same* outcome or they're well not the *same* outcome but they'll all judged by the .h ultimately by the same criteria

(aa)   I   yes

(bb)   D   at the end product .h so:o what you do in the meantime ultimately they've all got to end up (0.6)

(cc)   I   mm

(dd)   D   in the one place

(ee)   I   so it seems to me that you're saying you've got two lots of constraints

Examples 8.2 and 8.3 show that the interviewer listens with minimal interruption or disruption to the account. In particular, the interviewer's use of continuers, mainly in the form of the monosyllabic "yes" after each of the teacher's turns (see especially Example 8.3, lines (a)–(cc)), assures the speaker that she still has the floor and that the listener is interested in her point of view. Goodwin (1986) has shown that in some instances speakers use continuers in conversation ("mm hm," "yes," "right," "OK") to forego taking the floor, and this appears to be the case here. The interviewer's use of the token response "oh yes" in Example 8.2, line (f), as a change of state token (Heritage 1984) could signal that this complaint-like talk is heard as "safe" (Roulston 2000; Sacks 1995). Therefore, she aligns herself with the teacher. After the interviewer's elaborate attempts to position the interviewee (Bamberg 1997b) to be critically reflective, it would seem counter-productive for her to engage in conversational resources that could be heard as unreceptive and impeding the take-up of the critically reflective practitioner identity that the interviewer offered her in the opening stages of the interview (Example 8.1).

In the next segment of the interview (not included in this chapter) Desley continues to reflect on the dilemma she finds herself in regarding the implications for teachers trying to cope with a frequent mismatch between parental expectations and their children's (lack of) academic abilities. Her account can be heard as evidence for the difficult situation that the institution places her in – that is, she points to her inability to achieve an ideal teacher identity under these circumstances. Up to this point she does not pursue this as a personal identity, as the dilemma in which she is immersed is discussed as a general issue for "staff at the school."

8.5 Producing a personal teacher identity through an analogy

The next extract demonstrates how Desley shifts from a complaining or dilemmatic discourse to the production of a much more agentive good teacher identity. She proceeds through a brief positioning with an institutional teacher identity to a much more prolonged claim to a personal identity of good teacher practitioner; in the talk (which does not appear in the transcript) preceding Example 8.4, Desley begins shifting towards a description of teachers' practices in general and therefore orienting to an institutional teacher identity. This orientation is clearly displayed in turn (a) (see Example 8.4). However, in line (l) she moves from the institutional to the personal when she uses an analogy to offer a characterization of what counts as good teaching practice for her. Her claim to this identity is strengthened by her move to seemingly "ignore" the interviewer's preceding attempt to re-position her once again as embracing the critically reflective identity (beginning at line (e) and concluding in line (i)) in much in the same way she does in example 8.1 at the start of the interview. However, in describing her identity as a good teacher in a research interview whose purpose is to facilitate critical reflection, Desley is once again simultaneously taking up the interviewer's identity positioning.

Example 8.4

> I (Interviewer)
> D (Desley)
> Date: 26 April 2001

(a) D   so I've then I then moved on to because we looked at um this (.) idea of of *knowl*edge and I was then starting to think about teaching practice so I've sort of put our lovely tree of knowledge here ((describing page 3 of the picture book)) and talked about yeah well whose knowledge (h)

(b) I   mm(h)mm

(c) D   whose knowledge (h)is this we're about ta to explore now um and and ultimately at the end is there any knowledge (heh) [or has there any any been gained and just there a little bit of a a critical (.) comment about the fact that what we've just talked about how all students don't want to be here

(d) I   [yes

(e) I   I guess what I meant in the beginning with your picture book was that you know how in um literary theory we talk about sort of um some texts present sort of views of the dominant um [members of society and some don't well yours sort of presents ah non dominant views already you know [you're challenging the status quo and now I guess this talk (.) that we're having is um unraveling that challenging a bit more so

(f) D   [mm

(g) D   [mm

(h) D   mm

(i) I   that [(a bit better)

(j)   D   [(heh) okay heh so basically what I've now (0.4) attempted
                to *do* is look at (0.2) how I teach and it's and I've titled it you
                know teaching learning prac ah process ((describing page 4 of the
                picture book))
(k)   I   yeah
(l)   D   and it's basically how I (0.8) how I attack (0.4) like the unit of
                work when I'm going to when I'm going to actually introduce it .h
                and then I've said .hh the overview and I've I've being a little (.)
                you know (0.2) cynical over in the side here saying that after I've
                finished discussing all this I've still only got about twenty per(h)
                cent of the student because the eighty percent have been off with
                the pixies because they haven't been learn=ah listening or or
                whatever um I haven't actually you know turned the right but-
                tons to (0.4) to actually get them in included yet so it's just a
                general (1.2) um giving students an overview of of where they're
                going *trying to* because I I very much believe that (0.6) without a
                definite frame of reference (0.2) students (.) struggle (.) to (.)
                learn
(m)   I   okay
(n)   D   so my analogy is that if you think of a student as (0.2) um (0.2)
                the old the old rotary hoist
(o)   I   mm hm
(p)   D   I often look at that (0.2) um and the student is the pole
(q)   I   yes
(r)   D   the being is the pole and then *from* the time that they (0.4) you
                know are born I suppose that they start to grow (0.2) each little
                experience that they have builds um (0.2) a little *frame*
(s)   I   yep
(t)   D   around them
(u)   I   yeah
(v)   D   and so therefore when they have another one (0.2) they can peg a
                (0.2) *sock* for example
(w)   I   yeah
(x)   D   on their first little (0.2) frame of knowledge
(y)   I   mm hmm
(z)   D   um and as they go (.) all the way through life they their frames of
                reference get
(aa)   (0.6)
(bb)   I   big[ger
(cc)   D   [bigger and bigger
(dd)   I   yeah
(ee)   D   and and the arms that that support those frames of reference
                obviously likened to the poles of th(h)e the rotary hoist allow
                them to hang more and more
(ff)   I   oh that's
(gg)   D   clothes

(hh)	I	yeah
(ii)	D	if you like
(jj)	I	yeah
(kk)	D	on to
(ll)	I	or baggage heheh
(mm)	D	or baggage heh on to *no* knowledge we're talking about here Greer
(nn)	I	heh
(oo)	D	knowledge heh on to their on to their you know *being* so to speak
(pp)	I	yeah
(qq)	D	and (0.6) kids that don't have that frame of reference I think of my old grandma's (0.4) clothesline where she had a prop at one end
(rr)	I	yes
(ss)	D	you know a prop at the other end
(tt)	I	yes
(uu)	D	and (.) the *being* is the first prop but without any frames of reference all they've *got* (0.2) as they *hang* and move through life to their final prop are these (0.2) *isolated*
(vv)	I	yeah
(ww)	D	things you know
(xx)	I	yeah
(yy)	D	so like a whole line of socks (0.2) but none actually connected because they haven't (0.2) gone around in any sort of frame
(zz)	I	yeah
(aaa)	D	and so
(bbb)	I	it's a good metaphor
(ccc)	D	heh
(ddd)	I	it's a good metaphor for teaching and learning isn't it

Implicit in the identity work displayed in line (e) is the inter-viewer's added attribution to Desley as a member of a category of excellent research participant with desirable reflective practices. Line (l) is an important turning point in Desley's interactional production of a professional identity as good teacher. Although she describes at length her teaching practice, she never actually names herself as a good teacher identity. However, her repeated use of the first person and the attribution to herself of appropriate teaching practices (presumably designed to solve some of the dilem-mas set out in the earlier part of the interview) could reasonably be taken to support a claim to a personal identity as a good teacher.

This identity is constituted initially through a description of her plans for optimizing students' learning. As a good teacher, she attributes the following category-bound activities (Baker 1997; Sacks 1995) to herself. She explains in line (l) that she must focus on "the eighty percent [of students who] have been off with the pixies because they haven't been learn-ah listening or or whatever" and she has not, idiomatically, "turned the right buttons to (0.4) to actually get them in included." She describes "giving students an overview of where they're going" by providing them with a "definite frame of reference" without which students "(.) struggle (.) to (.) learn." In each of these activities this teacher is constituted as an active, thoughtful professional who gives generously of her time and professional capabilities so as to optimize student learning.

It has been argued that the process of identifying "is constituted by the practical activities through which people produce verbal 'markers' of who they are and the methods they use to assemble those markers into patterns while in interaction with others" (Hadden and Lester 1978: 335). The good teacher identity is produced in this segment of the talk through Desley's early naming of an analogy, in line (n), through which she describes the student learner as a "rotary clothes hoist" (see Figure 8.1).

I now look to Forceville (1996) and Cameron (1999) for confirmation of the identification and interpretation of metaphoricity and by extension, analogy. The literary tradition poses the following questions in identifying a metaphor:

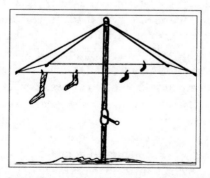

Figure 8.1. A rotary hoist. This appliance became something of a popular domestic icon in Australian backyards from post-World War II onwards.

1. Which of the two terms is the metaphor?
2. Which is the primary subject and which is the secondary subject?
3. Which feature(s) of the secondary subject is/are projected upon the primary subject? (Forceville 1996: 201).

Working within a Labovian perspective of personal narratives, this analogy or metaphor could be seen as an intensifier in that it selects an event in the telling and strengthens it (Labov 1972a). The clothes hoist analogy acts as "a bridge to the 'reality' of the professional or technical world" (Cortazzi and Jin 1999: 149) of teaching and learning for this teacher and her listener. Desley's explicit description of how the two terms "a student" and "the old rotary hoist," or rather "the [central] pole" of the old rotary hoist, relate to each other in terms of category-bound activities confirms her nomination of this segment as an analogy or a metaphor. The analogy also sets up an *"Identity-Rich Puzzle"* (Schenkein 1978: 66). Desley begins to solve this puzzle when she explains further that for a student, each new life experience contributes in building the concentric frames (of reference) of the hoist, on which further experience and knowledge can be "pegged," like socks on a clothes line. The clothes hoist analogy offers the view that the more frames (experience) you have, the more clothes (knowledge) you can peg on them. Desley then reinforces the importance of this analogy for effective teaching and learning practice by using a contrasting metaphor.

"My old grandma's clothesline" (Example 8.4, line (qq)), the linear, more traditional alternative, is used as a symbol for less effective, unconnected methods of (bad) teaching and learning. In this instance Desley has employed an analogy that has facilitated her description of herself as a caring, helpful kind of teacher who tries to do the best for her students in the circumstances. The choice of a domestic metaphor, the rotary clothes hoist, has the potential to negotiate an adjacent identity for the speaker within the domestic sphere. However, from very early on the analogy acts as an intensifier for the production of a personal identity as a good teacher who assists her students to connect their life experiences so as to heighten their knowledge base.

In doing a close reading of the talk-in-interaction, there is evidence in this segment to support the observation that the interviewer co-constructs the good teacher identity with the teacher as the analogy unfolds. As discussed earlier, the teacher proposes the rotary hoist analogy in line (n). The listener's next turn, line (o) signifies recognition of the analogy and she does not seek clarification by way of, for example, request for a repeat (Sacks 1995: 7). The listener/interviewer then follows the analogy through to turn (x) using minimal but various acknowledgment tokens, for example, "mm hm," "yes," "yep," "yeah" and "mm hmm," signalling at the very least that she is still on the teacher's side. The variants of "yes", especially, are strong response tokens of agreement (Gardner 2001: 113). After the 0.6 second pause by Desley (line (aa)), the listener displays even more active agreement by finishing Desley's turn at line (bb). The teacher then displays her agreement to this word through her overlap and repetition (line (cc)). In the extract below, the members work closely together to explicate the analogy.

(z)	D	um and as they go (.) all the way through life they their frames of reference get
(aa)		(0.6)
(bb)	I	big[ger
(cc)	D	[bigger and bigger
(dd)	I	yeah
(ee)	D	and and the arms that that support those frames of reference obviously likened to the poles of th(h)e the rotary hoist allow them to hang more and more
(ff)	I	oh that's
(gg)	D	clothes

The interviewer tries to fill in the gaps in the talk and is quickly overlapped by Desley in line (cc). Again, the two members are working harmoniously to construct a good teacher identity across the analogy nested within the research interview.

At one point in Example 8.4, the interviewer's talk offers to revive an identity (poststructuralist teacher) that was alluded to momentarily and then silenced in Example 8.1, line (w). In Example 8.4, line (ll), the interviewer describes the students' metaphorical clothes/knowledge as (cultural) baggage.

(hh)	I	yeah
(ii)	D	if you like
(jj)	I	yeah
(kk)	D	on to
(ll)	I	or baggage heh heh
(mm)	D	or baggage heh on to *no* knowledge we're talking about here Greer
(nn)	I	heh

This conversational move can be heard as a paired action known as a dispreferred turn shape (Pomerantz 1984). At first Desley shows her agreement with this identity construction, even to the point of following her full repetition of the interviewer's "or baggage" with laughter (line (mm)). However, in the same turn, the teacher repairs her former agreement with a strongly empha-sized "*no*." The interviewer's term "baggage" is related to the same type of English teacher professional identity called up earlier and the teacher rejects it, calling the interviewer by name. This topic is clearly outside the frame of reference of the analogy. Desley then reorientates to her good teacher identity through reference to a contrast description of those students who fail to succeed because "they haven't (0.2) gone around in any sort of frame" (line (yy)).

(yy)	D	so like a whole line of socks (0.2) but none actually connected because they haven't (0.2) gone around in any sort of frame
(zz)	I	yeah
(aaa)	D	and so
(bbb)	I	it's a good metaphor
(ccc)	D	heh
(ddd)	I	it's a good metaphor for teaching and learning isn't it

The interviewer's repeated formulation "it's a good metaphor" in lines (bbb) and (ddd) confirms recognition of the metaphor/ analogy and agreement between the members that these are appropriate analogies with which to produce the good teacher identity. This section has made a further close examination of the research interview talk-in-interaction, this time focusing on the teacher's shift from a complaining or dilemmatic discourse to a more agentive personal identity of herself as a good teacher/cap-able professional.

8.6 Concluding comments

This chapter has demonstrated how a teacher and an interviewer co-construct identities during their discursive interactions. These identities are produced within and across four sequential segments of the research interview. The focus of the analysis of the segments facilitates micro observations on how a teacher and an interviewer manage a range of conversational resources to propose, assume/adopt and extend or reposition identities ranging from the successful research participant as critical reflector to a good teacher identity.

Methodologically, the analytic process highlights how some concepts and practices belonging to ethnomethodology and conversation analysis can usefully inform the discursive identity work that takes place within the research interview. The discussion surrounding Example 8.1 of the talk displays the enactment of the concept that identity work can take place through members' positioning within the talk. In this instance the interviewer primarily positions the interviewee through the assignation of a teacher as excellent reflective practitioner category and the option is taken up by the teacher recipient in the ensuing conversational moves. This treatment of the data highlights the possibility for identity work to be instigated by the talk of others as opposed to the self. By Example 8.3 Desley has gained considerable confidence within the assigned identity as she fills out the details of her dilemma with an account of how she and the other teachers deal with the mismatch between high parental expectations and low student ability. In Example 8.4, a two-part analogy selected by the teacher is shown to act as an intensifier in the production of the good teacher identity. In a sense the teacher positions the interviewer to hear her as a good teacher and the alignment afforded her serves to demonstrate the discursive dexterity with which the two members co-construct identities inside the talk-in-interaction.

Overall, this chapter displays through a bottom-up analytic approach to interview talk that identity is an evolutionary discursive construction. By extension, identities shift and change according to the conversational resources available at particular points in time. Finally, it is possible to take the observations drawn from this understanding of identity (as a construction *within* discourse or talk) and insert those findings into the wider ideological framework within which the teacher is working (Johnson 2002b). Such a step would amount to bridging the two views of identity outlined at the beginning of this chapter.

Appendix 8.1 Transcription conventions

CAPITALS	stressed pitch or volume
emphasis	stressed word or part of word
.h	inbreath (.hhh = a longer inbreath)
(h)	injection of laughter into a word
heh	laughter (the more hehs the longer the laughter)
((turns page))	transcriber's description of non-verbal activity
[	utterances beginning simultaneously
=	talk running on from prior speaker without interval or overlap
::	stretching of sound of the preceding letter (::: more stretching of sound)
(.)	micro-pause (less than one-tenth of a second)
(0.2)	timed gap (in tenths of a second)
-	cut off of prior sound in a word

Becoming a mother after DES: Intensive mothering in spite of it all

Susan E. Bell

You know, I think I'd been thro- through so much with my daughter um, that it just really, the things that happened to me like you could probably throw darts at me and it really wouldn't bother me.

(Hannah Fisher, a DES daughter)

9.1 Introduction

For most of the twentieth century, the dominant North American view of mothering was that one woman – the biological mother – should take almost exclusive responsibility for taking care of children during their formative years, and conversely that children need "constant care and attention from one caretaker, their biological mother" (Glenn 1994: 3). This view is called "the ideology of intensive mothering" by Sharon Hays (1996). It "declares that mothering is exclusive, wholly child centered, emotionally involving, and time-consuming. The mother portrayed in this ideology is devoted to the care of others" and self-sacrificing (Arendell 2000: 1194). An intensive mother is held and holds herself accountable for keeping her children fed and housed and "for shaping the kinds of adults these children will become" (Hays 1996: 108). Intensive mothering ideology is dominated by and exhibits a logic of family and private life that requires a moral commitment to "relationships grounded in affection and mutual obligations" (Hays 1996: 152). Among other things, intensive mothering ideology assumes a seamless progression from conception to birth. However, some women's abilities to manage this trajectory is fragile and unpredictable; an easy pregnancy followed by the birth of a healthy infant cannot always be assumed. Indeed, the medicalization of pregnancy and childbirth in the early twentieth century US was in part a response to (and a contributor to the discourses of) this fragility and uncertainty (Layne 2003).

In this chapter I look at the story-worlds and identities produced by a woman I call Hannah Fisher in her narratives about becoming and being a mother. Hannah had difficulty becoming a mother. Her first child was born a month prematurely, and had severe health problems. Subsequently, she had three miscarriages and two more children. My analysis considers how Hannah Fisher positions herself in relation to the dominant ideology of intensive mothering, as well as how she produces herself as a mother.

Hannah Fisher was exposed prenatally to DES (diethylstilbestrol); her mother took DES when she was pregnant with Hannah to prevent having a miscarriage. DES is a synthetic estrogen that was prescribed in the US to prevent miscarriage from the 1940s to the 1970s, when it was banned for use in pregnancy by the US Food and Drug Administration. As it turns out, DES does not prevent miscarriage but it does cause cancer, reproductive tract differences, and fertility problems in DES daughters.[1] I interviewed Hannah in the early 1980s for my study of the social and emotional consequences for DES daughters of living with these negative effects, and well as with risk and medical uncertainty as a result of their prenatal exposure to DES (see Bell 1988, 1999).[2]

In my interpretation of Hannah's mothering experiences, I weave together the early 1970s when Hannah gave birth to her first child (the events Hannah tells about); the early 1980s when

---

[1] The relative risk of reproductive tract cancer – vaginal and cervical clear cell adenocarcinoma – for the roughly 2 million US DES daughters is very high, but the absolute risk is rare. The incidence has been estimated to be 1 in 1000 DES-exposed women (Swan 2000: 795). As of 1997, 680 women in the US had been registered with DES-related cancer and 80 percent of them were still living (http://www.descancer.org/des.html).

[2] Of the 20 women, four had children at the time I interviewed them. Two of them were DES cancer daughters and had adopted children; a third was a DES daughter who had given birth to a baby two months before I interviewed her; Hannah was the other DES daughter who had children. For the DES cancer daughters mothering cannot be disentangled from their experiences of cancer; the other mother had worried about the possibility of trouble conceiving and carrying a pregnancy to term but had not had any difficulties.

I interviewed Hannah (the storytelling interactions and context); and 2003 when I interpret the interview narratives. Disentangling and then weaving together these time periods emphasizes a dynamic conception of identity and enables me to explore how changing medical understandings of the effects of DES on pregnancy in DES daughters affected Hannah's mothering experiences as well as our interview and my interpretation. I can also identify images and conventions of mothering that Hannah drew upon to present and interpret her experiences, and explore my responses to them in the interview. Hannah's mothering identities are produced in interview narratives, performed in particular places and times to particular audiences; and constantly rewritten (see Mishler 1999).

I use narrative analysis because it provides a systematic way of understanding how people make events in their lives meaningful, as well as how they engage in the ongoing construction of their identities. As Riessman (2002: 705) put it recently, "Personal narratives are, at core, meaning-making units of discourse. They are of interest precisely because narrators interpret the past in stories rather than reproduce the past as it was." Narratives draw upon culturally shared images and conventions to present and interpret experiences, as well as to draw connections between individual and society (Hyden 1997; Mattingly and Garro 1994). In a narrative, one action is consequential for the next; the narrative's sequence is held together with a "plot," and the "plot" is organized temporally and/or spatially (Riessman 2002: 698).

A growing number of scholars suggest that the "form of stories (their textual structure), the content of our stories (what we tell about) and our storytelling behavior (how we tell our stories) are all sensitive indices" of our personal, social, and cultural identities (Schiffrin 1996: 170). Mishler (1999: 20) argues that narratives are performances in which individuals "speak" their identities.[3] This way of connecting narrative and identity challenges prevailing assumptions about the self.

---

[3] Elsewhere I have explored how narratives are produced visually as well as textually (Bell 2002, 2004). Riessman (2003: 6) argues that "much remains unspoken, inferred, shown and performed in gesture, association, and action. What narrators show, without language, [also] constitutes ways of making claims about the self."

The predominant (reigning) conception of the modern 'self' defines it as individualistic, unitary, rational, and active (Seidman 1994). This conception assumes that an individual becomes a "stabilized entity", one that "is generally imbued with a structure of self-descriptions (concepts, schemata, prototypes) that remains stabilized until subjected to external influences from the social surroundings" (Gergen and Gergen 1997: 162). It ignores the capacity of individuals to shape the configuration of this structure (Gergen and Gergen 1997: 162) as well as "the multiple, sometimes fractious sources of social identity constituted by one's gender, race, class, ethnicity, sexual orientation, and so forth" (Meyers 1997: 2).

Today, scholars challenge the modern conception of identity. For example, Elliot Mishler (1999: 8) argues that identity is a "collective term referring to the dynamic organization of sub-identities that might conflict with or align with each other." He prefers the notion of "formation" rather than "development" and emphasizes "process" over "state." In his view, identity consists of disjunctions, discontinuities, contingencies, and transitions; he uses the metaphor of a double arrow to capture the sense in which "present (and future) anticipations shape the past as well as the reverse" (Mishler 1999: 2; see also this volume). In its most extreme version, some scholars "reject the view that a 'life' is anything in itself and . . . believe that it is all in the constructing, in the text, or the text making" (Bruner 2001: 27).

Disenchantment with modern views of the self has led some scholars to narrative, because it emphasizes the active, self-shaping quality of human thought and the power of stories to create and refashion personal identity (Hinchman and Hinchman 1997: xiv). Jens Brockmeier and Donal Carbaugh (2001: 15) argue "that narrative proves to be a supremely appropriate means for the exploration of the self or, more precisely, the construction of selves in cultural contexts of time and space." As Freeman (2001: 287) writes, "simply put, 'my story' can never be wholly mine, alone, because I define and articulate my existence with and among others, through the various narrative models – including literary genres, plot structures, metaphoric themes, and so on – my culture provides." But at the same time, "there is a good measure of narrative freedom even amidst the constraints that are inevitably posed by culture" (287).[4] And in story-worlds made up by individuals, interactions between characters "provide a framework within which relationships – and hence the interacting self and other comprising that relationship – can be situated, displayed, and evaluated" (Schiffrin 2000: 1).

9.2 I've had fifty percent fetal loss

I interviewed Hannah Fisher in December 1982, about ten years after she had become a mother. When I first telephoned her late one Friday afternoon to describe my study and to arrange an interview, she was crisp and businesslike. She said that she had nine hours a week to herself, and that I would have to come during that time or she would never be able to talk for an hour and a half, since her preschool-age son would disrupt us. We were able to arrange two interviews, each lasting for about 1½ hours, the second interview about two weeks after the first.

Hannah Fisher lived in a middle- to upper-middle-class neighborhood just outside city limits in the Northeastern US, tucked in behind a very wealthy-looking neighborhood, with tree-lined streets, and mansions set back from the road. She and her husband were having their house renovated. The air smelled of paint, and the furniture in the house was in disarray. When I arrived, she led me through the house, through a room with photographs of her family covering one wall, apologizing for the state of the house, and on back to the kitchen, which had freshly painted white walls. We sat around a white table on two of the five chairs drawn up to it.

Hannah's immersion in intensive mothering was reflected in our initial telephone conversation and again at the start of the interview, when she turned to me after she had signed the informed consent form but before I asked her the first question and said, laughing, "10 after 10 okay we're on I've been moving since 6:30 s'nice to sit down what's next." She used precise amounts of time to tell me how time consuming mothering is for her. She had been moving for three hours, so busy that she had not been able to sit

---

[4] Mishler (1999: 51) puts it thus: "culture is not a template from which lives are stamped out but parallels the infinite variety of sentences formed from a limited grammar."

down and take a break until our interview. In the initial telephone conversation she had told me she had only nine hours a week to herself. Her laughing comment at the start of the interview reminded me of her family's demands on her time, as did the family photographs and the three empty chairs at the table where we sat. Hannah's laughter along with the comment was a friendly invitation to use her free time, and our time together, efficiently. Perhaps it was also "entry talk" to the interview frame.

I (SB) began the interview with a question, and she (HF) answered me with a story.[5]

Example 9.1

(a)	SB	uh the way I usually start is to ask
(b)	/HF	mhm/
(c)	SB	how you found out you were a DES daughter
(d)		and what that was like
(e)	HF	okay, uh my first child was born [in the early 1970s]
(f)		she was born with multiple abnormalities . . .
(g)		and she was one month premature
(h)		she wasn't expected to live
(i)		it was a terrible
(j)		it was the worst time of my life (p)

This is the abstract of Hannah Fisher's first interview narrative and it is deeply ironic. Hannah gave birth but prematurely. She gave birth to a baby girl – whom I call Grace – with multiple abnormalities. Her daughter's birth initiated the worst time of Hannah's life. For her, becoming a mother represented a loss of innocence (Layne

---

[5] The transcript is a translation of speech into text, and in this respect it is an interpretive practice. I preserve false starts, hesitations, and repetitions, and give each clause a separate (numbered) line. Brief pauses are indicated by a comma, ","; pauses lasting longer than one or two seconds are indicated by "p". Nonverbal sounds are given in parentheses "(inhale)." Words or syllables of words that are drawn out are indicated with double letters "aand"; emphasis on one syllable of a word is indicated with italics: When pitch is higher at the end of a word it is marked with a question mark "hysteroscopy?" In some places I have been unable to hear words clearly ("unclear-4" words). To preserve anonymity, I have used pseudonyms ("Hannah Fisher"); removed some identifying details such as the names of people and places "[a hospital]"; and changed some dates and ages.

2003, chapter 8). In this first story Hannah introduces characters, indicates that becoming a mother and learning about DES are connected for her, and that becoming a mother ironically initiated the worst time of her life. As the answer to my first question, telling a story also begins to establish a mutual understanding of how we will produce knowledge together.

Hannah Fisher continued, in her first story, to tell me that following Grace's birth, when Grace was still living in the hospital, her mother, father, husband and Hannah "really went through hell." During this hell, Hannah's mother asked, "I wonder if it was the DES I took that is the reason for this." Hannah Fisher soon asked this question of her gynecologist, who was "new at the time 'cause [she] had just kind of fired" her previous gynecologist "because of what happened." She ended the first story,

Example 9.2

(a) HF   Anyway I said to my new gynecologist (tch)
(b)   I think um you know my mother took DES
(c)   And that's how it all started.

Hannah enlists me in the performance of her story, when she says, "you know" ("you know my mother took DES") (Schiffrin 1987). Hannah repeats the adjective "new," emphasizing the dramatic switch from one gynecologist to the other. The word "fired" engages a consumerist discourse of employer (Hannah) and employee (gynecologist) and of employee incompetence (he had done a bad job, so she had fired him). Hannah's use of reported speech is a "performance feature"; she takes her experience and makes it into the experience of her audience (Langellier 2001: 150). The use of reported speech also connects the telling of this story to the events in the past that the story tells (Langellier 2001).

Hannah's new gynecologist responded to her by doing a complete DES investigation. During the early 1970s, when Grace was born, medical experts had connected prenatal DES exposure to reproductive tract cancer in DES daughters, and had also noted "benign epithelial changes of the vagina and cervix, as well as certain cervical and vaginal structural anomalies" in some DES daughters (US Department of Health, Education and Welfare 1978: 31). The extent to which these findings represented the frequency of such anomalies in all DES daughters was unclear. In addition, their effect on pregnancy and delivery was also unclear, because "normal pregnancy and delivery can occur in the presence of such anomalies" (US Department of Health, Education and Welfare 1978: 7–8). In the early 1970s, Hannah's mother's question ("I wonder if it was the DES I took that is the reason for this") could not be answered with any degree of certainty. The reasons for Grace's premature birth, and the effects of DES on Hannah's body, however, could be explored more fully.

Grace lived in the hospital for two months, was subsequently hospitalized ten times in ten years, and had two surgeries and five invasive medical tests. When Grace was a toddler, Hannah Fisher unexpectedly became pregnant again, but had a miscarriage in the second trimester of her pregnancy. She became pregnant again as soon as she could, and after an easy pregnancy she gave birth to a healthy daughter. After two more miscarriages, she gave birth to a healthy baby boy. As she put it to me during the interview, "I've had fifty percent fetal loss."

9.3 I guess I just underreacted to everything

The interview narrative from Hannah that I work with here emerged in answer to another question I asked her. She had just described what had happened between the time of her first and last child's births, including the "fifty percent fetal loss." I wondered how she had handled these experiences, so I asked her. We then collaborated to produce a narrative that embodied and performed what she did and why, how she felt, and what she learned. My analysis of the narrative continues a process that began when we met, during which we drew upon our "culturally shared stock of knowledge" (Mishler 1999: 110) and our mutual, locally situated knowledges achieved during the interview in which "we continually made and remade the sense of what we were saying and hearing" (Mishler 1999: 95).

Hannah's story began as part of a general discussion about her experiences in relation to DES. For her, the overriding theme of the experience was pregnancy and miscarriage, and mothering a child with severe health problems. She did not experience a seamless progression from conception to birth, or a healthy infant, in contrast to assumptions embedded in the ideology of intensive mothering. My question to her was "how did you, how did you get, how did you, *han*dle it during those *years* though?" (lines (a)–(c)). The "it" in my question refers to the premature birth of a very sick daughter, several years of going back and forth to the hospital with this child who had numerous life and death situations, and a second-trimester miscarriage. These terrible things did not fit with the future she had imagined since she was a child. Hannah had always wanted to be a mother, and after marrying and being happily married, she had been on her way to becoming the mother she imagined, until Grace was born.[6]

My question asks Hannah Fisher for two sorts of information. In one sense the word "handle" concerns actions (what did you do to handle or manage things) and in the other concerns emotions (how did you feel about the events happening to you, how did you handle your feelings). Hannah Fisher gave answers to both in her narrative:

Example 9.3

(a)	SB	how did you
(b)		how did you get
(c)		how did you, *han*dle it during those *years* though
(d)	HF	well what happened was (unclear-4)
(e)		well I'll tell you what happened um,
(f)		I had my miscarriage on [New Year's eve],
(g)		as soon as I could
(h)		I became pregnant again,
(i)		you know that's the best way to get over having a miscarriage, (inhale)
(j)		aand I had a hyst'
(k)		but after right after I had that
(l)		I had a hyste*ro*scopy?
(m)		that's or a *hyste*rogram?
(n)		something like that
(o)		to see if they could figure out why
(p)		I had the miscarriage
(q)		and it's something tha' I guess they do do to DES daughters, (inhale)
(r)		gives you a clearer picture of your uterus (inhale)

[6] In her study of pregnancy loss, Linda Layne writes that "a pregnancy that ends in miscarriage, stillbirth, or infant death . . . lends itself to ironic treatment, for the outcome is certainly worse, far worse, than what the would-be parents anticipated" (Layne, 2003: 174).

(s)		they wanted to see if
(t)		I had a double *ute*rus
(u)		or if it was you know "*T*" shaped
(v)		that I couldn't *ca*rry a *ba*by (inhale),
(w)		(voice getting softer) you know cause my my first daughter was prema*ture*
(x)		and now this baby, which appeared normal
(y)		um uh miscarried (tch),
(z)		(voice gets louder again) they found that
(aa)		I did have an unusual shaped uterus
(bb)		but it wasn't se*ve*rely malformed,
(cc)	SB	mmm
(dd)	HF	it wasn't, "T" shaped,
(ee)	SB	mhm
(ff)	HF	you know that I *should* be able to carry, a baby to term, (inhale)
(gg)		and, um (p)
(hh)		in between this time
(ii)		I also had adenosiss
(jj)		somewhere between Grace and the miscarriage
(kk)	SB	mhm
(ll)	HF	you know that was confirmed,
(mm)		through my first DES, examination
(nn)		that I had um, a cervix like hamburger
(oo)		that's what I remember
(pp)	SB	that's wh' who' the
(qq)	HF	yeah
(rr)	SB	gynecologist told you that
(ss)	HF	he said yeah
(tt)		it was like hamburger, raw hamburger,
(uu)		and he had to cauterize it
(vv)	SB	what was that like to hear that,
(ww)		how did that make you feel
(xx)	HF	well, you see,
(yy)		you know I had,
(zz)		I had spent a lot of time in [a hospital with Grace]
(aaa)		I had seen a lot of really gruesome thinngs, (inhale)
(bbb)		so somehow I,
(ccc)		I think it just rolled off my back,
(ddd)		it did
(eee)		I'd really been, you know through a lot?
(fff)		and um (p)
(ggg)		you know, I think
(hhh)		I'd been thro- through so much
(iii)		with my daughter
(jjj)		um, that it just really,

(kkk)		the things that happened to me
(lll)		like you could probably throw *darts* at me
(mmm)		and it really wouldn't bother me, (inhale)
(nnn)		you know I became,
(ooo)		probably isn't a good way to be
(ppp)		because um, (swallows)
(qqq)		I guess I just under reacted to everything
(rrr)		and maybe it was a defense,
(sss)		but that was how I handled things by under reacting
(ttt)		and just
(uuu)	SB	mhm
(vvv)	HF	you know (p)
(www)		you know there are so many instances
(xxx)		where you had to be calm
(yyy)		and you know speak to, physicians about different things

In this narrative, Hannah refers twice to herself as a DES daughter, implicitly (line (q)) and then explicitly in relation to a medical test "through my first DES, examination" (line (mm)). She talks about events that occurred in the early 1970s, when physician experts were just beginning to understand that DES was carcinogenic and that it changed the structure and function of DES daughters' reproductive tracts. Hannah refers to diagnostic tests that were beginning to be standard for DES daughters having trouble with pregnancies – a hysterogram (lines (j) and (m)), also known as a hysterosalpingogram, HSG, or tubogram, in which a dye or other contrast medium is introduced into the uterus through the cervix for an X-ray examination of the uterus;[7] and a hysteroscopy (line (l)) in which a fiberoptic telescope is inserted through the vagina and cervix into the uterus enabling its user to see inside a woman's uterus. In addition, she refers to effects that were beginning to be observed in DES daughters: adenosis (line (ii)) (a condition in which cells that ordinarily are found only in the uterus are found on the walls of the vagina and surface of the cervix) and a double uterus or "T"-shaped uterus (lines (u), (dd)) (the inside of the uterus is different from normal, shaped like a "T"). She describes a treatment as well, cauterization (line (uu)), a procedure in which abnormal cervical tissue is destroyed with a chemical or an electrically heated instrument.

---

[7] On-Line Medical Dictionary http://cancerweb.ncl.ac.uk/cgi-bin/omd

By the time of the interview in 1982, studies of the effects of DES-exposure on pregnancy in DES daughters were well underway. In 1978, researchers reported observations of "primary infertility, ectopic pregnancy, preterm delivery, and cervical incompetence" among DES daughters, but did not know "whether these conditions occur[red] more frequently in DES daughters than in the general population" (US Department of Health, Education and Welfare 1978: 36–37). Over the next few years, reports from several DES research centers about the ability of DES daughters to become pregnant were inconsistent. However, virtually all of them showed that when DES daughters became pregnant, they were more likely than non-exposed women to have an "unfavorable outcome" (Barnes *et al.* 1980: 609), most commonly ectopic pregnancy, miscarriage, or premature birth (Swan 2000). Hannah's uncertainty about the link between her exposure to DES – and the adenosis and unusual-shaped uterus associated with DES – and the premature birth of her first daughter (line (w)) and subsequent miscarriage (line (x)–(y)) reflects concomitant medical uncertainty and controversy.

Two main questions structure the narrative. The first is "How did you, *han*dle it during those *years* though? (line (c)). Hannah replies with a prototypical story opening, "well I'll tell you what happened" (line (e)) and answers that as soon as she could she became pregnant again (line (g)–(h)); and that she handled things by under reacting (line (sss). The second main question is "what was that like to hear that, how did that make you feel?" (lines (vv)–(ww)) Her answer is "it rolled off my back" (line (ccc)). The question asks more about feelings and reflections than the first question did. Hannah's answer to this question closes with a summary that ties back to the initial question, "but that was how I handled things by under reacting" (line (sss)). This exchange gives Hannah the opportunity to tell another example of how she under reacted: "like you could probably throw *darts* at me and it really wouldn't bother me," (lines (lll)–(mmm)). To her, the diagnosis ("cervix like hamburger") wasn't remarkable; only in the interview with me, when I reacted with surprise and offense on her behalf, did it become remarkable.

Hannah divides the narrative into two parts. The first part of the narrative (lines (a)–(c)) takes place from the time after her miscarriage until she "became pregnant again" (line (h)) for the third time. It uses medical language and is quite detailed in its description of what was done to and seen in Hannah Fisher's body, but is vague about who did and saw it. In it, she positions herself as a woman patient. Not identifying her caregivers, and referring to them only as "they" (lines (o), (q), (s), (z)), helps to construct an image of distanced, objective knowers, and disembodied knowledge. She uses visual images: they "see" into her body (line (s)) and try to get a "clearer picture" of her uterus (line (r)). What they find is "unusual" (line (aa)) but based on what her uterus looks like, still she "*should* be able to carry, a baby to term" (line (ff)), although she hadn't been able to do this in either her first or her second pregnancy. Hannah becomes a spectator. I, like she and "they," become a spectator too as she takes me on a visual tour of her uterus (lines (t)–(u), (aa)–(dd)).

With her use of visual metaphors, Hannah Fisher reproduces and locates herself in a world created on the basis of visual knowledge, which has traditionally been used to signify a way of knowing associated with modern science (Foucault 1980b). This visual way of knowing distances the observer from the observed, separates the observed from the contexts in which they are ordinarily situated, and removes the observed to a homogeneous, neutral space in which what is seen can be explained. In Hannah's story, physicians use medical technology to look into her body, to get a clear picture of her uterus, and to compare her uterus both with that of the anatomical normal female body (lines (aa)–(bb)) and with the (ab)normal anatomy of DES daughters' bodies (lines (tt)–(uu)) that was beginning to be understood "to see if they could figure out why I had the miscarriage" (lines (o)–(p)). Hannah names two different procedures for visual diagnosis: a hysteroscopy (line (l)) and a hysterogram (line (m)). Although she can name the procedures, Hannah does not know which of them was used or even whether the procedure was one of these or "something like" a hysterogram (lines (m)–(n)). She does know the results discovered: she should be able to carry a baby to term (line (ff)). To put it slightly differently, in the first part of the story Hannah describes medical tests, all of them designed to picture the uterus with the conclusion that the uterus wasn't severely malformed so the woman should be able to carry a baby to term. Neither the fetus nor the uterus was severely abnormal, therefore the miscarriage could not be attributed to them; it must be Hannah's fault ("you know that I *should* be able to carry, a baby to term" (line (ff))).

In the first part of the story she uses "you know" to invoke shared knowledge and appeal to relevance beyond the immediate experience (see Schiffrin 1987). In the first instance, with "you know that's the best way to get over having a miscarriage" (line (i)), she gains my involvement. The discourse marker also has referential meaning in repeating a "general truth" beyond the interview setting about how best to get over a miscarriage (Schiffrin 1987: 276–278). That is, it is a general truth that for a woman who wants to have a baby, the pain of losing a pregnancy and the failure of achieving motherhood (again) with a particular pregnancy can be relieved with a subsequent pregnancy (Layne 2003). (This general truth assumes that a lost pregnancy can be followed by a successful pregnancy, recuperating a version of the seamless progression ideology in intensive mothering.) In another instance, "you know cause my my first daughter was premature" (line (w)) reminds me of what we have already established together in the interview, which is now part of our mutual, locally situated knowledge (Mishler 1999).

In the 1970s, when Hannah became a mother, feminist discourse "established a harsh self-questioning about . . . motherhood" (Snitow 1992: 37). Second-wave feminists advocated changes in legal, political, and social conditions, and worked to produce a theoretical apparatus that could recognize the subjective dimensions of these changing conditions (Kelly in Iversen, Crimp and Bhabha 1997: 9). As part of this project, from the 1970s to the 1980s, feminists inside and outside of the academy dedicated themselves to demystifying the practice of mothering, the institution of motherhood, and the traditional nuclear family ideal (Glenn 1994; Snitow 1992; Umansky 1996). Hannah's persistence in becoming a mother placed her at odds with this feminist discourse of the 1970s, and so did the bargain she had with her husband. In her marriage, she and her husband made a decision to structure their lives by redividing their work after they became parents. She gave up her job to be a full-time, stay-at-home mother. He kept his to support the family. She told me: "I know marriages aren't supposed to be like that any more it's supposed to be sort of fifty–fifty equal, but he wor' he works hard and I work hard and we both enjoy what we're doing." The discourses of intensive mothering and feminist motherhood critiques infuse the mutual, locally-situated knowledge we achieve during the interview (Mishler 1999).

The second part of the narrative (lines (ggg)–(yyy)) begins with the voice of medicine (Mishler 1984), but starts to depart from this voice when Hannah uses the metaphor "a cervix like hamburger" (line (nn)) to describe what she "had." I respond to her, asking her if this metaphor was used by a gynecologist; express my surprise at the term and suggest with my question that it shouldn't/couldn't have been. She responds by confirming that the gynecologist had used it, and further elaborates the term in the medical voice as a medical term: "he said yeah it was like hamburger, raw hamburger, and he had to cauterize it" (lines (ss)–(uu)). In response to my next question, however, she switches to the voice of the life world and stops describing what she saw and what was done. She uses the word "things" four times (lines (aaa), (kkk), (sss), (yyy)) and the word "everything" once (line (qqq)) instead of naming or describing medical procedures.

The narrative develops without pauses until the end of the first part of the story (line (gg)) where a pause functions as a signal to the audience (combined with the words "and um") that Hannah is not finished and still holds the floor, but that a new idea is about to be begun. Hannah switches time (between the premature birth of Grace and the first miscarriage), setting (my first DES examination) and result (diagnosis of cervix like a hamburger and the need to cauterize it). When I interrupt Hannah by responding to the words "cervix like hamburger" – I ask her a three-part question (lines (pp), (rr), (vv)–(ww)): who told you that, what was it like, how did it make you feel? I become the "feeling" person in this story. My emotional response is indicated by the false starts and the question in three parts, inserted into a story in which the only question I have asked up to this point is the first one (lines (a)–(c)). In the interaction between us, Hannah Fisher performs a distanced, objective, visually adept self.

At the time I interviewed Hannah, I was doing women's health work, starting out on a career in sociology – I was a post-doctoral fellow – and I had just begun to find out that becoming a mother was not going to be easy for me. Along with my attempts and my desire for having children, I was giving a lot of attention in my work to empowering women through access to birth control, abortion services, and motherhood by "choice." Feminism of the 1970s was more than a "cultural climate" (Mishler 1999) for me; it was where I situated myself, a lens through which I engaged with Hannah and the other DES daughters I interviewed in the early 1980s. I missed cues Hannah gave to me about the overwhelming importance in her life of mothering, which I now see and understand more clearly. Instead, I picked up on other topics in her account, notably those related to her encounters with medicine. When I heard the diagnosis of "cervix like a hamburger," I was surprised and deeply offended on Hannah's behalf.

The words "cervix like hamburger" evoke particular meanings in the world of DES. Beginning in 1941, DES was used as a growth stimulant in chickens, sheep, and cattle. The Food and Drug Administration banned the use of DES in food-producing animals in 1979, because there was no way of determining what levels of exposure to DES might be safe for agricultural workers and consumers. There were reports of its covert use in food-producing animals through the early 1980s, and again in 2000.[8] In describing Hannah's cervix like a hamburger, her physician evoked this highly contested agricultural practice, and Hannah repeated it in her exchange with me. At the time of the interview, however, neither Hannah nor I made the connection between using DES in cattle and in pregnant women. My emotional response was to what I perceived as a dehumanizing term, evidence of the ways medicine (mis)treats women patients, and of a play for power between doctors and patients.

The second pause (line (fff)) occurs after Hannah has answered my interrupting question, signaling to me that her answer is complete, but just as it has the first time, she is not finished and the pause, along with the words, holds the floor for her. She returns to answer the question with which she began the story (how she handled it (lines (a)–(c)) and finishes her answer to it: she handled things by under reacting (line (qqq)). The third pause (line (vvv))

---

[8] DES Action Voice Winter 2000:1; http://www.descancer.org/timeline. html

occurs just before the coda to the story. The coda gives another explanation for why she handled things by underreacting – it was strategic. To speak to physicians caring for her daughter and herself, she had to be calm.

Hannah uses "you know" twice as often in the second part of the narrative as in the first, appealing to our shared knowledge about DES (lines (ll)–(mm)) and our mutual understandings already developed in the interview about what she had been through (lines (eee), (ggg)) (Schiffrin 1987). Here the discourse marker also seems to function interactionally, in her appeal to me to understand why she became calm (lines (vvv), (www), (yyy)) (Schiffrin 1987). Perhaps it also refers back to the end of the first part of the story, to appeal to me to understand her persistence in trying to carry a baby to term (line (ff)).

In contrast to the first part of the narrative, in the second part Hannah uses vivid, non-medical language to describe her response, saying she had "seen a lot of really gruesome thinngs" (line (aaa)) and then that "it just rolled off my back" (line (ccc)) and finally, "you could probably throw *darts* at me and it really wouldn't bother me" (lines (lll)–(mmm)). She then interprets her response by saying, first that this "probably isn't a good way to be" (line (ooo)) but she probably "under reacted" (line (qqq)) which "maybe was a defense" (line (rrr)). There's a striking contrast between the vivid metaphors she's using here and the response she's describing: to under react and "to be calm" (line (xxx)). She used the voice of medicine in order to be able to "speak to" (line (yyy)) physicians and speaking their language means more than words. Physicians adopt this language to be able to be distant from the "gruesome thinngs" (line (aaa)) they must see and do to their patients. So must Hannah, in order to protect and advocate for her child as a good (intensive) mother.

Hannah Fisher produces her identity as a mother in the story-world in a multi-layered use of contrasts. She compares what is happening to *her* body and her responses to this with what is happening to her *daughter's* body and her reaction to that. Both of these experiences affect her ability to be seen as a proper (intensive) mother. In response to her experiences of pregnancy, the premature birth of a very sick child, miscarriage, and the identification of DES effects, she becomes conversant and comfortable

with biomedical language (e.g. "hysterogramm" line (m), "adenosis" line (ii)) and logic (e.g. a severely malformed uterus can
cause premature birth or miscarriage (lines (s)–(ee))). In response
to gruesome things she sees happening to Grace (lines (hhh)–(iii))
and perhaps to other children in the hospital with Grace (lines (zz)–
(aaa)), she makes herself calm (lines (www)–(yyy)) and prepares
for an attack so that she can be a protective mother (lines (kkk)–
(ttt)). In another contrast, she lists procedures performed (lines
(l)–(m), (uu)) and diagnoses made about her body (lines (z)–(dd),
(ii), (nn)), but leaves the "gruesome things" (line (aaa)) performed
on her daughter's body to my imagination (lines (hhh)–(iii)). Not
speaking in this narrative about her daughter's body, in contrast
to having said a great deal earlier in it about her own body, is a
way of "wielding silence" (Pollock 1999: 189). It enacts resistance:
"As the guardian of secret ways, the self may or may not bare the
secrets she carries" (Pollock 1999: 189).

Withholding information is a form of power. In producing this
narrative with me, Hannah enacts one of the strategies she used to
deal with her own and her daughter's needs. She had had limited
options available to her for dealing with medical experts. Silence
was one of them. Here, she simultaneously demonstrates and
"does" silence, positioning me in the same location as the experts
who treated her and her daughter, against whom she wielded
silence. Elsewhere in the interview, she provided detailed descriptions of "gruesome things," that led to the strategy of silence, and
of strategies other than silence that she used in order to secure
and monitor medical care for her daughter. Immediately following
the end of this story, for example, I asked her what kinds of
"instances" she had in mind, repeating a word Hannah Fisher had
just used ("you know there are so many instances/where you had
to be calm" (lines (www)–(xxx)). In response she then described
an event very early in Grace's infancy. It began with several days
of worsening health. Her daughter "cried more and more and she
threw up more and more." Finally Hannah and her husband
brought Grace to the emergency room in the middle of the night.
The surgeon who was called to fix her told them that Grace was
near death and that they had "really failed as parents" because they
had waited too long to take her to the hospital.

Hannah Fisher becomes calm and enters a world in which the details of intensive mothering are left unsaid: "I had spent a lot of time in [a hospital with Grace] I had seen a lot of really gruesome things" (lines (zz)–(aaa)); and left inferred by the repetition of her talk: "I'd really been, you know through a lot? and um you know, I think I'd been tho- through so much with my daughter" (lines (eee)–(iii)).

9.4 Concluding thoughts

Hannah Fisher makes events in her life meaningful and engages in ongoing construction of her identities in narrative. She shows how cultural discourses of science (medicine) and mothering play a role in her sense making. She positions herself in relation to medicine and intensive mothering. At the same time she does intensive mothering she makes critical commentary on intensive mothering and medicine. She draws upon images and conventions to present and interpret her account of mothering.

Hannah Fisher's narrative contains culturally shared visual images and conventions of battle and butchery. These images help her to position herself as a heroic intensive mother. She was overwhelmed; she persevered, and she rejected the use of her emotions as a basis for action. She did what she had to do. She put up a shield that could absorb darts, and adopted a calm and distanced scientific stance. Ironically, in the narrative, her stance was even more distanced and unfeeling than one of her physicians in his description of her body. Her verbal images draw listeners into her story, puzzling over them, engaging them in the discourses of science and mothering.

Hannah Fisher enacts intensive mothering in strategic expertise. She has had three miscarriages and three children, one of them very sick. She worked hard to produce a baby and to mother a sick child. She is aware of this difficulty in meeting the standards of intensive mothering, but persists in claiming this identity in the everyday practices that for the most part remain unsaid in her narrative: going to the hospital, monitoring the medical care of her daughter, and sacrificing her own needs in favor of her daughter and other children.

My analysis of Hannah Fisher's narratives provides a way of showing how she engages, reproduces and resists cultural and scientific discourses of mothering. Looking at this narrative helps us to explore and bring to light practices of intensive mothering, simultaneously locating them in place and time and acknowledging their fluctuating meanings. This approach privileges positionality and subjectivity, the context, setting, and aims of her narrative – an interview; a DES daughter in the early 1970s and early 1980s; a woman with 50% fetal loss and a sick child. At the same time that it seeks to recognize the multiplicity of social experiences and perspectives, it tries to make statements about regularities in the social world and to develop systematic knowledge about embodied motherhood.

Part III

The gendered self: becoming and being a man

Editors' introduction

Part III of our volume consists of three contributions to the field of identity studies concerned with the more specific business of gender identity. Even more concretely, within the field of gender studies, all three chapters speak to what it means to be or become a young *man*. While other contributions in this volume similarly show how participants orient toward issues of gender (cf. Georgakopoulou's analysis of 17-year-old girls' identity formation in projective narratives, or Bell's study of a woman who is trying to make sense of herself as mother and as DES daughter), we decided to give these chapters their own categorical umbrella. They all show how male identities are formed discursively vis-à-vis particular hegemonic discourses of masculinity, but also vis-à-vis discourses of heterosexuality and whiteness – in positions of complicity but also in positions of resistance towards these discourses.

All chapters use narratives-in-interaction as their database to explore these identities as constructed and emergent, but the data collection techniques are different in each case. While Kiesling made use of the ethnographic interview as a story-elicitation technique with fraternity students, Moita-Lopes relied on a focus-group interview between three researchers and seven young adolescents. Wortham and Gadsden had young African-American researchers interview lower-class, urban African-American men who had become fathers as teenagers. Their semi-structured interviews resemble more the traditional biographic interview style used typically by sociologists.

In addition to the joint thematic focus on masculinity, a further common thread that ties these three chapters closely together is their focus of stories as told-in-interaction. This methodological stance enables the authors to treat the emerging stories as participants' own resources rather than as resources pre-defined by the analyst. At the same time, using forms of positioning analysis (see our Introduction to this volume) all three authors effectively document how the narrators in their stories also orient toward all participants present in the interview situations, including the interviewers. This methodological orientation enables the authors to connect aspects of the world that are constructed in the stories with aspects of the interactive local situation in which the stories are performed, resulting in the unveiling of some forms of complicity with or resistance to what can be seen as pre-existing master or dominant discourses. Such discourses, however, are drawn up and brought to bear locally by use of discursive means. The three chapters in Part III show effectively how these different levels of analysis interact.

Kiesling (Chapter 10) analyzes two stories told by two different fraternity members (male, white, heterosexual, middle class) to illustrate how narratives can be employed to construct hegemonic identities. His analysis underscores the action orientation of the participants involved in the interaction, i.e., demonstrates how the narratives are part of interview interactions, and how the resulting identities are situated and performed. Kiesling, in his role as analyst, convincingly shows also how the narrators in their local performance of their stories "rely on shared cultural knowledge" (or capital D-discourses, as he also calls them) in order "to structure the crucial context for their interpretation and performance of their local narratives, a practice which also reinforces these Discourses" (p. 261). He analyzes the narratives within the framework of indexicality, illustrating how the participants' use of particular story features indexes cultural models, which are qualified as more specific capital D-discourses. The participants' access to these models is guaranteed through shared social and meta-pragmatic knowledge structures. Kiesling points out that the relationship between indexicals (down to the use of phonological features) and the work they accomplish in story-telling processes is not direct, but rather, indirect and mediated by local and highly contextual processes of knowledge accessing and sharing that make it possible for meaning to be locally re-created. In the analysis of his first story, Kiesling nicely demonstrates how the narrator, by calling up particular personal experiences, not only convincingly (re)creates a vision of himself as "a person who is going somewhere," but also *produces* an understanding of his identity that enforces a model of hegemony that appears as an almost natural frame for it. The second example, a story that seemingly has become an icon in fraternity discourses, shows how the performance of a particular story plays itself out within story-routines and how the use of indexical means at the local level of one particular narrative functions within a wider indexicality "in which the practices and structures of masculinity and femininity, and Black and White, are structured by Discourses of identity" (p. 284).

Kiesling delivers in-depth insights into the processes of *how* identities are re-made (see Marecek's (2003: 55–57) distinction in qualitative research between the investigation of "how" versus "why" questions). He productively alternates between the participants re-making of themselves in their stories and their being re-made through means that are *always already* given. Furthermore, Kiesling also demonstrates convincingly how performance and repetition of indexical means (that seem to be crucial to this construction process) play out in praxis so that they can ultimately result in the valuing and reification of particular capital D-discourses.

In close proximity to Kiesling's focus, Moita-Lopes' analysis of one boy's stories within a focus group setting (Chapter 11) centers on the construction of hegemonic identities. Moita-Lopes singles out different stories in the interaction among the focus group participants (seven young male and female adolescents and three researchers in a Brazilian school), to illustrate the simultaneous construction of masculinity (gender), heterosexuality (sexuality and desire), and whiteness (race) in their discourse. Also, in line with Kiesling's argument, narratives and in particular narrative practices are taken to constitute a crucial site for the construction of identities and for the study of how these are called into existence. And although Moita-Lopes in his analysis also refers to features of indexicality (that he calls *indexation*), his frame of analysis is more firmly grounded in positioning analysis (see the Introduction to this volume). Accordingly, narrators (in this case Hans, a 14-year-old boy) locate themselves within a repertoire of emplotted stories, relying on existing storylines and master narratives that are culturally shared (see Kiesling's *culturally shared capital D-discourses*). These same narrators simultaneously engage (agentively) in the business of "legitimating particular social identities while rejecting others" (p. 294) positioning themselves as agentively producing these (local) storylines, and simultaneously being produced by these (culturally shared) master or dominant narratives.

What nicely unites the analyses of the three story segments ("Hans as *male*," "Hans as *heterosexual*," and "Hans as *white*") is the way Moita-Lopes lines up these three cases showing how in each instance Hans accomplishes his particular identity by positioning himself vis-à-vis the Other: He constructs a *male* sense of self vis-à-vis *the female*, a *heterosexual* sense of self vis-à-vis *the homosexual*, and a young *white* person's sense of self vis-à-vis *the black*. The construct of positioning within these analyses is applied in a very productive way to show how Hans produces multiple identities by reference to alterity at the very moment the narratives are told. The construction of one's own sense of self as the "unmarked," the normal and natural through an opposition to others, moves this type of storytelling discourse into a "hegemonic" practice – where race becomes "blackness," sexuality becomes "homoeroticism," and gender turns into "femininity."

An additional insight that the Moita-Lopes chapter provides is the demonstration of the interplay of larger socio-historical constraints (within existing plot lines or master narratives) with the situated, interactional construction of local plots (and its outcome in the form of hegemonic discourse). Moita-Lopes, in a similar way to Kiesling, nicely alternates between Hans' 'self' construction and his 'other' construction by forces that operate both within socially dominant discourses and local interactional structures. While Hans is analyzed as "constructing himself" by making use of reference to alterity, the interactional process between the teenagers is also called in as contributing pivotally to Hans "getting" or "being positioned" into his identities.

In contrast to the first two chapters of this section, where narrators are presented as sharing dominant discourses and master narratives, Wortham and Gadsden (Chapter 12) analyze the narratives of a lower-class, urban African-American man who had become a father as a teenager, and who positions himself in non-complicity with the dominant discourse of the street – and, one could add, of masculinity as a hegemonic discourse. More specifically, this man uses discursive means that allow him to draw up a position that is *not cool*, that is *old fashioned* and, in some interesting ways, *counter* to the types of *masculinity* that are valued in the street. The authors are quick to point out that these aspects of identity and self presentation may have to do with the situation within which they were produced. Moita-Lopes argues that "people take up different positionings and construct different SIDs [social identities] in the different discursive practices they get involved with" (p. 310). And similarly, Wortham and Gadsden point to the interview as a particular occasion that may have allowed the participant "to articulate this identity, in the company of another [black] man who rejects the values of the street" (p. 340). Nevertheless, this issue of producing counter narratives (cf. Bamberg and Andrews 2004), even if the conditions are specific (or unique), provides potential insights into constructive procedures that are of eminent relevance to discussions around issues of narratives as therapeutic tools as well as more general issues of intervention in adolescent development and the fight against prejudice, hegemony and violence.

A second notable contribution of Wortham and Gadsden's chapter lies in their detailed discussion and extremely insightful application of the positioning framework as a methodological tool. Although they are grounding their analytic frame firmly in indexicality, they show how indexicals not only function indirectly (as underscored by both Kiesling and Moita-Lopes), but may also be (better) understood as signifying something different according to the different types of positioning that are taken up. Indexical cues within the positioning framework are complex and indeterminate and need to be analyzed as components of the different layers of narrative positioning. The authors suggest four different layers: (i) narrators' positioning of themselves as experiencers, (ii) their positioning of characters within the represented, narrated world, (iii) their evaluation of these characters (including themselves as characters if the story includes them), and (iv) their self-positioning in interaction, within the local situation of the story-telling. In their analysis of several segments from a biographic, long interview with a young man called Robert, the authors extrapolate, in a very illuminating way, how symbolic spaces (the street, the home, and the system) are called into the horizon of understanding, to frame the claiming of an identity based on counter-hegemonic notions of masculinity.

Overall, Wortham and Gadsden's contribution to the field of identity studies presents an enormous step toward "a linguistically sophisticated account of how narrative discourse creates relevant patterns" for the construction of the self (p. 314), a contribution that is important for rethinking the identity–language tapestry in innovative ways.

The three chapters comprising Part III discuss issues of masculinity and hegemonic identity, topics that for quite a while have been neglected because of the belief that little could be learned from them in the formulation of progressive recommendations towards changing practices and ideologies. However, as these chapters convincingly demonstrate, a fine-grained analysis of how male identity formation processes take shape in compliance with, as well as in opposition to dominant, hegemonic ideologies proves extremely insightful. And in spite of the fact that the authors analyzed only a handful of interactive situations, their focus on particular narrative practices considerably increases the scope of methodological sensibilities by invoking what Hymes (1996: 19) called "comparative generalization." Reading the three chapters in synchrony will provide a much better understanding of the complexities of male identity formation, and more productively, serve constructive change in the long run.

10

Hegemonic identity-making in narrative

Scott F. Kiesling

> The individual cannot hold power, but (he) can exercise it through the dominant discourses of masculinity.
>
> Stephen M. Whitehead (2002: 109)

10.1 Introduction

In this chapter I explore the role of narrative in the construction of hegemonic identities by analyzing two narratives told by members of a college fraternity who are male, heterosexual, white, and middle class. I show that these men rely on shared cultural knowledge, or Discourses (as discussed by Fairclough 1992; Foucault 1980a, 1988) to structure the crucial context for the interpretation and performance of their local narratives, a practice which also reinforces these Discourses. I also explore how the narratives help the speaker create a local stance with respect to his hearers, and then how the local stances, the narrator's "story self," and Discourses interact to create identity and provide material for later identity performances. It is through this interaction among stances, identities, and Discourses, I argue, that hegemony works and Discourses circulate throughout society.

10.2 Hegemonic identities

I understand identity as a person's relationship to her/his social world, and I use the term "hegemonic identities" rather than "powerful identities" because people in hegemonic positions do not always feel powerful, and they in fact may not directly dominate anyone. Hegemony, as described by Gramsci (1994), involves maintaining dominant social positions through less obvious but more basic means than direct coercion: for example, by controlling the basic ideologies in a society rather than ruling by force. The most important facet of hegemony, other than dominance, is its ability to change in the face of challenge. That is, ideologies that challenge the status quo of a dominant group can be appropriated and changed slightly so as to allow the dominant group to remain powerful, and even to use the formerly challenging ideology as an argument to legitimize its power.

While Gramsci conceived of these ideologies as being largely controlled by an elite (intellectual) class, the notion of hegemony has undergone substantial revision, particularly in its use by scholars of men and masculinities. In their view (or views) hegemony does not function through ideologies controlled by elites, but is created and perpetuated by Discourses in the post-structuralist sense (Foucault 1980a, 1988; for a post-structuralist view on men and masculinities, see Whitehead 2002: 99–110). (I will always represent these Discourses with an initial capital letter to distinguish them from the more material spoken and written discourses.) These Discourses are not the same as ideologies, as ideologies imply a system of ideas only, while Discourses encompass what we are used to thinking of as practices, structures, *and* ideologies; a Discourse is the entire interlocking web of practices, ideologies, and social structures: a system of understanding and expectation that prefigures which practices and interpretations are available, and how practices and structures are understood. In addition, Discourses are always changing and changeable, and not controlled by any single person or group. Thus they are hegemonic in the sense of being powerful and changing, however those who engage in the production and reproduction of Discourses need not be powerful (or feel powerful even if they have power). A particular discourse (interaction, conversation, or text) is thus structured by, and interpreted through (one or more) social Discourses, and can be a site in which Discourses compete. Among the most basic definitions that Discourses provide there is the division of society into socially relevant groups such as men and women, Black and White, and heterosexual and homosexual.

The concept of cultural models makes it possible to think about Discourses in somewhat more concrete forms. Cultural models are more specific Discourses that can be distilled from the culture. They are more abstract than actual narratives told, but more specific than

Discourses (and ideologies). Holland and Skinner (1987) provide a textbook example of their functioning. They analyzed the terms women used to refer to men in an American college campus (stud, nerd, jerk, etc.). After interviewing a large number of women, they concluded that an explanation of the way these words were used and understood based on a particular cultural model worked better than an account based on semantic models such as Componential Analysis. According to Holland and Skinner, the women all shared a cultural model of romantic relationships according to which a man would be desirable because he was considerate to women or attractive; and dating was seen as a complex calculus involving the relative attractiveness of the man and the woman and the man's considerateness. The cultural model is thus a richly organized norm shared by the women. It is more specific than a general ideology dictating, for example, that women and men should be of similar attractiveness, because it specifies ways in which women and men act if they deviate from the norm (reflected in the terminology used by the women). Yet it is also more general than a list of specific cases. Cultural models can thus be seen as ways of representing specific Discourses, which allow us to connect these to discourses. In the cases discussed in this chapter, these models all represent some form of domination, and therefore they mediate between local stance-taking and global cultural Discourses.

Naturally, some mechanisms of linguistic domination may be fairly direct: people with hegemonic identities may talk about how to hold on to power, or explicitly denigrate those in subordinate classes. They may also develop markers of group identity and perform "acts of identity" (LePage and Tabouret-Keller 1985) in which they use linguistic features directly associated with their group. But such manifestations of identity still need to take place within a Discourse that defines them as dominant; and presuppose a division of society into specific groups to which the speaker of the dominant group may refer.

In this chapter, however, I argue that the in-group talk of one hegemonic group – White heterosexual fraternity men – does not work so directly. In fact, the men studied are not consciously attempting to be socially hegemonic, even as they successfully accomplish it. The kinds of meaning processes that they set in motion to accomplish their identities are much more indirect than simple claims

to a dominant social position based on skin color, or uses of unpro-
blematically defined "male" linguistic features. Rather, the men in this
group rely on other speakers' social and metapragmatic (Silverstein
1993) knowledge – Discourses, including cultural models – to indicate
their relationships with their current (in-group) interlocutors, and
they are also limited by these Discourses. However, in the process of
reproducing them, they can both reinforce or elaborate them. I am
thus concerned with how very local meaning processes of discourse
are dependent on, and (re)create hegemonic Discourses.

The mechanisms for hegemonic identity-making that I and others
have previously found at work in the fraternity men's discourse rely on
interlocutors accessing shared cultural models of race, sexuality, and
gender, in order to create stances and categories. The sharing of these
cultural models reflects, reinforces, and (re)creates these models and
the more abstract related Discourses. In Kiesling (2001) I focused on
two main processes used to create a White hegemonic identity, both
involving a Discourse in which a fictional Other is marked somehow
as non-White. One strategy used a linguistic feature associated with a
particular social group to momentarily claim some social or interactional trait associated with that group. In the case analyzed, the White
men claimed a stereotypical Black trait by using a Black linguistic
feature. (Similarly, during the fieldwork, I noted that men created a
stereotypical gay male stance by using language associated with gay
men.) In her groundbreaking work on hegemonic discourse, Jane Hill
(1995b, 1995c) makes a similar point. She shows that Anglo speakers
use Spanish and Spanish-like suffixes to signal that they possess desirable qualities, such as "a sense of humor, a playful skill with a foreign
language, authentic regional roots, and easy-going attitude toward
life" (Hill 1995c). However, this process also assigns undesirable
qualities to Spanish speakers, such as "gross sexual appetites, political
corruption, laziness, disorders of language, and mental incapacity"
(Hill 1995c). These uses rely on an interlocutor's knowledge about
language (metapragmatics) to create a stance and humor. The listener
must have access to this knowledge in order to make sense of the
speaker's utterance. Such uses of non-dominant linguistic forms by
hegemonic speakers thus reinforce the Discourses of hegemony.

Another (unconscious) hegemonic strategy consisted in "marking
the Other": a discursive meta-strategy which situates the speaker as a
member of a dominant, or central, social group by creating an "other,"

marginalized category. The latter was created in several ways, not all of which are direct. First, a group could be explicitly categorized as non-dominant (here I mean non-dominant as not White, male, young adult, or middle class). Second, members of a non-dominant group could be characterized through a description that highlights differences between them and the speaker. Finally, a co-present interlocutor – the "material" other in a conversation – could be labeled as a social Other by a speaker wishing to take a dominant stance. In the cases analyzed, these Others are in fact members of the fraternity, and hence such labeling functions metaphorically to create hierarchical difference within the fraternity.

In this chapter I am more concerned with how narratives are deployed in talk to create a hegemonic identity, and how the structure, content, and relationship to the surrounding discourse of narratives relies on dominant Discourses, recreates, or shapes them. However, these processes are similar in kind to those outlined above. Most importantly, they rely on speakers' access to Discourses in order for the stories to "make sense" or "have a point." Without these assumed discourses, the stories become non-sequiturs. Thus, the meaning process on which the narratives rely more generally is indexicality.

10.3 Indexicality, norms, and cultural models

As noted above, meaning and identities are created in actual daily performances against a backdrop of norms and expectations held by speakers about how actors in certain social categories do, or should, act and talk. Thus, speakers and hearers have knowledge about forms of language typically used by speakers of different identities in particular situations. These connections are then available to be used as resources that take on meanings associated with typical users and situations – they *index* these situations. Indexes, and knowledge of them, become part of Discourses that are shared widely in a culture, and are therefore resources which can be used in interaction for identity performances. Even a single linguistic feature might index an entire life trajectory because it indexes a certain cultural model.

For example, the address term *dude*, does not index the speaker only as young, White, and male, nor only as creating an unenthusiastic affiliative stance, but also as a drug user who is not particularly intellectually strong and is unconcerned with many of life's daily practicalities (this type of indexicality also allows it to be used in the title of a film – *Dude, where's my car?* – to indicate what kind of characters the film represents). The processes Hill observes, in which mock Spanish perpetuates stereotypes of Hispanics, rely on similarly shared, pre-existing (demeaning) norms and expectations – Discourses – about Hispanic identity. Without such shared Discourses, mock Spanish cannot index the kinds of meanings Hill elucidates.

These Discourses go beyond simple stereotypes, but are elaborate (though abstract) webs and scripts, including "cultural models" or "figured worlds" (as described by Holland and Quinn 1987). For example, Frankenberg (1997: 11) outlines some American racial cultural models in what she calls the "trope-ical" family of gendered White and Black Americans. These models represent ways in which Black and White men and women are repeatedly portrayed in American culture. Cultural models also exist for masculinity and femininity, working class and middle class, old age and youth, among others (and in fact these binaries interact to produce complex cultural models). We can find a connection between situated identities and abstract cultural models or Discourses by investigating how the stances taken and categories created in daily interaction rely on such cultural models to yield their full social indexicality.

Let me stress again that Discourses are *not* deterministic ideologies, but generally accepted ways of thinking about how the world works, which means that they encompass practices and structures as well as ideologies and, more importantly, that they can be challenged; new or revised Discourses can be proposed and indexed as well, while dominant Discourses can be deployed in new ways. As shown by Foucault (1980a), power is productive and useful for society. Discourses are an example of these characteristics of power since, being accessed through indexicality, they make interaction much more efficient as "background knowledge" does not need to be spelled out (cf. Fairclough 1992).

The story I analyze below is one told to an interviewer. As the interviewer, I could have challenged the value of the Discourse being indexed by the speaker: although the speaker presents the actions in the story as admirable, I could have suggested that I disapproved of such actions. However, I chose the role of a supportive interviewer, investigating and privileging the interviewee's world view.

10.4 Indexicality and discourse in narrative

Indexicality is usually discussed as a contextual meaning attached to linguistic items like phonological or lexical elements, i.e. isolatable linguistic features that have specific meanings because of their general association with an aspect of context (such as the speaker's identity). However, since a narrative is a unit of discourse (as discussed by Schiffrin 1984), we can look at what a particular narrative indexes, and ask whether it uses similar mechanisms of indexicality as words or sounds. What linguistic features of stories do the indexical work? How does the story as a whole do indexical work? How is this indexical work similar to and different from other instances of indexicality?

Narratives are a unit of discourse that have meaning, and perhaps more obviously than in other speaking genres, rely on Discourses for their meaning. Stories do not "mean" in the conventional (symbolic) way, but rather take their meaning from their relation to the context of speaking on both the micro and macro levels (see Schiffrin 1996). A story will always have a meaning on the level of the interpersonal relations of the storyteller and the audience, but it may also have significance in its relationship to wider social relationships and discourses. In fact, stories are often used to exemplify or challenge cultural models and Discourses.

The essential point is that hearers need to construct some kind of coherence around a story told within a conversation (on coherence strategies in general, see Halliday and Hasan 1976). In other words, a narrative is a unit that needs other material to make it interpretable. This material can be clearly related to the talk that has immediately preceded the story, but it can also be exophoric, that is, interpretable with respect to other information, such as "background knowledge." Because narratives often have explicit evaluative sections, and have material that can be related within the story, this exophoric sense-making can be less obvious to both interlocutors and analysts.

Another way of looking at this sense-making is through a conversational principle of relevance. Sperber and Wilson (1995) suggest that people rely on speakers' knowledge of this principle such that they craft their utterances to get the maximum amount of communication with the minimum amount of processing effort. Stories, in this view, are very effective, because they often do not explicitly evaluate their point, but make it very powerfully. However, in order to apprehend the point, a hearer must have access to shared and "unspoken" Discourses.

10.5 Discourses of masculinities

Since the late eighties, men and masculinities have become the focus of rapidly expanding research, and there has been considerable theoretical development along with this explosion in the volume of investigations. Most recently, authors in the so-called "third wave" of research (e.g. Petersen 1998; Whitehead 2002) have begun to theorize using analyses that rely on Discourses of masculinities, such that structures, practices, performances, biology, individual psychologies, and ideologies are not seen as separate, competing ways of looking at and explaining masculinities (and gender), but as an interlocking web-like Discourse, as discussed above. Such a view suggests that some of the most central ideas in research on men and masculinities can and should be understood as part of this web. Thus, the notion of hegemonic masculinity, which Connell (1987, 1995, 2000) first proposed and uses as one of his central concepts, can be seen as an effect of a Discourse that creates, and is created by, knowledge of social structures and practices. Although Connell does not take a post-structuralist view, his definition of hegemonic masculinity – the "most honored or desired" form of masculinity (2000: 10) – can indeed only be understood as part of a Discourse that valorizes one kind of identity over another. Hegemonic masculinity is usually not overtly discussed as such, but speakers do have knowledge about such dominant forms of masculinity, and this knowledge affects the practices they engage in, and helps to create the structures in which they find themselves. This Discourse in turn will influence other social concepts discussed by Connell: practices people engage in, the kind of structures they find themselves in, and the people and things they desire, among others. Most importantly, this hegemonic masculinity can be challenged and, as a result of that, change.

The view that there is a hegemonic masculinity and that it can change, also implies that there are different kinds of masculinity, and that they compete with one another for dominance. In fact, I argue that there are multiple competing hegemonic forms at any time, some compatible, but some in conflict. Thus, there is a Discourse about the working-class, hard-working man that presents him as powerful because of his discipline in the face of a struggle, which is at odds with a Discourse about a "playboy" man who is fun-loving, frivolous, and surrounded by comfort (although both are seen as heterosexually potent). The concept of hegemonic masculinity also suggests that masculine Discourses at their most abstract are about power and dominance, about being at the top of some perceived social hierarchy, even if that hierarchy is composed only of men, and even if being at the top of one hierarchy means being at the bottom of another one for a time. In addition, as pointed out by French and Raven (1959), there are multiple ways of claiming power, or multiple *sources* of power. One of the foci of my work has been to investigate how men use linguistic features to create identities that are powerful in different ways, by indexing different sources of power (see Kiesling 1997, 1998). In a post-structuralist view, however, we can look at these sources as different, interlocking Discourses of power, which speakers may or may not use to create dominant identities depending on other social resources at their disposal.

The kinds of Discourses we see described in the literature are numerous, but they can all be traced back to sources of power and meta-narratives of how one gains power. Thus, we find hegemonic masculinities based on physical power (sports stars), economic power (corporate CEOs), "solidarity" power (elected leaders and politicians), structural power (leaders such as generals, and fathers), and even intellectual power, although this latter category can be problematic if it is in contrast with heterosexual power. In addition, in American society power that is perceived to be achieved, i.e. earned, is generally more highly regarded than power that is simply inherited. Thus, many Discourses of hegemonic masculinity are possible, but they all need to place the protagonist at the top of some hierarchy, often through hardship and initial subordination or trial. For example, in the popular film *Rocky II*, the protagonist embodies a physical and mental hegemonic masculinity, as he wins a world championship boxing title through strength, perseverance, and even intelligence (in the boxing ring). Although very few people are as focused as the protagonist in reality, the Discourse allows many men to identify with this kind of identity and add it to their own inventory, as shown in Kiesling (1998).

It is tempting to find a single Discourse being used by a particular speaker in one stretch of talk. But the fact that multiple, competing Discourses are available means that a speaker can in fact draw on more than one of them, even if they are in conflict. Thus, a speaker may simultaneously try to be powerful physically and intellectually, and the two identities may in fact seem to contradict each other (for example, often the stereotypes of the "nerd" and the "jock" are in conflict). Such a situation is possible because the hierarchy of masculinities is never clear-cut (nor is it always clear where one ends and another begins), and most importantly because different kinds of masculinities are in competition.

Discourses of masculinities are "successfully" used by speakers to construct identities if their listeners have access to the same Discourses as they do. Only the ability to access a similar discourse can bring about a complete understanding of a speaker's indexes.

10.6 A narrative of masculinity

The first narrative that I will analyze is from a corpus of data collected in a year of participant observation in the early nineties in an all-male college fraternity in Northern Virginia. Fraternities, found at many North American universities, are essentially social clubs, with members joining to have access to the social interaction provided by the fraternity, not least to the relationship that fraternities often have with their all-female counterparts, sororities. Membership is selective, with men, usually in their first year of college, going through a process of "rush" in which they meet fraternity members at parties and other functions. The fraternity then extends an invitation to join, and if the invitee accepts, a period of probationary or initiate membership then follows, in which the probationary member or "pledge" is subjected to a number of tests before he is initiated into the community. The fraternity has a governing structure and budget, which affords the men opportunities to gain experience with working in corporate-like organizations to develop their "leadership skills." The other aspect of activity for fraternities is the performance of volunteer work both in the university and the wider community, and this work especially requires coordination and leadership. In doing this research, I was interested in the role of language in the men's identity creation, as well as the circulation of linguistic forms throughout the fraternity.

To that end, I carried out ethnographic interviews designed to find out how the men themselves organized different identities in the fraternity. The first narrative I will analyze is taken from one of these interviews. At the time of this interview, Mick had recently been elected president of the fraternity, and I had asked him why he had been chosen (even though his election was uncontested, the fact that no other member chose to challenge him shows that his election was nevertheless a consensus choice). After a pause, a vague answer, and a repetition of the question by me (SK), Mick responds in the following way:

Example 10.1

(a)	MICK	I:'m just a very:
(b)		Tha- the type of person that's goin' somewhere and and uh, whatever I mean.
(c)		This is merely just uh
(d)		I mean they- I- um
(e)		*Any*thing I do I do it . . . the best I can do.
(f)		I mean I have I have *not* watched television in I couldn't tell you how long.
(g)		I mean just don't do things that aren't very productive at all. I me-
(h)	SK	(?)
(i)	MICK	No I don't No I don't you're right I don't ha:ng out.
(j)	SK	(sit on the couch)
(k)	MICK	No even if I go to the townhouse I'll sit there for a whi-
(l)		I don't know if you've ever been there when I come in I sit there and I'm like
(m)		All right. What are we doin'.
(n)	SK	He he he he
(o)	MICK	It's like. I just can't- I can't just do *no*thing.

(p)	SK	Yeah
(q)	MICK	I could never, never satisfy my dad.
(r)	SK	Yeah
(s)	MICK	I tore down, wa- we had a chicken coop?
(t)		That- the end of it burned down.
(u)		It was, like, on my grandfather's farm
(v)		it wasn't really our farm it was the closest- our closest neighbor.
(w)		But ah, it was huge.
(x)		It was about three times the size of this house
(y)		It took me a whole summer to tear it down.
(z)		Hand- by my hand all- hand by-
(aa)		brick by brick I tore the damn thing down.
(bb)		And he was still like- he was bitchin' at me the whole time y'know.
(cc)		Like, if- I'd come in, yeah, What's takin' so long?
(dd)	SK	Yeah
(ee)	MICK	Yeah I mean he's- and he's-
(ff)		not that I hate him for that I'm very glad that he was like that, yknow.
(gg)		He built our whole house himself.
(hh)	SK	Wow
(ii)	MICK	The entire thing.

There are in fact two separate short narratives in this stretch of talk. Both are relevant to illustrate that Mick is "the type of person that's goin' somewhere" (line (b)), and ultimately to answer my question about why he was the consensus choice for president. His answer is thus not just about his own identity, but also about what type of identity is valued by the fraternity members. It is therefore about what kind of personality traits are seen as powerful. Note that because of its location in the structure of the interview, the narrative is necessarily understood as an answer, or an elaboration of an answer, to my question. Its status as a second-pair part in an adjacency pair is one of the local structures that give the story its meaning, and provide Mick with the opportunity to answer the question with the recounting of a personal anecdote. Note also that he is encouraged by my supporting behavior in lines (h) and (j), where I in fact co-construct the answers with him (although my speech in line (h) is not intelligible on tape, it is clear from Mick's speech in the next line "No I don't know I don't you're right I don't hang out" that I have suggested that he doesn't hang out).

The first narrative is very short, and occurs in lines (l)–(m), when Mick is illustrating his restlessness by relating his actions when he goes to the townhouse.[1] These lines technically form a narrative since, although Mick attempts to represent the *typical* (i.e. iterative) course of events when he goes to the townhouse, the two clauses in line (l) "when I come in I sit there and I'm like" are temporally ordered, and thus fit the definition of a narrative given by Labov and Waletzky (1967). Mick is illustrating a typical case and giving it specific details through constructed dialogue (Tannen 1989: chapter 4). He thus creates an image of himself within the narrative, most vividly through the character's talk, as somebody who "just can't do nothing." This is all fairly clearly related to the question that elicited the answer: Mick was elected because he is the type of person who accomplishes things, and because he doesn't waste time. I will address how this fact relates to masculinity below.

Mick's use of habitual narrative – a narrative that relates repeated or typical events (Carranza 1998) – is a discursive device that helps him make an argument about his hard-working identity. As Carranza (1998: 305) notes, "the textual effect of segments about habitual actions or continuous states is to build a holistic picture of the past that speaks for itself" which makes "the propositions and evaluations contained in a segment harder to challenge." This "holistic picture" is especially powerful for Mick, who is not only representing a past event, but an enduring quality of his identity. By illustrating a trait with habitual action, a speaker can present the trait as more difficult to challenge.[2]

Mick then continues with the abstract of a more involved narrative in line (p) ("I could never, never satisfy my Dad"). This move is less clearly related to the question of why he was elected, but it can be interpreted as his motivation for being the kind of person who "never does nothing." Note that I have not asked him how he

---

[1] The townhouse is one domicile where members of the fraternity, and only members of the fraternity, live. While some fraternities have their own houses, this fraternity did not. Nevertheless central places like houses did exist where members would "drop by" and "hang out" even if they didn't live there.

[2] I thank Anna De Fina for pointing this parallel out to me.

became that way, or what his father was like. He thus must have believed that this statement, and the following narrative illustration, was relevant to his depiction of his personality, and ultimately to the reasons for his election as president of the fraternity.

The narrative, despite its brevity, contains all the sections outlined for canonical stories by Labov and Waletzky (1967). I have already pointed out the abstract, which is followed by a long orientation in lines (q)–(v) describing the chicken coop. The complicating action is very brief, and the resolution is embedded in it: Mick tore the chicken coop down while his father "bitched" at him. Finally, there is embedded evaluation (Labov 1972a: 372) when the father is represented in constructed dialogue in line (cc), followed by a coda in line (ff).

This discussion clarifies the microstructure of the narrative. The next move in the analysis is to answer several questions that will help to understand how Mick creates an identity through this narrative: what do these narratives index, and how do they do it? If Mick belongs to the hegemonic categories of male, white, middle class, do his narratives help him maintain that hegemony? How? Since indexes are linguistic elements that point to a context, we need to understand how these stories call up a context, are appropriate to the current context, or bring up a new one. These questions entail a brief discussion about the notion of context. I do not subscribe to the narrow view of the relationship between context and identity as proposed by conversation analysts (Antaki and Widdicombe 1998b), according to whom contexts must be made relevant by the speakers of the conversation in order to become relevant to the analyst. I believe that speakers make contexts relevant in other ways besides referring to them directly. Although some CA scholars may argue that a context need not be *directly* referred to, such a perspective seems to dilute the "scientific rigor" argument that understandably motivates CA scholars and that forbids analysts from recruiting any context not referred to by the participants. However, one test for the relevance of an aspect of the context is whether the contextual information in question is necessary for the understanding and interpretation of a person's words in interaction. Speakers do not always articulate what contexts are relevant to produce this coherence, and in fact it would be inefficient for them to do so. In addition, contexts occur on

many levels: the preceding and following discourse, the relationship between the interactants, the speech event that the talk is
embedded in, the structural position of speakers in an institution,
and the societal categories occupied by speakers (gender, age, class,
race, ethnicity) are all possible relevant and interacting parts of
context (see Schiffrin 1996). Any or all of these may be indexed
by a particular linguistic item.

To return to Mick's narratives, then, we need to look at all of
these contextual possibilities to answer the questions posed above.
In essence, we want to understand (what we need to know about)
which aspects of the context of telling make these stories coherent,
and "tellable," in this conversation: How do they cohere with the
idea that Mick was elected to be president of the fraternity because
he is "the type of person that's goin' somewhere"? This utterance,
his initial attempt to answer the question, is notably vague: What
type of person is that? Where are you going? In what endeavor?
To answer these questions, let us work our way from the immediate, local contexts, to the more global considerations that relate
ultimately to the question of hegemonic identity categories.

At the most immediate level, these narratives are understood as
a second pair part – an answer to my question. This answer occurs
in an interview speech activity, in which I have been asking questions for some twenty minutes, and Mick has been giving me
answers about his past, his personality, and especially the fraternity.
So the speech event sets up his stance as an information giver,
an explainer. Thus the stories make sense if we are to understand
Mick's stance, which is generally cooperative. Mick answers questions fully, to the best of his ability, and in fact at one point suggests
my inclusion, to a limited extent, in his social sphere: in lines (k)
and (l) he refers to "the townhouse," and opens the possibility of
my presence there during his visits. "The townhouse," with the
definite article, refers to a particular house in which some members
live; there are many townhouses in the surrounding city, so Mick
is assuming that I have the knowledge, which can only be learned
through interaction within the fraternity, to grasp the referent of
the townhouse. This assumption, if correct, includes me in the
fraternity group and thus works to build solidarity.

Mick's talk in this stretch also follows the expected turn-taking and
adjacency pair pattern for such a speech event: Mick explains aspects

of his life to an interviewer, with expected extended turns at talk in response to questions. Moreover, I have repeatedly followed up with simple questions that require him to expand his answers, so his elaboration of these answers is not unexpected for the speech event. In relation to the structural discourse context, then, these narrative expansions of what it means to be "a person that's goin' somewhere" are coherent. Note that in other situations, even as an answer to the same question, these narratives would not be coherent.[3]

These local levels of indexicality for the stories are not surprising from a discourse analytic, or even conversation analytic, point of view. At the next level of context, however, much more knowledge must be recruited to understand why Mick's narratives are relevant. At the institutional level of the fraternity, he is relying on me to create an understanding that "a person that's goin' somewhere" is someone that the fraternity members want as president of their fraternity, and that furthermore, qualities of relentless productivity and extreme endurance characterize "a person that's goin' somewhere." Mick does, later in the interview, discuss the importance of having members who work hard (as well as members who are "people persons"). However, at this point in the interview he is relying on my knowledge that the fraternity values a serious work ethic when it comes to fraternity offices. Mick knows that I was present at elections in which these very themes were discussed and therefore may find it likely for me to be aware of the value of this hard work. Mick may also be assuming that I know this because I was a member of another fraternity when I was an undergraduate. But even if I am unaware of these facts, I could construct them afresh because such knowledge makes his statements coherent: if the fraternity didn't value hard work in its presidents then it wouldn't have elected him. In answer to my question, Mick does not list his qualifications, training, rhetoric skills

---

[3] For example, in a discussion of his role in the fraternity with other members, the members may ask Mick to recruit wrestlers from the University team (Mick is a former varsity wrestler). If Mick were to resist, the other member might reply "why do you think you were elected president"? To which Mick might reply "I'm just the kind of person that's goin' somewhere," but would less likely tell or even be afforded the opportunity to tell a story about tearing down a chicken coop. Such an answer in that situation would be incoherent.

or even his view that he is a "people person." Rather, he highlights his productive, hard-working personality, so in order to see his answer as coherent, we must assume that fraternity members value hard work.

Let me clarify that the men *do* use other criteria to evaluate a potential fraternity president, not the least of which is pure charisma and leadership, which is not always the same as working hard. As one member, Pete, described Mick's immediate predecessor: "I guess he's more charismatic and stuff like that, looks more like a president should. He was a really good leader and everything." Mick's characterization of why he was elected is likely, therefore, to be at odds even with the views held by other members of the fraternity. But he creates the connection between the personality traits he highlights through his narrative and the motivation for electing him president in his elaborated answer. Thus, Mick's narratives index a particular Discourse within the fraternity about valued personalities, which may in fact be at odds with other Discourses circulating in it. I discuss these competing discourses and their connections with wider Discourses of masculinity in Kiesling (1997), but it is important to note here that the Discourse of masculinity that needs to be drawn upon by the hearer to make the story coherent, is in fact a *particular* Discourse of masculinity. One danger in talking about gender is to assume that it can be conceived of simply as a categorical dichotomy of men and women, or masculine and feminine (on the difference between men and masculinities, see Connell 2000: 16, and Kiesling 2004). As shown above, Mick is relying on a Discourse of a particular type of masculinity.

We are now prepared to investigate the widest domains of discourse, that of cultural identity categories. Mick's categories at this level would be listed as: male (gender), early twenties (age), White (race), and middle class. These are all, as I have described above, categories of privilege and dominance in American society. How is it that these categories are relevant to creating coherence in Mick's narratives? In other words, if we did not have access to cultural models about how a young, White, middle-class man normatively acts, would the stories make sense?

The first step is to realize that the different ways of evaluating men in the fraternity are related to wider Discourses of society for evaluating men. That is, if we compare these to the Discourses of masculinity discussed above, we find that the sources of power in the fraternity mirror the ways in which men are valued in society. One of these Discourses of masculine power revolves around labor and labor markets, and another around physical power and the ability to physically control and discipline one's body. This physical *Rocky* masculine cultural model is something that Mick draws on in order to make the chicken coop narrative coherent in this conversation. Notice how he shifts "the type of person that's goin' somewhere," from someone who does everything "the best" to someone who doesn't do things that aren't productive, to, finally, someone who could never satisfy his father. He shifts from being evaluated in terms of the excellence of his activities to his endurance and persistence. Mick doesn't mark these shifts, but rather makes either brief statements or illustrates them with the two narratives. Presumably lines (f) and (g) (about not watching television and not doing things that aren't productive) are meant to illustrate line (e) ("anything I do I do it the best I can do"), but the connections are not made explicitly, and Mick relies on his listener to make use of relevance principles to make them coherent. In fact, there is no need to connect doing something the best you can do and not watching television, and not being able to satisfy one's father represents another step altogether. Therefore, line (q) ("I could never, never satisfy my dad") is one of the most difficult to make relevant in the entire segment. How is Mick's father and Mick's manual destruction of a large structure relevant to why he was elected president? One way of making this segment relevant is to see this as an explanation for why Mick is the way he is. This explanation provides yet another angle on the traits that make the speaker worthy of his place in the fraternity: if we draw on a Discourse of masculinity in which activity and the disciplining of one's body is valuable, then this narrative makes sense.

Note that one can deduce from the way Mick tells the story that he values these traits for a man, or maybe even a person in general, even if we don't already hold these views. This possibility of common sense deduction might suggest that the cultural knowledge need not be held *a priori*. However, Mick assumes that I already share these cultural presuppositions with him. It is this assumption of shared cultural models that makes up a Discourse; by relying on the cultural models, Mick recreates in another context the Discourses that have shaped his life.

This narrative illustrates one way in which hegemonic categories are recreated, and in the process, both changed and perpetuated. Mick does not, in fact, merely repeat a cultural model of masculinity through his report about the physical determination that led him to tear down the chicken coop; rather, he creates a new context, a new specificity in which the narrative takes place. His narrative is probably different from other instantiations of this kind of story in that his father serves as the model for his hard work, and in fact constitutes his motivation. Mick thus deftly weaves in a familiar narrative structure with details particular to him.

The significance of Mick's father's reaction to his work also relies on a culturally shared Discourse of fatherhood, although here we find more ambivalence. One model of fatherhood sees good (boys') fathers as demanding and distant. The ambivalence is shown in Mick's statement in line (ff) when he says that he doesn't hate his father for being demanding and distant, showing that he thinks that his father's actions could be construed as hateful. Mick explicitly states that he does not hate his father, and then continues to describe him indexing the same Discourse of masculinity that he has just used for himself (telling me that his father "built our whole house by himself"). This move extends the value of the cultural model by evaluating his father according to the same standards: Mick not only evaluates himself highly because he embodies this cultural model, but he also admires his father for embodying the same model and for passing it on.

Other models of masculinity that have been prevalent in other times do not valorize this kind of hard work. These other models might suggest that there is something wrong with the masculinity represented by Mick and his father if they have to work so hard, rather than relying, for example, on their good breeding or the historical economic power of their families. Hoch (1979) argues, for example, that these are two basic views of masculinity and that history shows an oscillation between the two. Although I believe that this theory is too general, the important point is that Mick's evaluation of himself and his father, and their relationship, relies on Discourses of masculinity in which (one form) of hegemonic masculinity values this kind of hard work.

The narrative that Mick tells therefore indexes not simply masculinity, but a particular model or Discourse of historically relevant hegemonic masculinity. It is through such tellings that these Discourses are circulated and mutated. Each new recreation (telling) both *relies on* the Discourse, in that it requires a listener to have access to that discourse, and *recreates* the Discourse, by giving it details particular to that telling and that person. The narrative gives the Discourse a unique voice, while echoing uncounted previous voices, in Bakhtin's (1981c) sense. In addition, the particular voice is anchored in a specific context, in both an institutional and a discourse sense, which makes it not only culturally relevant but also relevant at time of speaking as well. In this way, the telling of stories helps recreate hegemonic identities and Discourses, and helps maintain the hegemony of the Discourse.

10.7 A narrative of White heterosexual masculinity

The second narrative which I will analyze is hegemonic not just in its conception of masculinity, but also in its construction of sexual and racial identities for the protagonists. In this case, the teller of the story was not actually present to witness the events, but the story is an iconic narrative in the fraternity (i.e. it does not even need to be told in full, but is so well known – iconic – that a single phrase stands for the entire narrative). The narrative is told to explain how the term *Bitch boy* entered the lexicon of the fraternity. *Bitch boy* has come to be used to indicate a particular relationship between two men, and this is the reason why I asked to hear how it originated. Another member (Speed) exemplifies its use in a meeting when he says "I used to be Rex's little bitch boy [in the] graduate affairs [office]," meaning that Speed did mundane work for Rex in his capacity as Graduate Affairs officer. This narrative is thus very much like the wider discourse of which it is part because it has entered the consciousness of the fraternity members who were not even present at the time the incident took place.[4] In this narrative, I am interviewing Mack, a senior member, and have asked him to explain the term.

---

[4] The term is also used more widely than in the fraternity, particularly in gay men's discourse. I believe the two uses are related, probably such that the protagonist in the fraternity story borrowed it from gay men's discourse. However, here I am interested in how the narrative creates the meaning of the term in the fraternity, and not necessarily in its origin in gay men's culture, although such origin is intriguing and bears further investigation.

Example 10.2

(a)	MACK	So bitch boy um
(b)		Chicken hawk and I don't know if you've ever met him KW ((the member's name)) um
(c)		one time was tellin' a story
(d)		and I don't know if there were other people around
(e)		or if he's just told this story so many times
(f)		but um he apparently was at another school I think
(g)		maybe with his brother,
(h)		he was in a bar with his brother,
(i)		the details of it I'm not – I don't remember very well.
(j)		Anyway he was at this bar
(k)		and I think maybe he was talking to this – he was talking to a girl.
(l)		another guy some strange guy bigger than K though
(m)		um came over and started hassling him
(n)		either about the girl or he was standing in his place
(o)		you know the normal bar nonsense. and um
(p)		so K kinda left it be for a while and uh
(q)		he he I think he mentioned it to his brother
(r)		now they were there with a friend of his brother's
(s)		and apparently this friend of his brother's
(t)		they were at the bar
(u)		this friend of his brother's was quite a big man
(v)		very large you know
(w)		like six four you know like two hundred and fifty pounds or something
(x)		strong
(y)		big guy
(z)		and um so K went back over I think to talk to this girl
(aa)		and uh apparently this same guy started giving him problems again
(bb)		eh and this guy this big friend of Ks brother
(cc)		comes up behind – behind this guy this guy that's bothering K,
(dd)		and just puts his arm around him very gently
(ee)		and kind of pulls him in close
(ff)		and starts talking to him r:::really kind of
(gg)		y – you know I don't even wanna I don't even wanna try and do the voice
(hh)		that K does you're gonna have to ask K for it.
(ii)		but t – he starts really talkin to him
(jj)		like he's pimpin' this guy or somethin' you know
(kk)		**and he goes you know what we gon do?**
(ll)		**You gon be ma bitch boy fa the rest of the night**

(mm)	and then he just went down the list of things that he's gonna make=
(nn)	this guy do for him an
(oo)	it wasn't – it was demeaning things like
(pp)	you know you gonna get me drinks
(qq)	you're gonna come in and wipe my ass and
(rr)	you know nothing nothing like
(ss)	I'm gonna kick your ass or anything like that.
(tt)	he spoke real calmly and real coolly and
(uu)	**you know You gon be my bitch boy tonight.** you know
(vv)	and so that's where it came from and
(ww)	bitch boy you know it's pretty self explanatory
(xx)	you know it's just a little boy
(yy)	who's gonna do all the bitch work for me I dunno

I will not analyze this story in the detail of the previous narrative for reasons of space. I want to focus on lines (kk)–(ll) and (uu), which I have highlighted in bold. These lines are constructed dialogue, and it is within these vivid recreations of the protagonist's speech that the term *bitch boy* appears in the narrative. Before line (ll) in the narrative, the events in the narrative have been related in general terms, without providing much detail. For example, in lines (s) and (aa) "apparently" hedges Mack's recounting of events, and describes the brother as being "two hundred and fifty pounds or somethin'." These terms give the general outline of events and characters but without the specifics that make a narrative particularly vivid (see Tannen 1989 on the importance of detail in conversation). In this immediate context line (ll) stands out, because it is a representation of a specific statement. Although Mack suggests in line (gg) that he doesn't "even wanna try and do the voice," he does anyway. Line (ll) is thus the central clause in the narrative: it is the point at which the term is used, and the point at which the narrative becomes vivid in its details.

One of those details, as Mack suggests, is the phonology of the utterance. When Mack represents the voice of the dominant character, the amplitude becomes lower, and voice quality is almost breathy. More significantly, the pronunciation of *going to*, standardly reduced to *gonna* in American English, is reduced even further in three of its repetitions. Crucially, the two uses that also include *bitch boy* show this complete reduction. In fact, in line (ll) the reduction is such that the vowel is nasalized and the nasal consonant elided. Another aspect of lines (kk), (ll) and (uu) is the deletion of the copula. As Labov (1972c) shows, the deletion of the copula is related to the standard American English contraction of the copula, so that rates of deletion parallel rates of contraction to 're in similar contexts (e.g. *you gonna* is just a further step of reduction from *you're gonna*, just as *you're gonna* is a reduction of *you are gonna*). Most importantly, however, the deletion of the nasal and the deletion of the copula are aspects of African-American Vernacular English (AAVE) (Mufwene *et al.* 1998, Wolfram and Schilling-Estes 1998:171). These statements are presented as not just mimicking the actual words said, but also their precise phonology and intonation.

However, the character being described by Mack is White, even as he is represented as using AAVE phonology. Mack is thus using the AAVE phonology not as an index of race, but as an index of a typical stance associated with Black men. As shown in Kiesling (2001) and Bucholtz (1999b), and as discussed by Frankenberg (1997), the Discourse of race and gender in the US places Black masculinity in stances of sexualized physical power. In Frankenberg's terms: "'Man of Color' is sexually rapacious, sometimes seductive, usually predatory" (1997:11).

Here Mack uses the AAVE phonology to create a physically dominant stance in his character, and gender and sex are implicated as well. Important for the story is that the protagonist never directly threatens the man who becomes his bitch boy; he only implies the threat. In fact, Mack points out that the protagonist does *not* say he's "gonna kick your ass or something" where to "kick ass" is to physically assault someone. Rather, the protagonist refigures the relationship in sexual terms such that the dominated man is dominated as if he were a sexually dominated woman: Mack suggests that the protagonist is "pimpin' him or somethin'," which entails a male–female relationship within which the man "owns" the woman, who is used sexually (a pimp is a man who controls and protects female prostitutes and takes part of their income). The subordinate man in the story is metaphorically turned into a woman. Thus, by relying on his speakers' access to Discourses of sexuality and race, Mack is able to create a masculine character who dominates another feminine, but male, character.

All these aspects of the narrative are indexed by the term "bitch boy." The lexical items in the term are related to those meanings, as Mack implies when he says that a *bitch boy* "is just a little boy who's gonna do all the bitch work for me." The word "boy" encodes an age-based dominance,[5] providing the subordinate male part of the term (*boy*). The *bitch* part of the term (with *bitch* used as an adjective rather than a noun) indicates the female sexual subordination involved in the *bitch work*. While Mack suggests that the term is "pretty self explanatory," such clarity can only come from an understanding of the dominance relations of the sexes and dominance relations of masculinity by age. Both the term more generally, and the story more specifically and vividly, thus rely on Discourses of masculinity, race, and sexuality to become meaningful. The story is not coherent as an illustration for the term unless we have access to all of these Discourses. In this sense, it reinforces and continues to reify these Discourses of dominance relations in society: Black men as "predatory," and women (or feminine men) as "subordinate." It thus performs identity work not for the characters in the story, but for the teller who occupies a cultural Center, while the characters become Others.

This narrative also shows that the point of a story can actually be the illustration and elaboration of the meaning of a single word. But there is more to this narrative. In the fraternity, this story has become a Discourse of its own, and has become "packaged" in the indexicality of a single phrase. The story creates the original context of use for this term, and thus sets its indexicality, while the phrase continues to bring the narrative into new contexts, even if speakers do not necessarily have access to the original story. It is thus a particularly layered example of indexical meanings, and shows how stories can become iconic in a society, even if they do not come from literature. However, this kind of indexicality only works within a wider indexicality in which the practices and structures of masculinity and femininity, and Black and White, are structured by Discourses of identity. In this sense, the continued telling of the stories and the use of terms that are iconic of them recreate hegemonic identities.

---

[5] A race-based dominance may also be indexed here; see Ervin-Tripp 1972.

10.8 Re-making hegemonic identities

A person's identity is represented by the ways in which a person's self is related to other selves in the social world. Even enduring relationships such as maternal or paternal ones are continually recreated or reinforced, despite their existence as relevant cultural categories. Among the ways in which the creation of this relationship is accomplished is through narrative, either in the kind of conversational stories discussed by Schiffrin (1996), or in life stories (Linde 1993). I have suggested that for the narratives illustrated in this chapter to be properly understood, one must assume the teller's presumption that the audience shares cultural Discourses that help prefigure relationships among individuals and groups. For people who belong to hegemonic groups, these Discourses specify dominant and subordinate categories – the Center and the Other. By indexing the Discourses, the hegemonic teller can then fill a role in the dominant Center. In order to create these dominant categories, subordinate categories must also be created. In fact, it is by identifying and creating these subordinate categories that the dominant categories also become invisible and normative; they are "erased" in a sense, and the speakers can thus naturalize their power. This is one of the mechanisms of hegemony.

One question left unanswered up to this point is that of the exact working of this process: where do the discourses come from, and is the speaker just relying on pre-existing Discourses or is he/she doing something to the Discourses while the stories are being told? I introduced the chapter by asking the question (as Critical Discourse Analysts do): what is needed to make the story understandable, or coherent, within the local context of the speech event (whether that be an interview, meeting, or something more casual)? I have shown that some hegemonic Discourses are required for this understanding. But I have also shown how hegemonic Discourses are being *recreated*, not only presupposed. In this way, the hegemonic identity-making that takes place in narrative is not only the making of the *narrator's* identity, but is also in fact the re-making of *Discourses* of identity: categories and relationships that are repeated and reflected in social structure and practice. Mick is not just presenting himself as a hard-working man, he is also making this a relevant, valued category. Once an individual hears such evaluations several times, he can deduce the ideologies about masculine identities that dominate in this fraternity and culture. And as I have shown elsewhere (Kiesling 1997, 1998), as these evaluations are repeated, the Discourses and identities are re-made in the fraternity. The same process can be seen in the bitch boy narrative: we could deduce that a *boy* is small and powerless based on Mack's description, and that *bitch* work is of a certain demeaning sort; once we hear the term "bitch boy" used in a few contexts it will be clear how it is to be interpreted. The way the term is used then, will show us how this group thinks about gendered identities in a number of social dimensions (e.g. labor, sex, and age). The narratives are re-making the Discourse.

I am emphasizing the morphological separation in re-making (and re-creating) for a purpose. This term should not be taken to be a synonym for "repeating"; I mean precisely that while the Discourses may pre-exist in the listener's knowledge, the narrative is in fact "making the Discourses again," reifying them in a particular way for a specific purpose. This process also guarantees the possibility, in fact the need, for Discourse to change. There is a connection to previous Discourses and voices, but these previous Discourses and voices are being put together in a new way for a fresh context. These narratives, then, are truly *making* identities which are hegemonic, for both the speaker at the time of speaking and the social world they inhabit and will inhabit in the future.

Appendix 10.1 Transcription conventions

Each line is roughly a breath group, and unless otherwise noted there is a short pause for breath at the end of each line in the transcripts.

(TEXT)	indicates accuracy of transcription inside parentheses is uncertain
(?)	indicates an utterance that could be heard but was not intelligible
A:	indicates the segment is lengthened
. . .	indicates a short pause
=	indicates that the utterance continues on the next line without a pause

TEXT   indicates emphasis through amplitude, length, and/or
             intonation
BU-   indicates an abrupt cutoff of speech
((TEXT))   indicates comments added by the author

Acknowledgements

I would like to thank Anna De Fina and Michael Bamberg for their insightful comments on this chapter, that have strengthened it considerably and led to a deepening of my thought on the material. I also would like to thank the audience and participants of the 2001 American Association of Applied Linguistics Annual Conference panel for their attention and comments on the paper presented there which was the precursor to this chapter. I take the usual individual responsibility for any failings that remain.

11

On being white, heterosexual and male in a Brazilian school: multiple positionings in oral narratives

Luiz Paulo Moita-Lopes

Since many stories can be told, even of the same event, then we each have many possible coherent selves.

(Davies and Harré 1999: 49)

The ideological becoming of a human being . . . is the process of selectively assimilating the words of others.

(Bakhtin 1981c: 341)

11.1 Introduction

The theme of identity can be seen as one of the most popular topics in the media and in the Human Sciences today. This interest may be due in part to an effort to understand the social, cultural, technological and political changes that are affecting the way we live our everyday lives, in most parts of the world. These changes have led us to question traditional views of, for example, gender, sexuality and family life, in view of a new panorama in which to live social life. The ever-increasing presence of women in the job market, women's feminist consciousness and human reproduction technology, to name just three of these changes, have altered our perception of how families are organized, of what sexuality means and, consequently, of how the genders are performed.

On the other hand, the centrality of the theme of identity also seems to be motivated by the way the structures of power within which we live have been affected, in most parts of the world, by the so-called liberation movements, which began in the middle of last century (although in different degrees in different parts of the world), as well as by the intense migration from the old colonies of the southern hemisphere to the old colonies or to the rich countries of the northern hemisphere, in the so-called post-colonial world. All of these changes, side by side with the influence of the written media, the screens of international TV channels and the Internet, have brought about an awareness of the mosaic we are made of in such a way that the interrogation on who we are in the social world has become a constant and relevant pursuit. That is the reason why "identity matters, both in terms of social and political concerns within the contemporary world and within academic discourses where identity has been seen as conceptually important in offering explanations of social and cultural changes" (Woodward 1997: 1).

No wonder, therefore, research on masculinities has motivated so many scholars: gender can be considered one of the crucial categories to understand social and cultural changes in contemporary life. After years of concern with femininities, very much due to feminist movements,[1] one finds more and more emphasis on masculinities in the Human Sciences: Johnson and Meinhof (1997) in discourse analysis; Mac an Ghail (1994) and Lesko (2000) in education; Connell (1995 and 2000), Bourdieu (1999) and O'Donnell and Sharpe (2000) in sociology; Badinter (1992) and Frosh, Phoenix and Pattman (2002) in psychology are just a few examples.

But why focus on masculinity, heterosexuality and whiteness in a Brazilian school, as indicated in the title of this chapter? This concern springs mainly from results of previous research that I carried out in Brazilian schools (cf. Moita-Lopes 1998, 2002). Although the project did not center on any specific social identity (SID) in particular, the ethnographic analysis of the discursive construction of SIDs at school drew my attention to the fact that masculinity was one of the crucial identities in construction in the ethnographic situation. As I argue in Moita-Lopes (2002), although the analysis of the classroom discourse seemed to indicate, at first sight, that what was being constructed was sexuality, a more careful analysis

---

[1] It is true, however, that within some types of feminist movements the focus is/was on femininity as a political banner (just like the way other identities are/were conceived in other political movements), following, therefore, an essentialist perspective as if a unity called woman existed in isolation from social classes, ethnicities, sexualities, etc. (cf. Hall 1996: 15–16).

showed that, in fact, the crucial concern with which boys and girls were involved was the construction of hegemonic masculinity. The research showed that both sexuality and femininity were constructed in the school context through the definition of hegemonic masculinity. Masculinity (and by extension heterosexuality) was then taken as the comparison element and the SIDs of homoeroticism and femininity were defined in relation to it. As Bourdieu (1999:18) pointed out, "it has been many times noted that both in social perception and in language, masculinity shows itself as something unmarked, neutral to some extent, in opposition to femininity, which is explicitly characterized."

These results seemed still more interesting because, in common sense, masculinity, in the patriarchal societies in which we live, is equally understood as a given or as a natural feature of human nature (Badinter 1992; Bourdieu 1999; Epstein and Johnson 1998; Hollway 1984; Kimmel and Messner 1989, for example) against which femininity is defined. What is different from the norm, as it were, is femininity, which is defined in the light of masculinity. Likewise, homoerotic and black identities are also defined in relation to the norm: heterosexuality and whiteness, respectively. That is to say that what is different is homoeroticism and blackness. A similar point seems to be made by Mac an Ghail (1994:10): "there has been a tendency to conceptualize gender as something to do with women, sexuality as something to do with lesbians and gays, and 'race' as having something to do with black people."

My argument is that the SIDs which, in general, are in a position of hegemony constitute the center, which defines the margins or otherness. The SIDs which are understood as in a process of construction, in common sense, are blackness, femininity and homoeroticism because they are different from what I call here naturalized SIDs: the white, the male and the heterosexual. In a similar trend of thought, it would be possible to discuss issues related to normality in relation to how the whites are constructed in Euro-centered cultures or, perhaps now, in northern hemisphere-centered cultures such as the Brazilian cultures. The same could also be said in relation to the construction of the normalcy of heterosexuality in opposition to the social construction of the abnormality of the homoerotic person (cf. Katz 1996 and Freire Costa 1992, for example). The hegemony position guarantees that the other is the black, the feminine and the homoerotic, in such a way that, as Epstein and Johnson (1998: 26) have argued, "[the excluded categories] become the Other against which the Us is defined."

It is in this perspective, I think, that Giroux (1997: 286) refers to whiteness as a concept that, in the USA, was "displaced from its widely understood status as an unnamed, universal moral referent," and is now understood as "a category of racial identity." Although in the USA, according to Giroux (1997: 287), whiteness is no longer invisible, I would like to argue that this is not true in Brazil – where the research reported on here was carried out – since whites, in general, do not seem to be aware that they are privileged because of their race. As Sodré (1999: 196), in reference to Brazil, points out, "[whites] are semiotized through a vague notion of 'purity' and not as race (except in radical discourses): race is always the other." Therefore, race is blackness, and by extension, in the light of my argument above, one could say that sexuality is homoeroticism and gender is femininity.

In this chapter I want to focus on the social identities of whiteness, heterosexuality and masculinity so that I can show their socially constructed nature as "race," sexuality and gender. To use and extend Giroux's comments (1997: 286) about whiteness, such an analysis deprives whiteness, heterosexuality and masculinity of their status of "unnamed, universal moral referent[s]" or unmarked naturalized social identities. Following hooks' proposals (1992), I want to change the focus, so that I can reveal a different world: instead of showing how blacks, gays/lesbians and women are constructed, which would go along the lines of common sense, I want to objectify[2] a white heterosexual boy, by transforming or repositioning him into the other, so that I can make visible how he is constructed.

---

[2] In this connection, it should be noted that it is not usual for those socially situated in hegemonic positions to be the object of research. The middle classes, the whites, heterosexuals and men are not as likely to open their doors to researchers as are those marginally located. Probably, this is so because the role of object is normally given to those who "lack the capacity to see or recognize reality" (hooks, 1992: 168).

I focus on the social construction of SIDs by investigating how a particular boy, fictionally addressed here as Hans, – a focal subject – constructs himself and/or gets constructed as male, heterosexual and white by analyzing how he is positioned or positions himself in the narratives he tells or is told in a school. I first discuss the social constructionist approach to discourse and social identities, which informs this paper, presenting the theoretical framework for a social constructionist view of masculinities. I take the view that masculinities are discursively constructed (situated, accordingly, in history, culture and institutional life) in narrative practices and are fragmented, fluid and contradictory. To examine these narrative practices, I then introduce positioning as a theoretical construct that can show how multiple SIDs are constructed at the very moment the narratives are being told. Then I briefly present the research situation (a 5th grade Brazilian Portuguese reading classroom in the city of Rio de Janeiro) as well as the ethnographic mode of inquiry through which the stories analyzed were generated. The analysis reveals that whiteness, heterosexuality and masculinity are constructed in collective narrative practices in which both boys and girls are participants and that these faces of SIDs are created through the multiple positionings that narrative participants occupy in relation to characters, tellers and listeners. In particular, the analysis shows that these SIDs are not directly focused on or topicalized in the narratives as such, but they are constructed, instead, by reference to blackness, homoeroticism and femininity.

11.2 Discourse, narratives and social identities: a social constructionist approach to masculinities

I follow the view that discourse has a constitutive nature in the sense that, when we are engaged in discourse, besides representing the world, we are also constructing it in the discursive practices in which we act (Fairclough 1992; van Dijk 1997). This view also implies that when we use language we are in fact acting in the world, doing things to each other through the meanings we construct. That is to say that discourse has a social nature in the sense that discursive practices are dialogical (Bakhtin 1981a) since language use crucially implies otherness, and the fact that we use language in relation to one another, reflecting other voices we have been exposed to as well as our interlocutors. This implies that when we use language we place ourselves interactionally with other people (Wortham 2001).

The other important feature of the view of discourse that underlies this chapter highlights its situatedness, which implies that we use language under particular cultural, historical and institutional contingencies (Hall 1995; Lindstrom 1992; Wertsch 1991; etc.). Implicit here is the view that meaning is constructed and negotiated locally under the direct influence of sociohistorical constrains that make different kinds of meanings available on the basis of how people are positioned in power-infused discursive practices (Parker 1993) and, therefore, on the basis of their social identities (Hall 1995). Power, which crisscrosses the discursive construction of social identities as regards social class, gender, sexuality, race, etc., is inherent here.

That does not mean, however, that these sociohistorical constraints cannot be altered or that they are passively accepted as a matter of fate. People in their local discursive practices are building life on the basis of their meaning choices and are therefore constructing history. In the perspective I follow here, what is of interest are the discursive struggles between the meanings people bring to the discursive practices they are engaged with and the ways these meanings are or are not locally (re-)constructed in these practices. In other words, people are acting within meanings located at the level of socio-history (macro-level social processes) and within meanings situated at the level of local social interaction (micro-level social processes).

Therefore, at the same time that SIDs are taken into account in meaning negotiation, they are also being discursively (re-)constructed locally. I take a social constructionist view of SIDs: they are constructed in language use. This view of SIDs is anti-essentialist since there is no essence to be revealed about men, women, whites, blacks, etc. Our SIDs are constructed in the discursive practices in which we act and in which we get involved with particular SID projects. This makes it possible for men, for example, to perform hegemonic masculinity (Connell 1995) as in the case of the boy whose discursive practices are investigated here. This view also implies that other men are involved with other masculinity projects or that the same men may be performing different masculinities in different discursive practices: masculinities are fragmented, fluid and contradictory.

Another relevant theoretical construct in this chapter is the view that narrative practices are crucial sites for social identity construction or for the study of social identity construction processes since as Wortham (2001: 145), among others, points out: "people rely on 'storylines' from the culture to organize themselves." This view is taken by researchers coming from different fields of investigation and different theoretical frameworks: Bruner (1986, 1987, 1996, 1997), Schiffrin (1996), Sarup (1996), Munby (1997), Goodwin (1993), M. M. Gergen (1994), Somers and Gibson (1994), Brockmeier and Harré (1997) Linde (1993), Mishler (1999) and Wortham (2001), to name just a few. These researchers have shown that "stories guide action; that people construct identities (however multiple and changing) by locating themselves within a repertoire of emplotted stories" (Somers and Gibson 1994: 38).

Because narratives present characters in action, they have the potential for picturing people doing things to each other in the world, i.e., acting in social life through discourse, and, therefore, for constructing particular social identities in the story-world – in "the narrated event" – and in the very act of telling the story – in the world the story is being told or in "the storytelling event" (Wortham 2001: 19–20). Narrating is therefore a way of doing things to people both in the story-world and in the interactional context in which the story is being narrated. This view is in line with the approach to discourse as a mode of social action through which we act in and construct the world I discussed above.

Following this perspective, I approach narrative practices as ways of legitimating particular social identities while rejecting others. These practices are locally influenced by the sociohistorical contingencies that constrain the meanings with which tellers and listeners operate and that construct particular social identities although these meanings may also be contested. As I have indicated above, masculinities are constructed in discursive practices that promote particular gender projects for boys. I argue that the narratives boys get involved with in institutional life (with colleagues in schools, as the case of Hans here) are crucial in questioning or promoting particular masculinity projects.

11.3 Positioning in narratives

Positioning is a theoretical construct that has been used in similar ways in different areas of investigation. In general, it refers to how people are located in discourse or in conversation when they are engaged in meaning construction with others. In the field of Cultural Studies, it is used at a macro-level of analysis, referring to the situatedness of discursive practices and to the enunciation of the "I" (Hall 1990: 222). This view actually accounts for the sociohistorical contingencies that guide language use, as discussed above. A similar use of positioning is found in Holland *et al.* (1998), in anthropology, although these authors are guided by Vygotskian and Bakhtinian sociohistorical approaches. Positioning here is equated with perspective or angle through which people are trying to act in the world.

Positioning is also used at a more micro-level of analysis, but still taking into account sociohistorical factors, in a Foucauldian perspective (1971), in critical discourse analysis. For example, Fairclough (1992) conceives of positioning as a construct that accounts for the social effects of what people say to each other in the discursive practices in which they act. In this sense, "the social subject that produces a statement is not an entity which exists outside and independently of discourse, as the source of the statement (its 'author'), but is on the contrary a function of the statement itself. That is, statements position subjects" (Fairclough 1992: 43) as both speakers/writers and as listeners/readers. Fairclough (1992: 43–44) argues that in different discursive activities subjects are positioned differently through different enunciative modalities that account for the fragmentation of the subject.

A similar use, usually identified in the literature (van Langenhove and Harré 1999; Bamberg 1999) as the first introduction of positioning as a theoretical construct in the Social Sciences, is proposed by Hollway (1984), who was also influenced by Foucault. In her study of gender construction in discourse, she (1984: 236) argues that "discourses make available positions for subjects to take up." This view seems to imply that the social subject is a function of discourse – given meanings – just like in Fairclough (1992) above. Hollway (1984: 238) further states that people invest in particular "positionings in discourses, and consequently in relation to each other." Out of given or existing meanings, there is investment in some positionings and not in others on the part of discourse participants.

In social psychology (Bamberg 1999; Davies and Harré 1999; Harré and van Langenhove 1999; for example), positioning as a theoretical construct is used in a way that seems to incorporate both the meanings that are given by sociohistory (at a macro-social level) when people come to discourse engagement and the meanings they themselves generate (at a micro-social level). This duplicity accounts for the changing / dynamic / multiple positions discourse participants may occupy in discursive and in narrative practices and is fruitful to my approach because it accounts both for social history and agency. As Davies and Harré (1999: 52) indicate, "with positioning, the focus is on the way in which the discursive practices constitute the speakers and hearers in certain ways and yet at the same time they are a resource through which speakers and hearers can negotiate new positions," and be, as a consequence, re-positioned.

I argue that positioning is a useful construct in the analysis of narrative practices, to locate tellers, listeners and characters vis-à-vis one another (Bamberg 1999) in the meaning construction struggles they are involved with. It helps to illustrate how social identities are being discursively constructed in narrative practices as well as how their enactments can be fluid, fragmented and contradictory in nature. In this perspective, the SIDs one identifies with or is identified with depend on the positionings one has occupied/will occupy in the narrative practices one has been or is involved with. To investigate positionings in storytelling is a way to understand how people act when they are involved in narrative practices with others or in the discursive construction of SIDs both as agents and as people who live under sociohistorically given discourses.

This interactional view of positioning is also followed by Wortham (2001), whose analytical tools I use in the analysis of Hans' narratives below. Following Bakhtin very closely, Wortham (2001) argues that when a narrator takes up a particular interactional positioning, he acts like someone in that positioning and "becomes like that kind of person" (Wortham 2001: 9). That is to say that his words echo the words of others in that positioning:

he is in dialogue with the words of others who have been in that positioning, as well as with the words of interlocutors in the narrative practice itself.

Although the analytical tools suggested by Wortham (2001: 70–75) were conceived for the investigation of interactional positionings in autobiographical narratives, I find them useful in the analysis of the interactional positionings Hans takes up in the stories he tells to his interlocutors in school in the process of constructing himself as male, white and heterosexual. These tools make explicit the cues used by narrators, which are indexical of their interactional positionings to others both in the narrated story and in the storytelling event. They are reference and predication, metapragmatic descriptors, quotation, evaluative indexicals and epistemic modalization.

Reference and predication account for the elements of the world narrators choose to refer to and characterize in the stories they tell. Through these devices, narrators choose to position themselves towards characters, objects, facts, etc. that are included in their narratives. Predicating a noun through the use of adjectives or other devices is a way of placing a character, for example, in a particular social group and of ventriloquating those in that group.

Metapragmatic descriptors include "verbs of saying", which narrators use to refer to and predicate about how something was said in such a way that they evaluate what was spoken. Narrators can also use nouns, which are metapragmatic just like "verbs of saying," in the sense that they refer to and predicate language use. Note, for example, nouns such as *row, lie, quarrel*, etc. Again these nouns and verbs are indexical of how particular others (narrators and characters) used language in the narrated story and in the storytelling event.

Quotation is a cue which involves reference to who said what, to the verb used to characterize the speech event (i.e. the metapragmatic verb) and to the actual utterance quoted, which represents the event. When choosing the quotation, narrators are ventriloquating others and positioning themselves towards them.

Evaluative indexicals are "lexical items, grammatical constructions, accents, or any of a number of other linguistic patterns" (Wortham 2001: 73) which get associated with particular groups of people and when used by narrators and/or characters function as indices of these groups, in the sense that their voices are brought up into the narratives, therefore positioning narrators towards them.

The last type of analytic tool that Wortham (2001) suggests is epistemic modalization. Epistemic modalizers express the kinds of access narrators have towards the narrated event and position them in the storytelling event in particular ways. They show whether narrators are situated as privileged spectators/participants or as contingent participants in the narrated event and in the storytelling event. Some formulaic expressions ("Once upon a time") and verb tenses, for example, account for the epistemic access that narrators have towards the narrated event, and, therefore, indicate how they relate to the storytelling event, voicing characters and narrators in different ways.

Another point raised by Wortham (2001) is the fact that these cues have to be understood and, therefore, analyzed in relation to particular ethnographic contexts. As a consequence, before moving on to the analysis of Hans' multiple interactional positionings in narratives, I want to look into the ethnographic context and the general research methodological framework within which the stories analyzed here were generated.

11.4 Research context and methodology

The narratives I analyze below were generated within an ethnographic mode of inquiry in a school of the public sector in the city of Rio de Janeiro. Specifically, the research context were 5th grade literacy events in a Portuguese-as-a-mother-tongue classroom. The data were generated in the second semester of 1997 in a classroom in which there were 38 pupils between 12 and 14 years old.

I generated the data with two research assistants (two female undergraduate students) and audiotaped a total of 20 hours of classes and 4 hours of focus-group interviews. In addition, we took field notes during classes and interviews; both were literacy events since the interviews focused on the texts discussed in class and on the discussion they had generated. The texts were chosen by the teacher out of a collection of texts on issues of identity that I had given her. To these she also added a few of her own choice. In the focus-group interviews I also used some comic strips (therefore, also research instruments) about social identities to equally mediate their discussion.

The focus-group interviews were conducted in another class-room when the pupils had some free time. I asked the teacher to select 7 pupils of different ages, ethnicity, gender and academic standards. The pupils (4 boys and 3 girls) sat around in a circle, read a few lines of our class transcription data and I inquired about their ideas. Hans was one of the oldest pupils in class, i.e. he was 14 years old then. He has a working-class background and con-structs himself as white.

The stories below were spontaneously told by Hans in the focus-group interviews in his effort to make sense of the issues being discussed. The boy positions himself through the narrated events and in the storytelling event to six classmates (three boys and three girls), the researcher and two research assistants.

11.5 Analyzing Hans' interactional positionings

The aim of the analysis of Hans' interactional positionings is to show how Hans gets constructed as male, heterosexual and white in the stories he tells. I will analyze three narratives that were told by him to all the participants in the focus-group interviews. The focus is on his construction as male in Example 11.1, as hetero-sexual in Example 11.2 and as white in Example 11.3. These narratives were chosen because they clearly show his interactional positionings with respect to gender, sexuality and race.

The first narrative below[3] concentrates on the construction of Hans as male. The other overt participants[4] in the narratives are

---

[3] The transcriptions have been translated from Portuguese (cf. the original texts in the appendix) into English for the purpose of this paper. I use T for teacher, B for boy, G for girl, Ps for several pupils speaking at the same time. I also use ( ) to indicate something inaudible and . . . where there was some editing. Also, / means a short pause and // a longer pause. Also, note that for ethical reasons, all the pupils' names used here are fictitional.

[4] By overt participants I mean interlocutors who are actually helping Hans to narrate the story whereas other interlocutors (other classmates, the researcher and the two research assistants) are listening to him.

Peter and Gail, who will also be present as overt participants in other narratives, as will soon be shown. The characters in this story are Hans, his father and his sister. The narrative is motivated by previous conversation about the differences between men and women. The theme of the narrative is men's sexual incontinence, which has been widely raised in the literature as one of the main concerns in men's discourses (Badinter 1992; Hollway 1984; Moita-Lopes 2002).

Example 11.1

Hans as male

"Lock up your she-goats because my he-goat is free."

(a)	HANS	When Dad arrived/ and saw my sister outside,/ and she would be on the street
(b)		until late,/ then my father would say:/ "Go home!//This is not the time for
(c)		women/to be out on the street"./ Then I would say:/ "What do
(d)		you mean by this is not the time/ for a woman to be on the street?/ Don't you
(e)		keep telling me:/ 'Go and find a girlfriend!'/ How can I find a girlfriend/ if all
(f)		the fathers say/ that this is not the right time for girls/ to be on the street,/ if
(g)		they lock up their daughters at home?"//
(h)		Then/ my father would say:/ "Lock up your she-goats/ because my he-goat is
(i)		free."/ Because we have to lock up the women/ because the he-goat is free./ If
(j)		we let the women within easy reach ((laughter)), /the he-goat will go/ and
(k)		((makes the sound of an animal catching another))// ((laughter)).
(l)	PETER	Right,/ the he-goat is free,/ isn't he?//
(m)	HANS	They have to lock up the she-goats!//
(n)	GAIL	My mother always says that to me./ My mother always says that.//

Hans makes recourse to a story in which the characters are members of his family (his father and his sister), therefore voicing the referents as people who directly participate in his life and who will accordingly be responsible for the meanings under which he lives. Also, he places his father as someone who has the authority to

define how he ("Go and find a girlfriend!" (line (b))) and his sister
("Go home!/ This is not the time for women/ to be out on the
street," (lines (b)–(c))) should live their lives and, hence, as someone
who knows best about how men and women live. That is to say that
he positions himself in a specific way because he is voicing the
words of his father, who, as a male, should know about how men
go about the world in the performance of hegemonic masculinity, in
particular, as a protector of the women in the family. Hans is
positioning his father as a protector of the women in the family
and therefore he is positioning males and himself in the same way.

The authority on the father's part is also cued by the imperative
verb forms with which Hans frames his father's voices: "Go home!"
(line (b)); "Go and find a girlfriend!" (line (e)), "Lock up your she-
goats" (line (h)). That is to say that he voices his father as someone
who gives commands when he speaks. The use of these verb forms
consequently predicates his father's words by indexing him both as
a man and as a father, who is also involved with Hans' construction
as heterosexual.

Another device used by Hans to position himself in the narrative
is the use of direct quotations. By choosing to quote his father
and himself directly, he is adding verisimilitude to the narrated
event. The use of direct quotations, therefore, indicates that Hans
has epistemic access to the narrated event and that he actually
participated in it.

The quotations also indicate who is entitled to speak: he and his
father. Despite the fact that his sister is a crucial element in the story
since she is the motivating force ("When Dad arrived/ and saw my
sister outside" (line (a))), she is only spoken about or referred to.
Her voice is not quoted. By doing this, Hans is aligning himself as a
man with his father. He repeats his concluding statement in lines
(i) and (j), showing, therefore, that he positions himself like him:
"Because we have to lock up the women/ because the he-goat is
free./ If we let the women within easy reach ((laughter)), /the he-
goat will go/ and ((makes the sound of an animal catching
another))//."

The lexical items used in these sentences, which contain the
evaluation of the story, are also indexical of how Hans positions
himself towards men and women: men are "free" whereas women
should be "locked up." Also, the sound used by Hans (line (k)) to

describe how men attack women indexes men as animals and predators and women as passive victims, voicing, therefore, them as such.

The cues indicated above show that Hans interactionally positions himself as hegemonically male by voicing his father and himself in the narrated event as characters that know that men cannot control their sexuality. This same type of interactional positioning is consequently enacted to the other participants in the storytelling event, minimally Peter, Gail and the researchers. Note that both Peter (line (l)) and Gail (line (n)) are collectively and overtly telling the narrative with Hans and, therefore, collectively helping to construct Hans as hegemonic male and, therefore, as heterosexual.

Both positionings of males as protectors and as predators, co-existing within this narrative practice, are in fact contradictory; however, Hans as a male is occupying both. On the one hand, males are responsible for protecting women and, on the other, they cannot control their sexual desires, i.e. women are inevitable sexual targets. It could also be said that these two positionings are indicative of two different worlds in which men act differently: the private world of family life in which males are protectors of their families and of the women in their families, and the public world of the men in the street in which men chase women. It is also noteworthy that Hans positions himself to his interlocutors as someone who is aware of this contradiction since in the story-world Hans, as a character, questions his father about it, positioning himself as a clever young man who is free to do as he pleases and who is not subject to the rules which govern home life as his sister is.

I want to draw attention to the fact that the social construction of Hans as an hegemonic male in the narrative above is achieved through interactional positionings which refer to femininity. Hegemonic masculinity, as argued above, is the given or natural feature of human nature that gets constructed by reference to femininity, i.e. to the other.

The second narrative, Example 11.2, focuses on Hans' construction as heterosexual. The story is narrated by Hans with the help of other voices (secondary narrators such as Betina, Peter and Gail) who collectively help to construct Hans as heterosexual. They follow Hans' line of argument, and contribute to back it up. The

story is motivated by previous discussion on how homoerotic boys
behave (from Example 11.2, lines (a) to (f) below). It has four
characters: a boy in their class that they believe to be gay, the boy's
mother, Hans (i.e. "I") and the other co-narrators (i.e. "we"). The
theme of this narrative is the defamation of homoerotic people as a
way to construct hegemonic masculinity. This has been constantly
shown in the literature as typical of hegemonic masculinity performance (Badinter 1992; Mac an Ghail 1994; Moita-Lopes 2002
etc.).

Example 11.2

Hans as heterosexual

"He is that kind of mad queen."

(a)	HANS	Did you get it?/ He comes and talks to you:/ (in an affected tone of voice) as
(b)		if he spoke like a woman/. What would you think?/ Chap,/ this guy must
(c)		have a problem./
(d)	PETER	me too.//
(e)	HANS	My goodness!/ This is not normal!//
(f)	PETER	( )
(g)	HANS	Like this boy in our class./ He speaks in a totally different manner,/ do you
(h)		get it?//
(i)	PETER	Walks in a different manner.//
(j)	BETINA	He wiggles his ass.//
(k)	HANS	We tried somehow to play with him,/ but // to me this is wrong./ The chap
(l)		is 12 years old.//
(m)	RES	How old are you?//
(n)	HANS	I am 14,/ but when I was his age,/ I wouldn't go somewhere/ and use that
(o)		funny voice / and wiggle my ass.//
(p)	BETINA	And the worst thing about it/ is that he is a gossip!//
(q)	HANS	Right! Right!//
(r)	BETINA	He tells everything to everybody./ We can never rely on him.//
(s)	HANS	He can never see anything that [he gossips about it]//
(t)	PETER	He is that kind of mad queen.//
(u)	GAIL	We start with the fact that his mother is too strict with him.//
(v)	BETINA	His mother is//
(w)	RES	What?//

(x)	HANS	No, you know why/ his mother is too picky//
(y)	GAIL	with him,/ do you get it?//
(z)	BETINA	I think that's because he is the only child.//(. . .)
(aa)	BETINA	But sometimes he is like that just because of his mother.//
(bb)	RES	Right.//

The story begins in line (g) when Hans makes his first reference to the boy he describes as gay. Note that the boy is not referred to by his name, which may imply, on one hand, that Hans (as well as his co-narrators: Betina, Peter and Gail) does not want to say who he is for ethical reasons but, on the other, that he does not need to since all his classmates know who he is, for they are used to gossiping about him. This second implication is in fact warranted by the fact that they all engage in this narrative practice by helping to characterize the boy. The lack of explicit reference to the boy's name indexes that his alterity is so well-known/noticeable that he does not have to be singled out by his name.

Also, this is a device used by the narrator (Hans) to draw attention to this boy's otherness, in reference to which Hans is going to construct himself as heterosexual. It is a device to transform the boy into the other. His otherness has in fact been previously announced in lines (a)–(c) when some negative features characterizing the boy have already been stated ("as if he spoke like a woman/ . . . this guy must have a problem."). This goes on later in the narrative when the pronouns "I" and "we" (used to refer to other characters in the story), contrasting with "this boy," introduce propositions which clearly point to the boy's strangeness or unnaturalness ("I am 14,/ but when I was his age,/ I wouldn't go somewhere/ and use that funny voice / and wiggle my ass" (lines (n)–(o)); "We tried somehow to play with him" (line (k)); "We can never rely on him" (line (r)) and "We start with the fact that his mother is too strict with him." (line (u))).

Carrying on with this same kind of indexation of the boy, Hans and the other co-narrators use adjectives to characterize the boy that evaluate him negatively as "different" (lines (g) and (i)), "funny" (line (o)) and "mad" (line (t)). Other lexical items also describe his body ("walks in a different manner" (line (i)) and "wiggles his ass" (line (j)) and the nature of his character ("he is a gossip" (line (p)) and "We can never rely on him" (line (r)) negatively. Another device which cues Hans' (and his co-narrators') interactional positioning is expressed by the way he meta-pragmatically describes how Hans makes use of language: "He speaks in a totally different manner" (line (g)) and "He tells everything to everybody" (line (r)), which may echo that "he [speaks] like a woman," as put by Hans in line (b).

The narrators index the boy as someone whose voices they are positioned totally against because "this is not normal" (line (e)) or "wrong" (line (k)) or because "this guy must have a problem" (lines (b)–(c)). Note that Hans is one of the oldest boys in the class and actually looks older and more mature than the other boys and girls. Therefore, it could be said that in the storytelling event his co-narrators are asymmetrically situated in relation to him and that their interactional positionings in the narrative practice, by aligning themselves with his ideas, may be considered a reflection of this asymmetry.

Hans interactionally positions himself against the boy in the narrated event and in the storytelling event. He (and, in fact, his co-narrators) takes up a positioning that sets him/them totally apart from the boy, and therefore as people who deplore gays.

The epistemic status of Hans and of his co-narrators is that of people who are narrating an event in which they participated, i.e. they saw him "walk in a different manner" (line (i)) and "wiggle his ass" (line (j)), heard him "use that funny voice" (lines (n)–(o)) and "speak in a totally different manner"(line (g)); etc. This status situates them in the narrative and in the storytelling events as people who know what they are talking about and therefore have the right to say what they are saying.

This analysis shows that Hans interactionally positions himself to the characters and to the other participants in the narrative practice as hegemonic male by defining what gays are like and that by doing so he gets constructed as heterosexual.

The third and last narrative I want to focus on, Example 11.3, is used to show how Hans constructs himself as white. This story is told by Hans to further support the argument underlying Gail's narrative (in which he is also a co-narrator (lines (e) and (g)) – the introductory narrative in the excerpt below – which points out that blacks have a negative view of themselves and that they themselves agree on their inferiority. In other words, they themselves are aware of their alterity; both Gail's brother and Hans' father, who are black, share the same point of view about blacks. I will analyze Gail's and Hans' stories together because Hans' is an extension of Gail's and they have a parallel structure. The characters in the stories are Gail's brother (in Gail's story) and Hans' cousin and Hans' father (in Hans' story).

Example 11.3

Hans as white

"Things niggers do!"

(a)	GAIL	My brother/ my brother/ who lives with us/, you know what he says,/when we
(b)		arrive home/: "Go and do the dishes"//. If we don't do it all right/ he says:/
(c)		"See,/ you are acting like a nigger."//
(d)	RES	Right,/ what is he like?//
(e)	HANS	Things niggers do! /Things niggers do!//
(f)	RES	What is he like?//
(g)	HANS	He is also black!!/ (laughter) He is black./ He is dark-skinned,/ right?//
(h)	RES	Right.//
(i)	. . .	
(j)	HANS	I had a cousin who came,/ who came from/ I had a cousin who had come
(k)		from Bahia[5] / I had a cousin who had come from Bahia/ and was terrible./ Then/
(l)		my father also knows a few things. It is always good to teach some things from
(m)		Bahia culture//
(n)	RES	Is your father from Bahia?//
(o)	HANS	Right./ My father has driven cars to Bahia,/ trucks too./ My father has driven
(p)		there a few times/ how do I say?/ Do you know the trucks/ which carry cars one
(q)		on top of the other.//
(r)	RES	Right.//
(s)	HANS	My father has driven cars,/ trucks,/ he knows these places./ Bahia is something
(t)		we have in our culture,/ do you get it?/ And my father says that.//

[5] A Brazilian state with a large African-Brazilian population.

(u)	RES	Now why is it that your father/ why do you think your father,/ despite being black
(v)		says:/ "Only blacks would do something like that?"//
(w)	HANS	Because he thinks so

As in Example 11.1 above, the characters whose voices are brought into the stories are members of the narrators' families. They therefore populate their narratives with characters they are familiar with, and this immediately sets their epistemic status as narrators who have lived these stories and hence can stand by their truth. Note that Gail is black whereas Hans, a child of an inter-racial marriage, constructs himself as white.

Also, as in Example 11.1, the status Hans gives to his father is that of someone who defines the meanings under which he lives: in Example 11.1 meanings about hegemonic masculinity and here about race. The voice Hans brings into the narrative and through which he interactionally positions himself, as in Example 11.1, is his father's: "my father also knows a few things"(Example 11.3, lines (k)–(l)) and "Because he thinks so" (line (w)). This depiction is actually backed up by researchers' findings about how fathers are the initiators of their sons into the world of manhood (Badinter 1992; Connell 1995; Moita-Lopes 2002) and, in fact, into the world of other social meanings (as of race here). One could say that the construction of masculinity is racialized in this narrative practice.

Gail brings her brother's voice into the narrative by directly quoting him, "Go and do the dishes" (line (b)) and "See, you are acting like a nigger." (line (c)). She is therefore identifying him as someone who has a negative attitude against people who are black like himself by implying that they are lazy or lousy workers. The lexical item ("nigger") she uses to refer to blacks indexically eval-uates blacks negatively since it is a term that is normally used by racists. As Hans, as a co-narrator in Gail's narrative, indicates, her "brother is also black!! / He is black./ He is dark-skinned,/ right?//" (line (g)) and he has a racist attitude towards blacks because, as Hans says by echoing Gail's brother: these are "Things niggers do!" (line (e)). This is the evaluation of Gail's story provided by Hans, which in turn motivates his own.

Hans' story refers to his cousin who is from Bahia (a Brazilian state with a large African-Brazilian population), implicitly understood as black, and who is predicated as "terrible" (line (k)). In the light of Gail's previous predication of blacks as lazy "niggers" (line (c)), Hans interactionally positions himself in the same way about blacks by narrating a story about a "terrible" black man, whose actions also explain his statement above: "Things niggers do" (line (e)). To back up his argument and to close the story, he brings in the voice of his father as of someone who is indexically referred to as powerful: knows about things ("my father also knows a few things," line (l)); drives long distances ("My father has driven there [to Bahia] a few times" line (o)); has driven heavy trucks ("My father has driven cars to Bahia,/ trucks too" (line (s))), is himself from Bahia (line (o)), is black (line (u)), and has the same opinion about blacks as Gail's brother (lines (u)–(v)).

One could also understand Hans' story as a follow-up to Gail's story of her black brother in the sense that Hans follows it as an illustration of a story of a black person's engagement with defamation of blacks themselves. He does so by telling the story about his black father who also defames blacks. As a second story, his narrative has the function of supporting Gail's in the storytelling event. Hans' postioning as "supporter" protects him against possible accusations of racism, since Gail is black and she has the right to defame other blacks. Hans enacts his positioning by making use of his father's voice (i.e. his knowledge, power and blackness) to contrast himself with blacks and to interactionally position himself as male and as white.

The point I want to emphasize here is that when telling this story, Hans interactionally positions himself as white both in the narrated event and in the storytelling event by defining what blacks are like or by constructing blacks negatively. Of course, both Gail's and Hans' stories position blacks as people who are racist against themselves, which seems to indicate, on the one hand, the level of racism existing in Brazilian society, and, on the other, how fragile political awareness of racial relations in Brazil is.

11.6 Conclusion

The analysis of Hans' interactional multiple positionings in the narrative practices above shows the instantiation of the fragmented and heterogeneous nature of his social identities as male, heterosexual and white by pointing to the cues used by Hans when he interactionally positions himself vis-à-vis characters and interlocutors. The interactional positionings he takes up indicate that masculinity, heterosexuality and whiteness are not directly topicalized in these narratives as such. Instead, Hans' interactional positionings show that he constructs himself or gets constructed as male, heterosexual and white by reference to alterity: femininity, homosexuality and blackness. This is done as a response to crystallized and naturalized meanings about social identities. The analysis also illustrates an interactional process of social identity coconstruction in which the interlocutors' eyes are pivotal in creating the illusion of permanent and stable identities.

As argued above, the social identities situated in a position of hegemony are unmarked and naturalized and constitute themselves by constructing the margins: femininity, homoeroticism and blackness. This chapter tried to make visible how these naturalized social identities are constructed by showing how Hans wants to expel femininity, homoeroticism and blackness from within himself in the project of constructing himself as a member of hegemonic masculinity. He does so by occupying multiple positionings that show how gender is sexualized and racialized in his attempts to take up a hegemonic position in the stories he tells the other participants. Hans is narrating the world in such a way that he consistently positions himself as dominant in the three stories. In fact, the three narratives could be taken as a single story line about his efforts to interactionally position himself as hegemonic.

The local meanings which come about through Hans' interactional positionings reflect a patriarchal and racist society and therefore do not incorporate recent social and political changes about gender, sexual and racial identities which are found in some circles. His interactional positionings are indicative of traditional sociohistorical processes about the unmarkedness and naturalness of masculinity, heterosexuality and whiteness.

In the three narratives, Hans' positionings are supported by the other participants. The collective nature of these narrative practices indicates that Hans is not alone in the project of performing his white heterosexual masculinity. His co-narrators and the other participants in the storytelling event are corroborating such a project and consequently supporting the stability of his hegemony across the three narratives. That is to say that in these narrative practices he interactionally accomplishes the performance of hegemonic masculinity. The story about who he is becoming in these practices nevertheless could have been different if a participant had offered him an alternative story line he could have followed or made possible a different positioning. However, in the three narratives participants are supportive of his positionings. As I pointed out above, this may be explained by the fact that Hans is older and more mature than his peers and in fact looks so. He can more easily try out his dominant positionings as male, white and heterosexual in these practices.

It should also be indicated, accordingly, that in other discursive practices other meanings about his social identities could be constructed. As a participant in other narrative practices with different interlocutors, Hans himself could perform a different type of masculinity or could construct different story lines about himself. People take up different positionings and construct different SIDs in the different discursive practices they get involved with. If SIDs are interactional positionings in discourse, the same person in different discursive practices may perform contradictory identities since, as I argued above, SIDs are contradictory and in flux.

This chapter shows possible discursive positionings about who Hans is in the social world and how stability about the hegemonic positionings is collectively constructed. It cannot however account for other positionings Hans may take up in other different practices or for the other social meanings about who he is in the social world. The social identity positionings indicated here co-exist with others that may in fact contradict the meanings about who he is in the narrative practices above. This theoretical stance accounts for the fact that Hans may revise himself or that he may occupy positionings that question the ones above.

Appendix 11.1 (Example 11.1) – October 31, 1997

Hans as male

"Prende as suas cabras que o meu bode está solto."

(a) HANS Meu pai chegava lá,/ minha irmã ficava na rua até tarde,/ aí meu pai falava

(b)   assim:/ "Sobe que não é hora de mulher ficar na rua."// Aí eu falava,/ ué,/ isso

(c)   não é hora de mulher ficar na rua?// Você não fica falando assim:/ "Pô,/ vai

(d)   namorar,/ como é que eu vou namorar se todos os pais falam que isso não é

(e)   hora de mulher ficar na rua, prendem as filhas?"/ Aí meu pai:/ "Prende as

(f)   suas cabras que o meu bode está solto."//. Porque/ tem que prender a sua

(g)   mulher porque o bode do homem está solto./ Se deixar a mulher dando mole

(h)   ((risos)),/ vai o bode lá e craw (som de um animal caçando outro)!// ((risos))

(i)   PETER   É,/ o bode está solto,/ né?//

(j)   HANS   Tem que prender as cabras!//

(k)   GAIL   Minha mãe faz isso comigo./ Minha mãe sempre fala isso.//

Appendix 11.2 (Example 11.2) – October 31, 1997

Hans as heterosexual

"Ele é aquele tipo de bicha-louca."

(a)   HANS   Entendeu?/ Chegar e falar pra pessoa: "((imitando voz de bicha)) assim com voz

(b)   de mulher./ Tu vai pensar o quê?/ O cara /e esse cara aí/ deve ter algum

(c)   problema.//

(d)   PETER   Eu também.//

(e)   HANS   Pô,/ isso aí não é normal!//

(f)   PETER   ( )

(g)   HANS   Como esse menino da nossa turma aqui./ Ele tem um outro jeito de falar,/

(h)   entendeu?//

(i)   PETER   Jeito de andar.//

(j)   BETINA   Ele rebola.//

(k)   HANS   Poxa,/ de algum jeito,/ a gente procurou uma maneira de brincar com ele,/ mas,/

(l)   poxa,/ depende. / Pra mim,/ isso tá errado./ O cara tem 12 anos.//

(m)   RES   Quantos anos você tem?//

(n)   HANS   Eu tenho 14,/ mas com a idade dele,/ eu não chegava e ficava com aquela

(o)   vozinha/ que ele fica/ e rebolando.//

(p)   BETINA   E o pior de tudo é que ele faz fofoca!/ Ele é fofoqueiro!//

(q)   HANS   Isso! Isso!//

(r)   BETINA   Conta tudo pra todo mundo./ Não pode contar nada,/ nada.//

(s)   HANS   E ele também não pode ver nada que//

(t)   PETER   E ele é aquele tipo de bicha-louca.// ((risos))

(u)   GAIL   Começando por aí,/ a mãe dele é rigorosa.//

(v)   BETINA   ( ) a mãe dele é.//

(w)   RES   Vai virar o quê?//

(x)   HANS   Não, /sabe por quê?/ A mãe dele é toda fresca//

(y)   GAIL   Com ele,/ entendeu?//

(z)   BETINA   Eu acho que é porque ele é filho único.//(. . .).

(aa)   BETINA   Mas,/ às vezes,/ ele é assim só por causa da mãe dele.//

(bb)   RES   Ah!//

Appendix 11.3 (Example 11.3) – October 31, 1997

Hans as white

"Creolice! Creolice."

(a)   GAIL   Meu irmão/ meu irmão/ que mora lá em casa,/ ele fica falando assim

(b)   quando a gente chega/: "Vá arrumar a cozinha".// Se a gente não arrumou

(c)   direito/ aí ele diz/: "É,/ né!/ Já tá fazendo serviço de preto."//

(d)   RES   É,/ e ele é?/ E ele é o quê?//"

(e)   HANS   Creolice!/ Creolice!/

(f)   RES   Ele é o quê?//

(g)   HANS   Ele é preto também!//(risos) Ele é preto./ Ele tem pele escura,/ né?//

(h)   RES   Sei.//

(i)   . . .

(j)   HANS   Eu tinha um primo que veio,/ veio/ eu tinha um primo que tinha vindo da

(k)   Bahia/ e era terrível/. Aí meu pai também conhece algumas coisas./ É sempre

(l)   bom você ensinar algumas coisas da cultura de lá.//

(m)   RES   Teu pai é baiano?//

(n)   HANS   É./ Meu pai já dirigiu carros para a Bahia/ e caminhão também./ Ele já foi lá

(o)   algumas vezes./ Como é que se chama?/ Você conhece esses caminhões

(p)   que carregam carros?//

(q)   RES   Sei,/ sei.//

(r)	HANS	Meu pai já levou carros,/ caminhões,/ ele conhece assim esses lugares./ Bahia é
(s)		uma coisa que tem em nossa cultura,/ entendeu?/ E meu pai diz que//
(t)	RES	Agora por que seu pai,/ por que você acha que seu pai,/ apesar de ser negro,/ fala:/
(u)		"Isso tinha de ser coisa de preto?"//
(v)	HANS	Porque ele acha.//

Acknowledgements

I am grateful to CNPq (Brazilian National council for Research, 523548/96-6) and FAPERJ (The State of Rio Research Council, E-26/171-390/98 and E-26/151.687/2000) for grants which have made the research reported here possible. I am also grateful to Marlene Soares dos Santos (UFRJ) and Branca Falabelle Fabrício (UFRJ) for their suggestions on the first version of this paper.

Urban fathers positioning themselves through narrative: an approach to narrative self-construction

Stanton Wortham and Vivian Gadsden

12.1 Introduction

Many have argued that narrators can partly construct themselves when they tell autobiographical stories. For this reason, autobiographical narrative has been proposed as a therapeutic tool (Anderson 1997; Cohler 1988; White and Epston 1990), as a means to critique unjust social orders (Personal Narratives Group 1989; Rosenwald and Ochberg 1992; Zuss 1997), and as an educational tool (Cohen 1996; Witherell and Noddings 1991). This body of work makes at least two important points. First, the "self" is not an unchanging entity beyond the reach of everyday human action, but is something that can under some circumstances be changed with effort. Second, changing the self can happen through the social practice of narration, not just through the activity of an isolated individual.

Although this work on narrative self-construction promises both theoretical insight into the processes of self-construction and practical tools for changing the self, most of it has failed to provide a comprehensive account of how autobiographical narration can actually construct the self. A full account would require three components: a linguistically sophisticated account of how narrative discourse creates relevant patterns; an account of the mechanism through which these discursive patterns influence social and psychological processes; and a theory of what the self is, such that it can be partly constructed through some narrative mechanism. Most existing work on narrative self-construction includes only one or two of these components. Many rely on folk conceptions of how narrative discourse works, instead of systematic linguistic analyses (cf. critiques in Schiffrin 1996; Wortham 2001). Many presuppose implicit or implausible mechanisms through which narration can influence the self. And many fail to offer an account of the self.

This chapter focuses on the first component of an adequate account, and touches on the second (Crapanzano 1992; Wortham 2001 and others begin to describe a complementary account of self, but there is insufficient space here). We argue that any adequate analysis of narrative self-construction must offer more complex and specific accounts of narrative and of the mechanisms through which narrative influences the self. Drawing on "positioning" theory (Bamberg 2003; Davies and Harré 1990; Wortham 2001), the chapter describes four types of narrative positioning that might potentially be relevant to self-construction. Although any one of these might in principle contribute to self-construction by itself, in practice the different types of positioning generally depend on each other. Many plausible mechanisms for narrative self-construction also involve interrelationships across these different types of narrative positioning.

The chapter applies this work in positioning theory to an auto-biographical narrative told by one young, urban African-American man who became a father as a teenager. His narrative comes from a corpus of fifteen autobiographical narratives told by lower-class, urban fathers we have worked with. Our detailed analysis of one narrative explores how this narrator may be constructing himself, in part, through telling autobiographical stories. We describe one father's narrative self-construction by analyzing how he uses various linguistic devices to position himself and by sketching how this narrative positioning might partly construct his "self." In addition to applying positioning theory to the study of narrative self-construction, the chapter also illuminates the challenges faced by young urban men as they struggle to construct themselves as good fathers in a social context that often impedes good parenting.

12.2 Data and methods

This chapter draws on a pilot study of urban fathers, which included individual interviews with fifteen subjects and focus group interviews with about sixty (Gadsden, Wortham and Turner 2003; Gadsden, Wortham and Wojcik 2001). The fifteen subjects were selected from those who participated in focus groups based on their willingness, their articulateness, and the apparent richness of their stories. All of the fathers were participating in a father resource program, where they could talk to other young urban fathers and get advice from staff. They were all lower-class, urban African-American men who became fathers as teenagers.

The interviewers were relatively young African-American men who were graduate students or university-based researchers. The semi-structured interviews included questions about barriers to employment, their experiences and feelings as a parent, typical interactions with their children, their experiences with their own fathers and mothers, and their relationship with the mother(s) of their children. Interviewers also left substantial space for the fathers to tell stories about their lives. Over the course of these interviews, fathers told stories about their own childhoods, their relations with their parents, their relationships with the mother(s) of their children, their own activities with their children, and their goals both for themselves and their children.

We have analyzed these interviews using techniques drawn from Bakhtin (1981c), Bamberg (2003), Labov and Waletsky (1967), Schiffrin (1996), Wortham (2001) and Wortham and Locher (1996). As shown below, these techniques allowed us to uncover four different types of "positioning" that the narrators and interviewers accomplished. Before introducing these types of positioning, however, we first need background information on these fathers' lives and on the corpus of narratives.

12.3 Street, home and system

In order to understand the positions adopted by interviewers and fathers in these interviews, we need to understand the types of positions made available by the cultural context. As we have described elsewhere (Gadsden, Wortham and Turner, 2003; Gadsden, Wortham and Wojcik 2001), and as described by others (e.g. Anderson 1999; Bourgois 1995; Dance 2002), these urban African-American men often presuppose three salient realms in their stories: the street, the home, and the system. We do not claim that this taxonomy captures actual behavior in all respects, just that the fathers consistently make these presuppositions in their narratives. Whether the fathers' descriptions are accurate or not, the narrators and interviewers must take into account the fathers' common presuppositions about these three realms.

Almost all of the fathers in our study described the street as destructive, dangerous, and unproductive. Activities commonly associated with this realm included "hustlin'," "hangin' out," and "partying." A recurring theme was that life on the streets was free and unrestricted, with no responsibilities "holding one down." Several of the fathers associated the street with their youth: "I was still playin'. I was still bein' a boy." Several of the fathers characterized their transition from the street to the home as "slowing down." Street life is "fast" and involves concern primarily for oneself, while domestic life is "slow" and involves responsibilities for others.

Almost all the fathers represented their mother's home, and their children's primary home, as protected and nurturing. The domestic realm is an environment characterized by togetherness, with families spending quality time during meals and outings. A large proportion of time in the domestic realm is dedicated to child care, with parents cooking, cleaning, feeding, and playing with their children. The urban fathers in this study characterized the home as starkly different from the street. For example, whereas street life is characterized by the desire to circumvent responsibility (and the law), in the home fathers relinquish selfish ways and sacrifice for their children. Fathers spoke of putting their children first, as their "number one priority" at home. The domestic realm also offers stability.

This sort of grounded, settled behavior at home is opposed to typical street behavior. One father compared the two realms this way:

Example 12.1

Responsibility...that's the number one thing to me. Responsibility because, it's like I watch some of these fathers out there that just hang on the street all day, they'll be *wish*ing they could see their child, but me, on the other hand, that's my number one priority, you know, so. That's my responsibility is to deal with him and make sure *he's* all right before I go have *my* fun. That's the number one thing.

This father's response describes two key aspects associated with the home: responsibility and sacrifice. While street life is unbounded by external controls, home life requires sacrificing one's desires in order to follow rules and live up to responsibilities. Fathers spoke of following "the rules of the house" in their own childhood homes, as well as in their interactions with their own children.

Many narrators represented the system as biased and heartless. For instance, one said:

Example 12.2

Dealing with the court systems is like being public enemy number one. You know, it's like sometimes they don't care to know the situation. It's just automatically. Sometimes I just think fathers get a bad rap in court. I know I been to court one time. . . my child support was in arrears. I was working. Instead of just having me maybe pay five more dollars a week, they wanted me to do community service. Which, I was working at the time so I didn't do the community service. They locked me up and charged me $1000 for that. . . My son's mother was trying to tell them, even she was trying to be on my side and say hey, he's paying his support, he's been. . . But they didn't want to hear it. Just locked me up, you know.

This father characterizes the court system here as heartless and unproductive. They stereotype him, despite the fact that he has started to pay child support, as "public enemy number one." They also act in capricious and unproductive ways. Despite the fact that the system should want him to work and provide child support, they impose community service and lock him up, in ways that jeopardize his ability to do both. Thus the system is both unjust and ultimately self-defeating.

The fathers draw on the three realms of street, home and system in order to characterize spaces (e.g. the street corner vs. the living room), activities (e.g. hanging out vs. caring for children) and people (e.g. the drug dealer vs. the responsible father). Because these three realms are salient for them, and because their stories make these three realms salient in the interviewing situation, we can use these realms to characterize both the "voices" that they assign to characters in their narratives and the roles available to interviewers and fathers as they interact with each other.

Drawing on these three realms, almost all of the fathers in our sample present themselves as struggling with, or as having just successfully negotiated, a turning point in their lives – the transition from street to home. Their own fathers and they themselves most often lived on the street, and fathered children during this phase of

their lives. But they have now decided to become responsible
fathers, to move off the street and to get deeply involved in their
children's home lives. In this chapter we analyze how one young
urban father narrates this transition from street to home. Our
analysis has two goals. First, we model a more systematic approach
to studying narrative self-construction. We illustrate how systematic tools from positioning theory can be applied to analyze the
process of narrative self-construction. Second, through Robert's
narrative we describe some of the challenges and opportunities
facing young urban fathers in contemporary America.

12.4 Four layers of narrative positioning

Many, including one of us (Wortham 2000, 2001), have argued that
autobiographical narrative "positions" narrators and that such
positioning is crucial to narrative self-construction. We still find
this a plausible claim, but we now follow Bamberg (2003) in
making more careful distinctions among different types of patterns
that one might call "positioning." In this chapter we illustrate how
autobiographical narration can position narrators in at least four
different ways. First, narrators position themselves as having
experienced various narrated events in the past. Second, narrators
"voice" or position people represented in their narrative, including their own various narrated selves, as recognizable types of
people. Third, while voicing themselves and other characters, narrators also evaluate these voices, such that the narrator him or
herself often takes a position on the types of characters represented.
Fourth, through the telling of their stories, narrators position themselves interactionally with respect to their interlocutors in the
storytelling event. Any one of these positionings – and perhaps
other types of narrative patterns as well – could be central to
narrative self-construction. A systematic account must distinguish
between them and make clear how they individually or collectively
contribute to narrative self-construction.

12.4.1 Narrated events and voicing

Most accounts of narrative self-construction tacitly or explicitly
presuppose something like the following account: autobiographical

narrators describe themselves as having participated in certain events, and such representations have the power to construct the self. For instance, a narrator might represent him or herself as having developed from passively being a victim to actively struggling against injustice. Such narration might help accomplish a transition from passive to active in the narrator's life. This type of account focuses on what Jakobson (1971) called the "narrated event" – the events described in the narrative – as opposed to the "event of speaking" (sometimes also called the "narrating event"), which is the interactional event transacted between narrator and audience.

Accounts of narrative self-construction that focus on the narrated event actually presuppose two analytically distinguishable types of positioning. The first is reference to past events, accomplished through grammatical devices like those described by Labov (Labov 1972a; Labov and Waletzky 1967). A narrator positions him or herself by referring to a series of past events that s/he participated in. The second is "voicing," through which the narrator characterizes him/herself and other narrated characters as being recognizable types of people. In practice, reference to past events and voicing of the characters in those events almost always happen together. But the tools used to analyze them differ.

In the following example, one young urban father, "Robert Banks" (RB), describes the typical morning routine at his house.

Example 12.3

(a)   RB   okay, well my typical day starts at about *five* thirty a.m.
(b)   I get up, hit the showers. I have to be at work by seven,
(c)   so I hit the shower and either *Na*tasha or *I* will fix her
(d)   something to eat. fix her something to eat *be*fore we wake
(e)   her up, because she's hard to wake up in the morning. so,
(f)   we have to have a *sys*tem. the initial wake up, then the *go*
(g)   in there and take your shower. and then the, she actually
(h)   comes *out* of the shower, then the wake-up to get your
(i)   clothes on, get ready and then go to school. we have to get
(j)   her *two* to three times in the morning before she's *act*ually
(k)   awake.

By describing the sequence of events through which he helps his daughter get ready for school, Robert helps position himself as a particular kind of person. He gets up early, he has a system for accommodating his daughter's unwillingness to get up quickly, he helps take care of her food and clothes – and thus he positions himself as a responsible and accommodating parent. Note that he also uses "we" in lines (d), (f), and (i), to refer to his girlfriend and himself as they work together to help their daughter get ready for school. By referring to himself and his girlfriend in this collective way, he positions himself as part of a functioning relationship in which parents care for their child.

The positioning that Robert accomplishes in this segment depends both on reference to past events and on what Bakhtin (1981c) called "voicing." A voice is a recognizable social type, associated with a character primarily through indexical cues in a narrative. When Robert says "we have to have a system" (at line (f)), for instance, he presupposes that he and his girlfriend are organized, planful, responsible people. His utterance indexically presupposes this voice because speakers characteristically use the expression "have a system" to describe organized, planful, responsible people. In the segment above, Robert positions himself as responsible both by describing past events in which he takes care of his daughter and by using indexical cues like "have a system" that also presuppose this voice.

As described extensively elsewhere (Wortham 2000, 2001; Wortham and Locher 1996), characters get assigned voices through various types of cues. Quoted speech, for instance, often plays an important role in voicing (Voloshinov 1973). By putting words into a character's mouth, and by framing those words with a verb of speaking, the narrator has a rich opportunity to assign the character a voice. "Evaluative indexicals" – terms like "have a system" that associate characters with a recognizable type of person – also play an important role in voicing. Calling someone a "wolf," for instance, in the context of urban environments, may voice that person as predatory and associated with the life of the streets.

Although these brief illustrations do not capture it, we must emphasize that voicing is not solely a rule-based process. Indexical cues do not normatively establish voices, because any cue can be interpreted in multiple ways. "We have a system" might presuppose that Robert is responsible and organized, but it could also presuppose that he is obsessive. Indexical cues only come to presuppose a given voice over time, as patterns of cues collectively come to presuppose that voice. The complexity and indeterminacy of this process has been described over the last several decades by many people (e.g. Goffman 1976; Gumperz 1982; Sacks, Schegloff, and Jefferson 1974; Silverstein 1992; Wortham 2001).

12.4.2 Evaluation

After voicing their characters, narrators themselves take a position with respect to those voices. Labov and Waletzky (1967) gave a basic account of this process, under the term "evaluation" – an account extended by Schiffrin (1996). Bakhtin describes a similar process under the term "ventriloquation." In the following segment, Example 12.4, for instance, Robert voices his mother and then evaluates the voice.

Example 12.4

(a) RB my mom, she's just a flat out *drill* sergeant. until she
(b)   met *him*. until she met my stepfather, she was single mom
(c)   trying to make it so whereas most moms where like ooh,
(d)   little Johnny don't do that. and then spoilin' them rotten
(e)   to the core to where there just nothing she was *op*posite
(f)   spectrum.
          . . .
(g)   this is the woman that was like,
          . . .
(h)   I was second place in the spelling bee and
(i)   the girl that won was in *sixth* grade, but that's still no
(j)   excuse. I come home with my plaque after being all but
(k)   carried off the *stage* at school. I was the *man*. second place.
(l)   I was the man.
          . . .
(m)   they carried
(n)   me off the stage and this and that and this woman asked
(o)   me, why didn't you *win*? you know what I'm saying? can I
(p)   please this woman?
          . . .
(q)   this woman
(r)   was demanding and she's a perfectionist, and she gave the
(s)   best *to* her kids and she expected the best *from* her kids.
          . . .

(t)   and I think when she looks at me, she
(u)   knows that *all* the effort that she put in was *worth* it. she
(x)   knows that if there's one person in the world that she can depend
        on, it's *me*.

Robert voices his mother here, using evaluative indexicals like "drill sergeant" (line (a)). He contrasts her approach to parenting with mothers who just say "ooh, little Johnny don't do that" (lines (c)–(d)). His mother was so demanding that she expressed disappointment at his second-place finish in the spelling bee.

How does Robert evaluate this "drill sergeant" voice that he assigns his mother? He could lament it, or resist it, or ridicule it, or embrace it. She said "that's no excuse" (lines (i)–(j)) when Robert placed second in the spelling bee behind an older girl. This seems a bit extreme. He also uses the phrase "this woman" to refer to her at line (q), another cue that indicates a negative evaluation. Robert seems to be evaluating his mother as too demanding a parent. But toward the end of the segment he says "she gave the best to her kids and she expected the best from her kids" (lines (r)–(s)), which gives her more credit. And he ends by saying "all the effort. . .was worth it" (line (u)). Taken together with other segments in which Robert describes his own parenting as similar to his mother's – although a bit less extreme – these last few lines indicate that Robert evaluates his mother's parental voice positively. It was hard on both of them, but it was for the best in the long run.

12.4.3 Narrating interactions

Description of past events, voicing, and evaluation, then, can each "position" the narrator. As he describes events and voices himself and other people in his story, Robert has opportunities to position himself as a responsible parent. And while narrating these events and voices, Robert adopts a position with respect to the voices in his narrative. Robert himself evaluates his mother's "iron fist" approach to parenting as ultimately for the best, which positions him as having a similar value system. In addition to these three, there is a fourth type of positioning.

Like all speakers, narrators inevitably interact with their audiences. Even the driest lecture is a type of interactional event, with roles and expectations for different participants. By virtue of telling a particular story in a particular way, narrators position themselves interactionally with respect to their interlocutors. Such interactional positioning can help construct the narrator's self, if the interactional stances taken through narration become habitual. Bamberg and Marchman (1991), Gergen and Kaye (1992), Wortham (2001) and others have given such interactional accounts of narrative self-construction.

In Robert's case, he develops a particular type of relationship with the interviewer, and his position in the relationship might maintain or construct a particular kind of self for him. One type of interactional event going on throughout most of their conversation is a formal interview. Robert is a subject being paid to give information and the interviewer is a professional paid to collect that information, in the name of (applied) science. As the interview proceeds, Robert and the interviewer adopt other interactional positions as well. They struggle a bit over whether, because of his lower socioeconomic status and the stigma of early parenthood, Robert is a lower-status person than the interviewer.

A comprehensive account of narrative self-construction, then, must clearly distinguish among the types of narrative structure that might be relevant. The four types of positioning described above do not exhaust the types of narrative structure that might contribute to narrative self-construction, but they represent four important possibilities and illustrate how a more precise account is needed.

It is also important to note that the four types of positioning depend on each other. In principle, they can be analyzed as separate layers. But in any actual narrative they always occur alongside and often buttress one another. In order to voice a character, for instance, the narrator generally must describe that character as involved in narrated events; in order to evaluate a voice, the narrator must first presuppose that voice in the narrated events; in order to position him or herself interactionally in the event of speaking, the narrator generally uses patterns from all three other types of positioning. Going in the other direction, evaluation generally depends on information about the narrator and the audience members' interactional identities; voicing depends on a value system presupposed through evaluation; and the description of past events depends on information about voices and the event of speaking (coherent denotation can only be accomplished given information about the event of speaking – cf. Hanks 1990; Jakobson 1971; Silverstein 1976).

If autobiographical narration partly constructs the self, we must specify which narrative structures are doing the work. We have argued that the four layers of narrative positioning described here, and their interconnections, constitute a useful analytic tool-kit for studying narrative structures that play a role in narrative self-construction. A full account of narrative self-construction also requires a mechanism through which narrative might influence the self. If Robert describes and/or voices himself as a responsible parent, how might this affect or effect his self? If Robert evaluates his mother's "iron fist" as a good thing, or if he interactionally positions himself as inferior to the interviewer, how might these affect his self? Analysts will clearly give different accounts of the mechanism of narrative self-construction, depending on whether they focus on narrated events and voicing, or also on evaluation and interactional positioning. Describing or voicing oneself in characteristic ways might provide seminal representations of self, if one believes that the self is primarily a matter of how one represents the self. Or description and voicing in the narrated events might provide scripts for action, if one believes that habitual actions are central to the self. Types of evaluation or interactional positioning might provide characteristic stances that the self takes toward others, if one believes that habitual ways of relating or acting are central to the self. We discuss mechanisms of narrative self-construction further below, following our more detailed analysis of Robert's narrative.

12.5 Robert's narrative positioning

12.5.1 Narrated events

In his narrative Robert partly constructs himself using all four types of positioning. At the level of narrated events, Robert describes his life in three phases. From birth to age five, he lived alone with his mother. Robert can remember no more than five conversations with his biological father, and he feels that he was "more or less an afterthought" to him. When he was five, Robert's mother got married to the man who became Robert's adored stepfather. From age five to seventeen, home life was "joy" because his parents cared for each other and had good jobs. During this time, at age fourteen, Robert fathered his own child.

In the following segment, Example 12.5, Robert describes his relationship with his stepfather.

Example 12.5

(a) RB   . . . my *biological*
(b)   father, he didn't want anything to do with me at *all*. and
(c)   then, he a*dopt*ed me, changed my last *nam*e, was calling
(d)   me *son*, and then, he was *my dad*, the way I looked at it
(e)   . . .
(f)   I remember. I was *litt*le but I remember my
(g)   mom holding my *right* hand and him holding my *left* hand
(h)   and us walking into the courtroom, walking into the city
(i)   county building, and I came out and I said we're a *fam*ily
(j)   now. and he's like yup. I remember that. I remember that.

In this episode Robert describes the creation of his new family. Note the "us" at line (h) and the "we" at line (i), which presuppose that he is a part of a family now, together with his mother and stepfather. At this point in his narrative he positions himself as having made a transition from a (potentially stigmatized) single parent family to an intact nuclear family. This positioning gets communicated in substantial part through reference to past events – which is accomplished through various grammatical forms like past-tense verbs, plural first-person pronouns, etc.

At age seventeen, however, Robert's family discovered that his stepfather was a bigamist and had been keeping two families all those years. "Everything fell to pieces," his mother became poor, and Robert dropped out of college. He then made some bad decisions and left several jobs, such that he does not earn very much money. But at age twenty-three he nonetheless has a steady job. He also now lives with and is engaged to marry the mother of his daughter.

Robert's narrative thus describes two central crises or challenges, each of which was precipitated by one of his mother's men. First, she got involved with Robert's father, who continued his life on the street and did not contribute to the family at all. Robert and his mother overcame this challenge when she married his stepfather and they became a two-parent family. Second, after twelve years Robert and his mother discovered that his stepfather was a bigamist. They were emotionally wounded by this, and loss of the stepfather's income also meant financial hardship for them – among other things, Robert had to drop out of college and his mother lost her home. Robert has not fully recovered from this second challenge, and he has not forgiven his stepfather for the betrayal. But Robert nonetheless describes himself moving in a positive direction at this point in his life. He has a stable relationship with the mother of his child, and they are engaged to be married. He lives with and cares for his daughter. And he has a regular job.

12.5.2 *Voicing*

At the first layer, then, that of the narrated events described in his autobiographical narrative, Robert positions himself as someone who has overcome challenges to become a promising and responsible parent. Robert reinforces this sense of who he is at the second layer of positioning, by voicing his characters in distinctive ways. He describes and voices several characters in his story: his mother, his father, his brother, his stepfather, his daughter, his girlfriend and her family. By characterizing these people as recognizable types, Robert reinforces the sense of himself as a promising and responsible parent.

Voices presuppose types of identity that are recognized in a particular social context. As described above, the distinction between "street" and "home" is salient in the urban neighborhoods in which Robert and his peers live. As explained by Anderson (1999), people and their behavior often get characterized as either "street" or "decent" – with "decent" meaning the type of stable, responsible, rule-following behavior that characteristically takes place at "home." A narrator like Robert, then, generally must choose whether to voice his characters as "street" or "decent." His choices about these voices, and how he voices himself, position him in characteristic ways.

The voicing that Robert does, while describing the various characters in his story, reinforces the positioning that he accomplishes through his description of past events. Men like his father and brother are "street." Women like his mother, his girlfriend and his daughter are "decent." It is painful for Robert to discuss his stepfather, because this man was paradigmatically "decent" for Robert, and helped Robert construct himself as "decent," before the revelations about his bigamy. So Robert has faced challenges from the street – and from his stepfather's non-decent, self-centered behavior – but he has maintained his own position as a "decent" person who is now deeply involved in the prototypical "home" activity of childrearing.

Robert says only a few things about his biological father, but they suffice to voice him as completely irresponsible and uninvolved.

Example 12.6

(a)	RB	and that's how it was the *few* times, like I said, five
(b)		times, five conversations I had with my real pops, and he
(c)		was like, he was so cool, he could barely talk [RB changes
(d)		his voice to imitate his father. Interviewer laughs]. and it
(e)		made me uncomfortable. I'm used to, *talk* to me, I'm not *cool*.

Being out on the street, Robert's father is concerned to be "cool" (line (c)). He was so busy being cool, in fact, that he only spoke with his son five times in his life. His male friends out on the street knew Robert's father well. But Robert was not a part of that world.

Example 12.7

(a)	RB	my biological father died, and they leaning all over the
(b)		casket, and they cryin' and I'm sitting there, me, his *son*,
(c)		his *first* born and I *leaned* over the casket and it looked like
(d)		*me* with a low haircut. nothing. I'm looking around. I never
(e)		saw that many people at a funeral. that's what just *irked*
(f)		me. it just *irks* me. so many people knew him and I *did*n't.
(g)		my *mom* talks so fondly of him. *she* loved him.

Robert's father did have connections with other men out on the street, and these men wept for him. It turns out that many of them met and respected him for his skill at basketball, a prototypical game of the streets. But Robert's father chose to live with his friends on the street, and Robert was not a part of that world.

In contrast to Robert's biological father, we have already described Robert's mother above – the woman with the iron fist who demanded a lot. She sacrificed for Robert, and she demanded a lot from him, but in the end it turned out for the best. His stepfather, before his bigamy was revealed, was also a stable, responsible figure in Robert's life. Robert was proud of his family's respectability.

Example 12.8

(a)	RB	and it's all about how you *view* yourself
(b)		and how you *view* your family. I viewed my family as *tops*
(c)		of the block, none better. I mean, the Huxtables might have
(d)		had more money, but they didn't have more *know*ledge in
(e)		their home.

Because of his stable home, Robert was able to, as he says, "do his job" and focus on succeeding in school.

So Robert voices some people in his life as "street" – his father and, as we will see below, his brother. He voices others like his mother as "decent," as acting responsibly to create a home. In addition to voicing these others, the genre of autobiographical narrative also provides narrators like Robert a chance to voice their own past selves. We have already seen indications that he voices himself as "decent," but it turns out to be more complicated than this. He has been both self-centered and responsible, but he has moved from the former toward the latter.

Robert describes himself as having undergone a developmental transition, as he has dealt with his challenges. He voices his younger self as having had some characteristics of "street" people. For instance, he was negative and refused to make an effort, and this cynicism "soured" (Example 12.9, line (e)) him in his attitudes towards others. He has changed from this earlier cynical self, however, wanting to set a better example for his daughter.

Example 12.9

(a)	RB	but everything I *say*
(b)		and *do* and behavior, in front of her *mat*ters. I mean
(c)		everything, like my interaction with different types of
(d)		people, and races and colors and ethnic backgrounds and all
(e)		that stuff. I don't wanna *sour* her with what I was soured
(f)		with. then, my *temp*er. I used to have a, not a short fuse. it
(g)		would take a lot to get me upset, but *once* I was upset, you
(h)		could pretty much kiss it goodbye for the evening.

(i)   there would be no communicating or even, you know.
(j)   every little decision is a *lot* more crucial, because you have
(k)   more than just *you* that you're worrying about. you can't
(l)   just *haul* off and do something wrong and that because if
(m)   you're just by yourself, only person you have to worry
(n)   about pleasing is yourself. but it's not like that.

In addition to overcoming this cynicism, Robert has also overcome his temper. He used to think only of himself, getting upset and taking it out on others. But now he realizes his responsibility to think about his daughter's needs before his own. He now operates according to the rules of the home, not the street.

In the following segment Robert not only acknowledges that he was wrong in the past, but also that this has a continuing impact on his life.

Example 12.10

(a)   RB   whenever I would get to a point where I wasn't happy with
(b)   my *prog*ress in life, I automatically attached it to the *job*
(c)   that I was working at the time.
             . . .
(d)   I was working
(e)   the water company, and every time I see a water company
(f)   truck drive by I'm like, *man*, you were *nine*teen years old at
(g)   the water company, could a had it *made* in the *shade* by
(h)   now. I don't know. I guess thirty five *grand* a year, I don't
(i)   know, but that's *de*cent money to me. I'm a simple man.
(j)   It doesn't much to make me happy and I could a had it *made*
(k)   by now, but oh no. I wanna leave. I'm *ti*red. I don't *like* that
(l)   job. I don't like how this supervisor's *talk*ing to me. this is
(m)   the bottom line. and I *un*derstand that now

Robert voices himself clearly through the quotation at lines (k)–(l). He used to be the kind of person who complains about working hard and quits a job over minor slights. Because of this, he is not making as much money as he could.

Robert continues to feel the effects of his earlier decisions to quit jobs and leave college.

Example 12.11

(a)   RB   it
(b)   *does* kinda hurt me when I call the job line and it says that
(c)   they're hiring for this and this and this, and you must

(d)   possess a *bach*elor's degree and all of this, it kinda *hurts* me
(e)   a little bit that I don't have that. I feel that I'm *sharp*
(f)   enough to still get it if I wanted it but I don't have the *drive*
(g)   to get it anymore. I just have the *drive* to get paper and
(h)   make my ends meet.

Robert has the ability, but he does not have the "drive" to complete college (lines (f)–(g)). As he has developed, from self-centered, temperamental young man to responsible parent, Robert has also chosen a working-class life. Caring for his family is his first priority, and a job is simply a means to that end. He expects a job, not a career: "I am there for the green paper with the *eagle* on it."

12.5.3 Evaluation

Through the narrated events that he describes, and through the voices that he assigns to other characters and to himself, Robert communicates a sense of himself. He never was "street" himself, thanks to his mother and his stepfather. But he did face two crises when his mother's men left. And as a younger man he also thought primarily of himself. In recent years he has become a responsible parent, and he has started to put others' needs before his own.

Robert reinforces this positioning through the evaluation he does in his narrative. We can see this most clearly in the different evaluations he makes of his brother and himself.

Example 12.12

(a) RB and the deal is, when you rule with an iron
(b)   *fist*, your rule is *complete*, but when your *fist* isn't *iron*
(c)   anymore, *you* no longer rule. that's why I have a eighteen
(d)   or nineteen, no Brandon's twenty. he was nineteen, just
(e)   turned twenty. I have a *twenty* year old brother who *barely*
(f)   listens to anything my mom says. I can't really, I can't
(g)   relate to that because when I grew up, *her* word was *rule*.
(h)   from the time, five years on. I don't know what it *was*,
(i)   *diff*erent make up, he *never* had any *fear* in his *heart* of that
(j)   woman at *all*. ever. but maybe it was because she was he
(k)   was the *baby*. the *young* one. I know Brandon didn't do
(l)   that and this and that and blah, blah, blah.
       . . .
(m)   I got the more *call*oused hand so. I guess it all worked out
(n)   for the best. except the fact that he won't *list*en to her. he
(o)   *bare*ly listens to me.

Robert's mother had an iron fist with him. As described above, Robert evaluates this as having been for the best. His mother behaved differently with his brother, however. Brandon was spoiled, and as a result he "won't listen" (line (n)). Later on Robert describes how his brother has turned out to be "a thug," although he is "a thug with a heart."

A "thug" lives on the street. But how does Robert evaluate this voice? He could have some sympathy for the injustices that such people face, or he could blame them for their situation. Examples like the following show that he adopts the latter position.

Example 12.13

(a)	IVER	do you *see* getting
(b)		job as a barrier?
(c)	RB	no. all you gotta do is listen to the news. I mean,
(d)		unemployment is at a *all* time low in this city. I mean, all it
(e)		takes is a Sunday paper. nine times outta ten, it don't take
(f)		much. a *smile*, a Sunday paper and a *hair*cut and a *belt* to
(g)		put in your belt loops. nine times out of ten you can get a
(h)		nine-dollar an hour job. it's not hard. I don't see that as a
(i)		barrier. it's a barrier when you don't want to *work*. the
(j)		*prob*lem is when you *want* money, but you *don't* want to
(k)		work to get it.
		. . .
(l)		of course, it may be harder for some other
(m)		people, because they may *have* five, six, seven *gold* teeth,
(n)		hair in *corn* rows, *pants* sagging down, I mean, that's not
(o)		the type of English that some places. like if I had a
(p)		store and it was black owned and I'm proud to be black and
(q)		everything else, but you ain't going to be walking into my
(r)		store looking like a *hot* mess. you're going to *pick* your hair
(s)		out, *shape* it up, tuck your shirt in, look presentable. that's
(t)		all. that's where their problem is, that's *my* brother's
(u)		problem. he don't want to *cut* his hair, he got his *way* out to
(v)		here, and I guess that a *thing* with the young toughs or
(w)		whatever (hh). but, no, getting a job. that ain't no problem.
(x)		not for *me*.

In this segment Robert colorfully voices "street" people like his brother. They have gold teeth, distinctive haircuts, saggy pants, and they do not speak Standard English (lines (m)–(o)). Robert makes clear his position, by calling such self-presentation a "hot mess" (line (r)). He feels that such people should make a small effort to "look presentable" (line (s)). Then they could get jobs and join mainstream society.

In several similar segments, Robert negatively evaluates "street" people like his brother and his father. He positions himself as very different from such people.

Example 12.14

(a) RB I couldn't relate. I found myself not being able to
(b)   relate to guys at school because they's like, oh, I'm living
(c)   from place to place and I'm *hust*lin' is the only way I know
(d)   to survive, I was. *my* upbringing was *sto*rybook up until I
(e)   hit seventeen. mom and dad huggin' each other and it.

Although he himself has faced hardships, he cannot relate to street people who are "hustling" (lines (b)–(c)). He expresses sympathy at various points toward people who have genuine needs, but he is unsympathetic toward those who act "street."

We can see a similar evaluation in the following segment, where Robert is describing his own responsible behavior as a child.

Example 12.15

(a) RB my mother. we was talking about latch key kids and
(b)   stuff and *I* didn't *know* I was a *latch* key until they actually
(c)   labeled that. I thought that was being a *re*sponsible young
(d)   man. not burning the house *down* while your *mo*ther's
(e)   gone. fixing a ham sandwich, get some chips, turn on the
(f)   tv, wait for *mom* to get home, it's not that hard. I found out
(g)   oh you're latch key. *latch* key. I was like, am I? I was *latch*
(h)   key from fourth grade on, if that's what *latch* key is.

Unlike "street" kids today, he implies, Robert himself was a "responsible young man" (lines (c)–(d)). By using this phrase here, Robert the narrator positions himself as like responsible, adult, parental figures who talk this way. He has little sympathy for "street" people and others who cannot act responsibly – as he says, "it's not that hard" (line (f)). Through such evaluation, in this example and others, Robert positions himself as "old fashioned." He is not cool. He is working within the system and taking care of his daughter.

12.5.4 *The event of speaking*

In describing the narrated events, in voicing his characters, and in evaluating those voices, Robert adopts a consistent position for himself as someone who has become a "decent," responsible parent. His emerging relationship with the interviewer in the narrating event reinforces this positioning.

The interviewer and Robert begin their interaction with the presupposed roles of interviewer and interviewee. The interviewer has authority to direct the conversation and Robert has an obligation to provide information. They continue in these roles throughout the conversation, but there are other possible relationships that they might also be adopting. At times, for instance, the interviewer acts sympathetic toward the difficulties that Robert has faced. On hearing about Robert's stepfather's bigamy, for instance, he says: "and so it was really devastating when you found out." For most of the interview, the interviewer is primarily an interviewer, but a sympathetic one.

There is another interactional issue in play, however. The interviewer begins with the following comment:

Example 12.16

(a)	IVER	. . .we appreciate, when I say *we*, NCOFF [National
(b)		Center on Fathers and Families], we really appreciate your
(c)		taking *your* time out of your busy schedule to come in here.
(d)		although twenty-five dollars is not a *lot*, we at least want to
(e)		show that we respect your *time*.
(f)	RB	it's like I was telling Lisa, I said *twenty*-five dollars. I
(g)		could work *half* a day to make that, so it's plenty to *me*, so
(h)		it's *more* than enough.
(i)	IVER	oh, okay. so I'm going to start with some
(j)		background information. . .

When the interviewer apologizes for the small $25 payment, it becomes clear that Robert and the interviewer have different socioeconomic positions. Robert responds that "it's plenty to me" (line (g)), thus accepting the differing positions that he and the interviewer occupy. This issue of relative status remains presupposable throughout the interview. Robert and the interviewer must deal with or avoid tacit interactional questions like: Is the interviewer "better" than Robert? Does Robert admire or resent him for this?

Does the interviewer flaunt or try to minimize his socioeconomic privilege?

In the following segment, for instance, Robert engages the issue of credit and mentions the interviewer in passing.

Example 12.17

(a) IVER   how did she, and this is just an aside, how did
(b)   she deal with finding out your stepfather was a bigamist?
(c) RB   oh, man. she had a nervous breakdown. she lost her
(d)   *house.* she had to *file* bankruptcy. you don't find a whole
(e)   lot of black people, with, you may have decent credit, but
(f)   *per*fect, never had a late payment, anything. I never forget
(g)   1986. she walked into the showroom floor and saw a
(h)   eighty-six V8 Trans Am, with *all* the trimmings, and she
(i)   walked in and she looked at it and said, I want it. and
(j)   *drove off* with the car. no money. she didn't put any money.
(k)   that's what her credit was like. a *brand* new car. just signed
(l)   for it and took it *home.*

At line (e), Robert says "you may have decent credit, but." This presupposes the question of whether Robert's mother had better credit than the interviewer, and it potentially raises the issue of relative status. If socioeconomic status is a marker of worth – and it is often taken that way in the larger society – does his mother's good credit make Robert "as good as" or "better" than the interviewer? Such questions about interactional positioning are not necessarily conscious or important to the participants in an interaction like this, but they are presupposable and thus they may become important to the interactional positions of the speakers (Goffman 1959).

It turns out that Robert is not centrally interested in asserting his own status relative to the interviewer. We can see this near the end of the interview, when the interviewer makes a bid to establish solidarity with Robert. Despite their different socioeconomic statuses, and despite the fact that he is the interviewer and has authority to direct their conversation, the interviewer shares a story from his own experience. He describes how his own father left him when he was a child, and in doing so he expresses sympathy for what Robert went through when his stepfather left.

Right before the interviewer tells this story, he jokingly describes their interaction as having been like a therapy session:

Example 12.18

(a)	IVER	um, well, let's transition now out of this,
(b)		perhaps, and I hope that at least maybe it does you some
(c)		good to have someplace to talk about (hh) it.
(d)	RB	talk about it. it's *easi*er to talk about it because
(e)		Natasha, she *knows* my mom. you're hardly ever in a *fo*rum
(f)		where you're *asked* the questions to *prompt* discussion. it's
(g)		more like, you say something, then I say something, then
(h)		you say something, then I say something. but, it feels good.
(i)		you don't know how much, what a *weight* it feels like is
(j)		being lifted just being able to talk about this stuff. because I
(k)		*brew* on it all the time, I think about him leaving us like it
(l)		was yesterday.

Here Robert ratifies the interviewer's description of the interview as a therapy session. It feels good to "talk about this stuff" (line (j)), as one would do with a therapist. And the interview has been a therapeutic success, as it feels to Robert as if a weight "is being lifted" (lines (i)–(j)).

There are now two potential frames for the interaction: an interview and a therapy session. In what follows, the interviewer introduces a third potential frame – a sympathetic conversation among peers who have shared similar traumatic experiences with fathers who disappointed them.

Example 12.19

(a)	IVER	I mean I can understand the *fresh* vision of
(b)		that occurring because my father left my home when I was
(c)		nine years old and I can remember it as if it was yesterday.
		. . .
(d)		I can see myself playing with my mail
(e)		truck, and seeing my dad coming down the stairs with his
(f)		*suit*case, and I asked him, innocent child, dad, where you
(g)		going? I thought he was going on a vacation. he said, well,
(h)		you know son. I have to go away. and I said, well, when
(i)		you coming *back*? and he said, well, we'll talk about it. and
(j)		then when it *hit* me that he was gone, it was devastating.
(k)		like for me, fortunately, it happened at a time when, it
(l)		really changed my whole life, because then my mother
(m)		ended up sending me to military school and I never really
(n)		had that father figure. consequently I learned a lot from my
(o)		*peers*, ended up making a lot of mistakes. but I was

(p)		fortunate that by my sophomore year in college, I woke up
(q)		and decided it was time to buckle down.
(r)	RB	see that was the thing I didn't. I wish I could have
(s)		buckled down then. I just, by that point, I just, I said,
(t)		forget it. but like you said, *crys*tal clear. I remember the *last*
(u)		shirt he had on, the *blue* jeans with the work look on the
(v)		side, where he used to hang his hammer and stuff like that.
(w)		too much.
		. . .
(x)	IVER	yeah, and it was like, with my parents, it's
(y)		like they lived in two different worlds. my mother lived in
(z)		the *west* of the city, which was economically a lot better
(aa)		off, than the *north*. and so I would go to see him, and it was
(bb)		just different, because he liked to *drink*. he spent a lot of
(cc)		time in the *bar*, so you know, these kinds of things.
(dd)	RB	and that's how it was the *few* times, like I said, five
(ee)		times, five conversations I had with my real pops, and he
(ff)		was like, he was so cool, he could barely talk [RB changes
(gg)		his voice to imitate his father. Interviewer laughs]. and it
(hh)		made me uncomfortable. I'm used to, *talk* to me, I'm not
(ii)		*cool*. I think, it's *good* to get it out. like I said, I feel a lot
(jj)		better. I feel I *hand*led it extremely well, too. I gotta pat
(kk)		myself on the back because a lesser person would have
(ll)		crumbled. just like my *mom*, can you imagine just, you
(mm)		being married to this man for twenty years and then you
(nn)		wake up and you're *not* and he's *gone*? [snaps finger]
(oo)	IVER	let's transition a bit to . . .

By sharing his similar experience with Robert, the interviewer might be creating a friendly, peer-like relationship. He emphasizes the pain of his own experience, describing himself as an "innocent child" (line (f)) who went through this "devastating" experience (line (j)).

In interviewing one of the other young fathers, this same interviewer told the same story and created solidarity with him (cf. Wortham and Gadsden 2004). This other father responded to the interviewer's story by empathizing with him. They went on to finish each other's sentences while describing their shared reactions to the experience, and they thus developed both interactional synchrony and camaraderie. Because they had endured similar pain in their childhoods, they could now talk to each other as black men working to contribute as husbands and fathers. They were still interviewer and interviewee, but they had also developed some solidarity with each other.

Robert, however, responds differently to the interviewer's story. When he tells the story about his father leaving, the interviewer steps out of his role as a scientist gathering data, and he steps out of the role of therapist that he seems to have adopted earlier in the conversation with Robert. He could be more of a peer with Robert, talking like an empathic friend. But Robert does not ratify this (potential) friendly, peer-like relationship. Unlike the other father, Robert does not empathize with the interviewer. Furthermore, instead of picking up on the similarities between his experience and the interviewer's, he immediately picks up on the differences. His first response – "I wish that I could have buckled down then" at lines (r)–(s) – notes that, unlike the interviewer, he did not turn toward school and prosocial behavior after his stepfather left.

After saying this, however, Robert does note that, like the interviewer, he does remember "crystal clear" the day his stepfather left (line (t)). The interviewer takes this as an invitation to talk more about his own experience, and he goes on to describe his parents' neighborhoods and his father's drinking. This presupposes that he and Robert have established some solidarity as men who experienced similar painful experiences as children. Robert, however, cuts him off and begins talking about himself again. He changes the topic to his biological father, and he does not acknowledge the interviewer's description of his own experience. Immediately following, Robert gives some meta-commentary on the interaction he and the interviewer have been having: "it's good to get it out" (line (ii)) and "I feel a lot better" (lines (ii)–(jj)). This positions himself as a therapy client again, someone being given the opportunity to talk about his feelings. It also positions the interviewer as a therapist. If their relationship in the interview is like therapy, then the interviewer should not be sharing his own experiences as he did – he should be listening to Robert's problems.

The interviewer, then, made a bid to change the event of speaking from an interview, and perhaps also from a therapy session, into a sympathetic conversation between peers discussing similar traumatic experiences. Robert, however, shifts it back into a quasi-therapeutic event. As he did with his earlier response about $25 being a lot of money, Robert actively positions himself as lower status than the interviewer and as benefiting from the interviewer's help.

This interactional positioning fits with the other sorts of positioning that Robert has done. He does not challenge power structures, as "street" people do. He works within the system, focusing on doing his job and caring for his family. Thus he is not interested in being the interviewer's friend, and he does not care to establish solidarity with him. He is happy to position himself as subordinate to the interviewer, and to benefit from this positioning by having a quasi-therapy session in which he gets to discuss his own problems.

12.6 Conclusions

All four types of positioning work in concert in Robert's narrative, to construct him as a responsible parent who distances himself from the street and embraces his domestic responsibilities. He describes himself in the narrated events as having overcome the challenges raised by his father's and stepfather's irresponsible behavior, to become a good parent for his daughter. He voices most of the men in his narrative, like his father and his brother, as living on the street. But he voices himself as having developed from irresponsible to responsible, as a "decent" person who takes responsibility in the domestic sphere. He evaluates "street" people negatively, as lazy, selfish and incompetent, and he embraces a more "old-fashioned" identity for himself. As Robert evaluates things, it's best not to be cool. Finally, interactionally, Robert positions himself as lower status than the interviewer, as someone who is comfortable with his working-class identity. Instead of being concerned with status and resenting people like the interviewer who represent the system, Robert takes what they have to offer and concentrates on being a responsible parent and domestic partner.

By constructing himself in this way, using all four types of positioning, Robert is artfully struggling with a challenge faced by the young urban fathers in our sample. The street and the home are gendered domains. Men stereotypically gain status as Robert's biological father did. They win respect on the street by fighting, being loyal to friends and playing ball (Anderson 1999; Bourgois 1995; Dance 2002; Ferguson 2000). Women stereotypically gain status by being good mothers, maintaining a nurturing domestic space for their children. Young fathers like Robert – under pressure from government and their own paternal urges to care for their children – are pushed toward the stereotypically female domestic realm. But to leave the street and participate in home life can threaten their status as men. Robert's response is to position himself explicitly as "not cool," as not concerned to prove himself according to the values of the street, but instead concerned to embrace an identity as an "old fashioned" man who values domestic responsibility. The interview itself seems to offer him an opportunity to articulate this identity, in the company of another man who rejects the values of the street.

In Robert's case, the four layers of narrative positioning work together, to create a more coherent sense of who he is. How he describes and voices himself, how he evaluates others' voices, and how he interacts with the interviewer all work together to position him as an "old fashioned" responsible parent and domestic partner. In some other narratives, although not in Robert's, this sort of synergy across levels happens in an even more robust way. Wortham (2001), for instance, describes an autobiographical narrative which involves elaborate parallelism between the events described and the positions enacted. In this case the narrator represents herself as going through a developmental transition (from passive to active) in the narrated events, and she simultaneously enacts a parallel transition in her interaction with the interviewer. Such parallelism represents a more complex type of interconnection among the various types of positioning than we see in Robert's narrative. Wortham (2001, 2003) argues that this sort of parallelism can constitute a mechanism that connects narrative structures to a self that is partly transformed through narration.

The various layers of narrative positioning need not work together, however. A narrator might, for instance, describe and voice herself as warm and sympathetic, while interactionally positioning herself as short-tempered and hostile in the event of speaking. This might construct a contradictory, or at least complex, sense of self for her. More work needs to be done on how different mechanisms of narrative self-construction work. But whatever the mechanism, analyses of narrative self-construction must attend systematically to at least the four layers of positioning we have outlined.

Appendix 12.1   Transcription conventions

-	abrupt breaks or stops (if several, stammering)
?	rising intonation
.	falling intonation
ITALICS	stress
1.0	silences, timed to the nearest second
[	indicates simultaneous talk by two speakers, with one utterance represented on top of the other and the moment of overlap marked by left brackets
=	interruption or next utterance following immediately, or continuous talk represented on separate lines because of need to represent overlapping comment on intervening line
[...]	transcriber comment
:	elongated vowel
°...°	segment quieter than surrounding talk
,	pause or breath without marked intonation
(HH)	laughter breaking into words while speaking

Part IV

The in-between self: negotiating person and place

Editors' introduction

The chapters that form the closing part of this volume analyze narrative data produced by people who have gone through fundamental and, in certain cases, deeply traumatic changes in their life. De Fina and Baynham look at immigrant discourse, while Schiff and Noy study the life story of a Holocaust survivor. As noted by Baynham in the introduction to his chapter, the experience of change and of physical or moral displacement leads people to revisit and question their past inventory of identities in order to rebuild a sense of self. In this regard, the types of narratives analyzed in this section are an ideal locus to study the discursive construction and negotiation of identity. The three chapters deal with interview data and in all of them interviewers and interviewees are shown grappling with the need to understand and give meaning to complex past experiences that led narrators to claim their present identities, but also to establish common ground or differences and confront each other on the adequacy of categories socially established to describe human experience. In this process, the analysts, who were also interviewers, rediscover the importance of looking at identity as something that is done on the basis of both, the stable and the innovative, the known and the unknown.

Thus a common thread running through the three chapters is an interrogation on the nature of the relationship between individual and collective identities, creative expression and social mould, and therefore also a reflection on social constructionism as a frame of reference.

De Fina (Chapter 13) analyzes this question from the angle of the construction and representation of ethnic identities. De Fina shares with the other contributors to Part IV a vision of identity as socially and discursively constructed. However, she questions a form of social constructionism, represented in some conversation analytic/ethnomethodological approaches to discourse and identity (such as Membership Categorization Analysis, cf. Antaki and Widdicombe 1998b) that restricts the analysis of identity to the examination of the context at hand and of members' orientation to categories emerging locally. The author stresses the importance of ideologies and shared representations in the building and management of social identities, and the need to look at processes of identity formation that can only be recognized when examining both a collective discourse level and the social discourses that surround immigrant stories and lives. Thus, to understand the nature of identities produced in specific discourse occasions, analysts need to look at the wider context of social categorization, and to the constraints that such context places on individual freedom. One way of studying the impact of social ideologies on the formation of identification categories is to look for shared social representations. Drawing on van Dijk's work on ideology (1998), De Fina argues that stories embody basic schemata in which people represent social dimensions and social relationships. These schemata are central to the construction of their social identities in that they allow members of a group to present themselves as belonging to categories whose members have typical characteristics and defining ways of acting. Thus the study of schemata involving identities, actions and reactions in narratives affords analysts the possibility of looking at collective processes of identity formation.

The author exemplifies the existence of such schemata looking at the use of the category "Hispanic" by narrators to describe themselves in different stories. In the narratives of different Mexican immigrants, being Hispanic is related to being colored, being perceived as physically different and being subject to acts of rejection by other groups also ethnically defined. However, De Fina points to the limits of an analysis exclusively based on recursive schemata, since analysts

need to account for the fact that the construction and presentation of identity is a process in constant development and that one of its crucial sites of negotiation is interaction. It is indeed in concrete social activities and within specific instances of discourse that shared categories and beliefs about identity become the object of resistance, alternative formulations and renegotiation. (p. 355)

The close examination of the performance devices used by an immigrant, Ciro, in a story about ethnic conflict, exemplifies how individuals redefine existing categorizations, build conflicting stances with respect to them, and often deploy nuanced identities in response to social and local contextual factors.

Baynham addresses similar concerns (Chapter 14) since he illustrates how both personal agency and social positioning play a role in the identity that Moroccan immigrants in England perform in their discourse reconfiguration of past experience. The theoretical frames of reference for Baynham's work are approaches to identity developed within cultural studies (Barker and Galasinski 2001; Hall and du Gay 1996) and ethnomethodology, both of which stress the situated, contingent, constructed nature of identity and identification processes. However Baynham, like De Fina in her chapter, points to the need to recognize both the creative, local nature of identity construction and the shaping forces of social processes on the way individuals talk about and perform the self. In his view, narrators position themselves with respect to interlocutors, social roles and categories, but are also positioned by their interlocutors and by social processes that go beyond the specific circumstances in which they produce their narratives. The author argues that the notion of "speaking position" captures, better than other constructs used to analyze identity, the existence of links between the expression of identities in discourse and the ratification of rights and social roles in a wider sense. Performance devices and narrative resources allow speakers to occupy such positions both at a local and more global level, and therefore their analysis reveals the mechanisms by which these social relationships are created and strengthened through discourse.

One narrative resource that exemplifies how the construction of identities involves the acceptance or rejection of social roles is narrative genre. Baynham shows how the generic narrative, for example, is normally appropriated by immigrant males who take up the role of telling, and of ratifying, the socially accepted story about migration. Such narrative typically involves a protagonist who is a young, enterprising male who leaves his family behind to open the way for a better life in the host country. This narrative form becomes therefore the means through which individual narrators both create a position for themselves within society, and get positioned by dominant discourses about migration.

But narrators build discourse positions through a variety of performance devices. Baynham, as other contributors in this volume (see, for example, Kiesling and Moita-Lopes), argues that the discourse construction of identity is fundamentally relational and illustrates how immigrants use constructed dialogue, the representation of the voice of others, to enact their individual stances in opposition to religious or other ideological conceptualizations about the individual and the acceptability of social behavior and ways of being. The exploration of narrative performance devices opens the way to the analysis of many levels of identity construction: from the assumption or rejection of roles with respect to family and other social institutions, to the definition of reciprocal relations within the interview. The Moroccan immigrants interviewed by Baynham exploit narrative resources that go from constructed dialogue to the use of different languages to build identities as immigrants, as fathers, as men, and as Moroccans. They are, at the same time, enacting those identities against the backdrop of what their own families, societies and interlocutors expect them to be. The analyses of such narrative performances reveal a complex picture in which immigrants reinvent themselves and reinterpret their past in the light of the new experiences that have brought them to a new life.

In their contribution (Chapter 15), Schiff and Noy address the interaction between individual agency and social determination in autobiographical narrative looking at the case of an Israeli holocaust survivor: Bella Kaplan. The authors' work can be inscribed in a discourse approach to narrative analysis that regards life story-telling as a meaning-making process in which the individual is engaged in a constant reinterpretation of the past within the framework of the contexts in which s/he moves in the present. Within this tradition (represented in this volume by Mishler and Bell) telling one's story is doing identity since individuals by making sense of their past are also coming to terms with their interlocutors and present circumstances. Schiff and Noy stress the role of shared social knowledge and meanings embedded in metaphors, themes, symbols and stories in these processes of individual reconfigurations of the self. They argue that it is through the filter of these shared constructs that individuals are able to make sense of their own identity and to communicate their interpretations to others. In other words, tellers borrow many aspects of the social knowledge and incorporate them into their life stories. The processes through which the social is incorporated into the individual are, according to Schiff and Noy, interpretation and communication. Reviewing and reflecting upon their past, people strive to find a unity and a logic in their life, thus they reconfigure social knowledge in their own terms. At the same time, the process of communicating their interpretation of reality entails negotiations with others, and therefore a renewed sharing of personal meanings.

The significance of this interaction between personal and social in narrative is illustrated through Bella's autobiographical reconstruction of her Holocaust experience. The analysis of Bella's narrative shows how she appropriates a historical event, the public trial of John Demjanjuk, a Nazi guard accused of atrocities against the Jews in Jerusalem, to make sense and share her own story as a Holocaust survivor. Although the narrator never met Demjanjuk and was not aware of his existence at the time of her detention in a concentration camp, this figure becomes a recurrent and integrating theme of her biography. In fact the figure of Demjanjuk not only allows her to reinterpret her past and understand her sufferings, but also provides categories in which to place such experience and communicate it to her interlocutors in the interview. In this sense, the historical trial of Demjanjuk and its social meaning is appropriated by Bella to lend meaning to her individual experience.

An important point made by Schiff and Noy is that the interaction of social and individual meanings is especially significant in the analysis of Holocaust stories. The authors point to a tendency, among scholars of the Holocaust, to exclusively focus on questions of truth and historical credibility. Survivors' stories are usually treated as mere reconstructions of past experiences because of their importance as testimonies of the atrocities committed by Nazis, therefore their links to a multiplicity of contexts are normally ignored. However, as Schiff and Noy claim, Holocaust narratives are, like all autobiographical and personal stories, crucial sites for identity construction for their narrators. Cultural and historical knowledge play an important part in them and the role of experience after the Holocaust in survivors' stories cannot be overestimated.

The three chapters in this section contribute to spell out the multiple threads that unite individual tellings with the social contexts in which they are inserted. They illustrate, through the analysis of different contexts and communities, how identities are formed and enacted through the constant interactions between individuals, with their unique experiences and reflections, and societies, with their ideologies, institutions, accumulated knowledge and history.

Group identity, narrative and self-representations

Anna De Fina

13.1 Introduction

The last decade has seen a growing interdisciplinary interest in the formation, negotiation, and development of identities. This new focus on identity is, at least partially, the product of the intensified contact between different communities brought about in post-modern societies by such social processes as globalization and massive migrations. The multiplication of the occasions for contact with *the other* has brought with it a problematization of the concept of identity itself and an effort to understand the relationship between people's sense of membership in a community, the beliefs and social practices that define that sense of membership, and its expression and manifestation in social behavior.

For discourse analysts and sociolinguists the challenge has been to show not only the centrality of the role of language in the construction and transmission of identities, but also the concrete forms in which and through which language practices index such identities.

In this chapter, I focus on how group identity is represented and negotiated in narratives. I argue that narrators build shared representations about who they are by creating story-worlds in which identities are characterized in common ways and routinely related to specific actions or reactions. The analysis of how narrators build relationships between identities and actions affords us knowledge on the nature of group self-representations, because it allows the investigation of traits that are seen as salient in descriptions of self and others and of the consequences that category membership has for social action. Such knowledge is especially important to understand the repertoire of identities from which minorities and marginal groups draw in order to build images of themselves and their own interpretation and appropriation of mainstream labeling categories.

Narrative analysis based on detailed textual examination can help reveal how socially shared group representations are managed and replayed by members of particular groups and what kinds of conflicts and acts of resistance are associated with them. In this chapter, I argue for an approach that combines broad analyses of schematic relationships between actions and reactions in stories, with close textual analysis of the performance devices employed by narrators in the storytelling. To exemplify my approach I use self-representations in the narrative discourse of Mexican undocumented immigrants to the United States. Before I turn to my examination of the data, I provide some theoretical reflections on the relationship between narrative and identity, and a brief review of research on categorization. I also discuss the notion of self-representation and its application to group identity. Finally, I present my own approach to the analysis of group identity in narrative.

13.2 Identities in narrative

The stress on narrative as the locus for the study of identities is not new in discourse analysis. Researchers in the field have shown that by telling stories, narrators are able not only to represent social worlds and to evaluate them, but also to establish themselves as members of particular groups through interactional, linguistic, rhetorical and stylistic choices. Thus, for example, researchers in narrative have related identities to cultural ways of telling (Blum-Kulka 1993; Ochs and Taylor 1995) or culturally determined schemata (Wood 1999; Kiesling, this volume), to the choice of particular strategies such as reported speech (Hill 1989) or detail (Johnstone 1990), to the use of performance devices in general (Bauman, 1986), to the degree of discourse integration of stories (Sawin 1999), to the choice of language or language variety in the telling (Bucholtz 1999b; Holmes 1997). These studies of narrative have shown that what defines people as members of a group is not only the content of their stories, but the way in which they use socially established resources to tell them.

In other analyses, the focus has been on the way in which social categories and beliefs are put into play through the construction and evaluation of story-worlds. Researchers investigating the representation of self in story-worlds have pointed to the kinds of agency that narrators attribute to themselves as figures in the story-world by looking at linguistic choices indexing particular roles such as action verbs and referential expressions (O'Connor 1994; Schiffrin 1996), or voicing devices (Hamilton 1998; Hill 1995a; Relaño and De Fina 2005).

Another way of analyzing the relationship between identities and narrative has been to examine how linguistic resources are used by narrators to index their positioning with respect to social categories such as gender, ethnicity, or race (Bucholtz 1999b; De Fina 2000, 2003; Kiesling, this volume; Moita-Lopes, this volume). Analyses of the use of these kinds of social constructs in stories have shown that narrators give situated meanings to categories describing race, ethnicity and gender, that these categories are often interconnected in intricate ways in the discourse of narrators, and that the latter negotiate through stories their sense of belonging or opposition to groups represented by those categories. The studies just discussed support a widely accepted social constructionist conception of identity in which identity is seen as situationally motivated and achieved (Bauman 2000: 1). Within this vision, amply represented in this volume, people do not possess one identity related to the social categories to which they belong, but rather they present and re-present themselves, choosing within an inventory of more or less compatible identities that intersect and/or contrast with each other in different ways and in accordance with changing social circumstances and interlocutors. Social constructionist perspectives have also influenced our view of identity construction and attribution as a process grounded in different kinds of social practices and activities. In that sense, it has become generally accepted that different types of narratives emerging in different types of interactional contexts provide specific loci for the construction of particular inventories of identities. The recognition of the "polyphonous" (Barrett 1999) nature of identity should not, however, lead to a vision of the construction of identity as an entirely creative and locally managed process, since, as I will discuss below, the identities that people display, perform, contest, or discuss in interaction are based on ideologies and beliefs about the characteristics of social groups and categories and about the implications of belonging to them. These ideologies and beliefs underlie in complex ways the discourse produced in interaction by social actors. Thus, situated displays of identity relate in many ways to the more general identities that are built by social groups.

13.3 Identity and categorization

Among recent developments in identity studies, one of the most influential is an approach that focuses on categorization as a central discourse process for the construction and negotiation of identities. As categorization reflects ways in which members of a culture organize experience into categories with associated features, the analysis of how these processes are managed in discourse, i.e. of how categories for identification are produced and made relevant by participants in interaction, has become one of the main areas of interest within this kind of analysis of identity. Proponents of this approach, which has become known as Membership Categorization Analysis (MCA – see for example Antaki and Widdicombe 1998b; Hester and Englin 1997), have worked around ideas on categorization first developed by Sacks (1972, 1995) to explain the rules according to which interactants create and use "membership categories" and routinely link certain activities to them. Among the most important principles proposed within this approach are the centrality of the local occasioning of identity categories, the stress on the activities that make relevant certain identity categories, and the idea that the use of categories in discourse is consequential for the interaction at hand (see Antaki and Widdicombe 1998a: 3). Along with these basic principles, proponents of MCA have also given voice to their rejection of "cognitivist" explanations of how categorization works (Edwards 1998: 18) since their stress is on local relevance and construction. They have therefore invited analysts to "hold off from using all sorts of identities which one might want to use in, say, a political or cultural frame of analysis" (Antaki and Widdicombe 1998a: 5).

Most scholars working on identity share some of the ideas put forth by proponents of MCA since there is a generalized consensus on the value of Social Constructionism as an approach to social and discursive phenomena. Many discourse analysts look at identities as built and negotiated in discourse, agree on the situated nature of the processes of attribution and negotiation over identities, and consequently reject a conception of identity as a stable feature characterizing individuals or groups independently of social activities and interaction. However, recognizing the centrality of interaction and of member's orientation to the study of identity, does not, in my view, automatically entail the rejection of the existence of cognitive aspects in the management of identity categories and concepts, nor does it resolve the analytic problem of how categories are interpreted by interactants, given that much of what is being conveyed about category membership is a matter of shared understanding and implicit meanings. Thus the study of categorization and identity should avoid two equally misleading assumptions: one is that the meaning of categories is exclusively managed at a local level and is in some sense "manifest" only within the interaction at hand; the other is that speakers hold in their minds a certain number of well-defined categories with associated meanings and that all they do in specific interactions is apply them. Analysts need instead to be able to link local identities to shared ideologies and beliefs, but they also need to account for the fact that the construction and presentation of identity is a process in constant development and that one of its crucial sites of negotiation is interaction. It is indeed in concrete social activities and within specific instances of discourse that shared categories and beliefs about identity become the object of resistance, alternative formulations and renegotiation.

13.4 Narratives and group identity

As we have seen in the previous section, central to identity is a sense of belonging to social categories. According to Tajfel (1981: 255), for example, identity is "that part of an individual's self-concept which derives from his knowledge of his membership in a social group (or groups) together with the value and emotional significance attached to that membership." However, membership loyalties are continuously revised according to historical and local circumstances, and both the way in which people relate to social groups, and the meaning given to social categories, change through time and in different social contexts. Likewise, identities can be expressed not only at a collective, but also at an individual, level:

these two facets of identity never completely overlap. In this chapter I focus on the forms through which narratives present and construct group identity.

According to van Dijk (1998), although group identity is related to the cognitive representations of a group, it cannot be reduced to representations, since social practices and forms of organization play an important role in its definition, redefinition and reproduction. However, van Dijk argues, cognitive representations form basic schemata in which people represent social dimensions and social relationships. These schemas allow members of a group to answer questions on who they are, what the criteria for membership in their group are, how they relate to members of other groups and what their goals and values are (1998: 129). Self-representations are, therefore, the basis for ideologies, and for this reason their investigation is of primary importance for an understanding of the constitution and functioning of social groups.

The role of discourse and, more specifically, the role of story-telling in these processes can be approached at two levels. First is the level of schematic representations. At this level, narratives are loci for the display of self-representations because they build story-worlds in which narrators introduce themselves and others as figures and use categories to define their identity (or the identity of others) that are often presented (implicitly or explicitly) as playing crucial roles in the explanation of the actions themselves. Thus, stories provide models of the world in which actions and reactions are related to identities and therefore represent and conceptualize social relationships. The analysis of the relationships between actions and identities leads us to implicit (or explicit) self and other representations.

The second level of analysis proposed here is that of interactional negotiation. At this level, stories present an arena for the negotiation of stances vis-à-vis shared (or unshared) representations of group identity. Narrators convey implicit stances towards social definitions of who they are through the use of performance devices. Central to the study of these stances is the narrator's weaving of a polyphony of voices (Bakhtin 1981b) into the story-telling. Voicing devices, such as alternations between dialogue and narration, pronoun switches, tempo, pitch, loudness, rhythm, are central to strategies of involvement or distancing, to the display of "otherness" with respect to characters and actions, to the communication of irony, surprise, sarcasm. At the same time, inter-actional moves of alignment or disalignment between narrators and audiences may point to local renegotiations of meanings related to identity.

13.5 Membership categories: being Hispanic in the United States

In the previous section, I have introduced the idea that stories allow narrators to develop and circulate self-representations, i.e. images about collective identities. What is the nature of these con-structs? Based on van Dijk's proposal, it is possible to conceptualize these representations as including membership categories and asso-ciated defining properties (who are we? who are others? what do others call us?), ways of relating actions to identities (how do Xs usually act?), ways of representing relationships with others (how do Xs usually act towards others, how are they treated by others, how close are they to others?), belief systems (what kinds of beha-viors are right or wrong for Xs?). Through these representations, narrators convey not only their own way of looking at themselves and at the members of their groups, but also interpretations of how others categorize them. These complex interrelationships result in definitions and redefinitions of the categories socially available for the apprehension of reality. By looking at these implicit definitions we can thus gain knowledge on group identities.

The case that interests me here is that of ethnic identity and its negotiation among Mexican undocumented workers. I have shown elsewhere (De Fina 2000) that ethnicity is a central category for the ascription of identity in the case of Mexicans (and of immigrant groups in general) in the US. I have also discussed the fact that the label *Hispanic* is not self-chosen, but is applied to Mexican immi-grants through social categorization processes with which they need to come to terms in order to define a new identity.

Little qualitative research exists on the formation and mainte-nance of ethnic identities in the case of Mexicans and other Latin Americans in the United States. Some studies have attempted to es-tablish how the choice of ethnic labels for reference to self or others reflects group identification on the premise that labels are asso-ciated with attitudes that groups hold toward each other (Buriel and Cardoza 1993). Although there are no studies of Mexican immigrants, the choice of labels has been analyzed in the case of Mexican Americans. The selection between terms such as *Chicano* or *Latino* for self-identification, for example, has been related to different social factors such as age, social class and generation (Hurtado and Arce 1986; Gómez 1992; Buriel and Cardoza 1993; Estrada 1993; Berry 1993). Most of the studies devoted to this topic are quantitative, except for Oboler (1995) who looked at the different perceptions of the term *Hispanic* as expressed in interviews by 21 Latin Americans of different origin and social class. However, many investigators take for granted that being *Hispanic* has the same meanings for everybody, and therefore they give us no information about the self-representations that Mexicans (or other groups) associate with the label itself. In contrast, one of the most important questions that a study of identity in the case of Mexican undocumented workers raises is, crucially, what being *Hispanic* means to them. That question leads to more specific questions: how do Mexican undocumented workers conceptualize being *Hispanic*? What kinds of self-representations are associated with this category in discourse? How do different contexts affect these representations?

Narratives can help us answer those questions through the investigation of the relationship that Mexican speakers create in story-worlds between being *Hispanic* and the representation of experience, and through the examination of stances and alignments displayed by storytellers. I will use two narratives told by two Mexican undocumented workers to illustrate this point. The stories come from a corpus of 41 narratives and 13 chronicles of the border crossing collected during one year of fieldwork among Mexican undocumented immigrants in Langley Park, Maryland between 1997 and 1998 (De Fina 2003).

13.6 Self-reference and social representations

The analysis presented in this section focuses on the level of schematic representations by looking at the connections implicitly established by narrators between characters categorized through ethnic or color labels and actions and reactions in the story-world. The analysis shows, besides differences in tone and content of the narratives, some common elements in narrators' representations of being Hispanic. These include a conception of Hispanics as colored, an action schema in which "looking" Hispanic sets in motion acts of discrimination, and an implicit acceptance of a color/ethnic hierarchy in which Hispanics are closer to blacks than to whites.

The first story is told by an immigrant (for whom I use the pseudonym Ciro[1]) within a chronicle of his border crossing experience. The interview was conducted by me, with the assistance of a young Mexican immigrant, called Ismael. In the chronicle, elicited by a question on how he had managed to arrive in the US, Ciro recounted how he left Mexico with a group of young immigrants, how he crossed the border illegally, how he met with other young people from Mexico and how they went from town to town in search of a job. During this period, Ciro and his friends decided to go to Florida. They had bought a van and were traveling together. At this point the story starts:

Example 13.1
Ciro's story[2]

(a)	c	Allá vamos que pa' Florida,
(b)		nos perdimos,
(c)		fuimos a dar allá a Atlantic City donde está una playa,
(d)		"Bueno muchachos pus- y la camioneta?"
(e)		pus se nos jodió de la cruzeta,
(f)		"Mientras le cambio la cruzeta vamos a la playa,"
(g)		"Orale ahí cobran cinco pesos,"
(h)		"Pus órale."
(i)		puro *gringo*,[3] puro *blanco*!
(j)		((blows lightly))muchachas *blancas* también,
(k)		((faster tempo and higher pitch))u::y y uno que viene del campo,
(l)		dice ((whispering))"Viste esta muchacha?"
(m)		"Si!"
(n)		y, "Empezamos a meternos?"

---

[1] All names in the narratives are pseudonyms. The only person who asked me to mention his real name is Ismael, the young immigrant who helped me collect the data.

[2] Terms referring to ethnicity or color are reproduced in bold in order to make them more easily identifiable.

[3] The term *gringo* is used to refer to Americans. It often has a pejorative connotation in Mexican Spanish.

(o)   @ "Orale?"@
(p)   I   @@@
(q)   @ todos *hispanotes*, llegan @@@@
(r)   sale,
(s)   íbamos los ocho,
(t)   entramos al agua
(u)   y había hartas muchachas y chavos bañándose acá,
(v)   y mira en menos de cinco minutos solitos est[ábamos!
(w)   I   [@@@
(x)   A   @@@
(y)   C   @"Vamos a seguir a la bola!"@
(z)   @"Pus órale!"@
(aa)   íbamos para allá y otra vez solitos!
(bb)   A   @@
(cc)   C   no había ni un *moreno* puro *güero*[4]
(dd)   y ah ya nos bañamos,
(ee)   y, "Vámonos ya está la camioneta, vámonos!"
(ff)   nos fuimos.
(gg)   ya pos si, nos daba risa ya! tsk!(.)

Translation of Ciro's story

(a)   C   And there we go to Florida,
(b)   we got lost,
(c)   we ended up close to Atlantic City where there is a beach,
(d)   "Okay guys well- and the van?"
(e)   the head stick broke,
(f)   "While I change the head stick let's go to the beach,"
(g)   "Let's go there they charge five pesos,"
(h)   "Ok let's go."
(i)   only *gringos* only *white* people!
(j)   ((blows air lightly)) *white* girls too,
(k)   ((faster tempo and higher pitch)) o::h and one comes from the
            country,
(l)   says, ((whispering)) "Have you seen that girl?"
(m)   "Yes!"
(n)   and, "Shall we go in?"
(o)   @"Let's go!"@
(p)   I   @@@
(q)   @all *Hispanics* ((hispanotes)) there they go, @@@

[4] The word *güero* (literally "blond") is used in Mexican Spanish to desig-
nate people who are "fair" in skin, besides being blond. On the other
hand, the term *moreno* (literally "dark") is routinely used by Mexicans in
the US as the "politically correct" description for "black."

(r)   ok,
(s)   there we went the eight of us,
(t)   we went into the water
(u)   and there were lots of girls and guys swimming and all,
(v)   and look in less than five minutes we were al[one!
(w)   I   [@@@
(x)   A   @@@
(y)   C   @"Let's follow the crowd!"@
(z)   @"Well let's go!"@
(aa)   we went that way and again alone!
(bb)   A   @@
(cc)   C   there was not ((even)) one *black* person only *fair* people
(dd)   and so we had a swim
(ee)   and, "Let's go, the van is ready, let's go!"
(ff)   we went.
(gg)   yea, that's it, at that point it made us laugh! Tsk! (.)

The narrative starts with Ciro and his friends leaving towards
Florida and getting lost (lines (a)–(c)). In lines (d) to (h), Ciro uses
reported speech to recount how the van broke down and the friends
decided to go to a beach while it was being fixed. The style of the
reporting is vivid, with fast exchanges between the interlocutors.
Notice that Ciro treats the protagonists as a collective agent since
no quotative verbs are used to specify who, among the friends, is
speaking and answering. The orientation clauses describing the
people that were at the beach (lines (i)–(j)) specify that there were
only *gringos*, only *white people* and *white girls*. The introduction of
identification categories in orientation clauses creates an expectation of relevance to the action taking place in the story (De Fina
2000). Thus color is presented in this orientation as a relevant
category for the understanding of the events that follow.

In line (k) Ciro mentions that he and his friends came from the
country and describes their surprise and excitement when they saw
the girls. The placing of the information that they are *country boys*
and the description of their reaction when they saw the women,
plus the relevance space opened by the mention of their whiteness,
all lead to the implication that the presence of white people (and
white girls more specifically) was a novelty to them, and that the
girls being white was a source of particular excitement. At this
point Ciro has already established the tone of the story, as can be
seen by the audience reaction of laughter (line (p)). Laughter by the

audience or the teller himself accompanies the telling of this story throughout (lines (o), (p), (q), (w), (x), (y), (z), (bb)) and is an indication of the fact that the tale is designed to be funny and is received as such. Ciro describes the decision-making process and the entrance into the water of the eight men in a very lively and burlesque tone. Here again, reported speech is used to convey the Mexican friends' surprise and optimism about joining the crowd. See for example the sequence in lines (l)–(o):

(l)   says, ((whispering)) "Have you seen that girl?"
(m)   "Yes!"
(n)   and, "Shall we go in?"
(o)   @ "Let's go!"@

In line (q), stepping out of the story action, Ciro describes himself and his friends as *Hispanic*, not as Mexican. He uses the term *hispanote*, a combination of the Mexican term *Hispano* + the suffix *-ote*. The suffixation of words with *-ote* usually (and also in this case) has the effect of presenting the referent as endearingly clumsy. We will discuss the implications of this choice later. At this point, an implicit contrast has been created between the physical appearance of the people on the beach (defined by their being white) and the physical appearance of the friends, who are seen by the others as *Hispanics*.

The action that follows presents the eight friends following the crowd and the crowd moving away (lines (t)–(v)). Nothing explicit is said on this point, but Ciro has succeeded in presenting the reactions of the crowd as a consequence of the actions of the protagonists. His ironic tone is met again with laughter (lines (w) and (x)). In lines (y)–(aa), he depicts the boys' repeated attempts to join the crowd and their outcome "y otra vez solitos," "and alone again." The embedded orientation (line (cc)) restates the fact that there were no black people, only *fair people*, thus conveying again the importance of this detail for the comprehension of the story. Ciro uses the expression *ni un moreno*, that I have rendered with "not (even) one black person" because although the word *even* is not in the original, the sense of *ni* is stronger than that of the simple negation *not*. This wording of the contrast is important because it allows Ciro to convey a sense of extreme opposition between the whites who were on the beach and the Hispanic boys, suggesting that the presence of just one black person would have made a difference and would possibly have adjusted the color balance. Such an implication also signals that Ciro feels somewhat closer to blacks than to whites in terms of color, otherwise he would not have mentioned the absence of blacks in opposition to the presence of whites.

Ciro provides the conclusion of the action and the resolution in lines (dd)–(ff). The boys have their swim (line (dd)) and decide to go since their car is ready. The decision is conveyed again through the use of reported speech. Line (gg) represents an evaluation of the implicit meanings that the story has carefully constructed: "it made us laugh," where the pronoun "it" ambiguously refers to the whole episode, or to the boys' reaction to being left alone in the water.

Ciro has presented this episode as laughable in many ways: through his own laughter, through the use of irony (the *hispanotes*), and through the sequential placement of actions and reactions. However, the content of the story is not funny since the narrative clearly deals with color and discrimination. The relevance of color as a category for the interpretation of the story is established in three ways. It is set in the first orientation section (lines (i)–(j)) through the stress on the presence of only white people on the beach as an element that creates expectations about the development of events. Notice that the adjective *gringo* (a slightly pejorative term for American) is strongly associated with the adjective *blanco* through repetition of the same structure in the two utterances containing the adjectives (*puro gringo puro blanco*, "only gringos/only white people," line (i)). It is then strengthened through the placement of actions and reactions (lines (t)–(v) and (y)–(aa)) that imply an opposition between Hispanics and whites, since the boys (described as Hispanic in line (q)) repeatedly try to join the crowd in the water and the crowd (described as *gringo* and white in the orientation section) repeatedly isolates them. Finally, it is emphasized through repetition of the contrast between whites and other colored people in the embedded orientation near the end of the story (line (cc)) that takes up again the initial theme of the presence of *fair* people only and the absence of any colored person.

Although funny and really enjoyable because of the way it is told by Ciro (see laughter as a sign of audience appreciation in lines (p), (v), (w), (bb)), this narrative dramatically shows how Mexicans concretely feel the rejection that they sometimes provoke among the *gringos*, but also how they attribute such rejection, at least in part, to a perception of difference in color.

Summarizing, this story has presented elements of a schema of self-representation. As proposed by van Dijk (1998) such a schema includes among other things, membership categories, and the representation of relations with others. In this case, we find the following elements of self-representation:

a. *Membership categories*: one of the categories that Mexicans use to classify themselves is the label *Hispanic*.
b. *Defining properties*: a defining property of being Hispanic is being colored.
c. *Relations with others*: in terms of relationship with other groups, based on the way identities are connected to actions in the narrative, the schema seems to include a causal effect between *looking Hispanic* and being rejected by whites since there is no action or verbal exchange in the succession of events that may explain the white people's reaction to the boys, other than their appearance.

Another element of the schema in terms of categories is an implicit assumption about the way ethnic categorizations relate to each other. The assumption is that there is a scale of color/ethnicity in which colored people are closer to each other than they are to white people.

A question that immediately arises at this point is: to what extent can we say that these elements are shared by this group of Mexican workers? In other words, to what extent are these schematic elements part of a group's self-representation, and therefore part of the group's represented identity? We can say that these elements are shared to the extent that they reappear in other stories.

In the remainder of this chapter I analyze another story told by a younger immigrant, Sergio, which shows similar elements of schematic representation. The excerpt containing the narrative comes from a part of an interview that also involved Sergio's brother Leo, his sister in law, Evelina, and Ismael (the young immigrant who assisted me in the data collection). The narrative was told during a section of the interview in which I had started asking Sergio if he had had personal experiences with discrimination and he had answered positively. At that point all three participants collaborated in explaining to me what kind of discrimination they had suffered. Sergio tells the narrative discussed below as an *exemplum* (Martin and Plum 1997) in support of a thesis that he proposes. The thesis is the same as the one that Ciro implicitly conveys in his story: Mexicans are rejected because of their color. However, this time the rejection is attributed not to whites, but to blacks.

Example 13.2
Sergio's story

(a) A Pero tu has tenido experiencia directa de eso?
(b)   de que la gente the ve mal [por ser mexicano?
(c) S   [Si:.
(d) L No por ser mexicle yo di[go,
(e) S   [No por ser este-
(f) E Hispano.
(g) A [Hispano
(h) S [Por ser hispano, ser diferente a ellos, de diferente colo:r,
(i)   hasta con negros he tenido así.
(j) A Por ejemplo no te acuerdas de algo?
(k) S el viernes [o jueves, [cuando estábamos trabajando en
(l) A   [uh   [uh
(m)   el museo en Bethesda, nos venimos en bus,
(n) A uhu,
(o) S y: yo llegué
(p)   y me senté donde es- en la parada no?
(q) A uhu
(r) S pus me, estaban unas señoras platicando unas *negras*, platicando,
(s) A uhu
(t) S platicando
(u)   yo me, pasé atrás de ellas no para sentarme?
(v)   y volteó una,
(w)   y se me quedó viendo así como,
(x)   y como venía sucio y todo, dijo, "Uh!",
(y)   con su cara dijo todo no?
(z)   como se me quedó viendo dije, "Mm:!"
(aa) L Mejor the cambiaste de asiento@.
(bb) S No. me quedé allí no?
(cc)   pero ps me sentí mal,
(dd)   porque se me quedó viendo así como "Ahi!" viéndome con mala cara.

Translation of Sergio's story

(a)	A	But have you had a direct experience of that?
(b)		that people despise you [because you are *Mexican*?
(c)	S	[Ye:s.
(d)	L	Not for being *Mexican* I [say.
(e)	S	[No, for being-
(f)	E	*Hispanic.*
(g)	A	[*Hispanic.*
(h)	S	[For being, *Hispanic*, being different from them, of a different colo:r,
(i)		even with *blacks* I have had that.
(j)	A	For example do you remember something?
(k)	S	On Friday [or Thursday,[when we were working in the
(l)	A	[uh [uh
(m)		Bethesda Museum, we came on the bus,
(n)	A	uhu,
(o)	S	a:nd I got there
(p)		and sat down where the stop is right?
(q)	A	uhu.
(r)	S	Well, some ladies were chatting, some *black* ladies,
(s)	A	uhu
(t)	S	chatting,
(u)		I went, I went behind them to sit down?
(v)		and one of them turned around,
(w)		and she started staring at me like,
(x)		and since I was dirty and all, she said, "Ugh!"
(y)		with her face she said everything right?
(z)		and since she stared at me I said to myself, "Mm:!"
(aa)	L	You decided to change seats@.
(bb)	S	No, I stayed there right?
(cc)		but I felt bad,
(dd)		because she stared at me like, "Oh!" looking at me with disgust.

The question eliciting the narrative (line (a)) pointed to the experience of discrimination for being Mexican, but the answer by Sergio came after some collective reformulation on the presupposition that the reason for the experience of social rejection was being Mexican. Leo reformulated my wording of the question explaining that discrimination was not related to being Mexican and Sergio started to elaborate on this answer, but Leo's wife, Evelina, interrupted his utterance. She took her turn in order to state that the reason for the discrimination was that he was Hispanic (line (f)). Sergio repeated the explanation, but he also added that he had been discriminated *for being of a different color* (line (h)). Thus, like Ciro, Sergio proposes that being Hispanic means *looking* different and being colored. To summarize, my question about discrimination produced a negotiation among the immigrants through which they identified *looking different*, and specifically *having a different color*, as a perceptible divide between them and others. They also negotiated the point that this different look characterizes "Hispanics" in general, not only Mexicans.

Sergio's story is argumentative[5] in that its main function is to back up the position offered between lines (e) and (h), according to which he had been rejected by people in the US for "being, Hispanic, being different from them, of a different color." Sergio also specified: "even with blacks I have had that" (line (i)).

We must notice that the position itself has important implications because of the way it is worded, specifically because of the meanings associated with the word *hasta*, the Spanish equivalent of *even* in English. *Even* has been analyzed by Karttunen and Peters (1979) and by Kempson (1975) as a word carrying what Grice called "conventional implicatures" (1975: 44), that is, implicatures that are not derivable from a breach of the Cooperative Principle, but rather from the conventional meaning of the word itself. According to these authors, *even* prefacing a NP (X) implies that:

a) there are other Xs besides the one(s) under consideration that realize the same action or have the same property
b) it is surprising that this particular X realizes that action or has that property.

If we apply this analysis to our case, we can say that Sergio is implying that:

---

[5] For an analysis of the way stories function in everyday arguments see Günthner (1995) and Müller and Di Luzio (1995). These authors show that narratives have an important function in "documenting, detailing, dramatizing claims that narrators want to affirm in everyday argument" (Müller and Di Luzio 1995: 114). Narratives provide a sort of common-sense proof that, although different from strictly logical argumentation, works as convincing evidence in conversation.

a) he has had problems not only with blacks but also with other
    ethnic groups,
b) it is surprising that he might have had problems with blacks.

Implicature a) indicates that Sergio feels that his color constitutes a problem in the relationships with other people, while implicature b) indicates that he would in principle consider blacks unlikely to show contempt for his color.

The latter implicature points to a representation of race and color that we have also encountered, although less explicitly, in Ciro's story, which involves the existence of a social hierarchy of color/ethnicity in the United States. Within that hierarchy blacks are not better off than Hispanics, and therefore they are closer to them than to whites.[6]

The story is opened through an orientation (lines (k)–(m)) establishing the time and place of the action:

(k)   s   On Friday [or Thursday, [when we were working in the
(l)   A   [uh [uh
(m)   Bethesda Museum, we came on the bus,

Another orientation line ((r)) provides the ethnic identification of the antagonists in the story: "Well, some ladies were chatting, some black ladies." The identification of the ladies as black is discourse related in that it ties the story back to the position: 'I have had problems even with black people' ("even with blacks I have had that," line (i)). The complicating action starts in line (u) where Sergio goes to sit behind the ladies and then one of them starts staring at him. After that, she makes a face of disgust (lines (v)–(w)). Sergio uses reported speech, or rather reported "response cries" (as Goffman (1978) called sounds like *ugh*! in line (x), and *Mm*! in line (z)), to convey respectively, the woman's rejection of his

---

[6] This color scale can be seen as a kind of ethnic hierarchy. According to Hagendoorn (1993: 32), ethnic hierarchies are scales of preference towards other ethnic groups. The author quotes a number of studies in different countries showing that members of a group report having common "preference sequences" towards members of out-groups. For example, young Dutch tend to place northern European immigrants highest but Turks lowest on a preference scale. Thus ethnic hierarchies can be seen as "collective representations" or "shared cultural models."

looks and his own reaction to the humiliation. He performs the woman's disgust with the sound "*ugh*" that also evokes in the listener's imagination a "face" of disgust, as confirmed by line (y) in which Sergio comments: "With her face she said everything, right?"

There is some ambiguity in the report of events as described in lines (w)–(y), which I reproduce below:

(u)   I went, I went behind them to sit down?
(v)   and one of them turned around,
(w)   and she started staring at me like,
(x)   and since I was dirty and all, she said, "Ugh!"
(y)   with her face she said everything right?

In line (x), Sergio seems to imply that the lady's response cry was due to his dirty appearance. However, the action of *staring* (which in Spanish is described through the verb *quedarse viendo*, literally *stay looking*) is presented as following Sergio's move of sitting behind the antagonists, and appears therefore as a consequence of his physical closeness. Furthermore, although being dirty is presented as related to the lady's response cry, it is not necessarily proposed as the only cause of her reaction. While he is describing the way the lady was staring at him, Sergio interrupts the description since he does not finish his utterance ("she started looking at me like," line (w)) and then adds more information, as signaled by *and since* preceding the utterance *I was dirty and all*. In other words, given the way he formulates the sequence of events and his choice of words, Sergio seems to convey that the lady stared at him for no reason other than the fact that he was sitting behind her, and that her disgust was further, not solely, prompted by his appearance. Finally, if we consider that the narrative is told as an exemplum of the fact that Sergio has experienced discrimination because of looking different and having a different color, the mention of his clothes and his state can be seen, in a sense, just as a description of a further element of humiliation for him.

Going back to the complicating action, the story does not have the resolution anticipated by Leo, that of Sergio moving away, since the protagonist stays where he was, but feels bad about the whole episode (lines (bb)–(dd)).

At this point it is interesting to compare the two stories. With respect to tone, there are clear differences in the narratives since Ciro's narrative is very humorous and funny, while Sergio's narrative is sad. With respect to the story-world recreated, there are also differences in the categorization of antagonists. In Ciro's case the antagonists are white, while in Sergio's case, they are black. With respect to the action structure, the story-world protagonists are presented as reacting in very different ways towards the actions of their antagonists: in Ciro's story they laugh about what happened and then leave; in Sergio's story, the protagonist does not leave, but feels frustrated and angry.

However, there are similarities in the action structure and in self-categorization, which support the hypothesis of the existence of common schematic representations. Sergio's story rests on the same elements of self-representation that we have seen in Ciro's story. Both narrators categorize themselves as *Hispanic* and this categorization implies a perception of being colored, which in turn determines a specific relationship between actions and reactions: people who look *Hispanic* are rejected by other social groups. In Ciro's story such rejection is presented as entirely predictable and the story-world protagonists are teased for not having realized that. In Sergio's story, on the other hand, the rejection is not expected (as we saw in the analysis of use of *even* in line (i). However, both the predictability and unpredictability of the antagonists' reactions in the two stories confirm the presence of an implicit assumption about color/ethnic hierarchies, presumably reflecting differences in power and status. In this hierarchy there is a scale that goes from white at the top to black at the bottom. It implies that colored people are closer to blacks than to whites, therefore while prejudice or rejection is expected from members of the white community, it is not expected from members of the black community.

To summarize: these two stories present interesting similarities. First, Mexican narrators refer to themselves in protagonist roles as *Hispanics*. Second, they imply that a defining category of being *Hispanic* is being colored. Third, they either imply or state that merely looking *Hispanic* causes them to suffer discrimination since the fact that the protagonists in the story are viewed as *Hispanic* is related in causal ways to negative reactions: avoiding physical closeness and staring in a disapproving fashion. We also saw that narrators implicitly conveyed the existence of hierarchies of color that define ethnic relations. Thus, comparisons of schemas implying typical relationships between identities, actions and reactions allow analysts to look at possible shared representations that include both membership categorizations, and scenarios typifying inter-group relations.

13.7 Narrative performance and the display of stances towards identity

From the previous schematic analysis we have seen that Mexican narrators seem to accept the notion that they are *Hispanics*, and represent their being *Hispanic* as often provoking rejection among white or black interactants. However, a close look at performance devices in the stories reveals more subtle elements of conflict and/or resistance to common wisdom about identity and the display of resistance towards this kind of self-categorization.

Let us examine Ciro's story again. The story is, as we saw, skillfully told through the use of voicing devices, in the Bakhtinian sense (Bakhtin 1981b) of linguistic and paralinguistic means through which a narrator weaves into his own narrating voice a polyphony of other voices representing different points of view on the events. The main voicing device here is constructed dialogue (Tannen 1989). Ciro uses dialogue to represent the negotiations and debate among friends taking place at different points in the story. For example in lines (d) and (f)–(h) he uses this device to show how and why the decision to go to the beach is reached:

(d)   "Okay guys well- and the van?"
(e)   the head stick broke,
(f)   "While I change the head stick let's go to the beach,"
(g)   "Let's go there they charge five pesos,"
(h)   "Ok let's go."

He then goes back to the use of a more neutral narrator's voice to signal a return to the orientation of the story, where he introduces the crucial information about the presence of only white people on the beech (*only gringos, only white people*, line (i)).

Different performance devices are used to emphasize other aspects of Ciro's stance toward the events in the narrative as can be seen in the fragment below:

(j)   ((blows air lightly)) *white* girls too,
(k)   ((faster tempo and higher pitch)) o:::h and one comes from the country,

Surprise and excitement at the sight of the white girls are signaled in line (j) through a light blow of air that juxtaposes the voice of the protagonist to the apparently neutral narrator's description. In the following line the elongation of the u sound in *u::y* (which I translated as *o::h* in English), the use of the discourse marker itself, and the faster tempo and pitch of the whole utterance signal an emphasis on the contrast between the white girls and the bunch of *country boys* (line (k)), thus stressing both the surprising nature of the encounter, and the separation between the two groups of story figures. The boys' excitement is conveyed again through whispering, as an enactment of the protagonists' voice in the story (line (l)). Constructed dialogue is used again in lines (l)–(o) both to move the action forward and to display the protagonists' stance of excitement, surprise, indecision towards the events. All these performance devices contribute to the creation of audience involvement in the story-world (Tannen 1989) and identification with the protagonists.

As Ciro is creating involvement, however he is also distancing himself from the story-world, by stepping out of it and ironically looking at himself and his friends from outside. He achieves this effect not only by abandoning constructed dialogue, but also by switching from the *we* form to the *they* form (as seen in the use of the third-person plural form of the verb *arrive, llegan,* in Spanish). His utterance (line (q)) roughly translates: "All *Hispanics,* there they go," where the protagonists are depicted as *they.* The ironic effect is also achieved through the use of the affix *-ote,* to the word *hispano.* The typical effect of this suffix is that of an affectionate teasing, since it usually means "big," but by extension it may indicate clumsiness. Ciro's use here combines an affectionate look with an implication of clumsiness. By saying: *There they go,* he conveys the image of this group of *Hispanic* boys happily and naïvely getting in the water in the middle of a white crowd. Laughter accompanies this utterance, thus underlining the irony of the situation. Ciro steps back into the story through the use of the pronoun *we* (lines (s), (t), (v)), and uses laughter again to introduce the dialogue in lines (y) and (z).

The point being underlined through the use of these indicators of irony is that the Mexican boys were being naïve in thinking that they would be able to join white people without being rejected. It is interesting that Ciro describes himself and his friends as *Hispanic* instead of Mexican in this episode. But it is particularly telling that this self-description coincides with his stepping out of the story-world and with a clustering of ironic devices: laughter, use of the affix *-ote*, and use of the pronoun *they* to self-refer. Through these linguistic clues, Ciro is performing the 'otherness' of this group with respect to the rest of the people on the beach. Yet at the same time, he is enacting a certain distance from the scene. As a narrator he steps out to look at himself in the same way as people on the beach would look at him. Thus, he treats the whole episode as an instance of naïveté, but he does so by virtue of assuming the point of view of someone who does not belong to the group.

In sum, Ciro seems to be conveying two meta-messages, "We were so naïve in thinking that we could mix with white people," but also, "For people who do not belong to our group we Mexicans are Hispanics. That's the way we are seen by whites." Ciro's distancing from the story-world may also serve the interactional purpose of presenting a more "mature" self, a self that has gone through many experiences in the host country and has learned from them. Thus, the choice of certain performance strategies shows the complex intersection between personal and social identities that storytelling sets in motion.

Space restrictions prevent me from developing this particular point since my focus is on group identities, but it is important to stress that performance devices are powerful tools to convey individual identities as much as collective ones. With respect to the latter, the implicit associations with the description *Hispanic* that we have uncovered seem to carry elements both of acceptance and of resistance.

Although the other story presented is less rich in performance devices, it is somewhat similar to Ciro's narrative also in this respect, since self-categorization as *Hispanic* combines with the representation of a look cast by members of an outer group. In

Ciro's story it is the look of the people on the beach, while in Sergio's story it is the look of the African-American woman on the bus.

In sum, the analysis of performance devices in Ciro's story and the comparison with the other story shows not only that Mexicans do describe themselves as *Hispanic* and that they feel that being *Hispanic* provokes a rejection among members of other communities, but also that they are aware of the stereotypical and discriminating nature of the category itself. They accept it as part of an inventory of identities available to them, but they also resent it as a label applied by people who cannot, and will not, distinguish between them and other Latin-Americans. Resentment and resistance are embodied in the two narratives in different ways: while Ciro uses irony both to depict his protagonists and his antagonists, Sergio openly describes his feelings of anger and humiliation at being rejected for his appearance.

13.8 Conclusions

The analysis of stories reveals how narrators' local displays of identity relate to more global conceptualizations about the self and its membership into groups. I argued that to fully account for this link we need to study self-representations that emerge through the establishment of connections between identities and actions. Such connections, if reproduced in different stories, may point to schemata about identity that are shared by members of a community and form the basis for ideologies about self and others. At the same time I argued for a close textual examination of story structure itself and of performance devices as a means of uncovering narrators' stances about socially shared self-representations. This kind of close text analysis can help avoid easy generalizations about the way communities portray themselves and their relationships with others. The analysis has important methodological implications for sociolinguistics and for the study of identity in that it tries to build a bridge between accounts of identity that focus on the connections between identities and ideologies, and more interactionally based accounts that stress the processual, locally managed nature of the phenomenon and its dependence on concrete occasions of interaction.

Appendix 13.1 Transcription conventions (adapted from Sacks, Schegloff and Jefferson 1974)

↑	rising intonation
↓	falling intonation
CAPS	Louder than surrounding talk
.	at the end of words marks falling intonation
,	at the end of words marks slight rising intonation
-	abrupt cutoff, stammering quality when hyphenating syllables of a word
!	animated tone, not necessarily an exclamation
ITALICS	emphasis
:::	elongated sounds
@	laughter
(.)	micropause
[ ]	overlapping speech
(( ))	transcriber's comment
( )	non-audible segment
=	no interval between adjacent utterances

14

Performing self, family and community in Moroccan narratives of migration and settlement

Mike Baynham

The desert-like world commands life to be lived like a pilgrimage. But because life is a pilgrimage, the world at the door-steps is desert-like, featureless, as its meaning is yet to be brought into it by the wandering which would transform it into the track leading to the finishing line where the meaning resides. This "bringing-in" of meaning has been called "identity-building."

(Z. Bauman 1996: 22)

14.1 Introduction

Narratives of migration and settlement are narratives in which, almost by definition, settled and stable senses of self are unsettled and challenged. Thus, they confront the discourse analyst and cultural theorist with the task of finding new ways of understanding traditional categories of identity and voice. In this chapter, I use the concepts of speaking position and performance to analyze, in narrative, this unsettling of identities characteristic of migration and diaspora, and I show how narrative has a crucial role in the discursive "bringing-in" of meaning through which the sense of a life is continually made and re-made. The narrative speaking position is necessarily retrospective: to transpose Bauman's words, the narrative of wandering transforms it into discourse, through it speakers articulate retrospectively both their journeys and the senses that can be made of them. Less obviously, the narrative speaking position is also both current and prospective: through narratives speakers construct versions of themselves in current and projected future time. So narrative is not a transparent vehicle that conveys "what happened," but rather, a structured and structuring genre that shapes and constructs the story that is told and the self-presentations that it involves.

I start the chapter by outlining the background of the study from which the data is drawn, then go on to review a number of theoretical perspectives on identity, subject position and discourse, developing a performance perspective on identity. I then discuss the notion of speaking position, showing how two kinds of narratives of migration, generic and personal, imply different narrative speaking positions, with accompanying issues of entitlement and right to speak. Finally, I go on to show how narrative resources enable speakers to perform identities discursively and how such identities are relational, not absolute, since they involve comparisons and oppositions with present interlocutors, but also with past identities.

14.2 Background

The life stories of migration and settlement examined in this chapter were told by Moroccan economic migrants (*muhajjirin li ajl al-aish*, that is, migrants for food and life, to use the Arabic term), who settled in London, UK in the 1960s and 1970s.[1] The narrators are married men who migrated leaving their families in Morocco while they established themselves in London.[2]

The construction of these narratives involves intricate shifts between presentations of self, family and community (and indeed of religious and national identities) with correspondingly interesting shifts in narrative speaking positions. In the following sections, I examine the role of two distinctive genres in these life stories: performed oral narrative and generic narrative, showing how these different types (personal and generic narrative) imply different speaking positions with associated assumptions of identity, entitlement and rights to speak, suggesting that identities can be understood as performed in discourse. A key discourse analytic insight from such a performance perspective on identity in narrative is that it is precisely through performance features that speakers will display

---

[1] They migrated during the post-Second World War period of intensive recruitment of migrant labour to Western European countries such as West Germany, France, Switzerland and the UK (cf. Castles and Kosack 1973; Sassen 1999).

[2] For an account of migrations that do not fit this hegemonic generic account see Baynham (2005).

and play out identities. I then go on to illustrate how a performance feature, constructed dialogue, serves explicitly to perform identity in discourse. The data presented will be drawn from narratives of three "moments" of the migration and settlement process:

- decisions to migrate
- early days in London
- return visits to Morocco

14.3 Identity, speaking position and performance in narrative

As many other contributors to this volume suggest, narrative is a rich source for identity work. In this chapter, I explore this theme in relation to a corpus of narratives that, as suggested earlier, challenge fixed and stable notions of identity.[3] They were generally elicited through a variant of the question: "What made you decide to come to England?" Writers on ethnographic research methodology (for example Maranhao 1993; Mishler 1986) have pointed out how in fieldwork conversations a question will very often, and sometimes unaccountably, elicit a narrative as an answer to it.[4] In order to frame the data, it is necessary to keep in mind this interview context with its dimension of communication across ethnic and cultural boundaries: Moroccan migrant worker speaks to Anglo professional, Muslim to Christian, school-educated to educated in the "School of Life," etc. This context becomes relevant when we consider issues of identity and categorization below.[5]

By pluralizing the notion of identity, we unsettle and problematize the notion of the stable, unitary subject. Not a new move

---

[3] Hall (1996: 4) writes: "We need to situate the debates about identity within all those historically specific developments and practices which have disturbed the relatively 'settled' character of many populations and cultures, above all in relation to the processes of globalization. . .and the processes of forced and 'free' migration which have become a global phenomenon of the so-called 'post-colonial' world."

[4] Compare also Labov and Fanshel's (1977) account of similar phenomena in their study of therapeutic discourse.

[5] As an instance of this, I recall an occasion during my fieldwork when I had called to interview Mr. R and was waiting in his sitting room for him to arrive home. I heard the front door open and Mr. R call out cheerily to his wife, "*Ja dak an-nasrani?*" (Has that Christian arrived?).

theoretically, to be sure,[6] and one on which there are by now a range of angles.[7] However, assuming that identity is a social psychological construct, how do we show the role of discourse in its construction, in other words, how do we theorize the connections between identities and discourse?

Perspectives relevant to the position I take on identity in discourse come from cultural studies (Barker and Galasinski 2001; Hall and du Gay 1996) and ethnomethodology (Antaki and Widdicombe 1998b). Both of these approaches emphasize the situated, contingent, constructed nature of identity and identification, constituted in discourse, set against intrinsic, essentialist notions.[8] Where these two perspectives differ perhaps is in ethnomethodologists' unwillingness to theorize the shaping impact of the macrosocial on the micro-social, as Bourdieu (1977) argues in his famous critique of social interactionism.

From theoretical perspectives such as these it is useful to think of the relationship between identity(ies) and discourse, here narrative, in terms of performance (Butler 1997): identities are performed, played out in discourse.[9] If we see the relationship

---

[6] It is now a commonplace that a person's social identity is not unitary but a configuration of identities; so that we can see the external negotiation of difference with others as continuous with – and rooted in – the internal negotiation of difference in the struggle to constitute the self (Fairclough 1996: 8, cited in Lillis 2001: 49).

[7] See, for example, Harré's insightful and instructive treatment of the notion of multiple identities from a realist perspective (Davies and Harré 1990). For post-structuralist arguments against the unitary subject see Weedon (1997) and Norton's analysis (Norton 2000) of the non-unitary and conflicting identities in the life situations and language learning of migrant women in Canada. Indeed Norton (2000) gives an accessible account of these arguments, particularly in her discussion of "Identity as a site of struggle" and "Identity changing over time" (127–129).

[8] For a summary of this position from a Cultural Studies perspective, see Barker and Galasinski (2001, Chapter 5).

[9] Butler (1997: 43) writes:

The title of J. L. Austin's *How to Do Things With Words* poses the question of performativity as what it means to say that 'things might be done with words.' The problem of performativity is thus immediately bound up with a question of transitivity: What does it mean for a word not only to name, but also in some sense to perform and, in particular, to perform what it names?

between identity(ies) and discourse as one of performances in which identities are played out, it follows that the discursive features through which speakers perform specific speech genres will be those of interest in establishing and exploring the identity/discourse connection. This is not a point that has gone unnoticed among those who have concerned themselves with the poetics of everyday speech.[10] In the case of narrative, we can therefore examine the playing out of identity(ies) in the stylistic features of narrative performances. However, from this perspective, it is not enough, theoretically, to bring together identity(ies) and discourses. We need some linking construct which can capture the ways that identity(ies) are articulated in discourse. Here I want to make use of the notion of *speaking position* to illustrate how identities are constructed moment by moment in different contexts.

Again, the literature on position and positioning has become quite diverse, with different theoretical perspectives on the construct (see Ribeiro, this volume; Wortham, this volume; Moita-Lopes, this volume). Davies and Harré (1990) propose, for example, a realist version, which is taken up in narrative studies by Schiffrin. The latter demonstrates how displays of self in storytelling "interactionally position speakers within a story-world" (1996: 196). Norton (2000) draws on another theoretical account of positioning, derived from post-structuralist feminist theory (Weedon 1997). Parallel perspectives can be found in cultural theory (cf. Barker and Galasinski 2001), in critical discourse analysis (Fairclough 1989, 1992) and in discourse theories based on a Foucauldian perspective. In the latter, discourses position speakers or create positions for them, generating affordances within which particular roles become possible. According to Foucault (1972) every discourse has its general politics of truth, its regime of truth, constituted by the rules that govern who can say what in what circumstances. The same can also be said of genres such as narrative, as has been insightfully demonstrated by Amy Shuman

---

[10] I am thinking here of the work of Polanyi 1985, of Hymes's ethnopoetics (Hymes 1996), the work of Barbara Johnstone (cf. Johnstone 1990) on style and narrative performance and indeed the work of R. Bauman and others on verbal art and performance more generally.

in her work on storytelling, entitlement and right to speak (Shuman 1993). So in considering identity in narrative, the notion of speaking position is useful to characterize, for example, social roles, ideological stances, and the inter-personal alignments taken up by speakers in order to perform identities. As Ivanič (1998: 10) puts it:

The socially available resources for the construction of identity are multiple, and that of an individual's identity is a complex of interweaving positioning.

A Foucauldian account of speaking position in discourse might lay itself open to accusations of sociological pessimism. Where are the possibilities of agency in the regimented discourses posited by this theory?[11] Some might want to react to this account by constructing narrative as a free zone for unregulated voice outside the political economy of discourse that Foucault adumbrates. However, an exploration of the construct of speaking position in narrative, even in apparently unregulated vernacular settings, does, as Shuman (1993) suggests, uncover quite complex regulations of discourse, for example around notions of what counts as tellable and who is allowed to tell it. An approach based on speaking rights can be set against a more straightforward, libertarian politics of voice, as it is articulated, for example, in Hymes:

In my own mind I would unite the two kinds of freedom in the notion of *voice*: freedom to have one's voice heard, freedom to develop a voice worth hearing. (Hymes 1996: 64)

The advantage of the notion of speaking position over that of voice is that the former can capture both how speakers take up certain roles in discourse and how they are placed in particular sites by society. To be sure, Bakhtinian dialogism provides a more complex and interesting account of voice, in which speakers routinely appropriate and echo earlier personas, but it still does not capture how speakers position themselves and are positioned. An adequate description of the role that storytelling has in constructing identities needs therefore to work with the ways through which discourse

---

[11] For a discussion of identity, agency and the Foucauldian perspective, see Barker and Galasinski (2001: 45).

both shapes and enables particular speaking positions and disables others, including an account of speaker agency as both shaped by and shaping the communicative agenda.[12]

From this perspective, narrative is therefore not a "free communicative zone" indifferent to the regulations of the discursive economy. We can, on the contrary, expect to uncover, through discourse analytic techniques, and complementary methodologies such as ethnography, complex and powerful regulations of what can and cannot be said and by whom, and ways in which speaking positions are made available in particular discourses and genres. An illustration of how a speaking position operates can be found through a consideration of the case of the generic narrative.

14.4 Personal narrative and generic narrative: issues of entitlement and right to speak

Sometimes a speaker, instead of recounting a unique and singular sequence of events, will recount events that happened regularly, repeatedly, to a particular group of participants over time. If we imagine that one of the conditions on "canonical" narrative is that its sequence of events occurred once and once only to a determinate set of participants (a uniqueness condition), then, we can say that in *generic* narratives the uniqueness condition is suspended.[13] What is emphasized is typicality, iterativity.

In the following extract, Example 14.1, MA, a worker with a prominent position in the community at the time when I carried out my fieldwork, describes a typical migration pattern, starting with the resettlement of the head of the family who, once established, brings the other members over to join him.

---

[12] The work of LePage and Tabouret-Keller (1985) on acts of identity is relevant here.

[13] Generic narrative can be linked to Laberge and Sankoff's notion of generalizing discourse: "The utterances we are concerned with are generalizations involving an indefinite person, and they all have the effect of locating this person in a potentially repeated activity or context. Anyone's experience may constitute the basis for generalization, though most often it is the speaker's" (Laberge and Sankoff 1979: 428).

Example 14.1

the head of the family works for a while sends the money to the family and the family arrives to London mostly to in a just a small room the husband sometimes has to go and work during the day he has got nobody to inform him the even if there was any leaflets in Arabic or anything they could not read it most of them so they rely on word of mouth mostly and they try to get together it was very difficult for them but they did have a couple of cafes in the west end they were run by Algerians and they used to get there and they used to get together and drink coffee and talk about various things that they can help them like for instance how do they communicate with their relatives back in Morocco how do they how can they send money back home erm what immigration what the home office think about the various things what er if there is any hassle of bringing families what is the cheapest fare etc.[14]

Linguistically the generic narrative claims typicality through features such as the general present ("works . . . sends. . . arrives" etc.) and the generalized actors ("the head of the family . . . the family . . . the husband" etc.). This type of narrative raises interesting questions of authority, authorization and rights to speak, questions about who has or claims the right to make generalizations.[15] As an instance of an entitlement issue, we can consider the question of who gets to tell generic narratives, those representing the experience of a group. Overwhelmingly in my data the tellers of these kinds of narratives were men who were active in the public life of the community, in the community associations, and articulated in different ways the needs of the community to the dominant group. MB, for example, one of the subjects in this study who is quoted below, was interviewed for a local newspaper article on housing conditions and spoke for the community, *represented* them as a leader. So taking on the right to tell generic narratives implies taking on a public-speaking position, a resource in a sense made

---

[14] All the men whose stories are drawn on in this chapter provide instances of the hegemonic account, in that they migrated here as married men earning money to set up a base to bring over their families.

[15] Not least is the fact that these generic narratives produce a kind of hegemonic account, excluding other types of account, for example those of single women or indeed single men migrating, which are evidenced in my data (Baynham 2005).

available by the genre itself but bespeaking also a social role of leadership.[16]

14.5 Performance features and the performance of identity

I have suggested earlier that, if we develop a performance account of identity in narrative assuming that identity isn't an inherent essence, or even a multiplicity of essences, but rather something that people do, then we need to analyze the role of performance features in the discourse enactment of identities. I am going to explore this by looking at some instances of narrative where a speaker mimics another's voice, in order to show how this resource helps both to animate a particular speaking position in the narrative, but also to refine and bring into relief the narrator's own position. For it is a crucial insight of identity theory that we define ourselves in terms of what we are not as much as in terms of what we are. As Barker and Galasinski (2001: 123) write of ethnic identity:

> Ethnicity is a *relational* concept concerned with categories of self identification and social ascription. What we think of as our identity is dependent on what we think we are *not*.

14.5.1 Decisions to migrate

The relational nature of identity and identification is well captured in the following extract, Example 14.2, where ML describes his father's reaction to his decision to go to work in England:

Example 14.2

(a) I   so what did he say when you left
(b) ML   well I left and he say I going to England or going to France I no want to still here that what I thinking
(c) I   yeah and what did your father think about

---

[16] I am not of course suggesting that there is anything necessary about this gendered division of rights to speak, more that it is contingently produced by a particular stage of settlement and community organization. Another visit to this migrant community, ten or twenty years after this data was collected, would reveal many women active in community organizations and local agencies actively claiming the right to speak and represent.

(d) ML he say you no Muslim
(e) I   yeah
(f) ML you go any place is no Muslim yes he said to me you no Muslim
(g) I   yeah
(h) ML you maybe *kaffar* (= unbeliever)

Example 14.2 gives a powerful example of positioning by others and shows how constructed dialogue, the bringing into narrative of the voices of 'others,' is a central linguistic tool for constructing speaking positions. ML's father positions him as a potential apostate from Islam. For ML's father, even to contemplate leaving a Muslim country is an act of apostasy, and he thus sets his son's Muslim identity (what he is) against what he is not (an unbeliever). Part of the risk of migration, for this man, is precisely the potential for destabilization of a settled and core religious identity. The speaking position that ML's father constructs, draws on powerful religious discourses, harnessed as it were, in support of his argument that his son should not migrate. What are the linguistic resources that ML draws on to articulate his father's views? The narrative is built around an extended strip of constructed dialogue in which his father's reaction is dramatically presented, with its opposition between Muslim and *kaffar*. The initial utterance "you no Muslim" is repeated and expanded "you go any place is no Muslim you no Muslim you maybe *kaffar*" to emphasize the significance and weight of the father's utterance.

In the following extract, Example 14.3, from a more extensive life story, MB talks about his decision to migrate arising out of a series of life choices made once he started working. An interesting and complex parallel is set up between his own achievement of independence and the independence of Morocco from colonial rule.

Example 14.3

(a) MB so yeah when they left that time they left er I remember nineteen fifty s-seven they was the last time when I we saw the Spanish government ruling our country and er when they left Mohammed the Fifth he you know he was the king at that time well recognized official by the world wide he was a king and the country was ruled and that our kingdom
(b) I   yeah
(c) MB so by that time when we took independence I was already working
(d) I   yeah fishing

(e) MB fishing so when you to inde- when you got experience and you making your own bread in that time in '57 it was er it was actually is as a heaven

(f) I yeah

(g) MB that is was educa- a part of education because a part of the whole education is they teach you how to make your own life

(h) I yeah to be independent

(i) MB that's it

(j) I yeah

(k) MB so in that time I was independent that's I was educated enough

In addition to the theme of independence, in which political independence is explicitly linked with the speaker's personal independence to live and earn his own living, this life story is interwoven with another theme about the nature of education, which can be linked back intertextually to an earlier interchange in the interview. There, the interviewer had asked: "So when did you leave school?" to which MB had replied: "no I never been in school" and had then gone on to explicitly link his lack of schooling to the political and economic situation:

because in that time it was you know all the whole world even in UK it was desperate actually for just for people for work and er there wasn't much in the time of er education we talking about five years after the the second world war

To understand the significance of these themes in the development of the life story, we have to refer back to preceding discourse and understand something of the socio-political context of the times when MB was growing up. We must also take into account the social role of the interviewer as a professional worker in education. MB is in effect saying to the interviewer, "Don't think that education is only schooling. Work and standing on your own two feet is also education." He is thus implicitly positioning himself as educated enough in the "school of life" rather than in the education system represented by the interviewer. In this sense the identity work here is as much *positional* as relational: MB is positioning me as interviewer within the expectations of conventional schooling, while he himself is positioned somewhere else, as educated in the school of life. Again, identity and identification can be understood in terms of articulating what we are in relation to what we are not. Here the effect is that of interactionally positioning the interlocutor in discourse.[17]

In the following narrative, Example 14.4, MB explains his reasons for eventually migrating to London.

Example 14.1

(a) MB   but I had a pressure when I had the first daughter because you know the fisherman he's got he gamble with his life in the sea and if you haven't got a courage you will make no money

(b) I   yeah

(c) MB   so I start actually thinking about ah dry land is to bring your your kids and to to look after your kids proper well you have to be with them so I start thinking where I can raise a family in a dry land if I was in the sea well you can say it's fifty fifty chance of loss of life you could come back you can not well you know about that anyway

(d) I   my dad was in the navy so I know the

(e) MB   you know the situation and how long they stay away from the families and everything

(f) I   so your wife didn't like that

(g) MB   my mother she's the one she didn't like it my wife at that time she didn't bother it at all well only when when was making her living and she was decent family so she didn't 'terfere my life but my mother she who was wroting writing to my sister to her daughter telling her about me you know (MIMICS) one day he going to die he going to leave his wife and his kids widow and all that you know and especially in my town you know it is a small in that time and er if you one family husband he miss in the sea it's really dreadful you know because see the young wife desperate and you know finished her life young and to get married again and another husband beating the children of the other person so that's why actually I decide to come to England.

The narrative in Example 14.4 presents the conflict between MB, the free young male and the powerful figure of his mother, reminding him forcefully of his duties and responsibilities as a father, dramatically performed in the mimicry of his mother's voice,

---

[17] The distinction made, among others, in Chafe (1980) between story-world and interactional world is relevant here. MB is positioning me within the interactional world of the sociolinguistic interview. In ML's narrative his father positions him within the story-world.

in which she writes about him to her daughter. The written text is interestingly represented by mimed constructed dialogue:

(g)   my mother she who was wroting writing to my sister to her daughter telling her about me you know (MIMICS) one day he going to die he going to leave his wife and his kids widow.

The narrative, however, also represents this change of job as being due both to an external pressure from the mother and an internal pressure coming from within, as MB considers the dangers of a life at sea for a father with children:

(c)   so I start actually thinking about ah dry land is to bring your your kids and to to look after your kids proper well you have to be with them so I start thinking where I can raise a family in a dry land if I was in the sea well you can say it's fifty fifty chance of loss of life you could come back you can not

Here the emergence of internalized thought processes ("I start thinking") dramatizes the protagonist's changing perspective, brought about by his responsibilities as husband and father. In the fragment MB is performing himself not as the young, carefree youth enjoying his freedom and ability to work, but rather as an individual in transition to an identity as a thoughtful planner, weighing up the options and benefits for his family. The narrative presents a complex social field within which his decision is taken considering both pressure from his mother and also his own wish to find a safer form of work, alert to the potential dangers of a life at sea.

At the end of the narrative, MB appropriates this perspective in a strip of generic narrative, sketching out, as it were, a sociological scenario, a social worker's case story:

(g)   if you one family husband he miss in the sea it's really dreadful you know because see the young wife desperate and you know finished her life young and to get married again and another husband beating the children of the other person

Here again we see the characteristics of the generic narrative discussed earlier, the general present to signal a typical, repeated state of affairs, the generalized actors ("one family husband . . . the young wife . . . another husband . . . the children"). It is this appropriated generalization that forms the basis for the conclusion:

(g)   so that's why actually I decide to come to England

This account can be linked to notions of identity and speaking position in a number of ways. First, in MB's positioning himself in the "school of life," which interactionally positions me as interviewer and educator, second in his evolving masculine identity, the emerging identity of responsible father, replacing the carefree exhilaration of the youth as expressed earlier in the life story at being free to gain his independence and earn a living in the (masculine) world of work as a fisherman:

(e)   so when you to inde- when you got experience and you making your own bread in that time in '57 it was er it was actually is as a heaven.

Thirdly, although interrelated with the second strand, in the identity work involved in the conflict with his mother (constructed as a conflict between the free-ranging male and the domesticating female) over whether he should stay at sea. The latter is ultimately resolved when MB takes on and appropriates that position as expressed in the generic narrative, performing himself as the responsible adult male, thoughtful about the impact of his actions on his family. In this narrative we see a complex interaction of speaking position, both positioning by others and self positioning: MB represents the developing concern with his life at sea as coming both from within himself and from his mother. The narrative, however, obscures somewhat the extent to which his internalized worrying about work at sea was produced independently from or as a result of his mother's pressure.

14.5.2 Arrival in London

The above narratives concerned the processes through which decisions to migrate were made. In the following extract, Example 14.5, Mr. R describes his first hours in London and his fortunate encounter with a Spanish-speaking man who picks him up at the airport and offers to take him to "where the Moroccan work." Two aspects of his sociolinguistic repertoire are relevant to the discussion: the first, typical in a speaker of Mr. R's age and background, is competence in Spanish, derived from his upbringing in the pre-independence Spanish protectorate, the second is his ability to represent mimetically a variety of Arabic that is not his own, as in the quotation of the typically Lebanese address form *"ah habibi"* in describing his encounter with a speaker of Lebanese Arabic.

Example 14.5

(a) MR.R then he drop me in Green Park is another company same company name Hatches

(b) I yeah

(c) MR.R club night e was open from seven till four o'clock a disco well I find that place first then the Spanish bloke I remember he come in with the car I f- he's English then he talk to me in Spanish then I feel very happy

(d) I yeah

(e) MR.R cos you know I find somebody that speak my language then he drive me with the car in the restaurant then I don't like it I feel very horrible is a bloke from Lebanon he speak to me in Arabic (MIMICS) *ah habibi tfaddal qsa qahwa* and he give me that coffee s very different taste of the Moroccan

(f) I Yeah

(g) MR.R type then I don't like it then in the restaurant it was very small and very warm very hot

(h) I yeah

(i) MR.R so he said to me I thinks you don't like to work here well I say to him if is any better than this place ( ) yes I like to change it says come with me I take you where the Moroccan work

The contingent and unstable nature of identity is well illustrated here in this very early stage of the migration process. In this disorienting new environment, the former language of the colonial rulers, Spanish, becomes the familiar tongue, "my language":

(c) then he talk to me in Spanish then I feel very happy. . .

(e) cos you know I find somebody that speak my language

The former language of colonialism is revalorized as a migrant lingua franca in the hotels, restaurants and hospitals of London. In contrast, Lebanese Arabic represents here the unhomely other, a shibboleth of the Lebanese dialect of Arabic. The tendency to use the term of affection *habibi* (my darling) as a term of address, combines with the strange-tasting, unhomelike Lebanese coffee to create the feeling of discomfort from which Mr. R's companion releases him in the resolution of the narrative:

(i) come with me I take you where the Moroccan work

What does this example tell us about linguistic and cultural identity (the language you speak, the coffee you drink)? First, that the unsettlement of migration, characterized so well by Hall, revalorizes old identities and identifications: in the new environment the language of colonialism becomes a familiar home language, while a dialect of Arabic which is not the home dialect, is estranging and contributes to the disorientation felt by the immigrant. Second, as underscored in ethnomethodological approaches (cf. Antaki and Widdicombe 1998a: 3), identity work is closely linked with categorization phenomena, which in this case implies the unsettlement of received sociolinguistic categories.

14.5.3 *Returning home for the summer holidays*

In the final excerpt, Example 14.6, we examine the narrative of another, much later moment in the migration process, in which MM is describing one of the final stages of the long drive south through France and Spain, undertaken by many thousands of workers in Western Europe every summer, to spend the holidays in Morocco. In this narrative, the narrator/protagonist is queuing for the ferry at Algeciras:

Example 14.6

(a) MM   well I in s- in eighty when I go there I find too many people I ask the people some of them said me two days some of them said three days

(b) I   blimey

(c) MM   you know and the people all of them angr- angry and shouting with uh Spanish uh soldiers and uh w- warms or something like the people who do keep the guards

(d) I   guardia civil

(e) MM   yeah guardia civil then before when I go to I find some people eh work with agency said ticket ticket ticket you want ticket to Tangier I said yes I say he say I said what time can I take the boat said well for example in 'at moment I f- find myself about six o'clock full up twelve o'clock full up something like that is one one clock I said ok I take the ticket for one clock but one o'clock pass no no chance to that boat

(f) I   yeah

(g) MM   in that moment I take the ticket and going to find someone to talk I find Spanish one with eh some man al grads

(h) I   yeah like an officer

(i) MM   yeah officer I tell him 'scuse me sir he said well what happen
          I said uh I pay the ticket for one o'clock this morning or tonight
          for to cross the channel waiting for one o'clock or another day he
          start laughing to me he said what happened I said well someone
          said me one o'clock now is one o'clock pass already said uh he
          said to me you no make any trouble with that people for to take
          the place I said how can I because 's my car is cost uh money I'm
          not have uh for example uh for horse or mule or donkey for to
          that is you know the car is cost money you must be keep him
          don't thinks just for to come now must be go back again well he
          said well uh which part you work in Europe I said in England he
          said how long you been in England I said uh oh 'bout twelve
          years he said well you see French people who working in France
          or Belgium or he make nosing and for to take uh by force you
          know but you take it kind of uh English people always calm you
          know I said yes then he send me two guards for to help me to
          take the the boat I'm lucky for to take him in four o'clock in the
          morning

     The interviewer's prompt

(j) I   you said sometimes you have to wait a long time on the boat

initiates a general response describing the return to Morocco on
holiday of migrant workers from all over Europe

(j) MM   because you know the summer times all workers out abroad take
          in for example in last day of June or first of uh August

The focus of discourse shifts, at the prompting of the interviewer, to
an actual instance of a return journey to Morocco, rather than the
initial generalization, and MM continues with a personal retelling:

(k) MM   well I in s- in eighty when I go there I find too many people

In the earlier part of the narrative, MM describes angry queues for
the ferry:

(c) MM   you know and the people all of them angr- angry and shouting
          with uh Spanish uh soldiers

     Perhaps the most distinctive and most evaluated episode is MM's
conversation with the Spanish officer, in which we see him
constructing a speaking position as a reasonable man, in contrast
to the impatient and dangerous pushing and shoving which other

drivers are demonstrating. This patient, reasonable calmness on the part of MM is also constructed through the speech of the other protagonist, as being distinctly English, and something which MM has presumably acquired during his time working in England.[19] This is a rather unassailable position, since the evaluative comment is attributed to an authoritative outsider, not present in the current interactional world within which MM is telling me the story.

MM is using the narrative to construct himself as a particular kind of traveler, patient, reasonable and rewarded by the approval of authority. The narrative provides evaluation of this self, embedded in constructed dialogue, his own and that of the other protagonist. For example, MM's comparison of the treatment of a donkey or a mule with the treatment of a car, indicates perhaps the veiled suggestion that the other more disruptive drivers are behaving in a rather ignorant way towards their cars, like the owners of a horse, a mule or a donkey rather than of the high status, expensive car:

(i)   I said how can I because 's my car is cost uh money I'm not have uh for example uh for horse or mule or donkey for to that is you know the car is cost money you must be keep him don't thinks just for to come now must be go back again

In the narrative, MM performs himself as a careful, thoughtful driver, in contrast to the others, mindful not just of the emotions of the moment but of the need to consider the value of the car and the need to keep it in good condition for the return journey. This identity construction is, again, activity, in that the narrator is constructing it in contrast to the impatient, disruptive drivers. The performance is jointly constructed in his own words (he is a character in his own narrative) and those of the Spanish official he talks to. MM is constructing a narrative speaking position of a sensible, reliable person, who has been changed by his long years in London,

---

[19] I'm not aiming to suggest here some grand narrative of acculturation, but more that in the complex and diverse social settings produced by the unsettlements of migration, identities become more complexly laminated. A young Moroccan woman told me how, on her yearly visits back to her town in Morocco with her family, she was nicknamed l-ingliziyya (the English girl) by her friends and family there.

having taken on some of the stereotypical characteristics of the English:

(i) he said well uh which part you work in Europe I said in England he said how long you been in England I said uh oh 'bout twelve years he said well you see French people who working in France or Belgium or he make nosing and for to take uh by force you know but you take it kind of uh English people always calm you know I said yes

In contrast with the theoretical parsimony of the ethnomethodological perspective, in which everything must be accounted for in the moment of discourse, much contextual information from previous conversations with MM is taken here as relevant in making sense of this narrative. (Z. Bauman's bringing in of meaning suggests not just the immediate context of interpretation, but the long sequence of events and actions through which meaning is accumulated intertextually.) On earlier occasions, for example, MM had told me of his struggles to get his driving test in England, while speaking very little English, and the achievement of succeeding. The blue Peugeot in which he drives his family back to Morocco is a symbol of life achievement, making sense both of the contrast with the riders of mules and donkeys in the narrative and, more broadly, of his struggles to make his way in London, the long-term narrative of migration. The relational terms out of which this identity is produced are here: angry and shouting/calm, car owner/rider of donkeys. As Barker and Galasinski (2001) pointed out in their relational treatment of identity, what we are not is significant in defining what we are. MM constructs a narrative speaking position for himself as calm, reasonable, thoughtful. He is able to draw on the dialogic resources of narrative in so doing, when he uses the constructed dialogue of the Spanish official to position himself in this way.

14.6 Discussion

The tellers of these stories are engaged in developing narrative speaking positions in which identities get performed, sometimes explicitly through the mimesis of speech representation, which captures a key moment of identity work, sometimes through other narrative resources. These speaking positions literally talk up identities. We understand identity construction in discourse from a relational perspective as involving as much what we are not as what we are. This relational construction of identity can involve religion, ethnicity, gender, age, the distinction between a car owner and a rider of donkeys. As well as being relational this identity work is positional: conversational partners, characters in a narrative can be and are, frequently, positioned on either side of an identity category. While appreciating the ethnomethodological perspective on identity as something achieved interactionally,[20] I argue against the theoretical parsimony that leaves aside the broader contextual perspective provided by the cultural studies and indeed critical discourse analysis perspectives on identity construction in which macro-social processes are played out in micro-interaction. Such analytical restrictions ultimately limit the possibilities of ethnomethodological perspectives.

I have shown how different kinds of narrative, personal and generic, imply different kinds of speaking position and corresponding identity choice, relating this to a political notion of "representation." The generic speaking position is in its own way hegemonic, writing out of the account other types of experience such as that of single women migrating. The "typical" migration pattern presented by MA is certainly not the only one.

I have examined ways of taking up identity, both interactionally, in the sense that taking up particular speaking positions in discourse can position conversational partners as 'other' (the school-of-life theme in MB's life story), but also within the story-world itself in which the narrator provides richly evaluated accounts of key moments where the membership categorization aspects of identity are fore-grounded. We saw examples of these strategies in ML's account of his father's reaction to his decision to migrate, or in Mr. R's description of how he sets foot in the "unhomely" restaurant and is greeted in the unhomely variety of Arabic.

At the beginning of this chapter I suggested that narratives of migration and settlement unsettle and challenge stable senses of self. In this process particular identity affiliations (moments of

[20] Once we are at a scene, the ethnomethodological argument runs, we shall see a person's identity as his or her display of, or ascription to, membership of some feature-rich category (Antaki and Widdicombe 1998a: 2).

"suture" as Hall describes them) can be revalorized, as when, paradoxically, for Mr. R the former language of colonialism becomes the language of home. MM's story of his return home in the car he has bought and learnt to drive in London can be seen to characterize part of the "success story" of migration: you return home with more than you set out with, in this case not just a car but a set of social attitudes. In the narrative of his encounter with the Spanish border guard, MM presents himself as having acquired some "anglicized" features, explicitly linked to his migration to London, rather than France or Belgium (he returns home with a different linguistic/cultural baggage than the one he set out with). As I argued earlier, we should resist an easy grand narrative of acculturation, invoking instead the notion of identity lamination (cf. Hill and Zepeda 1993), through which identities can be added and layered to existing identities, provoking their revalorization, but also providing a more complex and rich account of processes of settlement and the changes they bring.

It is clear that narrative as a genre privileges identity-work simply because of the central role of voices and speaking positions in its construction. Narrators take on narrative speaking positions that involve different types of authorization or entitlement to speak, such as in individualized or generic narrative. Speaking positions also involve the relational construction of identities by opposition or contrast with others. Such is the case with MB's narrative when he opposes his former identity as a young man who took pleasure in independence and freedom to a later assumed identity determined by the cares and responsibilities of the family man. The narrator positions himself also through the voices of others that are brought into the narrative to reject, ratify or problematize narrative identities. For example, MB uses his mother's voice and ML his father's voice to present problematic aspects related to their identity choices. MM uses the voice of the Spanish officer who compliments him on his restraint in the queue for the ferry, to ratify his positioning as an anglicized, "calm" northerner who is too sensible to risk his car by pushing and shoving in the queue. If it is true, as de Certeau suggests, that "every story is a travel story – a spatial practice" (de Certeau 1988: 115), then these narratives of migration and settlement surely highlight pervasive characteristics of self-presentation and identity work, particularly perhaps in relation to the revalorization of existing identity categories and the integration of new and emergent ones into complex laminations of the self, thus providing a rich source of insights into the construction of identities in discourse.

Appendix 14.1 Transcription conventions

Modified CA transcripition
Arabic in *italics*
English in roman
– = Self interruption
(CAPS) = Non-verbal

15

Making it personal: shared meanings in the narratives of Holocaust survivors

Brian Schiff and Chaim Noy

15.1 Introduction

The focus on narrative studies across the humanities and social sciences reflects a shared concern with the interpretation of subjective experience. Life stories may be, as Mark Freeman asserts, our best "inroad into the phenomenon of self-understanding and selfhood" (1993: 6). Indeed, by listening closely to talk, how tellers describe who they are and where they come from, life stories allow us to explore subjective understandings in great complexity and draw interpretations about how persons make sense of self and world. If we accept the premise that narratives allow us special insight into the process of identity, then, a more adequate understanding of life narratives should help us to better understand the character of identity. We might, therefore, begin by asking, what is a life story? How are we to read and interpret life stories? Are life narratives the product of the person, the situation of telling, or something else?

When interpreting a life story, it is common practice to consider the individual level of analysis. After all, there is a real person who is sitting before us, describing the details of her/his past. Tellers, typically, use the first-person singular and speak with their own distinct voice. Elements of personality and our unique life experience are important contexts in understanding a life story (McAdams 1996). Such a tradition, beginning with Freud's case studies, and on through Henry Murray and Robert White's work, allows us to see how the contours of the past are shaped through the eyes of single persons with their unique developmental history and life circumstances (Runyan 1982). However, interpreting the meaning of a narrative requires more than a consideration of the person. Narrative is more than personality writ large. Social constructionists have made a forceful argument that narrative is a performance tailored to meet the needs of the conversation before us; it is flexible, responsive to a given audience and to the game of talk (K. J. Gergen 1994; Mishler 1999; Shotter 1993; Wortham 2000).

We agree that person and situation are central in any interpretation of life stories. However, we argue for the consideration of an additional level of analysis in understanding all life stories. When telling the story of their personal past, tellers make use of the wide array of shared meanings available through their contact with others, including idioms, themes, works of art, symbols, stories, and so on; what Schutz and Luckmann (1973) have called the "social stock of knowledge." Shared meanings are so prevalent that, when carefully listening to a life narrative, one can hear a chorus of social voices intoning new melodies through the voice of the teller (Bakhtin 1981b, 1986). These shared meanings are not set apart from our life story but are the essence of our stories, giving us the terms for configuring a personal narrative; shared meanings provide the means for interpreting and communicating the personal past. Lives are narrated and identities are fashioned out of the raw material of shared meanings.

But, how do shared meanings become a part of our personal narratives? Of course, shared meanings are a very basic aspect of our experience. They are, in part, a consequence of growing up in a family, a peer group, a time in history, a language community, and a culture (Miller 1994). We inherit the values and stories that are esteemed in these contexts through our participation, with others, in a shared horizon of meaning. Our lives are entangled in the lives of others and so are our stories. As Paul Ricoeur (1992) writes, "the life history of each of us is caught up in the histories of others" (1992: 161). Alasdair MacIntyre has, similarly, argued that stories provide us with the terms for shaping the plot of our life stories and comprehending the actions of others. "Deprive children of stories," MacIntyre writes, "and you leave them unscripted, anxious stutterers in their actions and their words" (1984: 216).

Although people typically regard culture as affecting members of a given community in the same manner, the study of personal narratives allows a different conceptualization of the relationship between the shared and the personal. From the perspective of life storytelling, culture is not hegemonic. Rather, we make the social personal. Shared meanings are not only imposed upon us, but are also maneuvered into, tried on, chosen, and used (Mishler 1999, this volume). The act of taking over the terms of culture and history should be thought of as both intentional and non-intentional; some meanings are chosen to selectively fashion a self and others we seem to "slide" or even "fade" into. The social world is, metaphorically, a text that is quoted in the narrative of our personal past. We, the tellers, are prolific collectors, drawing upon our experiences in the world, both those that are direct or first-hand and those that are communicated to us through our participation in a social world. In talking about our lives, we "borrow," "collect," or "quote" from a wide variety of shared resources such as words, meanings, stories, expressions, and symbols. These aspects of the social world are then incorporated into the fabric of our personal stories.

The research presented here aims at describing the function of shared meanings in the telling of stories of personal identity. We argue that shared meanings are a significant part of all life storytelling, even in the context of conversations about the personal past, because they are always relevant to the life and story of individuals. In the following, we study the role of shared meanings in forming personal narratives through a careful interpretation of the life narrative of Bella Kaplan. Bella, an Israeli Holocaust survivor, makes use of a fortuitous historical event, the public trial of John Demjanjuk in Jerusalem, in order to tell and reflect upon the story of her own experience during the Holocaust. Although she never heard of Demjanjuk, or the person who Demjanjuk was accused of being, "Ivan the Terrible," until well after the war, she uses the figure of Demjanjuk as an integrating theme that recurs at numerous moments throughout her story of the Holocaust. In fact, Demjanjuk becomes a central protagonist in Bella's story.

We begin by describing how and why Bella uses the story of John Demjanjuk in her personal account of life during the Holocaust. Because Demjanjuk is easily traced as being outside Bella's direct, first-hand, experience, we are given a unique opportunity to inquire into the function of shared meanings in personal narratives. Based on a careful analysis of Bella's life story, we argue that Demjanjuk serves a clear purpose in configuring Bella's narrative identity. Without Demjanjuk, Bella's narrative would be very different. In a very real sense, the figure of Demjanjuk provides her with the language for interpreting and communicating her personal experiences. We then address the implications of our analysis of Bella's life story for thinking about survivors of the Holocaust, in particular, and identity stories, in general.

If narrative is a proxy for identity, then, identity must be something quite different than our current notions of the concept suggest. On the one hand, identity is not selfhood in the traditional sense of the word, an independent, coherent, entity with internal consistency over time (Erikson 1968). On the other hand, the life story is not just the product of a situation in which the teller has the freedom to create any kind of fantasy or "believed-in imagining" (de Rivera and Sarbin 1998), which fits the demands of our current context. Writing the story of our lives entails taking up the terms of history and culture in order to interpret and communicate our personal experiences. However, our affinity with particular shared meanings is not haphazard; we take up, and use, shared meanings for specific reasons.

The life story is like a cyborg that is constantly in the process of collecting and recollecting, arranging and rearranging, an amalgam of meanings from our personal and collective experience and then grafting these bits and fragments together into an account of the past, present, and future which makes sense. When telling our life narrative, we bring these found elements into the fold of our personal story and provide them with a new voice. Our identity, even the means for building it, are part of this vast resource of shared meanings, the "social stock of knowledge" (Schutz and Luckmann 1973), which are taken up and integrated into our subjective understanding of the self. Narrative identity, in the most concrete fashion, is part person, part situation, and part culture and entails relations between these three levels of analysis.

15.2 Collecting meanings that resonate

In previous work, we described the relevance of shared meanings to personal narratives as "resonance" (Schiff, Noy and Cohler 2001).

The term connotes something more than an intellectual understanding of shared meanings. We use the word "resonate" as people use it colloquially, in our day-to-day conversations. When someone says, "that resonates," s/he means something like "that appears true in my experience" or "that fits my perspective of the world." It is this sense of "fitting" or "working" that we wish to capture in the term. Within a life story, the idea of resonance has a similar meaning. Aspects of the social world are incorporated into a life narrative because they are congruent with, or relevant to, personal intentions and meanings and the situation of telling.

Our reading of the life story of Bella Kaplan has led to a deeper understanding of the function of shared meaning in shaping personal identity. Bella's life vividly demonstrates ways in which shared meanings can function in life stories in order to interpret and communicate personal experience. Shared meanings are similar to James' (1988 [1907]) "ideas" in *Pragmatism*; they are "instrumental." As James writes, "*Ideas. . .become true just in so far as they help us to get into satisfactory relation with other parts of our experience*" (1988: 30, italics in original). In other words, shared meanings serve a purpose both for the person and for the situation of telling, as they enter into "satisfactory relation with other parts of our experience" and, we would add, satisfactory relations with others.

The two functions that we describe for shared meanings are interpretation and communication. Shared meanings are instrumental in understanding aspects of our personal past in new and innovative ways and in clarifying our life and identity to our listeners. We are certainly aware of the complexities of using the terms interpretation and communication as distinct concepts. It is probably more accurate to think about interpretation and communication as simultaneous or dual processes, with each process having consequences for the other. As we interpret our past, we explain our lives to others. At the same time that we communicate the past, we clarify our reasons and justifications for past events and actions. Although it may be expedient to understand a given utterance as more or less responsive to either interpretation or communication, both are essential in explaining how shared meanings are used. An approach that reduces shared meanings to individual processes is as inadequate as one that focuses exclusively on social dynamics. However, for the sake of clearly describing the function of shared meanings, there is an advantage to keeping the two terms separate.

15.2.1 Interpreting

Gerontologists have long argued that retrospection is a way of reorienting ourselves to the past in order to find new insights and meaning (Butler 1963). However, singling out older adulthood probably overstates the importance of this developmental period for a process which occurs throughout the life course (Webster and McCall 1999). Telling the story of one's past, at any developmental epoch, provides the imperative for putting together a story that makes sense. In Kenyon and Randall's (1997) words, we are given the opportunity for "restorying" the past. Certainly, other people are important in the creation of this sense of meaning. However, it is also true that reviewing and reflecting upon our past has a logic of its own. The teller engages the world of the past in an attempt to provide her account with, as McAdams (1996; McAdams and Bowman 2001) puts it, "unity and purpose."

In a sense, shared meanings function to provide us with a framework for restorying the past in a way that imbues our account with significance, with "unity and purpose." The social world provides us with the tools for understanding the foundations and course of our lives and, consequently, our identity. Certainly, cultural stories can be blueprints for making sense of a past that was, previously, without order or pattern, leaving us with a feeling of desperation, anxiety or lack of direction. Psychotherapy, arguably, operates as a set of rich cultural narratives from which the client can learn a more functional way of interpreting the past, present, and future (Schafer 1992). Shared meanings provide tellers with the tools for envisioning a living world in which one's personal experiences can be seen in light of what other people thought and experienced. We are able to understand what happened before our own eyes in relation to what historical actors accomplished, or died trying to accomplish. In other words, shared meanings are the means for understanding the self as part of an ever-changing world of meaning and social intercourse. It is only through our immersion in a social world that we gain insight into the past and are provided with the various options, and tools, for storying identities.

15.2.2 Communicating

Shared meanings are relevant not only to the person but also to the situation of telling. Mishler (1986, 1999) has argued that speech must be understood as part of the dialogic context where interviewer and interviewee work together to negotiate coherence and meaning. Johnstone (1990), similarly, underscores the importance of situation as one of the key determinants for why certain stories are told. According to Johnstone, stories are pertinent to particular "rhetorical contexts" or "rhetorical situations." Which story is told and how one goes about telling it are influenced not only by the speaker, her life experience, and storytelling intentions, but also by the listener. Linde (1999) has noted that stories of second-hand experience are tailored to the situation in which they are told and are congruent with the immediate demands of context. It is only within a particular, transient, context of speech that stories are embodied and performed and that they assume their interpersonal intensity and effectiveness (Noy 2002). As Wortham (2001) and Stromberg (1993) argue, intelligible personal narratives require establishing common grounds between narrator and audience.

15.3 Truth in testimony

Although shared meanings are significant aspects of all life narratives, their analysis has a special importance when applied to the lives of Holocaust survivors. It is interesting that despite sympathies for postmodern thought in the humanities, few researchers have applied social constructionism to the study of Holocaust survivors. Few scholars have called for a contextualist interpretation of the stories of survivors (Mintz 2001; Young 1988). For example, Mintz (2001) has criticized the dominant perspective on Holocaust survivors for ignoring the role of history, culture, and tradition in interpreting the experiences of concentration camp survivors. LaCapra (1994) has argued for the importance of later cultural experiences in coming to terms with the Holocaust. Other researchers have argued that we have to understand not just the traumas expressed by survivors but also their resilience and success in America and Israel (Hass 1995; Helmreich 1992). In previous work, we have argued that researchers have focused on survivors' lives during the war while ignoring the impact of later life experience on self-understanding (Schiff and Cohler 2001). We have also shown the importance of cultural stories in survivor narratives (Schiff, Noy and Cohler 2001).

However, for the most part, social constructionism has been absent from the study of survivor narratives. Indeed, the most influential works on Holocaust survivors emphasize the representative nature of Holocaust narratives, the stark reality of the concentration camp experience which defies all context. For psychiatrist and survivor Dori Laub (Felman and Laub 1992), recounting Holocaust memory, in testimony, is a way of recovering the reality of the experience and working through the experience of trauma. Laub has argued that the process of giving testimony, and being listened to, is a mode of reintegrating, however incompletely, those events of the past that continue to live inside the survivor. Giving testimony is a way of reaffirming the self that witnessed the events of the war, but remained silent in the postwar years, in order to recover a semblance of wholeness. In a similar vein, Langer (1991), whose *Holocaust Testimonies* remains the most important work to date on survivor testimony, emphasizes the force of wartime experience in creating life narratives of a particular kind. Langer, similar to Laub, argues that Holocaust memories continue to maintain a presence in the survivor's life. However, for Langer, unlike Laub, it is an uncanny presence. Holocaust memories are vigilant; their "mental eyes have never slept" (1991: xv). Memories of the Holocaust are split off from the survivor's present and past lives, and continue to be preserved in the same, unaltered, form. These memories resurface during testimony, obstructing the survivor's ability to construct a meaningful narrative of the past. Talking about the Holocaust serves to break apart the coherence of the survivor's day-to-day existence. The harsh reality of the experience beckons survivors to repeat and re-experience the most emotionally devastating aspects of the catastrophe.

This focus on the representative quality of survivor narratives is so prevalent that the study of the lives and stories of Holocaust survivors is referred to as the study of "testimonies," rather than some variation of personal narratives or life stories. From this perspective "witnesses," through the work of "memory," provide "testimony" to what they have experienced. The reader should note that these concepts possess a myriad of connotations. In naming Holocaust survivors "witnesses," and the telling of their experiences during the Holocaust "testimony," scholars emphasize the connection between their words and past events. Indeed, testimony and witness have both legal and religious connotations of factualness; the first use of the word, testimony, was to bear witness to the deeds of God (Young 1988).

Notions of representativeness are also crucial to the political aims of survivor testimony. It is often claimed that survivor testimony is an effective weapon in combating the anti-Semitic denial of the Holocaust by "let[ting] those who were not there hear from those who were" (Lipstadt 1990: 219). If we lose sight of the facts, then, the actual experience is lost, shrouded in mystery and open to the winds of revisionism. Indeed, for survivors, what could be more frightening than the negation of the murder of their families, their camp experience, and the destruction of their communities of origin? All that is left are the stories of these people and places. It is, therefore, of utmost concern to survivors, and those of us charged with keeping watch over the legacy of the Holocaust, that the representative character of Holocaust stories be strongly affirmed.

If the life stories of Holocaust survivors, and indeed, all life stories, are, in part, socially constructed, what becomes of the meaning of "truth" and of representativeness in their accounts? What becomes of the reality of personal experience? Social constructionism may, as Hartman (1994) argues of some postmodern thinkers, "contribute to anti-memory in a particular way" (1994: 11): by eroding the connection between reality and our representation of that reality. The sense of losing the reality of personal experience is a problem for social constructionist thought in general. If our account of the past is heavily influenced by context, then, how can we know what really happened? Typically, this disconnection is not problematic; in some ways, the thought is very liberating. However, it is interesting that theoretical arguments, which appear so natural applied to one domain of study, begin to lose their appeal when applied to other subject matter such as the Holocaust. If there is no notion of reality anchoring our words, then can we tell any story that we like? If we can construct any story that we like, does that mean that survivors' accounts might not be "true"?

Survivor narratives, like all accounts of the past, have elements that maintain fidelity to past events and actions and other elements, which reframe, reinterpret, and reconfigure the events, and meanings, of the past. In this chapter, we do not directly address the consistency of survivor narratives. However, there are strong indications that survivor stories maintain a high degree of fidelity with previous tellings, suggesting a faithful depiction of past events (Schiff 2005; Wagenaar and Groeneweg 1990). In this chapter, we emphasize the power of later cultural experiences in shaping Bella Kaplan's Holocaust narrative. However, our theoretical description is complex. Social, cultural, and historical factors are central, but are only half the story. Shared meanings are articulated in the context of life story conversations for a reason, they resonate with personal intentions and the immediate situation of telling. In other words, even in the process of integrating shared meanings, we maintain a connection to the reality of the past; we are not permitted to tell any story that we wish, that is, without consequences. Rather, shared meanings are told because they are helpful in interpreting and communicating the past. Although some stories or meanings might not have been the product of their subjective experiences, the words of Holocaust survivors continue to respond to the events of the past.

15.4 Narrating Bella's life

In the summer of 1998, Bella Kaplan was interviewed by Schiff and an Israeli graduate student in Psychology at the Hebrew University of Jerusalem. Because Schiff is not a native speaker of Hebrew, the graduate student led the interview while Schiff listened intently and asked questions only as necessary. Both interviewers are young Jewish men; Schiff is American and the primary interviewer is Israeli. The decision to include a native speaker was made to ensure that the nuances of Bella's story would be completely understood during the course of the conversation. The number of interviewers present as well as differences in language, culture, and generation all contribute to Bella's clear efforts at testing the existence of a shared understanding of the social world.

The interview itself covered a wide range of topics including: Bella's family life before the war; her experience during the war; migration to Israel; profession, marriage, and children; current feelings of pain as well as accomplishment. We also asked Bella to explain her thoughts on living through the Holocaust and to reflect on religious belief and doubt.

The interview was transcribed and interpreted in Hebrew. The translation of selected passages from the interview into English was carried out by Noy for inclusion in this chapter.

Bella was in her early seventies at the time of the interview. She was born in 1927 in a small town close to Chernovitz, Staneshti, in Bukovinia, a region that at the time was part of Romania and today is part of the Ukraine. During the war, Bukovinia was first under the control of the Romanians. It then fell under the influence of the Soviets in June 1940, and when the Soviets retreated one year later, it was again controlled by Romanians who were aligned with the Nazis. The Romanians accused the Jews of collaborating with the Soviets and unleashed a murderous, and bloody, wave of violence against them (Ioanid 2000).

Bella was only fourteen years old at the time when she and her family were forced to leave their home and began a journey to the region east of Bukovinia, between the Dniester and Bug rivers, which came to be known as Transnistria. In total, more than a quarter million Jews died in Transnistria through various means; many Jews were massacred by Romanians, Germans, and Ukrainians while others died of starvation and disease as a result of forced dislocation, inadequate food and clothing, and filthy living conditions (Ioanid 2000). The killing grounds of Transnistria are at the center of Bella's Holocaust story since the majority of her immediate and extended family were murdered there.

In December of 1944, at the age of 17, Bella migrated to Israel. She soon married, raised two girls, and began a career as a high school teacher. She has several grandchildren. Bella's daughters are not far away; one of them lives in Jerusalem and the other in Tel Aviv. However, Bella lives alone; her husband passed away seventeen years before the interview.

Bella describes her life in Israel as full and rich. She is proud of her accomplishments in family and career, and for the most part, appears to be content with her present life. She approves of her daughters' lives, families, and careers and is clearly proud of the fact that they all chose to live in Israel even after extended stays in the United States. She is also proud that her older grandchildren are serving dutifully in the Israeli army.

Despite these accomplishments, Bella is still haunted by her wartime experiences. She also appears to be troubled by the fact that it is quite difficult for her to imagine the city where she was born. There are no physical artifacts from her family, home or childhood; as Bella stresses, "not even a button" from her past remains and no one is alive to remember the past along with her.

Bella is strongly identified as both a Holocaust survivor and an Israeli. She told her Holocaust story on a regular basis to various groups including Israeli youth and the Israeli Defense Forces. Bella, herself, also interviewed Holocaust survivors for Yad Vashem, the Israeli national authority for Holocaust remembrance. As she commented during our conversation, speaking with survivors is both "a duty and a privilege." As the reader will soon realize, Bella's life story is creative and articulate. She leaves the impression of an intelligent older woman, with charm, sophistication, and a rare gift for words and self-expression.

15.4.1 The historical Demjanjuk

Our discussion of Bella's life concentrates on her use of the story of John, formerly Ivan, Demjanjuk in order to interpret and communicate her experience during the Holocaust. The figure of Demjanjuk is a significant aspect of Bella's life story. His name is reiterated, time and again, throughout Bella's description of her Holocaust experience.

The historical figure of John Demjanjuk is that of a Cleveland autoworker who was deported to Israel in 1986 to stand trial as "Ivan the Terrible," the sadistic Ukrainian guard at the Treblinka death camp who was known for executing Jews in the most ghastly fashion. According to witnesses, Ivan the Terrible used his sword to slice off the body parts of Jews waiting for their death in the gas chamber and smashed their skulls open with iron piping (Nathan and Haaken 1996). He then relished in gassing his victims. Estimates of the number of Jews murdered at Treblinka begin at about 750,000 (Hilberg 1985). Only a handful of Jews survived Treblinka as walking corpses sorting valuables and carrying bodies from the gas chambers to bury or burn the dead.

Demjanjuk was only the second person to be tried in Israel for Nazi war crimes. The first, Adolf Eichmann, who was tried in 1961, played a central role in organizing trains for the deportation and executions of millions of Jews. The Eichmann trial was viewed by the government of Israeli Prime Minister David Ben-Gurion as an opportunity to teach the history of the Holocaust and to remind the world of the importance of a Jewish state as a safe harbor from anti-Semitism. Like the Eichmann trial, the Demjanjuk trial was seen by the Israeli government as an opportunity to retell the collective story of the Holocaust (Douglas 2001). The trial, which lasted over a year, was extensively covered by the Israeli media (Cohen *et al.* 2002). Although the name "Demjanjuk" might sound obscure to non-Israeli ears, inside Israel it is well known.

Unlike Eichmann, who was born in Austria and, therefore, is of Germanic heritage, Demjanjuk is Ukrainian. The trial turned public attention toward the role of European communities, other than Germans, in the murder of Jews. Also unlike Eichmann, who participated in the central command and orchestration of the Final Solution, Demjanjuk was accused of being a *rosh katan* (a small head) (Segev 1993), who, literally, executed orders.

In 1988, an Israeli court sentenced Demjanjuk to death. However, the sentence was overturned in July of 1993 on appeal to the Israeli Supreme Court. New evidence from the former Soviet Union indicated that Ivan the Terrible, the Treblinka guard, was more than likely another Ivan, Ivan Marchenko, and not Ivan Demjanjuk. Demjanjuk wasn't in Treblinka. He was identified in Soviet archival testimony as a guard at the Sobibòr death camp, as well as other camps, who was involved in Ghetto-clearing activities, herding Jews from the trains to the gas chambers with whips, and guarding the gas chamber (Sereny 1992). He was not, by any stretch of the imagination, innocent, but he wasn't *The* Ivan the Terrible. Rather, as *Time* magazine quipped, Demjanjuk was "Ivan the Not Very Nice" (Beyer and Johnson 1993).

By the time that the Israeli Supreme Court had reached a decision on the case, Demjanjuk had already served seven years in prison. Although he was acquitted of the original charges, there was some discussion about a retrial on new charges. However, the Supreme Court decided against this option and Demjanjuk was sent back to the United States where he won back, and then lost again, his citizenship.

15.4.2 Why Demjanjuk?

Exactly how, and why, Bella uses the figure of John Demjanjuk in telling her Holocaust story is the central question that we investigate in her life narrative. The story of John Demjanjuk is an organizing theme in Bella's life narrative that recurs numerous times as she recounts her wartime experience. However, it is important to underline the fact that during the war, Bella was neither imprisoned in Treblinka (where Ivan the Terrible reigned) nor Sobibòr or other camps (where Demjanjuk was stationed). She spent the war in Transnistria rather than in the death camps in Poland. It was also in Transnistria where most of Bella's family was murdered. In other words, neither Bella, nor her family, had any immediate connection with either of the Ivans, Marchenko or Demjanjuk. In all likelihood, she never heard of "Ivan the Terrible" until after she emigrated to Israel in 1944 or Demjanjuk until his trial in 1986.

It is important to note that not only did Bella read about the trial of Demjanjuk in the newspapers, but she also was present in the courtroom. The trial was a significant event for Bella both as a survivor and as a teacher. Although she had to pull some strings, Bella was able to accompany two classes of students to witness the court proceedings. She talked with her students about living through the Holocaust, but also "showed" them her experience in the courtroom. As Bella recounts, "not only did I tell my students about my experiences. For example, I took them [to the courtroom]." Although Bella's personal encounter with the Demjanjuk trial is certainly important, it can not explain the centrality of Demjanjuk within her personal story of the Holocaust. Why has Demjanjuk become such a significant part in Bella's narrative? In other words, if Demjanjuk is part of Bella's cultural experience in

Israel, four decades after the war, but not part of her direct first-hand experience, why does he show up in Bella's story of her personal past?

We argue that the figure of John Demjanjuk has an important, and legitimate, place in Bella's life story. He shows up for a reason. In a sense, the encounter with Demjanjuk reconfigures Bella's story of the Holocaust. It helps her tell the story of the past in a way that was not possible before encountering Demjanjuk. The story of Demjanjuk is a tool that allows Bella to interpret her life in a new way and serves as a bridge to recount her story to others within a given cultural and historical scope. In other words, Demjanjuk serves a dual function in Bella's life story, helping in problems of interpreting and communicating the personal past.

15.4.3 Bella's Demjanjuk

One of the main themes in Bella's interview is the recurrent problem of describing the nature of her wartime experience. In this regard, the problem is not unique to Bella. Concern over being mis-understood is a general problem in conversations with Holocaust survivors. Survivors will often call attention to problems in com-municating the depth and meaning of their experiences. In the case of Bella, these problems are accentuated since her experience dur-ing the war is complex, detailing various movements across Eastern Europe, but also obscure. The number and prominence of survivors from certain camps, Auschwitz in particular, has made accounts of these camps into icons for survivor experience as a whole (Lagerwey 1998; Mintz 2001; Wieviorka 2000). Despite the fact that each survivor's story is, in many ways, unique, the figure of "Auschwitz" has come to stand for "death camp experience" and variations on this canonical or prototypical account are down-played. It is within this framework that we must begin to under-stand Bella's account, which departs in significant ways from the canonical narrative. The experience of Romanian Jewry during the Holocaust, in contrast to Polish or German Jews, is not well known. Therefore, it is difficult for the listener to anticipate the path that Bella's narrative will follow.

Our interpretation of Bella's life follows the related themes of *balagan* and "Demjanjuk." In using the Hebrew word *balagan*, which is a common slang term meaning *utter mess, chaos, confusion,* or *disorder,* we retain some of the nuances that do not exist in an English translation of the word. It is also an idea that is central to Bella's story. Bella uses the word "*balagan*" repeatedly in our conversation. Her experience was an utter mess, chaotic, disorderly, and confused; so are aspects of our conversation together. Bella's use of "Demjanjuk" in her account of the Holocaust follows the sense of confusion inherent in her story and in the interview situation. Striving to communicate her Holocaust experience, Bella invokes the figure of John Demjanjuk. She offers a transformed version of the historical Demjanjuk, but some essential qualities remain intact. Conversational turns, between interviewer and interviewee, which attempt to clarify the nature of Bella's story and the meaning of her use of Demjanjuk, underline the negotiated nature of the conversation. Bella's description of Demjanjuk serves as a bridge to imagining the kind of experiences that she underwent. If one can imagine Demjanjuk, then, one can imagine Bella's tormenters. Demjanjuk is an aid in making her experience painfully clear. Following the interconnected themes of *balagan* and Demjanjuk, it also becomes evident that the encounter with Demjanjuk has allowed Bella to interpret her past in a new way. With the help of Demjanjuk, Bella can argue that she is a "survivor" of the same caliber as others who survived the death camps such as Auschwitz. In other words, Demjanjuk serves as an aid in interpreting her experience.

After speaking about her current life in Israel and her life before the war, Bella begins describing the first days of occupation. She attempts to describe her movements from place to place with the help of the sugar, cups, and plates on the coffee table, which stands in between her and the interviewers. She stops using the makeshift map for a moment to say:

Example 15.1

Cause what's Transnistria, do you know at all this term Transnistria? It's the ABCs of the entire matter, since we know Birkenau and Auschwitz and Bergen-Belsen and Majdanek and Chelmno and all these camps. Transnistria is a camp. It's "trans," like beyond, the Dniester. It's a term that doesn't exist at all, other than in the Holocaust Encyclopedia, because it's not a geographical location that existed previously. . . We were in all kinds of places [there].

As a descriptive statement of the geography of the Holocaust, Example 15.1 is informative. However, killing grounds or region is probably a better description of Transnistria than camp. Still, Bella's command of the history of the Holocaust, in general, and Transnistria, in particular, is impressive.

Although the "literal geography" is crucial, the "metaphorical geography" is even more important. In order to describe Transnistria, Bella invokes the prototypical narrative of the Holocaust, the "Auschwitzs" and the "Bergen-Belsens," and begins the project of distinguishing her experience from the prototype. Knowing the canonical tale of the Holocaust, Bella informs us, will be no help in understanding her experience. In a sense, Bella's life story is like learning the ABC of the Holocaust all over again. It also means understanding that the canonical story of the Holocaust is not applicable to all survivors; Bella is pointing out that there are multiple versions of survival with different imagery and unique languages. Indeed, her story of survival is one of these variations on the canonical story.

One has to know what Transnistria is in order to understand Bella's story. At the time, the interviewers had never heard of Transnistria. However, we quickly learned that Bella would provide us with the terms of her experience rather than relying on the fact that we share a common lexicon. In this fashion, Bella distinguishes between her experience and the image she suspects that we have about the Holocaust. The direct question she addresses to the interviewer, "Do you know at all Transnistria?" which digresses from the narrative flow, may thus be read as a request for common language, a shared "ABC."

The distinction between the narrative of Transnistria and the prototypical survivor narrative, which includes experience in the death camps such as Auschwitz, is clever. The play between Transnistria and the canonical narrative of the Holocaust is not only a distinction but also an analogy. Her experience is different but of the same variety as the experiences of other survivors who lived through the death camps.

Bella consistently distinguishes between the canonical tale of the Holocaust and her experience. For example, when thinking about deportations, we picture trains. In the canonical or prototypical narrative, Jews were transported from ghettos to death and concentration camps on trains. Both the United States Holocaust Memorial and Museum (USHMM) in Washington DC and Yad Vashem feature real train cars as significant parts of the museum narrative; cattle cars become icons of the deportation of Jews during the war. In Jerusalem, a train car hangs over the edge of a hillside as if charging off a cliff into nowhere. At the USHMM, one can walk through the cattle car and continue viewing the exhibit on the other side (Linenthal 1995; Young 1993). However, trains are not part of Bella's narrative. Bella and her family were forced to move from place to place, mostly on foot. She marks this distinction linguistically; in contrast to train transports, she was subjected to "foot transports" (*transport'im reglay'im*).

Bella also distinguishes between the experience of Jews living in concentration camps, which maintained the pretense of orderliness, and her experience living in makeshift camps.

Example 15.2

We lived in the camp which was an abandoned *kolhoz* (collective farm). And I lived. And there were a few hundred people. And I lived in the pigsty. . .Do you know what a *kolhoz* is? It's not a kibbutz because many people think it's a kibbutz. I lived in a pigsty. What I'm trying to say is that it's not that a pigsty is less honorable than a horse stable but in a horse stable you can enter almost at your own height, bent a little bit, because the horse is like that, the cow is like that, but the pig is like this. Then we had to lie down to crawl inside because we couldn't. . . So there we slept very crowded, one near another, and the lice were having a party. We were full, absolutely full of lice.

Imprisonment was disorderly. Farms were turned into makeshift camps, not like Auschwitz, but still horrible and disgusting. Bella lived in a pigsty. It is interesting to note, as in the case of cattle cars, that barracks are a prominent feature of some Holocaust museums. In the USHMM, the cramped barracks from Auschwitz were brought to the museum to give visitors a visceral experience of life in the death camp. For our purposes, it is interesting to note that a pigsty, in Bella's experience, is juxtaposed against the barracks from the canonical story of survival.

Her words, "It's not a kibbutz," can be heard in two ways. There is a literal sense; a kibbutz is different from a *kolhoz*. There is also a figurative sense in which *kibbutz'im* are now often vacation destinations. By saying, "it's not a kibbutz," she also implies, "it was no vacation." She teaches us, again, the lexicon of her survival story. Bella's image of living in a pigsty is, principally, claustrophobic. However, it is hard to imagine that Bella is indifferent, like she claims, to the fact that the animal was a pig rather than another small farm animal. For a young Jewish girl there is a difference. Living for over a year in a pigsty, meant literally becoming a beast, an animal, and losing her humanness. Bella's story is not one of radical mechanization, but of beastly disorder.

The sense of confusion in understanding Bella's experience is echoed in the questions posed by the interviewer. As if assuming a more prototypical narrative, the interviewer asks: "All the stories that you told about being expelled were these already the Germans?" Bella responds:

Example 15.3

No, not at all. I didn't see Germans during the war, other than once or twice or three times which was a coincidence. No, no, the Romanians. In the meantime the Romanians came in, the Romanians and the non-Jews (*goyim*), the "Demjanjuks" of sorts (*Demjanjuk'im ka'elu*). Did you see the Demjanjuk trial? Did you see what Ivan is? Such Ivans walked, and such Ivans killed, and such Ivans clubbed, and did all kinds of things like that.

In a sense, a "Demjanjuk" can be seen as a descriptive term for Bella's perpetrators. Bella's questions, "Did you see the Demjanjuk trial? Did you see what Ivan is?" press for a shared level of experience, even if Bella cannot take for granted that the listeners share the same cultural resources. Making the assumption of shared experience, Bella moves to typify the figure of a "Demjanjuk." Once again, there is poetry in her use of language. Bella marks this typification by adding the plural suffix "*im*" to Demjanjuk and later to Ivan. Using the plural form of "*im*" in Hebrew is the English equivalent of adding an "s" to the root. In this move, Demjanjuk is no longer one person but a class or variety of person. Demjanjuk, thus typified, is then read back into Bella's life story and the "Demjanjuks" are able to do all sorts of horrible things. The language that she uses to describe these actions is also brutal and violent; they walked and killed and clubbed. They "did all kinds of things like that."

The next time that Bella uses Demjanjuk's name is in response to a question about the constant movements from place to place,

"So were you still a group of several hundred people from the beginning?" Bella adds:

Example 15.4

Yes. But what was left was that all the time people died. Died, fell, murdered, and others joined [our group]. We found on the way, for example, all kinds of body parts because they would put [people] into a big barn where they put the food in for the cows, in the winter so that it won't rot. So let's say they put in there one hundred, two hundred, three hundred, twenty, doesn't matter how many Jews, and when he felt like it, some Demjanjuk like that, some Ivan like that, he poured a little gasoline on it, closed the doors tight, poured gasoline on top, and lit it. Well, OK so one leg could be found here, and a head here, or some other part. This is what we saw on the way. . .Do you know what body parts are? We have, we all have [body parts] but it's not like they cut it here and what you got left. Yeah, yeah, listen, that's the way it was. So I don't know what was better, to be burned in Auschwitz when there's a number and you're called by the number, or when it's an utter mess (*balagan*) like this. I don't know what's better. I'm not saying that this is better or that this is better. . . Is that enough for you? No?

The image of body parts strewn through the countryside is graphic and disturbing. Typified, anonymous, Demjanjuks again enter her story and appear to have a life of their own. The horrific description is reinforced by Bella's comparison between the orderliness of the killing operations at death camps such as Auschwitz and the chaos, the *balagan*, of Transnistria. Here, too, Bella directly addresses the interviewers with a question that searches for shared understandings. "Do you know what body parts are?" The question here is rhetorical in that finding fragmented body parts in the way she did is not something her interviewers would, hopefully, share. The utter mess of Bella's experience is repeated in the experience of the body parts that she describes. When she explains that the body parts were severed unnaturally, she suggests a radically different experience of what a human body is and what it was during the Holocaust; the utter mess of her experience is embodied.

The sentence beginning with "So I don't know what was better," is the pivotal passage in the above quote. The move is provocative, equating survivors' experiences in Auschwitz with Bella's experience, with those "Demjanjuks," in Transnistria. In equating Auschwitz with Transnistria, Bella does not challenge the authenticity or brutality of Auschwitz. Rather, she is claiming that her experience, like Auschwitz, was among the worst. Her final question "Is that enough for you?" appears to intensify this claim to a past that has witnessed much momentous suffering. On the one hand, Bella challenges her interlocutors, as if asking "Aren't I overwhelming you?" in making the case for the survival stories of Romanian Jews. On the other hand, she is also gently inquiring as to whether she, someone who wishes so deeply to educate, has fulfilled her mission in telling her story. Did she get her point across the linguistic abyss?

The transcript continues with the interviewer (IVER) asking yet another clarification question.

Example 15.5

(a)	IVER	I want to get clear, to organize, something else. It's not so clear to me, these deportations, were these Romanian soldiers who were with you all the time?
(b)	BELLA	Gendarmes. They weren't the same Gendarmes. They changed from time to time.
(c)	IVER	Who were these? Was it really run by Romanians, were the operations run by Romanians?
(d)	BELLA	Yes.
(e)	IVER	But you keep on saying Demjanjuks all the time.
(f)	BELLA	I call them Demjanjuks. These are kind of non-Jews (*goy'im*) Ukrainians, that's Ivan. I call them Demjanjuks. At the time, I taught 10th, 11th, and 12th grades. Have you been in Israel for a long time? When I talk about the. . .
(g)	IVER	I understand what you mean by Demjanjuks, that's why I'm inquiring about it.
(h)	BELLA	It's shut [the tape recorder], I think?
(i)	IVER	No, no.
(j)	BELLA	No? But I'm talking now in a disorderly fashion (*betsura balaganistit*)
(k)	IVER	No, not at all. And the order is not so important. But in addition to these Gendarmes that expelled you was there anyone else who committed these atrocities
(l)	BELLA	Right, we walked. Perhaps, I will show it to you. You'll see it. I have the Holocaust Encyclopedia. At least there's a little about it in there. As you can see, we walked like beasts (*behemot*), walking, walking. And there were several Gendarmes on horses with rifles. And especially there were Ukrainians who were posted on the sides. . .But they were wearing civilian clothing. Only the Gendarmes wore uniforms. But we

were afraid of these Ukrainians – they were not the same guards who walked from Staneshti all the way up to the end – much more than from the Gendarmes. Generally speaking, when the army came in we were frightened, but much less so than from the local population. (pause) So what do you want me to tell you? (In a quiet voice) How I lived in a pigsty?

Interviewer and interviewee are in the process of negotiating the terms of their conversation. The interviewer is apparently confused about the connection between Demjanjuk and Bella's Holocaust experience. He asks her directly about her use of the term "Demjanjuk." At this point, the interviewer interrupts Bella's response and asks a different question, perhaps an empathic lapse in the conversation. Bella begins to answer the interviewer's question and then clarifies her previous point, by underlining that although there were others present, the Ukrainians, in her words, the Demjanjuks, were to be feared the most. In other words, from Bella's perspective, there is good reason for calling such people Demjanjuks.

The horrific mess that she describes spills over, so to speak, from her story to the conversation, from the text to the context. Like Bella's experience during the war, the interviewers are lost too. They want to "clarify" or "arrange" the troubling chaos. And, in reply, Bella suggests that she is talking in a "disorderly fashion," interestingly, using the same root, *balagan*, which she previously used when describing the burning of body parts in Transnistria.

A few moments later, as if summarizing her thoughts, Bella steps outside the "taleworld" (Young 1987) of the Holocaust in order to reflect on the content of the conversation.

Example 15.6

And there, too, Ivans guarded us. Not all of them are named Ivan, and not all of them are named Demjanjuk. But very often they are called Ivan and something else. I call them this way. For me, they all have the same face.

The story of Demjanjuk is not only something that Bella uses to communicate her experiences to others but is, indeed, a mould to interpret her past. For Bella, there is an essential quality about the actions of Ukrainian perpetrators during the war, which is captured by the figure of Demjanjuk. He expresses an aspect of her lived experience that is difficult to describe and integrate. Bella's narrative is rewritten to include this observation. As she says, they all have "the same face."

15.4.4 Taking up Demjanjuk

Talking about her Holocaust experience, Bella provides us with a creative example of how and why shared meanings are used in the course of life storytelling. Although Bella never encountered John Demjanjuk or Ivan the Terrible during the war, her encounter with the event of the Demjanjuk trial gives her the opportunity to reconfigure the story of her Holocaust experience in new ways. By virtue of Demjanjuk's trial in Jerusalem, Bella has been provided with a productive symbol, widely understood throughout Israeli society, of the harsh brutality and cruelty of the Ukrainian collaborators. It is a symbol which helps her to understand her personal history in a new light and to share this understanding with others.

In order to understand the place of Demjanjuk in Bella's life story, we have argued, it is necessary to understand the thematic contrasts which run throughout our conversation. Bella's narrative is not told, as she recounts, in a "disorderly fashion" (*betsura balaganistit*). Rather, Bella clearly establishes a host of related distinctions which reveal a complex interpretation of her personal past in light of the larger historical and cultural context. As we have argued, Bella's life story is told through a series of oppositions to the canonical story. She contrasts the canonical story of Holocaust survivors with her experience, which is confusing and disorderly (*balagan*). Unlike the experience of Jews in the "Auschwitzes," Bella was deported in "foot transports" and not in trains, she lived in a pigsty and not in barracks, killing was random and messy and not mechanized, her tormentors were civilians from the surrounding region and not German military from elsewhere. It is within the context of these distinctions that Demjanjuk is typified and used. Demjanjuk forms part of this dialectic and symbolizes the disorder of Bella's wartime experience. Table 15.1 reviews these thematic contrasts as found in our conversation with Bella.

The two streams of *balagan* and Demjanjuk are not separate but facets of the same idea. In a sense, Demjanjuk as Ivan the Terrible typifies the murder process that Bella witnessed. The figure helps to convey the chaos, brutality and barbarism of Bella's perpetrators.

Table 15.1. *Contrasts between Bella's life story and the canonical survivor narrative*

Bella's life story	The canonical survivor narrative
Transnistria	Auschwitz
Balagan (utter mess)	Order
Foot transports	Trains
Pigsty (beasts [*behemot*])	Barracks
"Demjanjuks"	"Eichmanns"
Civilian	Military
Ukrainians	Germans

The listener or reader is given help in imagining this atypical account and Bella is provided with a productive frame to interpret her personal past.

Shared meanings function within particular social and cultural contexts. Bella distinguishes between the canonical story and her personal experience when telling her life story to two young men, one Israeli and one American. Bella appears to be sensitive to the fact that these young persons might not know a lot about a trial that began in 1986. Also, one of the interviewees is American and might not share the same social stock of knowledge. She tests the interviewers' knowledge at sensitive moments in the conversation "Do you know Demjanjuk? Do you know what an Ivan is?" and "Were you in Israel during the trial?" These questions are directed toward determining whether or not teller and listeners are working from a shared knowledge base. Given an intersubjective understanding of Demjanjuk, Bella is able to place the character of Demjanjuk within the "taleworld" of her Holocaust experience.

Without this shared knowledge, Demjanjuk does not make sense. He would communicate nothing. Within the frame of intersubjectively shared meanings, Demjanjuk stands for something. There aren't any Germans, gas chambers, or trains in Bella's story. One might be tempted to think that the absence of such central components of the prototypical survivor narrative might indicate that Bella's experience was less horrible. However, through the symbol of Demjanjuk, Bella is able to communicate the opposite. We listeners, who know Demjanjuk, are offered a mental, and emotional, tool (Vygotsky 1978; Wertsch 1991) to help us follow

Bella's story. Indeed, we are offered a vivid means of imagining the non-Nazi perpetrators in Bella's account. If you know Demjanjuk, then, you can begin to understand the brutality that Bella endured.

Shared meanings function to interpret the personal past. The figure of Demjanjuk provides Bella with a creative means for understanding her Holocaust experience. For Bella, those "Demjanjuks" explains something about her wartime experience. The protagonists of aggressive acts against Bella, her family, and other Jews were brutal Ukrainians, just like Demjanjuk. In fact, they are all Demjanjuks. They all have "the same face." In erasing the distinction between those Ivans in the camps (Ivan the Terrible and Ivan Demjanjuk) and those Ivans in Transnistria, Bella is able to better understand her torturers. By consequence, with each insight from the trial, she is given the opportunity to sort through the utter mess of the past. She is able to give a name, a face, and meaning to those persons who destroyed her family and community. Although she was not in the death camps, she makes the argument that she was with the same kind of perpetrator as *The* Ivan the Terrible. In such a fashion, the figure of Demjanjuk functions within Bella's life story to stake her claim, her identity, as a true survivor like those who survived Auschwitz. Just like survivors of Auschwitz, Bella claims that she survived the worst. In some ways, there is an advantage to the fact that Demjanjuk was not Ivan the Terrible; Bella is able to make the argument that, rather than the exception, Demjanjuks were the rule and such brutal actions can be seen in all non-Jews in the region during the war.

The shared meaning of Demjanjuk both functions in the social situation of telling Bella's life narrative and fits with her understanding of the personal past in order to fashion a convincing and articulate identity narrative. As we have argued, shared meanings resonate with person and situation. However, one of the rules of narrative identity is that we cannot tell any story that we desire – at least not without consequences. We are at liberty to a wide range of choices in cultural meanings that have been carved out for us by our contemporaries and ancestors. However, there are limits to their use.

Narratives are constantly framed by our social context and our past experiences. On the one hand, narrative identity is written in the context of conversations with other human beings. In the rules of the game, others also have the opportunity to influence, and sometimes determine, facets of our identity by affirming or denying our authority to narrate certain tales of the past and identity (Holland *et al.* 1998; Schiff 2002). On the other hand, narrative identity is written from a script that extends back in time, if not to the actual event, at least to previous articulations of our identity. Our account is constantly brushing up against these footprints, no matter how ephemeral, of previous tellings.

Narrative identity, in Paul Ricoeur's (1992) words, is both "*idem*" and "*ipse*"; it is both character and continuity. Articulating identity in words is, in part, a process that lends continuity over time to disparate periods of our lives in order to create a vision of the self as something consistent, despite change. According to Ricoeur, the sense of consistency through time, the "*ipse*" of narrative identity, derives from the will to maintain fidelity to previous self conceptions, literally to "keep one's word" or to "keep one's promise." As this author writes, "keeping one's promise. . .does appear to stand as a challenge to time, a denial of change: even if my desire were to change, even if I were to change my opinion or my inclination, 'I will hold firm" (1992: 124).

Change is important and narrativists have made a convincing case for the prominence of construction in life storytelling. However, we must consider change in light of strong tendencies to "hold firm" to the past, to previous events and self-understandings. Change takes place in the context of significant continuity. In theorizing about human identity, we must account for both tendencies. We suggest considering shared meanings as functioning against the background of individual interests, intentions, beliefs, and other forms of "promise keeping," which extend across long stretches of time. The social context of communicating one's life story is important, but so are previous modes of interpreting the past.

What does our interpretation of Bella's life story argue about the study of Holocaust testimony? Our analysis of Bella's life challenges the notion of "testimony" but not the notion of "truthfulness." The fact that we use shared meanings to describe personal experience does not imply that the experiences that we describe were not actual. If we relegate all stories that use shared meanings to the realm of fantasy, all stories, and histories, would be unhinged from an actual past. What kinds of meanings are there other than shared meanings? Even the most basic units of expression, utterances, are shared (Bakhtin 1981b, 1986; Wertsch 1991). Bella's use of the figure of Demjanjuk does not mean that Ukrainians did not imprison her or that her family was not wiped out, murdered, in Transnistria. However, we believe that this research seriously questions the concept of "testimony." Obviously, life narratives, which integrate shared meanings, are much more than the direct representation of painful memories in words. Later life experiences, including later cultural experiences, are extraordinarily important in the creation of meaning. We view the incorporation of such shared meanings, evident in all life narratives, positively; the addition of shared meanings allows the person to restory the past in a new, and hopefully, more useful manner.

What does our interpretation of Bella's life say about narrative identity? We argue that an understanding of life storytelling needs to include a consideration of culture. Typically, narrative research has focused on either the person or the situation of telling without an adequate account of the role of culture in shaping personal storytelling. We view narrative identity as a process which involves person, situation of telling, and larger cultural and historical meanings. Our interpretation of Bella's life points to a "personalized" conception of culture. Certainly, meanings are, largely, shared within a given community. However, viewed from a narrative perspective it is evident that some meanings are more salient to particular individuals while others are, in some respects, irrelevant. We choose to "collect" or "quote" aspects of the social world because they are significant to our lives, our intentions in communicating with others, and central to our identities; these collected resonances of the social world are functional in our subjective understanding of self, other, and world. In the process of bringing meanings found in the social stock of knowledge into our subjectivity, we create an individualized version of the larger historical and cultural world, which is both similar to that of others in our family and community but it is also unique to our life and identity. Thus, in talking about the past to others we make the social world personal.

Acknowledgements

Brian Schiff would like to thank the Lady Davis Fellowship Trust for a wonderful year of postdoctoral research and discussion at the Hebrew University of Jerusalem. Chaim Noy would like to thank the Rothschild Postdoctoral Fellowship for a most fruitful year of research and writing at Swarthmore College and the University of Pennsylvania. Both Schiff and Noy would like to recognize the contribution of Amia Lieblich to this research. Amia has been an inspiring mentor and role model. Her voice resounds through our work.

References

Anderson, E. 1999. *Code of the street: decency, violence, and the moral life of the inner city*. New York: W.W. Norton.

Anderson, H. 1997. *Conversation, language and possibilities*. New York: Basic Books.

Antaki, C. and S. Widdicombe 1998a. Identity as an achievement and as a tool. In C. Antaki and S. Widdicombe (eds.) *Identities in talk*. London: Sage, pp. 1–14.

Antaki, C. and S. Widdicombe (eds.) 1998b. *Identities in talk*. London: Sage.

Anzaldúa, G. 1987. *Borderlands/La frontera: the new mestiza*. San Francisco: Spinsters/ Aunt Lute.

Arendell, T. 2000. Conceiving and investigating motherhood: the decade's scholarship. *Journal of Marriage and the Family*, 62: 1192–1207.

Auer, P. 2002. *Acts of identity. Background and some questions for the 2002 Freiburg Workshop*. Unpublished manuscript.

Badinter, E. 1992. *XY, Sobre a identidade masculina*. Rio de Janeiro: Nova Fronteira.

Baker, C. 1983. A "second look" at interviews with adolescents. *Journal of Youth and Adolescence*, 12(6): 501–519.

1984. The "search for adultness": membership work in adolescent-adult talk. *Human Studies*, 7: 301–323.

Baker, C. D. 1997. Membership categorization and interview accounts. In D. Silverman (ed.) *Qualitative research: theory, method and practice*. London: Sage, pp. 130–143.

Baker, C. D. and G. Johnson 1998. Interview talk as professional practice. *Language and Education*, 12(4): 229–242.

Bakhtin, M. 1981a [1929]. *Marxismo e filosofia da linguagem*, São Paulo: Editora Hucitec.

1981b [1935]. *The dialogic imagination*. (C. Emerson and M. Holquist, Trans.). Austin: University of Texas Press.

1981c [1935]. Discourse in the novel. (C. Emerson, and M. Holquist, Trans.). In M. Bakhtin (ed.) *The dialogic imagination*. Austin: University of Texas Press, pp. 259–422.

1986. *Speech genres and other late essays* (V. W. McGee, Trans.). Austin: University of Texas Press.

Bamberg, M. (ed.) 1997a. Oral versions of personal experience: three decades of narrative analysis. Special issue of *Journal of Narrative and Life History*, 7(1–4): 1–415.

Bamberg, M. 1997b. Positioning between structure and performance. In M. Bamberg (ed.) Oral versions of personal experience: three decades of narrative analysis. Special issue of *Journal of Narrative and Life History*, 7(1–4): 335–342.

1999. Is there anything behind discourse? Narrative and the local accomplishments of identities. In W. B. Maiers, B. Bayer, B. Duarte Esgalhado, R. Jorna and E. Schraube (eds.) *Challenges to theoretical psychology*. North York ON: Captus Press, pp. 220–227.

2003. Positioning with Davie Hogan – stories, tellings, and identities. In C. Daiute and C. Lightfoot (eds.) *Narrative analysis: studying the development of individuals in society*. London: Sage Publications, pp. 135–157.

2005. Encyclopedia entry on 'Positioning.' In D. Herman, M. Jahn and M. L. Ryan (eds.) *The Routledge encyclopedia of narrative theory*. New York: Routledge, pp. 445–446.

Bamberg, M. and M. Andrews (eds.) 2004. *Considering counter narratives: narrating, resisting, making sense*. Amsterdam: John Benjamins.

Bamberg, M. and V. Marchman 1991. Binding and unfolding. *Discourse Processes*, **14**: 277–305.

Barker, C. and D. Galasinski 2001. *Cultural studies and discourse analysis: a dialogue on language and identity*. London: Sage.

Barnes, A. B., T. Colton, J. Gundersen, K. L. Noller, B. C. Tilley, T. Strama, *et al.* 1980. Fertility and outcome of pregnancy in women exposed in utero to diethylstilbestrol. *North England Journal of Medicine*, **302**: 609–613.

Barrett, R. 1999. Indexing polyphonous identity in the speech of African American drag queens. In M. Bucholtz, A. C. Liang and L. Sutton (eds.) *Reinventing identities*. Oxford: Oxford University Press, pp. 313–332.

Bastos, L. C. 1997. Power, solidarity and the construction of requests in service encounters. *The ESPecialist*, **17**(2): 151–174.

2002. Identity in service interactions: the situated affiliation to social groupings. In A. Duszak (ed.) *Us and others: social identities across languages, discourses and cultures*. Amsterdam and New York: John Benjamins, pp. 429–446.

Bateson, G. 1972. *Steps to an ecology of mind*. New York: Ballantine.

Bauman, R. 1986. *Story, performance and event: contextual studies of oral narrative*. Cambridge: Cambridge University Press.

2000. Language, identity, performance. *Pragmatics*, **10**(1): 1–5.

Bauman, R. and C. Briggs 1990. Poetics and performance as critical perspectives on language and social life. *Annual Review of Anthropology*, **19**: 59–88.

Bauman, Z. 1996. From pilgrim to tourist – or a short history of identity. In S. Hall and P. du Gay (eds.) *Questions of cultural identity*. London: Sage, pp. 18–36.

Baynham, M. 2005. Network and agency in the migration stories of Moroccan women. In M. Baynham and A. De Fina (eds.) *Dislocations/relocations: narratives of displacement*. Manchester: St. Jerome, pp. 15–35.

Beach, W. A. 1993. Transitional regularities for 'casual' "Okay" usages. *Journal of Pragmatics*, **19**: 325–352.

Beardsworth, A. and T. Keil (eds.) 1997. *Sociology on the menu: an invitation to the study of food and society*. London and New York: Routledge.

Beck, S., L. Bertholle and J. Child 1966. *Mastering the art of French cooking*. New York: Knopf.

Becker, A. L. 1984. The linguistics of particularity: interpreting superordination in a Javanese text. *Proceedings of the Tenth Annual Meeting of the Berkeley Linguistics Society*. Berkeley CA: The Department of Linguistics, University of California, Berkeley.

Bell, S. E. 1988. Becoming a political woman: the reconstruction and interpretation of experience through stories. In D. Todd and S. Fisher (eds.) *Gender and discourse*. Norwood NJ: Ablex, pp. 97–123.

　　1999. Narratives and lives: women's health politics and the diagnosis of cancer for DES daughters. *Narrative Inquiry*, **9**: 2, 347–389.

　　2002. Photo images: Jo Spence's narratives of living with illness. *Health*, **6**: 1, 5–30.

　　2004. Intensive performances of mothering: a sociological perspective. *Qualitative Research*, **4**(1): 45–75.

Benveniste, E. 1971[1966]. L'appareil formel de l'énonciation. In E. Benveniste (ed.) *Problèmes de Linguistique Generale*. Paris: Gallimard, pp. 79–90.

Berger, P. and T. Luckman 1967. *The social construction of reality*. Harmondsworth: Penguin.

Berry, J. 1993. Ethnic identities in plural societies. In M. Bernal and G. P. Knight (eds.) *Ethnic identity. Formation and transmission among Hispanics and other minorities*. Albany NY: State University of New York Press, pp. 272–296.

Beyer, L. and J. Johnson 1993. Ivan the not-so-terrible: was John Demjanjuk a victim of mistaken identity? *Time*, **142**: 41.

Billig, M. 1999. Whose terms? Whose ordinariness? Rhetoric and ideology in conversation analysis. *Discourse and Society*, **10**(4): 543–558.

Bloomfield, D. 2000. Voices on the web: student teachers negotiating identity. *Asia–Pacific Journal of Teacher Education*, **28**(3): 199–214.

Blum-Kulka, S. 1993. "You gotta know how to tell a story": telling, tales and tellers in American and Israeli narrative events at dinner. *Language in Society*, **22**: 361–402.

Bourdieu, P. 1977. *Outline of a theory of practice* (R. Rice, Trans.). Cambridge: Cambridge University Press.

1999. *A dominação masculina*. Rio de Janeiro: Bertrand Brasil.

Bourgois, P. 1995. *In search of respect: selling crack in El Barrio*. Cambridge: Cambridge University Press.

Britzman, D. P. 1992. The terrible problem of knowing thyself: toward a poststructural account of teacher identity. *Journal of Curriculum Theorising: An Interdisciplinary Journal of Curriculum Studies*, **9**(3): 23–46.

Brockmeier, J. and D. Carbaugh (eds.) 2001. *Narrative and identity: studies in autobiography, self and culture*. Amsterdam and Philadelphia: John Benjamins.

Brockmeier, J. and R. Harré 1997. Narrative: problems and promises of an alternative paradigm. *Research in Language and Social Interaction*, **30**(4): 263–283.

Brown, G. 1995. *Speakers, listeners and communication*. Cambridge: Cambridge University Press.

Brown, P. and S. Levinson 1979. Universals in language usage: politeness phenomena. In E. Goody (ed.) *Questions and politeness: strategies in social interaction*. Cambridge: Cambridge University Press, pp. 56–289.

1987. *Politeness: some universals in language usage*. Cambridge: Cambridge University Press.

Bruner, J. 1986. *Actual minds, possible worlds*. Cambridge MA: Harvard University Press.

1987. Life as narrative. *Social Research*, **54**: 11–32.

1990. *Acts of meaning*. Cambridge MA: Harvard University Press.

1996. *The culture of education*. Cambridge MA: Harvard University Press.

1997[1990]. *Atos de significação*. Porto Alegre: Artes Médicas.

2001. Self-making and world-making. In J. Brockmeier and D. Carbaugh (eds.) *Narrative and identity: studies in autobiography, self and culture*. Amsterdam and Philadelphia: John Benjamins, pp. 25–37.

Bucholtz, M. 1999a. "Why be normal?": language and identity practices in a group of nerd girls. *Language in Society*, **28**: 203–223.

1999b. You da man: narrating the racial other in the production of white masculinity. *Journal of Sociolinguistics*, **3**(4): 461–479.

Bucholtz, M., A. C. Liang and L. Sutton (eds.) 1999. *Reinventing identities*. Oxford: Oxford University Press.

Buriel, R. and D. Cardoza 1993. Mexican American ethnic labeling: an intrafamiliar and intergenerational analysis. In M. Bernal and G. P. Knight (eds.) *Ethnic identity. Formation and transmission among*

Hispanics and other minorities. Albany NY: State University of New York Press, pp. 197–210.

Bury, M. 1982. Chronic illness as biographical disruption. *Sociology of Health and Illness*, 4(2): 167–182.

Butler, J. 1990. *Gender trouble: feminism and the subversion of identity.* New York and London: Routledge.

    1997. *Excitable speech: a politics of the performative.* London: Routledge.

Butler, R. N. 1963. The life review: an interpretation of reminiscence in the aged. *Psychiatry*, 26: 65–76.

Cameron, L. 1999. Identifying and describing metaphor in spoken discourse data. In L. Cameron and G. Low (eds.) *Researching and applying metaphor.* Cambridge: Cambridge University Press, pp. 105–132.

Capps, L. and E. Ochs 1995. Out of place: narrative insights into agoraphobia. *Discourse Processes*, 19: 407–439.

Carranza, I. 1998. Low-narrativity narratives and argumentation. *Narrative Inquiry*, 8(2): 287–317.

Castles, S. and G. Kosack 1973. *Immigrant workers and class structure in Western Europe.* Oxford: Oxford University Press.

Chafe, W. 1980. The deployment of consciousness in the production of a narrative. In W. Chafe (ed.) *The pear stories.* Norwood NJ: Ablex, pp. 9–50.

Charmaz, K. 1987. Struggling for a self: identity levels of the chronically ill. In J. A. Roth and P. Conrad (eds.) *Research in the sociology of health care, Vol. 6: The experience and management of chronic illness.* Greenwich CT: JAI Press, pp. 283–320.

    1991. *Good days, bad days: the self in chronic illness and time.* New Brunswick NJ: Rutgers.

Cicourel, A. V. 1999. The interaction of cognitive and cultural models in health care delivery. In S. Sarangi and C. Roberts (eds.) *Talk, work and institutional order. Discourse in medical, meditation and management settings.* Berlin and New York: Mouton de Gruyter, pp. 183–224.

Claiborne, C. 1961. *The New York Times cookbook.* New York and Evanston: Harper and Row.

Clark, H. and D. Wilkes-Gibbs 1986. Referring as a collaborative process. *Cognition*, 22: 1–39.

Coates, J. 1996. *Women talk.* Oxford: Blackwell.

Cohen, A. A., T. Zemach-Marom, J. Wilke and B. Schenk 2002. *The Holocaust and the press: Nazi war crimes trials in Germany and Israel.* Cresskill NJ: Hampton Press.

Cohen, J. 1996. Rewriting our lives. *Journal of Narrative and Life History*, 6: 145–156.

Cohler, B. 1988. The human studies and the life history. *Social Service Review*, 62: 552–575.

Collins, P. H. 1994. Shifting the center: race, class, and feminist theorizing about motherhood. In E. N. Glenn, G. Chang and L. R. Forcey (eds.) *Mothering*. New York: Routledge, pp. 45–65.

Connell, R. W. 1987. *Gender and power*. Malden MA: Blackwell.

1995. *Masculinities*. Malden MA: Blackwell.

2000. *The men and the boys*. Berkeley CA: University of California Press.

Cook-Gumperz, J. and J. Gumperz 1997. Narrative explanations: accounting for past experience in interviews. In M. Bamberg (ed.) Oral versions of personal experience: three decades of narrative analysis. Special issue of *Journal of Narrative and Life History*, 7(1–4): pp. 291–298.

Cortazzi, M. and L. Jin 1999. Bridges to learning. In L. Cameron and G. Low (eds.) *Researching and applying metaphor*. Cambridge: Cambridge University Press, pp. 149–176.

Crapanzano, V. 1992. *Hermes' dilemma and Hamlet's desire: on the epistemology of interpretation*. Cambridge MA: Harvard University Press.

Dance, J. 2002. *Tough fronts*. New York: Routledge/Falmer.

Davies, B. and R. Harré 1990. Positioning: the discursive construction of selves. *Journal for the theory of Social Behaviour*, 20: 43–63.

1999. Positioning and personhood, R. Harré and L. van Langenhove (eds.), *Positioning theory*. Oxford: Blackwell, pp. 32–52.

de Certeau, M. 1988. *The practice of everyday life*. Berkeley CA: University of California Press.

De Fina, A. 2000. Orientation in immigrant narratives: the role of ethnicity in the identification of characters. *Discourse Studies*, 2(2), 131–157.

2003. *Identity in narrative: a study of immigrant discourse*. Amsterdam and Philadelphia: John Benjamins.

de Rivera, J. and T. R. Sarbin 1998. *Believed-in imaginings: the narrative construction of reality*. Washington DC: American Psychological Association.

Doctorow, E. L. 2000. *City of God*. New York: Random House.

Douglas, L. 2001. *The memory of judgement: making law and history in the trials of the Holocaust*. New Haven: Yale University Press.

Drew, P. 1998. Complaints about transgression and misconduct. *Research on Language and Social Interaction*, 31(3–4): 295–325.

Drew, P. and E. Holt 1988. Complainable matters: the use of idiomatic expressions in making complaints. *Social Problems*, 35(4): 398–417.

1998. Figures of speech: figurative expressions and the management of topic transition in conversation. *Language in Society*, 27(4): 495–522.

Dubar, C. 2000. *La crise des identités, l' interpretation d'une mutation*. Paris: PUF.

Durkheim, E. 1964 [1902]. *The division of labor in society.* New York: Free Press.
  1966 [1895]. *The rules of sociological method.* New York: Free Press.
Dyer, J. and D. Keller-Cohen 2000. The discursive construction of professional self through narratives of personal experience. *Discourse Studies,* 2(3): 283–304.
Eckert, P. 2000. *Linguistic variation as social practice.* Malden MA: Blackwell.
Eckert, P. and S. McConnell-Ginet 1999. New generalizations and explanations in language and gender research. *Language in Society* 28: 185–201.
Edwards, D. 1997. *Discourse and cognition.* New York: Sage.
  1998. The relevant thing about her: social identity categories in use. In C. Antaki and S. Widdicombe (eds.) *Identities in talk.* London: Sage, pp. 13–33.
Ellsworth, E. 1989. Why doesn't this feel empowering? Working through the repressive myths of critical pedagogy. *Harvard Educational Review,* 59(3): 297–324.
Epstein, D. and R. Johnson 1998. *Schooling sexualities,* Buckingham: Open University Press.
Erickson, F. 1966. Ethnographic microanalysis. In S. L. McKay and N. Hornberger (eds.) *Sociolinguistics and language teaching.* Cambridge: Cambridge University Press, pp. 283–306.
Erickson, F. and J. Shultz 1977. When is context? Some issues and methods in the analysis of social competence. *The Quarterly Newsletter of the Institute for Comparative Human Development,* 1(2): 5–10.
  1982. *The counselor as gatekeeper: social interaction in interviews.* New York: Academic Press.
Erikson, E. H. 1950. *Childhood and society.* New York: W. W. Norton.
  1968. *Identity: youth and crisis.* New York: W. W. Norton.
Ervin-Tripp, S. 1972. On sociolinguistic rules: alternation and co-occurrence. In J. Gumperz and D. Hymes (eds.) *Directions in sociolinguistics: the ethnography of communication.* New York: Blackwell, pp. 213–250.
Estrada, L. 1993. Family influences on demographic trends in Hispanic ethnic identification and labeling. In M. Bernal and G. P. Knight (eds.) *Ethnic identity. Formation and transmission among Hispanics and other minorities.* Albany NY: State University of New York Press, pp. 162–179.
Fairclough, N. 1989. *Language and power.* London: Longman.
  1992. *Discourse and social change.* Malden MA: Blackwell.
Farmer, F. M. 1896. *Boston cooking-school cook book.* Boston: Little, Brown and Company.

Felman, S. and D. Laub 1992. *Testimonies: crises of witnessing in litera-ture, psychoanalysis, and history*. New York: Routledge, Chapman and Hall, Inc.

Ferguson, A. 2000. *Bad boys: public schools in the making of black masculinity*. Ann Arbor MI: University of Michigan Press.

Fine, G. 1988. Sexuality, schooling, and adolescent females: the missing discourse of desire. *Harvard Educational Review*, 58: 3–32.

Fisher, M. F. K. 1968. *With bold knife and fork*. New York: Paragon.

Fletcher, J. 1999. *Disappearing acts: gender, power and relational practice at work*. Cambridge MA: MIT Press.

Forceville, C. 1996. *Pictorial metaphor in advertising*. London and New York: Routledge.

Foucault, M. 1971. *L'ordre du discours*. Paris: Gallimard.

1972. *The archaeology of knowledge*. New York: Pantheon.

1980a. *Power/knowledge: selected interviews and other writings 1972–1977*. In C. Gordon (ed.), New York: Pantheon Press.

1980b. The eye of power. In C. Gordon (ed.) *Power/knowledge: selected interviews and other writings, 1972–1977*. New York: Pantheon, pp. 146–165.

1984. *The history of sexuality*. Harmondsworth: Penguin.

1988. Technologies of the self. In *Technologies of the self: a seminar with Michel Foucault*. L. H. Martin, J. Gutman and P. Hutton (eds.) Amherst: University of Massachusetts Press, pp. 16–49.

Frank, A. W. 1995. *The wounded storyteller: body, illness, and ethics*. Chicago IL: University of Chicago Press.

Frankenberg, R. 1997. Introduction: local whitenesses, localizing white-ness. In R. Frankenberg (ed.) *Displacing whiteness: essays in social and cultural criticism*. Durham NC: Duke University Press, pp. 1–34.

Freeman, M. 1993. *Rewriting the self: memory, history, narrative*. New York: Routledge.

1998. Mythical time, historical time, and the narrative fabric of the self. *Narrative Inquiry*, 8(1): 27–50.

2001. From substance to story: narrative, identity, and the reconstruc-tion of the self. In J. Brockmeier and D. Carbaugh (eds.) *Narrative and identity: studies in autobiography, self and culture*. Amsterdam and Philadelphia: John Benjamins, pp. 283–298.

Freire Costa, J. 1992. *A inocência e o vício*. Rio de Janeiro: Relume-Dumará.

French, J. R. P. and B. Raven 1959. The bases of social power. In D. Cartwright (ed.) *Studies in social power*. Ann Arbor: University of Michigan, pp. 150–167.

Frosh, S., A. Phoenix and R. Pattman 2002. *Young masculinities*. New York: Palgrave.

Fussell, B. 1999. *My kitchen wars: a memoir*. New York: North Point Press.

Gadsden, V., S. Wortham and H. Turner 2003. Situated identities of young, African American fathers in low-income urban settings. *Family Court Review*, **41**: 381–399.

Gadsden, V., S. Wortham and T. Wojcik 2001. How urban fathers represent the transition to fathering: a discourse analysis of fathering narratives. Paper presented at the meeting of the American Education Research Association, Seattle WA, April.

Gallois, C. and V. J. Callan 1981. Personality impressions elicited by accented English speech. *Journal of Cross-Cultural Psychology*, **12**(3): 347–359.

Gardner, R. 2001. *When listeners talk*. Amsterdam and Philadelphia: John Benjamins.

Gee, J. P. 1996. *Social linguistics and literacies: ideology in discourses*. London: The Falmer Press.

1999. *An introduction to discourse analysis*. London: Routledge.

Georgakopoulou, A. 1998. Conversational stories as performances: the case of Greek. *Narrative Inquiry*, 8: 319–350.

2001. Arguing about the future: on indirect disagreements in conversations. *Journal of Pragmatics*, **33**: 1881–1900.

2002. Narrative and identity management: discourse and social identities in a tale of tomorrow. *Research on Language and Social Interaction*, 35: 427–451.

2003. Looking back when looking ahead: adolescents' identity management in narrative practices. In J. Androutsopoulos and A. Georgakopoulou (eds.) *Discourse constructions of youth identities*. Amsterdam and Philadelphia: John Benjamins, pp. 75–91.

Gergen, K. J. 1994. *Realities and relationships: soundings in social construction*. Cambridge MA: Harvard University Press.

Gergen, K. and J. Kaye 1992. Beyond narrative in the negotiation of therapeutic meaning. In S. McNamee and K. Gergen (eds.) *Therapy as social construction*. London: Sage, pp. 166–185.

Gergen, K. J. and M. M. Gergen 1997. Narratives of the self. In L. P. Hinchman and S. K. Hinchman (eds.) *Memory identity community: the idea of narrative in the human sciences*. Albany NY: State University of New York Press, pp. 161–184.

Gergen, M. M. 1994. The social construction of personal histories: gendered lives in popular autobiographies. In T. R. Sarbin and J. I. Kitsuse (eds.) *Constructing the Social*. London: Sage, pp. 19–44.

Giddens, A. 1991. *Modernity and self-identity: self and society in the late modern age*. Stanford: Stanford University Press.

Giles, H. and N. Coupland 1991. *Language: contexts and consequences*. Pacific Grove CA: Brooks/Cole.

Gilligan, C. 1982. *In a different voice*. Cambridge MA: Harvard University Press.

Gioia, D. A. and J. B. Thomas 1996. Institutional identity, image, and issue interpretation: sensemaking during strategic change in academia. *Administrative Science Quarterly*, 41(3): 370–403.

Giroux, H. A. 1997. Rewriting the discourse of racial identity: towards a pedagogy and politics of whiteness. *Harvard Educational Review*, 67(2): 265–320.

Givón, T. 1989. *Mind, code, and context: essays in pragmatics*. Hillsdale NJ: Lawrence Erlbaum Associates.

Glenn, E. N. 1994. Social constructions of mothering: a thematic overview. In E. N. Glenn, G. Chang and L. R. Forcey (eds.) *Mothering*. New York: Routledge, pp. 1–29.

Goffman, E. 1959. *The presentation of self in everyday life*. New York: Doubleday.

1963. *Behavior in public places*. New York: Free Press.

1967a. On face work. In E. Goffman (ed.) *Interaction ritual: essays on face to face behaviour*. New York: Pantheon, pp. 5–46.

1967b. The nature of deference and demeanor. In E. Goffman (ed.) *Interaction ritual: essays on face to face behaviour*. New York: Pantheon, pp. 49–95.

1971. *Relations in public*. New York: Basic Books.

1974. *Frame analysis*. New York: Harper and Row.

1976. Replies and responses. *Language in Society*, 5: 257–313.

1978. Response cries. *Language*, 54: 787–815.

1981. *Forms of talk*. Philadelphia: University of Pennsylvania Press.

1983. The interaction order. *American Sociological Review*, 48: 1–17.

1989[1959]. *A representação do eu na vida cotidiana*. Petrópolis, Brazil: Vozes.

Gómez, L. 1992. The birth of the "Hispanic generation." Attitudes of Mexican-American political elites toward the Hispanic label. *Latin American Perspectives*, 75(19): 45–38.

Goodwin, C. 1984. Notes on story structure and the organization of participation. In J. M. Atkinson and J. Heritage (eds.) *Structures of social action*. Cambridge: Cambridge University Press, pp. 225–246.

1986. Between and within: an alternative sequential treatment of continuers and assessments. *Human Studies*, 9: 205–217.

Goodwin, M. H. 1990. *He-said-she-said: talk as social organization among Black children*. Bloomington: Indiana University Press.

1993. Tactical uses of stories: participation frameworks within girls' and boys' disputes. In D. Tannen (ed.) *Gender and conversational interaction*. Oxford: Oxford University Press, pp. 110–143.

1999. Constructing opposition within girls' games. In M. Bucholtz, A. C. Liang and L. Sutton (eds.) *Reinventing identities*. Oxford: Oxford University Press, pp. 388–409.

Gould, S. J. 1987. *Time's arrow/time's cycle: myth and metaphor in the discovery of geological time*. Cambridge MA: Harvard University Press.

Gramsci, A. 1994. *Prison notebooks*. New York: Columbia University Press.

Greatbatch, D. and R. Dingwall 1998. Talk and identity in divorce mediation. In C. Antaki and S. Widdicombe (eds.) *Identities in talk*. London: Sage, pp. 121–132.

Green, G. 1989. *Pragmatics and natural language understanding*. Hillsdale NJ: Lawrence Erlbaum Associates.

Grice, H. P. 1975. Logic and conversation. In P. Cole and J. L. Morgan (eds.) *Syntax and semantics Vol. 3: Speech acts*. New York: Academic Press, pp. 41–58.

Griffiths, S. and J. Wallace (eds.) 1998. *Consuming passions: food in the age of anxiety*. London: Mandolin.

Grimes, W. 1998. Menus: challenging the old order. *The New York Times*. February 4: B1.

1999. The new American service: easygoing, not French and formal. *The New York Times*, February: B1.

2002. Critic's notebook: waiter, please put a lid on it. *The New York Times*, January 16: F1.

Grönroos, C. 1995. *Marketing: gerenciamentoe serviços*. Rio de Janeiro, Brazil: Campus.

Gumperz, J. 1982. *Discourse strategies*. Cambridge: Cambridge University Press.

Günthner, S. 1995. Exemplary stories: the cooperative construction of moral indignation. *Versus*, 70–75: 148–175.

Hadden, S. C. and M. Lester 1978. Talking identity: the production of "self" in interaction. *Human Studies*, 1: 331–356.

Hagendoorn, L. 1993. Ethnic categorization and outgroup exclusion: cultural values and social stereotypes in the construction of ethnic hierarchies' models. *Ethnic and Racial Studies*, 16(1): 26–51.

Hall, J. K. 1995. (Re-)creating worlds with words: a sociohistorical perspective of face-to-face interaction. *Applied Linguistics*, 16: 206–232.

1990. Cultural identity and diaspora. In J. Rutherford (ed.) *Identity: community, culture, difference*. London: Lawrence and Wishart, pp. 222–237.

1996. Who needs "identity"? In S. Hall and P. du Gay (eds.) *Questions of cultural identity*. London: Sage, pp. 1–17.

Hall, S. and P. du Gay (eds.) 1996. *Questions of cultural identity*. London: Sage.

Halliday, M. A. K. and R. Hasan 1976. *Cohesion in English*. New York: Longman.

Hamilton, H. 1998. Reported speech and survivor identity in on-line bone marrow transplantation narratives. *Journal of Sociolinguistics*, 2(1): 53–67.

Hanks, W. 1990. *Referential practice*. Chicago: University of Chicago Press.

1992. The indexical ground of deictic reference. In A. Duranti and C. Goodwin (eds.) *Rethinking context*. Cambridge: Cambridge University Press, pp. 43–76.

Harré, R. and L. van Langenhove 1992. Varieties of positioning. *Journal for the Theory of Social Behaviour*, 20: 393–407.

Harré, R. and L. van Langenhove (eds.) 1999. *Positioning theory*. Oxford: Blackwell.

Hartman, G. H. 1994. Introduction: darkness visible. In G. H. Hartman (ed.) *Holocaust remembrance: the shapes of memory*. Cambridge, MA: Blackwell, pp. 1–22.

Harvey, M. R., E. G. Mishler, P. A. Harney and K. Koenen. 2000. In the aftermath of sexual abuse: the narrativization of identity in survivor accounts of trauma and recovery. *Narrative Inquiry*, 10(2): 291–311.

Hass, A. 1995. *The aftermath: living with the Holocaust*. New York: Cambridge University Press.

Hays, S. 1996. *The cultural contradictions of motherhood*. New Haven: Yale University Press.

Heath, S. B. 1986. Taking a cross-cultural look at narratives. *Topics in Language Disorders*, 7(1): 84–94.

Helmreich, W. B. 1992. *Against all odds: Holocaust survivors and the successful lives they made in America*. New York: Simon and Schuster.

Heritage, J. 1984. *Garfinkel and ethnomethodology*. Cambridge: Polity Press.

Herman, D. 2001. Spatial reference in narrative domains. *Text*, 21(4): 1–27.

Hesser, A. 1998. Golden beets, blood oranges and other salads of winter. *The New York Times*, February 11: B1.

Hester, S. and P. Englin (eds.) 1997. *Culture in action*. Lanham MD: University Press of America.

Hilberg, R. 1985. *The destruction of the European Jews*. New York: Holmes and Meier.

Hill, J. 1989. The cultural (?) context of narrative involvement. In R. Graczyk and C. Wiltshire (eds.) *Papers from the twenty-fifth annual regional meeting of the Chicago Linguistic Society*. Chicago: Chicago Linguistics Society, pp. 138–156.

1995a. The voices of Don Gabriel: responsibility and moral grounds in a modern Mexicano narrative. In B. Mannheim and D. Tedlock (eds.) *The dialogic emergence of culture*. Chicago: University of Illinois Press, pp. 97–147.

1995b. Junk Spanish, covert racism, and the (leaky) boundary between public and private spheres. *Pragmatics*, 5(2): 197–212.

1995c. Mock Spanish: a site for indexical reproduction of racism in American English. *Language and Culture Symposium* 2, http://www.language-culture.org/colloquia/symposia/hill-jane.

Hill, J. and O. Zepeda 1993. Mrs. Patricio's trouble: the distribution of responsibility in an account of personal experience. In J. Hill and J. Irvine (eds.) *Responsibility and evidence in oral discourse*. Cambridge: Cambridge University Press, pp. 197–226.

Hinchman, L. P. and S. K. Hinchman 1997. Introduction. In L. P. Hinchman and S. K. Hinchman (eds.) *Memory identity community: the idea of narrative in the human sciences*. Albany: State University of New York Press, pp. vii–xxxii.

Hoch, P. 1979. *White hero, black beast: racism, sexism, and the mask of masculinity*. London: Pluto Press.

Hogg, M. A. and D. Abrams 1988. *Social identifications: a social psychology of intergroup relations and group processes*. London: Routledge.

Holland, D. and N. Quinn 1987. *Cultural models in language and thought*. New York: Cambridge University Press.

Holland, D. and D. Skinner 1987. Prestige and intimacy: the cultural models behind Americans' talk about gender types. In D. Holland and N. Quinn (eds.) *Cultural models in language and thought*. New York: Cambridge University Press, pp. 78–111.

Holland, D., W. Lachicotte, D. Skinner and C. Cain, 1998. *Identity and agency in cultural worlds*. Cambridge MA: Harvard University Press.

Hollway, W. 1984. Gender difference and the production of subjectivity. In J. Henriques, W. Hollway, C. Urwin, C. Venn and V. Walkerdine (eds.) *Changing the subject. Psychology, social regulation, and subjectivity*. London: Methuen, pp. 227–263.

Holmes, J. 1995. *Women, men and politeness*. London: Longman.

  1997. Women, language and identity. *Journal of Sociolinguistics*, 1(2): 195–224.

  1998. Victoria University's Language in the Workplace project: goals, scope and methodology. *Te Reo*, 41: 178–181.

  2000a. Victoria University of Wellington's Language in the Workplace project: an overview. *Language in the Workplace Occasional Papers* 1.

  2000b. Doing collegiality and keeping control at work: small talk in government departments. In J. Coupland (ed.) *Small Talk*. London: Longman, pp. 32–61.

  2000c. Women at work: analysing women's talk in New Zealand workplaces. *Australian Review of Applied Linguistics (ARAL)*, 22(2): 1–17.

Holmes, J. and M. Marra 2002. Having a laugh at work: how humour contributes to workplace culture. *Journal of Pragmatics*, 34: 1683–1710.

  2004. Relational practice in the workplace: women's talk or gendered discourse? *Language in Society*, 33(3): 377–398.

  2005. Narrative and the construction of professional identity in the workplace. In J. Thornborrow and J. Coates (eds.) *The sociolinguistics of narrative*. Amsterdam: John Benjamins, pp. 193–213.

Holmes, J. and M. Meyerhoff 1999. The community of practice: theories and methodologies in language and gender research. *Language in Society*, 28(2): 173–183.

Holmes, J. and M. Stubbe 2003. "Feminine" workplaces: stereotype and reality. In J. Holmes and M. Meyerhoff (eds.) *Handbook of language and gender.* Oxford: Blackwell, pp. 573–599.

Holmes, J., M. Stubbe and B. Vine 1999. Constructing professional identity: "doing power" in policy units. In S. Sarangi and C. Roberts (eds.) *Talk, work and institutional order. Discourse in medical, meditation and management settings.* Berlin and New York: Mouton de Gruyter, pp. 351–385.

hooks, b. 1992. Representations of whiteness in the black imagination. In b. hooks (ed.) *Black looks: race and representation.* Boston: South End Press, pp. 165–178.

Hoyle, S. and B. T. Ribeiro 1993. Roles and footings: a frame analysis of two genres of spoken discourse. Paper presented at the American Association of Applied Linguistics, Atlanta, Georgia.

Hurtado, A. and C. Arce 1986. Mexicanos, chicanos, Mexican Americans, or pochos . . .? Qué somos? The impact of nativity on ethnic labeling. *Aztláan,* **17**(1): 103–130.

Hyden, L.-C. 1997. Illness and narrative. *Sociology of Health and Illness,* **19**(1): 48–69.

Hymes, D. 1996. *Ethnography, linguistics, narrative inequality: toward an understanding of voice.* London: Taylor Francis.

Inness, S. A. (ed.) 2001. *Kitchen culture in America.* Philadelphia: University of Pennsylvania Press.

Ioanid, R. 2000. *The Holocaust in Romania: the destruction of Jews and Gypsies under the Antonescu regime, 1940–1944.* Chicago: Ivan R. Dee.

Ivanič, R. 1998. *Writing and identity: the discoursal construction of identity in academic writing.* Amsterdam: John Benjamins.

Iverson, M., D. Crimp and H. K. Bhabha 1997. *Mary Kelly.* London: Phaidon.

Jakobson, R. 1971[1957]. Shifters, verbal categories and the Russian verb. In *R. Jakobson, Selected Writings Vol. 2.* The Hague: Mouton, pp. 130–147.

James, W. 1988[1907]. *Pragmatism.* Indianapolis: Hackett Publishing.

Jefferson, G. 1978. Sequential aspects of storytelling in conversation. In J. Schenkein (ed.) *Studies in the organisation of conversational interaction.* New York: Academic Press, pp. 219–249.

1984. Transcription notation. In J. M. Atkinson and J. Heritage (eds.) *Structures of social action.* Cambridge: Cambridge University Press, p. ix.

Johnson, G. C. 2001. Accounting for pre-service teachers' use of visual metaphors in narratives. *Teacher Development,* **5**(1): 139–165.

2002a. Taking up a post-personal position in reflective practice: one teacher's accounts. *Reflective Practice,* **3**(1): 21–37.

2002b. A cautionary tale: a dialogic re-reading of a student teacher's visual narrative. *Narrative Inquiry*, 11(2): 451–478.

Johnson, S. and U. H. Meinhof 1997. *Language and masculinity*. Oxford: Blackwell.

Johnstone, B. 1990. *Stories, community and place*. Bloomington IN: Indiana University Press.

1993. Community and contest: Midwestern men and women creating their worlds in conversational storytelling. In D. Tannen (ed.) *Gender and conversational interaction*. Oxford: Oxford University Press, pp. 62–80.

1996. *The linguistic individual: self-expression in language and linguistics*. New York: Cambridge University Press.

Karttunen, L. and A. Peters 1979. Conventional implicature. In C. Oh and D. Dinnen (eds.) *Syntax and semantics, Vol. 3: Presupposition*. New York: Academic Press, pp.1–56.

Katz, J. N. 1996. *The invention of heterosexuality*. New York: Penguin Books.

Kempson, R. 1975. *Presupposition and the delimitation of semantics*. Cambridge: Cambridge University Press.

Kenyon, G. M. and W. L. Randall 1997. *Restorying our lives: personal growth through autobiographical reflection*. Westport, CT: Praeger.

Kerby, A. 1991. *Narrative and the self*. Bloomington: Indiana University Press.

Kermode, F. 1967. *The sense of an ending: studies in the theory of fiction*. New York: Oxford.

Kern, S. 1983. *The culture of time and space: 1880–1918*. Cambridge MA: Harvard University Press.

Kiesling, S. F. 1997. *Power and the language of men*. In U. H. Meinhof and S. Johnson (eds.) *Language and masculinity*. Oxford: Blackwell, pp. 65–85.

1998. Variation and men's identity in a fraternity. *Journal of Sociolinguistics*, 2: 69–100.

2001. Stances of whiteness and hegemony in fraternity men's discourse. *Journal of Linguistic Anthropology*, 11(1): 101–115.

2004. Men in language in woman's place. In M. Bucholtz and R. Lakoff (eds.) *Language and woman's place*. New York: Oxford University Press, pp. 229–236.

Kimmel, M. S. and M. A. Messner (eds.) 1989. *Men's lives*. New York: Macmillan.

Kotthoff, H. 2000. Gender and joking. On the complexities of women's image politics in humorous narratives. *Journal of Pragmatics*, 32(1): 55–80.

Kristeva, J. 1980. *Desire in language: a semiotic approach to literature and art*. New York: Columbia University Press.

Kronfeld, A. 1990. *Reference and computation*. Cambridge: University Press.

Kroskrity, P. 1993. *Language, history and identity*. Tucson: University of Arizona Press.

2000. Identity. *Journal of Linguistic Anthropology*, 9(1–2): 111–114.

Kyratzis, A. 1999. Narrative identity: preschoolers' self-construction through narrative in same-sex friendship group play. *Narrative Inquiry*, 9: 1–28.

Laberge, S. and G. Sankoff 1979. Anything you can do. In T. Givon (ed.) *Syntax and semantics Vol. 12: Discourse and syntax*. New York: Academic Press, pp. 419–440.

Labov, W. 1972a. *Language in the inner city*. Philadelphia: University of Pennsylvania Press.

1972b. *Sociolinguistic patterns*. Philadelphia: University of Pennsylvania Press.

1972c. The transformation of experience in narrative syntax. In W. Labov (ed.) *Language in the inner city*. Philadelphia PA: University of Pennsylvania Press, pp. 354–396.

Labov, W. and D. Fanshel 1977. *Therapeutic discourse*. New York: Academic Press.

Labov, W. and J. Waletzky 1967. Narrative analysis: oral versions of personal experience. In J. Helm (ed.) *Essays on the verbal and visual arts*. Seattle: University of Washington Press, pp. 12–44.

LaCapra, D. 1994. *Representing the Holocaust: history, theory, trauma*. Ithaca NY: Cornell University Press.

Lagerwey, M. D. 1998. *Reading Auschwitz*. Walnut Creek CA: Alta Mira Press.

Langellier, K. M. 1989. Personal narratives: perspectives on theory and research. *Text and Performance Quarterly*, 9: 243–276.

2001. Personal narrative. In M. Jolly (ed.) *Encyclopedia of life writing Vol. 2*. London and Chicago: Fitzroy Dearborn Publishers, pp. 699–701.

Langer, L. L. 1991. *Holocaust testimonies: the ruins of memory*. New Haven CT: Yale University Press.

Layne, L. L. 2003. *Motherhood lost: a feminist account of pregnancy loss in America*. New York: Routledge.

Lee, M. and F. M. Ulgado 1997. Consumer evaluations of fast-food services: a cross-national comparison. *Journal of Services Marketing*, 11(1): 39–52.

LePage, R. and A. Tabouret-Keller 1985. *Acts of identity: Creole-based approaches to language and ethnicity*. Cambridge: Cambridge University Press.

Lesko, N. (ed.) 2000. *Masculinities at school*. London: Sage.

Levinson, S. 2000. *Presumptive meanings*. Cambridge MA: MIT Press.

Lillis, T. 2001. *Student writing: access, regulation, desire.* London: Routledge.

Linde, C. 1993. *Life stories: the creation of coherence.* New York: Oxford University Press.

1999. The transformation of narrative syntax into institutional memory. *Narrative Inquiry,* 9: 139–174.

Lindstrom, L. 1992. Context contests: debatable truth statements on Tanna (Vanuatu). In A. Duranti and C. Goodwin (eds.) *Rethinking context.* Cambridge: Cambridge University Press, pp. 101–124.

Linenthal, E. 1995. *Preserving memory: the struggle to create America's Holocaust museum.* New York: Penguin Books.

Linklater, K. 1976. *Freeing the natural voice.* New York: Drama Book Publishers.

Lipstadt, D. 1990. Afterward. In R. G. Lewin (ed.) *Witnesses to the Holocaust: an oral history.* Boston: Twayne Publishers, pp. 217–221.

Lucius-Hoene, G. and A. Deppermann 2000. Narrative identity empiricized: a dialogical and positioning approach to autobiographical research interviews. *Narrative Inquiry,* 10: 199–222.

Lupton, D. 1998. *The emotional self: a sociocultural exploration.* London: Sage.

Lutz, C. and L. Abu-Lugod (eds.) 1990. *Language and the politics of emotion.* Cambridge: Cambridge University Press.

Lyons, J. 1977. *Semantics.* Cambridge: University Press.

Mac an Ghail, M. 1994. *The making of men. Masculinities, sexualities and schooling.* Buckingham: Open University Press.

MacIntyre, A. 1984. *After virtue* (2nd edition). Notre Dame IN: University of Notre Dame Press.

Marecek, J. 2003. Dancing through minefields: toward a qualitative stance in psychology. In P. M. Camic, J. E. Rhodes and L. Yardley (eds.) *Qualitative research in psychology.* Washington DC: American Psychology Association, pp. 49–69.

Maranhao, T. 1993. Recollections of fieldwork conversations, or authorial difficulties in anthropological writing. In J. Hill and J. Irvine (eds.) *Responsibility and evidence in oral discourse.* Cambridge: Cambridge University Press, pp. 260–288.

Marra, M. 2003. Decisions in New Zealand business meetings. Unpublished Ph.D. thesis. Wellington, New Zealand: Victoria University of Wellington.

Marra, M and J. Holmes, 2004. Workplace narratives and business reports: issues of definition. *Text* 24, 1: 59–78.

Martin, J. R. and G. Plum 1997. Construing experience: some story genres. In M. Bamberg (ed.) Oral versions of personal experience: three decades of narative analysis. Special issue of *Journal of Narrative and Life History,* 7(1–4): 299–308.

Mattingly, C. 1998. *Healing dramas and clinical plots: the narrative structure of experience*. New York: Cambridge University Press.

Mattingly, C. and L. C. Garro 1994. Introduction. *Social science and medicine*, 38(6): 771–774.

Mauss, M. 1967. *The gift*. New York: Norton.

Maybin, J. 1996. Story voices: the use of reported speech in 10–12-year-olds' spontaneous narratives. *Current Issues in Language and Society*, 3: 36–48.

McAdams, D. P. 1996. Personality, modernity, and the storied self: a contemporary framework for studying persons. *Psychological Inquiry*, 7(4): 295–321.

McAdams, D. P. and P. J. Bowman 2001. Narrating life's turning points: redemption and contamination. In D. P. McAdams, R. Josselson and A. Lieblich (eds.) *Turns in the road: narrative studies of lives in transition*. Washington DC: American Psychological Association Press, pp. 3–34.

McWilliam, E. L. 1994. *In broken images: feminist tales for a different teacher education*. New York: Teachers College Press.

Mead, G. 1934. *Mind, self and society*. Chicago: University of Chicago Press.

Meyerhoff, M. 1996. Dealing with gender identity as a sociolinguistic variable. In V. L. Bergvall, J. M. Bing and A. F. Freed (eds.) *Rethinking language and gender research: theory and practice*. New York: Longman, pp. 202–227.

Meyerhoff, M. and N. Niedzielski 1994. Resistance to creolization: an interpersonal and intergroup account. *Language and Communication*, 14(4): 313–330.

Meyers, D. T. 1997. Introduction. In D. T. Meyers (ed.) *Feminists rethink the self*. Boulder CO: Westview Press, pp. 1–11.

Miller, G. 1997. Building bridges: the possibility of analytic dialogue between ethnography, conversation analysis and Foucault. In D. Silverman (ed.) *Qualitative research: theory, method and practice*. London: Sage, pp. 24–44.

Miller, J. B. 1986. *Towards a new psychology of women*. Boston: Beacon Press.

Miller, J. B. and I. Stiver 1997. *The healing connection*. Boston: Beacon Press.

Miller, P. J. 1994. Narrative practices in self-construction. In U. Neisser and R. Fivush (eds.) *The remembering self: construction and accuracy in the self-narrative*. New York: Cambridge University Press, pp. 158–179.

Mintz, A. 2001. *Popular culture and the shaping of Holocaust memory in America*. Seattle: The University of Washington Press.

Mishler, E. G. 1984. *The discourse of medicine: dialectics of medical interviews*. Norwood, NJ: Ablex.

1986. *Research interviewing: context and narrative*. Cambridge MA: Harvard University Press.

1992. Work, identity, and narrative: an artist-craftsman's story. In G. C. Rosenwald and R. L. Ochberg (eds.) *Storied lives: the cultural politics of self-understanding*. New Haven CT: Yale University Press, pp. 21–40.

1995. Models of narrative analysis: a typology. *Journal of Narrative and Life History*, 5(2): 87–123.

1997. A matter of time: when, since, after Labov and Waletzky. In M. Bamberg (ed.) Oral versions of personal experience: three decades of narrative analysis. Special issue of *Journal of Narrative and Life History*, 7(1–4): pp. 69–74.

1999. *Storylines: craftartists' narratives of identity*. Cambridge MA: Harvard University Press.

Moita-Lopes, L. P. 1998. Discursos de identidade em sala de aula de leitura: a construção da diferença. In I. Signorini, *Língua(gem) e identidade*. Campinas: Mercado de Letras, pp. 303–330.

2002. *Identidades fragmentadas*. Campinas: Mercado de Letras.

Morris, C. 1938. Foundations of the theory of signs. In O. Neurath, R. Carnap and C. Morris (eds.) *International encyclopedia of unified science*. Chicago: University of Chicago Press, pp. 77–138.

Mufwene, S., J. Rickford, G. Bailey and J. Baugh (eds.) 1998. *African American English: structure, history, and usage*. New York: Routledge.

Müller, E. and A. Di Luzio 1995. Stories as examples in everyday argument. *Versus*, 70–75: 114–145.

Munby, D. (ed.) 1997. *Narrativa y control social. Perspectivas críticas*. Buenos Aires: Amorrorty Editores.

Nathan, D. and J. Haaken 1996. From incest to Ivan the Terrible: science and the trials of memory. *Tikkun*, 11: 29.

Norton, B. 2000. *Identity and language learning: gender, ethnicity and educational change*. Harlow: Pearson Educational.

Noy, C. 2002. "You *must* go trek there": the persuasive genre of narration among Israeli backpackers. *Narrative Inquiry*, 12: 261–290.

Oboler, S. 1995. *Ethnic labels, Latino lives*. Minneapolis: University of Minnesota Press.

Ochs, E. 1989. The linguistic expression of affect. In E. Ochs (ed.) *Culture and language development*. Cambridge: Cambridge University Press.

1992. Indexing gender. In A. Duranti and C. Goodwin (eds.) *Rethinking context*. Cambridge: Cambridge University Press, pp. 335–358.

1993. Constructing social identity: a language socialization perspective. *Research on Language and Social Interaction*, 26(3): 287–306.

Ochs, E. and L. Capps 2001. *Living narrative*. Cambridge MA: Harvard University Press.

Ochs, E. and C. Taylor 1992. Family narrative as political activity. *Discourse and Society*, 3: 301–340.

1995. The "father knows best": dynamic in dinnertime narrative. In K. Hall and M. Bucholtz (eds.) *Gender articulated. Language and the socially constructed self*. New York and London: Routledge, pp. 97–120.

Ochs, E., R. Smith and C. Taylor 1989. Dinner narratives as detective stories. *Cultural Dynamics*, **2**: 238–257.

O'Connor, P. 1994. You could feel it through the skin: agency and positioning in prisoners' stabbing stories. *Text*, **14**(1): 45–75.

O'Donnell, M. and S. Sharpe 2000. *Uncertain masculinities: youth, ethnicity, and class in contemporary Britain*. London and New York: Routledge.

Paoletti, I. 2000. Being a foreigner in primary school. *Language and Education*, **14**(4): 266–282.

2001. Teaching Italian in Australia to second generation Italian–Australian students, Kalbu Studijos. *Studies About Languages*, **1**: 44–47.

2002. Essere impopolare: la costruzione conversazionale dell'esclusione. In G. Klein and I. Paoletti (eds.) *La costruzione conversazionale dell'inclusione e dell'esclusione*. Napoli: Edizioni Scientifiche Italiane, pp. 27–56.

Parker, I. 1993. Discourse and power. In J. Shotter and K. J. Gergen (eds.) *Texts of identity*. London: Sage, pp. 56–69.

Personal Narratives Group 1989. *Interpreting women's lives*. Bloomington IN: Indiana University.

Petersen, A. 1998. *Unmasking the masculine: 'Men' and 'Identity' in a sceptical age*. Thousand Oaks CA: Sage Publications.

Polanyi, L. 1985. *Telling the American story: a structural and cultural analysis of conversational storytelling*, Norwood NJ: Ablex.

Pollock, D. 1999. *Telling bodies performing birth*. New York: Columbia University Press.

Pomerantz, A. 1984. Agreeing and disagreeing with assessments: some features of preferred/dispreferred turn shapes. In J. M. Atkinson and J. Heritage (eds.) *Structures of social action*. Cambridge: Cambridge University Press, pp. 57–99.

Potter, J. 2003. Discursive psychology: between method and paradigm. *Discourse and Society*, **14**(6): 783–794.

Psathas, G. 1995. *Conversation analysis: the study of talk-in-interaction*. Thousand Oaks CA: Sage.

Relaño Pastor, A. M. and A. De Fina 2005. Contesting social place. Narratives of language conflict. In B. Baynham and A. De Fina (eds.) *Dislocations/relocations. Narratives of displacment*. Manchester: St. Jerome Publishing, pp. 36–60.

Ribeiro, B. T. 2001. Por que ouvir estórias na entrevista psiquiátrica? De quem e do que estamos falando? In B. T. Ribeiro, C. C. Lima and M. T. Dantas Lopes (eds.) *Narrativa, identidade e clínica*. Rio de Janeiro: Edições IPUB/CUCA.

Ricoeur, P. 1980. Narrative time. *Critical Inquiry*, 7(1): 169–190.

1992. *Oneself as another*. K. Blamey (Trans.). Chicago: University of Chicago Press.

Riegel, K. 1997. The dialectics of time. In N. Datan and H. W. Reese (eds.) *Life-span developmental psychology: dialectical perspectives on experimental research*. New York: Academic, pp. 3–45.

Riessman, C. K. 1993. *Narrative Analysis*. Newbury Park: Sage Publications.

2002. Analysis of personal narratives. In J. F. Gubrium and J. A. Holstein (eds.) *Handbook of interview research*. Thousand Oaks: Sage, pp. 695–710.

2003. Performing identities in illness narratives: masculinities and multiple sclerosis. *Qualitative Research*, 3(1): 5–33.

Rimmon-Kenan, S. 1983. *Narrative fiction: contemporary poetics*. London: Methuen.

Robins, L. N. and M. Rutter (eds.) 1990. *Straight and devious pathways from childhood to adulthood*. New York: Cambridge University Press.

Rombauer, I. and M. R. Becker 1964. *The joy of cooking*. Indianapolis: Bobbs-Merrill.

Rosch, E. 1978. Principles of categorization. In E. Rosch and B. B. Lloyd (eds.) *Cognition and categorization*. Hillsdale NJ: Erlbaum, pp. 27–48.

Rosch, E. and C. B. Mervis 1975. Family resemblances: studies in the internal structure of categories. *Cognitive Psychology*, 7: 573–605.

Rosenwald, G. and R. Ochberg 1992. *Storied lives*. New Haven CT: Yale University Press.

Roulston, K. 2000. The management of 'safe' and 'unsafe' complaint sequences in research interviews. *Text*, 20(3): 307–345.

Rumelhart, D. 1980. Schemata: the building blocks of cognition. In R. J. Spiro, B. C. Bruce and W. F. Brewer (eds.) *Theoretical issues in reading comprehension: perspectives from cognitive psychology, linguistics, artificial intelligence, and education*. Hillsdale NJ: Erlbaum, pp. 33–58.

Runyan, W. M. 1982. *Life histories and psychobiography: explorations in theory and method*. New York: Oxford University Press.

Sacks, H. 1972. On the analyzability of stories by children. In J. Gumperz and D. Hymes (eds.) *Directions in sociolinguistics: the ethnography of communication*. New York: Blackwell, pp. 325–45.

1995. *Lectures on conversation*, 2 vols. G. Jefferson (ed.). Oxford: Blackwell.

Sacks, H. and E. Schegloff 1979. Two preferences in the organization of reference to persons in conversation and their interaction. In G. Psathas (ed.) *Everyday language: studies in ethnomethodology*. New York: Irvington, pp. 15–21.

Sacks, H., E. Schegloff and G. Jefferson 1974. A simplest systematics for the organization of turn-taking in conversation. *Language*, 50: 696–735.

Sarangi, S. and A. Clarke 2002. Zones of expertise and the management of uncertainty in genetics risk communication. *Research on Language and Social Interaction*, 35(2): 139–171.

Sarangi, S. and C. Roberts (eds.) 1999. *Talk, work and institutional order. Discourse in medical, mediation and management settings.* Berlin and New York: Mouton de Gruyter.

Sarup, M. 1996. *Identity, culture and the postmodern world.* Edinburgh: Edinburgh University Press.

Sassen, S. 1999. *Guests and aliens.* New York: The New Press.

Saussure, F. 1994[1972]. *Course in general linguistics* (2nd edition). La Salle, IL: Open Court.

Sawin, P. 1999. Gender, context, and the narrative construction of identity: rethinking models of women's narratives. In M. Bucholtz, A. C. Liang and L. Sutton (eds.) *Reinventing identities.* Oxford: Oxford University Press, pp. 241–258.

Schacter, D. L. (ed.) 1995. *Memory distortion: how minds, brains, and societies reconstruct the past.* Cambridge, MA: Harvard.

Schacter, D. L. and E. Scarry (eds.) 2000. *Memory, brain, and belief.* Cambridge, MA: Harvard University Press.

Schafer, R. 1992. *Retelling a life: narration and dialogue in psychoanalysis.* New York: Basic Books.

Schegloff, E. 1997. Whose text? Whose context? *Discourse and Society*, 8(2): 165–187.

Schenkein, J. 1978. Identity negotiations in conversation. In J. Schenkein (ed.) *Studies in the organisation of conversational interaction.* New York: Academic Press, pp. 57–78.

Schiff, B. 2002. Talking about identity: Arab students at the Hebrew University of Jerusalem. *Ethos*, 30: 273–304.

2005. Telling it in time: aspects of consistency and change in the life stories of Holocaust survivors. *International Journal on Aging and Human Development*, 6(3): 189–212.

Schiff, B. and B. Cohler 2001. Telling survival backward: Holocaust survivors narrate the past. In G. M. Kenyon, P. G. Clark and B. de Vries (eds.) *Narrative gerontology: theory, research and practice.* New York: Springer, pp. 113–136.

Schiff, B., C. Noy and B. Cohler 2001. Collected stories in the life narratives of Holocaust survivors. *Narrative Inquiry*, 11: 159–194.

Schiffrin, D. 1982. *Discourse markers.* University of Pennsylvania Dissertation in Linguistics.

1984. How a story says what it means and does. *Text*, 4(4): 133–146.

1987. *Discourse markers.* New York: Cambridge University Press.

1993. "Speaking for another" in sociolinguistic interviews: alignments, identities, and frames. In D. Tannen (ed.) *Framing in discourse*. New York: Oxford University Press, pp. 231–263.

1994. *Approaches to discourse*. Oxford: Blackwell.

1996. Narrative as self-portrait: sociolinguistic construction of identity. *Language in Society*, 25(2): 167–203.

2000. Mother/daughter discourse in a Holocaust oral history. *Narrative Inquiry*, 10(1): 1–44.

2002. Mother and friends in a Holocaust survivor oral history. *Language in Society*, 31(3): 309–354.

2006. *In other words: variation in reference and narrative*. Cambridge: Cambridge University Press.

Schneider, B. and D. E. Bowen 1999. Understanding customer delight and outrage. *Sloan Management Review*, 41(1): 35–45.

Schutz, A. and T. Luckmann 1973. *The structures of the life-world, Vol. 1*. R. M. Zaner and H. T. Engelhardt Jr. (Trans.). Evanston IL: Northwestern University Press.

Segev, T. 1993. *The seventh million: the Israelis and the Holocaust*. H. Watzman (Trans.). New York: Hill and Wang.

Seidman, S. 1994. *Contested knowledge: social theory in the postmodern era* (3rd edition). Cambridge MA: Blackwell.

Sereny, G. 1992. John Demjanjuk and the failure of justice. *The New York Review of Books*, 39: 32–34.

Shotter, J. 1993. *Conversational realities: the construction of life through language*. Thousand Oaks, CA: Sage.

Shuman, A. 1993. "Get outa my face": entitlement and authoritative discourse. In J. Hill and J. Irvine (eds.) *Responsibility and evidence in oral discourse*. Cambridge: Cambridge University Press, pp. 135–160.

Silverstein, M. 1976. Shifters, linguistic categories, and cultural description. In K. Basso and H. Selby (eds.) *Meaning in anthropology*. Albuquerque NM: University of New Mexico Press, pp. 11–55.

1992. The indeterminacy of contextualization: when is enough enough? In P. Auer and A. Di Luzio (eds.) *The contextualization of language*. Amsterdam and Philadelphia: John Benjamins, pp. 55–75.

1993. Metapragmatic discourse and metapragmatic function. In J. A. Lucy (ed.) *Reflexive language: reported speech and metapragmatics*. New York: Cambridge University Press, pp. 33–58.

Simmel, G. 1950 [1908]. *The sociology of Georg Simmel*. K. Wolff (Trans. and ed.). New York: MacMillan.

Smyth, J. 1992. Teachers' work and the politics of reflection. *American Educational Research Journal*, 29(2): 267–300.

Snitow, A. 1992. Feminism and motherhood: an American reading. *Feminist Review*, 40: 32–51.

Sodré, M. 1999, *Claros e escuros. Identidade, povo e mídia no Brasil*. Petrópolis: Editora Vozes.

Somers, M. R. and G. D. Gibson 1994. Reclaiming the epistemological 'other': narrative and the social construction of identity. In C. Calhoun (ed.) *Social theory and the politics of identity*. Oxford: Blackwell, pp. 37–99.

Sperber, D. and D. Wilson 1995. *Relevance: communication and cognition*. Malden MA: Blackwell.

Stromberg, P. G. 1993. *Language and self-transformation: a study of the Christian conversion narrative*. New York: Cambridge University Press.

Stubbe, M. 1998. Researching language in the workplace: a participatory model. Proceedings of the Australian Linguistics Society Conference, Brisbane, University of Queensland. http://english.uq.edu.au/linguistics/als/als98/.

2000. "Just do it . . .!": discourse strategies for "getting the message across" in a factory production team. Proceedings of the Australian Linguistics Society Conference, University of Western Australia September 1999. www.arts.uwa.edu.au/LingWWW/als99/.

Swan, S. H. 1992. Intrauterine exposure to diethylstilbestrol: long-term effects in humans. *Acta Pathologica, Microbiologica et Immunologica Scandinavica*, 108: 793–804.

Tajfel, H. 1981. *Human groups and social categories: studies in social psychology*. Cambridge: Cambridge University Press.

Tannen, D. 1980. A comparative analysis of oral narratives strategies: Athenian Greek and American English. In W. Chafe (ed.) *The pear stories*. Norwood NJ: Ablex, pp. 51–87.

1986. *That's not what I meant!* New York: Ballantine.

1989. *Talking voices: repetition, dialogue and imagery in conversational discourse*. Cambridge: Cambridge University Press.

Tannen, D. (ed.) 1993a. *Framing in discourse*. New York: Oxford University Press.

Tannen, D. and C. Wallat 1993. Interactive frames and knowledge schemas in interaction: examples from a medical examination/interview. In D. Tannen (ed.) *Framing in discourse*. New York: Oxford University Press, pp. 57–76.

Taylor, C. 1991. *The ethics of authenticity*. Cambridge MA: Harvard.

Thorne, B. 1993. *Gender play: boys and girls in school*. New Brunswick NJ: Rutgers University Press.

Tobias, S. 1998. Early American cookbooks as cultural artifacts. *Papers on Language and Literature*, 34.1: 3–19.

Toulmin, S. and J. Goodfield 1965. *The discovery of time*. Chicago IL: Chicago.

Umansky, L. 1996. *Motherhood reconceived: feminism and the legacies of the sixties*. New York: New York University Press.

US Department of Health, Education and Welfare 1978. *DES task force summary report*. DHEW Publication No. (NIH) 79–1688. Washington DC: US Government Printing Office.

van Dijk, T. A. 1997. Discourse as interaction in society. In T. A. van Dijk (ed.) *Discourse as social interaction*. London: Sage, pp. 1–37.

1998. *Ideology. a multidisciplinary approach*. London: Sage.

van Langenhove, L. and R. Harré 1999. Introducing positioning theory. In R. Harré and L. van Langenhove (eds.) *Positioning theory*. Oxford: Blackwell, pp. 14–31.

Voloshinov, V. 1973[1929]. *Marxism and the philosophy of language*. I. Matejka and I. Titunik (Trans.). Cambridge MA: Harvard University Press.

Vygotsky, L. S. 1978[1930]. *Mind in society: the development of higher psychological processes*. M. Cole, V. John-Steiner, S. Scribner and E. Souberman (eds.). Cambridge MA: Harvard University Press.

Wagenaar, W. A. and J. Groeneweg 1990. The memory of concentration camp survivors. *Applied Cognitive Psychology*, 4: 77–87.

Waters, A. 1996. *Chez Panisse vegetables*. New York: HarperCollins.

Webster, J. D. and M. McCall 1999. Reminiscence functions across adulthood: a replication and extension. *Journal of Adult Development*, 6: 73–85.

Weedon, C. 1997. *Feminist practice and poststructuralist theory*. Oxford: Blackwell.

Wenger, E. 1998. *Communities of practice*. Cambridge and New York: Cambridge University Press.

Wertsch, J. V. 1991. *Voices of the mind: a sociocultural approach to mediated action*. Cambridge MA: Harvard University Press.

White, H. 1980. The value of narrativity in the representation of reality. *Critical Inquiry*, 7: 5–27.

White, M. and D. Epston 1990. *Narrative means to therapeutic ends*. New York: Norton.

Whitehead, S. M. 2002. *Men and masculinities*. Malden, MA: Blackwell.

Widdicombe, S. and C. Antaki 1998. Identity as an analyst's and a participant's resource. In C. Antaki and S. Widdicombe (eds.) *Identities in talk*. London: Sage, pp. 191–206.

Widdicombe, S. and R. Wooffitt 1995. *The language of youth subcultures: social identity in action*. Hemel Hempstead: Harvester Wheatsheaf.

Wieviorka, A. 2000. *L'ère du témoin*. Malesherbes, France: Plon.

Williams, G. 1984. The genesis of chronic illness: narrative reconstruction. *Sociology of Health and Illness*, 6(2): 175–200.

Wilson, J. 2001. Who needs social theory anyway? In N. Coupland, S. Sarangi and C. Candlin (eds.) *Sociolinguistics and social theory*. Malaysia: Pearson Education Ltd, pp. 334–349.

Witherell, C. and N. Noddings (eds.) 1991. *Stories lives tell*. New York: Teachers College.

Wolfram, W. and N. Schilling-Estes 1998. *American English*. Malden MA: Blackwell.

Wood, K. 1999. Coherent identities amid heterosexist ideologies: deaf and hearing lesbian coming out stories. In M. Bucholtz, A. C. Liang and

L. Sutton (eds.) *Reinventing identities*. Oxford: Oxford University Press, pp. 46–64.

Woodward, K. 1997. *Identity and difference*. London: Sage.

2000[1997]. Identidade e diferença: uma introdução teórica e conceitual. In T. T. da Silva (ed.) *Identidade e diferença*. Petrópolis, Brazil: Vozes, pp. 7–72.

Wooffitt, R. and C. Clark 1998. Mobilizing discourse and social identities in knowledge talk. In C. Antaki and S. Widdicombe (eds.) *Identities in talk*. London: Sage, pp. 107–120.

Wortham, S. 2000. Interactional positioning and narrative self-construction. *Narrative Inquiry*, 10: 157–184.

2001. *Narratives in action, a strategy for research and analysis*. New York: Teachers' College Press.

2003. Accomplishing identity in participant-denoting discourse. *Journal of Linguistic Anthropology*, 13: 1–22.

Wortham, S. and M. Locher 1996. Voicing on the news: an analytic technique for studying media bias. *Text*, 16: 557–585.

Wortham, S. and V. Gadsden 2004. The complexities of "similarity" in research interviewing: a case of interviewing urban fathers. *Working Papers in Educational Linguistics*, 19: 1–32.

Young, A. 1995. *The harmony of illusions: inventing Post-Traumatic Stress Disorder*. Princeton NJ: Princeton.

Young, J. E. 1988. *Writing and rewriting the Holocaust: narrative and the consequences of interpretation*. Bloomington IN: Indiana University Press.

1993. *The texture of memory: Holocaust memorials and meaning*. New Haven: Yale University Press.

Young, K. 1987. *Taleworlds and storyrealms: the phenomenology of narrative*. Dordrecht: Martinus Nijhoff.

1999. Narrative embodiments: enclaves of the self in the realm of medicine. In A. Jaworski and N. Coupland (eds.) *The discourse reader*. London, New York: Routledge, pp. 428–441.

Zarifian, P. 2001. Comunicação e subjetividade nas organizações. In E. Davel and S. Vergara (eds.) *Gestão com pessoas e subjetividade*. São Paulo: Atlas.

Zeithaml, V. and M. J. Bitner 1996. *Services marketing*. NewYork: McGraw-Hill.

Zimmerman, D. H. 1998. Identity, context and interaction. In C. Antaki and S. Widdicombe (eds.) *Identities in talk*. London: Sage, pp. 87–106.

Zimmerman, D. H. and D. L. Wieder 1970. Ethnomethodology and the problem of order: comment on Denzin. In J. D. Douglas (ed.) *Understanding everyday life: toward the reconstruction of sociological knowledge*. Chicago: Aldine Publishing, pp. 285–298.

Zuss, M. 1997. Contesting representations. *Theory and Psychology*, 7: 653–656.

Index

Index